THE
DILLON
ERA

THE DILLON ERA

Richard Aldous

*Douglas Dillon
in the Eisenhower,
Kennedy,
and
Johnson Administrations*

McGill-Queen's University Press

Montreal & Kingston | London | Chicago

© The Dillon Fund 2023

ISBN 978-0-2280-1887-2 (cloth)
ISBN 978-0-2280-1938-1 (ePDF)
ISBN 978-0-2280-1939-8 (ePUB)

Legal deposit fourth quarter 2023
Bibliothèque nationale du Québec

Printed in Canada on acid-free paper that is 100% ancient forest free
(100% post-consumer recycled), processed chlorine free

Library and Archives Canada Cataloguing in Publication

Title: The Dillon era : Douglas Dillon in the Eisenhower, Kennedy,
    and Johnson administrations / Richard Aldous.
Other titles: Douglas Dillon in the Eisenhower, Kennedy, and
    Johnson administrations
Names: Aldous, Richard, author.
Description: Includes bibliographical references and index.
Identifiers: Canadiana (print) 20230222269 | Canadiana (ebook)
    20230222315 | ISBN 9780228018872 (cloth) | ISBN 9780228019381
    (ePDF) | ISBN 9780228019398 (ePUB)
Subjects: LCSH: Dillon, C. Douglas (Clarence Douglas), 1909-2003. |
    LCSH: Government economists—United States—Biography. |
    LCSH: Ambassadors—United States—Biography. | LCSH: United
    States—Economic policy—1945-1960. | LCSH: United States—
    Foreign relations—1953-1961. | LCSH: United States—Politics and
    government—1953-1961. | LCGFT: Biographies.
Classification: LCC HB119.A55 A43 2023 | DDC 330.092—dc23

Contents

Dillon with President Eisenhower. In 1959 *Time* magazine described Dillon as having "nailed down a top place in Ike's regard." Dillon Fund Archive.

Awkward encounter: President Eisenhower and President-elect Kennedy in the Cabinet Room, with Secretary of the Treasury Robert Anderson and Secretary of the Treasury–designate Dillon, January 19, 1961. Ike pronounced himself "surprised" when Dillon took the job. John F. Kennedy Presidential Library. Abbie Rowe, National Park Service.

Dillon and President Kennedy at an IRS conference, May 1, 1961. "Douglas Dillon he liked very much," Robert Kennedy said. John F. Kennedy Presidential Library. Abbie Rowe, National Park Service.

"Well, Doug, I guess I'm going to have to find you your billion dollars." Kennedy greets Dillon (with Dean Rusk in the background) after the Inter-American Economic and Social Conference at Punta del Este, August 19, 1961. John F. Kennedy Presidential Library. Robert Knudsen, White House.

Dillon at the height of his powers. White House, 1962. "He was an exceptionally
skilled operator ... ready to pull every stop and cut many corners," Arthur
Schlesinger Jr. said, "always (and justifiably) confident that his charm could heal any
feelings hurt in the process." John F. Kennedy Presidential Library. Abbie Rowe,
National Park Service

"Dillon wants to leave. I sure don't want him to." With President Johnson in the Oval Office, c. 1964. Dillon Fund Archive.

THE
DILLON
ERA

Prologue

Friday, November 22, 1963. 7:30 a.m. Hawaii–Aleutian Standard Time; 11:30 a.m. Central Standard Time. For around thirteen minutes that day, three Boeing C-137 Stratoliners from the presidential air transport fleet flew at the same time. The newest of them, Special Air Mission (SAM) 26000 – call sign Airforce One – carried President John F. Kennedy and the First Lady Jacqueline Kennedy on the short hop from Fort Worth to Love Field, Dallas, Texas, where they arrived at 11:38 CST. Making the same journey, SAM 86970 – Air Force Two – carried the vice president Lyndon B. Johnson and his wife Ladybird Johnson to Love Field, where on arrival they had to scramble to be at the bottom of the steps of Air Force One to meet the Kennedys as they disembarked. Such were the indignities that a vice president had to endure – indignities that Johnson felt more keenly than most.

Then there was the third aircraft. By now SAM 86972 was ninety minutes into a flight from Honolulu to Tokyo, with a possible refueling required mid-Pacific at Wake Island, depending on the headwinds. On board was the treasury secretary, Douglas Dillon, along with five other cabinet secretaries – Dean Rusk (State), Stuart Udall (Interior), Orville Freeman (Agriculture), Willard Wirtz (Labor), and Luther Hodges (Commerce) – as well as the chair of the Council of Economic Advisers, Walter Heller, and White House press secretary Pierre Salinger. The delegation was headed to the annual US-Japan economic conference. In light of what happened before they even reached Tokyo, investigators would pore over every detail of these flights. Soon enough, both pragmatists and conspiracy theorists alike wondered why it was that half the Kennedy cabinet was airborne at the same time and how so many senior advisers could be out of the country when a crisis hit.

Secretary of State Rusk, by order of cabinet precedence, had access to the private cabin usually reserved for the president on aircraft 86972, but if Douglas Dillon, accompanied by his wife Phyllis, was bothered about such things, he was certainly not showing it. As heir to one of the biggest fortunes in the United States, his vast wealth meant he was used to more luxurious travel arrangements. Government service, however, meant sacrifices and these included his own comfort. The usual round of meetings and telephone calls, of rushing to the Hill for conversations with obdurate members of Congress about a major tax bill, and the general tyranny of the calendar were removed at 30,000 feet. Yet meetings intruded with a wearisome inevitability even midair, for here came a steward approaching to ask if the secretary would mind stepping up front to see Rusk. Other members of the cabinet, along with Heller and Salinger, were similarly approached.

When Dillon arrived in the staterooms, he sensed immediately that something was desperately wrong. The taciturn Rusk was quiet even by his own low-key standards. Looking at him, Dillon felt that the Soviets must have dropped a nuclear bomb on an American city. Rusk shuffled awkwardly on the spot, fingering a yellow teletype message as he waited for everyone to assemble. When they were all there and the door was shut, he read out the message in his hand: "KENNEDY WOUNDED PERHAPS FATALLY BY ASSASSINS BULLET."

"My God!" gasped the agriculture secretary Orville Freeman, who began to weep. The legs of the commerce secretary, Luther Hodges, buckled at the news and he slumped to the floor. As to Dillon, the White House press secretary Pierre Salinger recalls that he "just shook his head back and forth in disbelief."

"What shall we do?" Rusk asked.

It was Dillon who gave the answer.

"We've got to turn this plane around."

In his classic account of the Kennedy assassination, the journalist and historian William Manchester uses the word "decisively" here to describe Dillon's instructions. It represents the general tenor of his account of the flight that day. Dillon knew Jack Kennedy better than any of the other cabinet members on board and was the only one who was a personal friend. But what struck everyone about Dillon's conduct was how commanding he was in the moment. When news came soon afterwards that the president was dead, Rusk made a short announcement on the intercom system but then seemed to suffer some kind of nervous collapse. Dillon's daughter Joan recalls her father telling her the next day that "Rusk became frozen and incapable of speech." It was Dillon who would fill the void.

After twenty-two minutes on the ground in Honolulu to refuel, the plane took off for Washington. Dillon told the exhausted Rusk to rest. The secretary of state took a sleeping pill and Dillon personally put him to bed. When calls came in over the radio from George Ball, the undersecretary of state, "the secretary of the treasury," writes Manchester, would "double as secretary of state." While Rusk slept, Dillon (now fourth in line to the presidency) gathered the other cabinet members with subcabinet officials to game out various scenarios. He urged caution, emphasizing Johnson's long experience. His tone was one of constant reassurance. He divided everyone "in pairs and threes and groups," Hodges recalled, with the instruction to think about "the new president's desires and plans." It was, Manchester says, "probably the first thoughtful assessment of the Johnson Presidency."

At 12:31 a.m. EST, after an eight-and-a-half-hour flight from Honolulu, the plane touched down at Andrews, where six hours earlier Air Force One had arrived with Kennedy's body. The six cabinet members, led by the recently awoken Rusk, descended the steps into a throng of officials and reporters. In the harsh illumination of the TV lights and camera flashbulbs, all looked wan and drawn. A microphone was set up for Rusk to speak – the same microphone from which the new president had spoken to the nation just hours earlier. Dillon hung back, but both Udall and Freeman pushed him forward to stand beside Rusk. "President Johnson needs and deserves our fullest support," the secretary of state said in a flat monotone. Throughout the statement, Dillon's eyes never left him.[1]

All anyone watching the television news would have noticed about Douglas Dillon, if they noticed anything about him at all, was a tall, grim-faced figure, hat in hand and silent. He drew no attention to himself. Certainly, he had not contrived to maneuver the ineffectual Rusk aside to make the statement himself. The forceful character who had taken the lead aboard the plane was not visible on the tarmac at Andrews. Instead, Douglas Dillon had faded to gray.

That would be Douglas Dillon's fate in the history books too. In the story of the fifties and sixties he has become, if not a forgotten figure, then a largely overlooked and underappreciated one. This has had much to do with his low-key style that did not draw attention to itself as did that of such larger-than-life cabinet figures as John Foster Dulles and Robert McNamara. Even those at a lower level such as George Ball or Chester Bowles, who both occupied the position of undersecretary of state that Dillon held in the 1950s, have been more prominent in public awareness. But his lack of recognition also has to do with history itself. The assassination of John F. Kennedy would change the nature of what government had been until that time. Everything about the period, including initially even the Eisenhower presidency, would be swept up overnight into The Age of Camelot. Even as Kennedy's Cold War liberalism came to be tarnished by the trauma of the Vietnam War and when revelations about the president's personal life – the "dark side of Camelot" – raised doubts about his character, public fascination with the tragic young president never dimmed. Quieter, less glamorous figures such as Dillon quickly receded into the shadows as the headlights of history focused on the martyred commander-in-chief and the Texan who succeeded him to preside over the Vietnam War.

Yet Dillon was a commanding figure and widely admired by those he worked with during the fifties and sixties. Robert Kennedy, attorney general in his brother's administration, said that JFK "thought he [Dillon] was a brilliant man" and that "I don't know anyone who has contributed more to the president." The close connection between JFK and Dillon was more than just professional. "Of all the cabinet once we were in the White House, they [Douglas and Phyllis Dillon] really were our best friends," the former first lady, Jacqueline Kennedy, recalled. For John Foster Dulles, Eisenhower's secretary of state, Dillon was "someone with whom I can talk with intimacy and confidence and on a statesmanlike basis." Walter Hallstein, the first commission president of the European Economic Community and a founding father of European integration, proclaimed that they were all living in "The Dillon Era." The New York Times picked up the quote and ran an editorial in March 1960 under a headline using the same phrase. Other contemporaries eagerly pointed to Dillon's achievements as treasury secretary, not least in delivering economic prosperity spurred by the then biggest tax cuts in American history and bringing unemployment down to record lows. Even Paul Samuelson, the Nobel Prize–winning economist who had been a sparring partner in the early days of the Kennedy administration, wrote that "posterity will rise to call Dillon's name blessed." The journalist Theodore White noted that Dillon had presided over a "revolutionary" moment in American economic life. His tax cuts would have been the crowning glory of the Kennedy administration's domestic agenda "had [they] not been overshadowed by … the civil rights bill."[2]

"Overshadowed" is a word that characterizes Dillon's historical reputation and his achievements: overshadowed by more flamboyant, grandstanding characters, by the public fascination with Camelot and the assassination of a president, and by the pressing nature of issues such as civil rights and Vietnam that dominated politics in the period after he left office.

So how was it that this understated American – a Republican who served in the Eisenhower, Kennedy, and Johnson administrations – came to be seen as a figure of such stature by his contemporaries? It seemed inevitable to them that Dillon would be secretary of state in a Nixon administration. Instead, it was his opponent who appointed Dillon secretary of the treasury. Whichever way they split it, by 1960, no one wanted to govern without Douglas Dillon.

Chapter One

An American in Paris
Paris, 1953–1954

Soon after the 1952 presidential election, the victorious Republican candidate, Dwight D. Eisenhower, general of the army, called Clarence Dillon, "Baron" of Wall Street, to his temporary offices in the Commodore Hotel, New York, to discuss political appointments. Cynical observers would have seen it as classic payback. Dillon, one of the fifty richest Americans, had been generous to the Eisenhower campaign, as well introducing him "to some of the lawyers and bankers from downtown." His firm, Dillon Read, served a range of blue-chip corporations including Goodyear, Standard Oil, and Chrysler, as well as public municipalities. Now Clarence could expect some reward. Eisenhower actively wanted to recruit successful figures from business into his administration rather than "failures, college professors [crossed out and replaced by 'political hacks'], and New Deal lawyers." All these latter figures, he complained, "would jump at the chance to get a job that a successful businessman has to sacrifice very much to take." By the end of the meeting the two men had agreed that a Dillon would be United States ambassador to France. But it was not Clarence who would be credentialed; the Baron had in fact secured the post for his son, Douglas.[1]

Did Eisenhower offer Clarence the job first? "I don't doubt it's right," noted August Belmont IV, later president of Dillon Read investment bank and a close friend of Douglas Dillon. For Clarence, however, the job offered an ideal opportunity to solve the problem of what to do about his eldest son, who even he recognized had become deeply unhappy working on Wall Street.

Paul Nitze, a protégé of Clarence Dillon's and vice president at Dillon Read until 1941, recalled a conversation with Douglas Dillon on a boat trip in Maine not long before the election. "I remember kind of a rough day in talking to Douglas about the relative merits of working at Wall Street or working the right job in government," he said. "And I think I was persuasive to him that there was more real excitement to be had working for the government than in Wall Street." It was a path that Nitze himself had taken with great success. During the Second World War, he had been recruited by another Dillon Read figure, James Forrestal, who had gone to Washington as a special assistant to President Franklin D. Roosevelt before being nominated as deputy to Frank Knox, secretary of the navy, and replacing him on the secretary's death in 1944. By the 1950s, Nitze was the director of policy planning at the State Department and responsible for producing the National Security Council's NSC-68 analysis that had provided President Truman with a strategic blueprint for conducting the Cold War.

For Douglas Dillon in 1952, that conversation was like "opening a door," Nitze judged, adding that Dillon had told him it was "instrumental in persuading him that he would like to get into government." By the beginning of the next decade, Dillon would be in the cabinet and outrank him. "Forrestal and I were the only ones to get to Cabinet level," Dillon would later tease the other Dillon Read partners who had worked in government, including Nitze.[2]

Clarence had never hidden the fact that he wanted his son to head up Dillon Read. Born in 1909 in Geneva, Switzerland, while his parents were traveling, Clarence Douglas Dillon was educated at Pine Lodge (alongside Nelson, Laurance, and John Rockefeller III), Groton, and Harvard. He was always known by middle name, Douglas, although he dropped the extra "s" from the name on his birth certificate – Douglass – which came from his mother Anne's maiden name. As soon as he graduated in 1931, Clarence brought him into his private office. Initially he worked as his father's personal liaison with Forrestal, who would be responsible for restoring the firm's fortunes during the Depression. It became in effect a Wall Street apprenticeship. His father paid $185,000 for a seat on the Stock Exchange to give him experience working as a floor broker before bringing him back to Dillon Read. Even during the Second World War, Clarence initially managed to keep his son within the Dillon Read family by sending him in 1940 to work for Forrestal, now undersecretary of the navy. Douglas was part of a bitter negotiation with the British after the Roosevelt administration forced them to sell the world's largest producer of rayon in return for American wartime aid. By the time the United States prepared to enter the war in 1941, Dillon received a commission in the naval reserve. Before going on active duty at sea, he worked briefly in the office of William "Wild Bill" Donovan as he set up the Office of Strategic Services (oss, the precursor to the cia); it was a connection with the intelligence agency that Dillon would maintain throughout his political career. From 1942, he began flying onboard B-24 bombers and more often on reconnaissance or search and rescue missions in the Pacific. "I know what tracers look like," he would say understatedly.[3]

Once the war ended, Dillon returned to Wall Street to be president of Clarence's closed-end investment trust, United States & Foreign Securities Corp (US&FS), where much of the family's personal wealth was invested. By 1952, Dillon was controlling assets that Nitze estimated were up to $250 million – "a big chunk of money." Yet Dillon was bored with life on Wall Street. "I didn't like the investment bank business," he would recall. "I wanted to go off and do something else." In part this was because he felt that the Depression had changed banking, making it "more salesmanship than crafting an investment package." There was something else too: the suffocating presence of his father and the expectations that went with being the heir apparent. "He had to argue with his old man all the time," August Belmont IV remembered. Nitze concurred. "I don't think he felt very happy [working] with his father," he judged. Nitze thought Dillon recognized he lacked the "inner drive" needed for "slaying rivals" that his father, a second-generation Polish-Jewish immigrant who had clawed his way to the top on Wall Street, possessed in abundance. "I just did not have the feeling that he wanted to take charge of Dillon Read & Co.," Nitze said. "And then when he got into the great world, he did a hell of a lot better."[4]

Clarence recognized his son's restlessness and made a deal with him. Douglas would be allowed to go off to play a public role but would return to run Dillon Read once he had shown his paces. It was a decision Clarence came to regret. "He was disappointed, because when I went to France as the American ambassador he was thrilled – that was fine," Douglas recalled. "But when I came back to work in the State Department and then went on to be the secretary of the treasury, he thought those were a waste of time. He thought the real thing to do was to be in business and create something." Clarence would live until 1979, dying at the age of ninety-six, his displeasure having only partly dissipated after Douglas returned from the Treasury department to run, if not Dillon Read, then at least US & Foreign Securities Corp and to manage the family's money.[5]

Dillon *fils* was announced as envoy to Paris on January 17, 1953, three days before Eisenhower's inauguration. "C. Douglas Dillon, who has been named Ambassador to France by Gen. Dwight D. Eisenhower, will bring to the critical Paris post an experienced hand in international finance," the *New York Times* reported, "at a time when the new administration must chart new economic and mutual aid policies." Not everyone was impressed. The influential commentator James Reston noted that "Eisenhower's diplomatic appointments are being watched here [in Washington, DC] with more than usual interest," noting that the nomination of Harvard president James B. Conant as ambassador to West Germany was being greeted "with more approval than the reports that Clare Boothe Luce was to get the post in Rome and Douglas Dillon, the young New York banker, the mission in Paris." The *Times* reported that Howard Alexander Smith and Robert C. Hendrickson, the senators from Dillon's home state of New Jersey, were outraged at his being chosen "without consultation."[6]

Luckily for Dillon, any drama about his appointment was overshadowed by difficulties in confirming "Engine Charlie" Wilson, the head of General Motors, as secretary of defense, and former Nebraska governor Val Peterson as ambassador to India. It meant that his appointment sailed through the Senate Foreign Relations Committee, helped by his friendship with Democrat J. William Fulbright of Arkansas – a rising star on the committee.

In fact, the toughest grilling Dillon got during the confirmation process was from Clare Booth Luce, married into the *Time, Life, Fortune,* and *Sports Illustrated* magazine empire, who was set to become the first woman appointed to a major overseas ambassadorial post. Waiting outside the Foreign Relations committee room, Dillon sprawled on a sofa next to Luce, who asked him sharply whether he intended sitting like that for the photographers. "She taught me then, right away, how I should take care of my legs when I was being photographed," he recalled. "So I always remembered that [if] your feet stick out they look as big as the rest of you." After this encounter with Luce, it was no wonder that his time before the committee seemed like a walk in the park. His one newsworthy observation at the hearing was that it was "vital" that further American aid should be given to "anti-Communist Vietnamese in Indo-China, particularly in the training and arming of more troops."[7]

For all the ease of Dillon's confirmation, there were still reservations about his appointment. To start with, he had no experience of foreign policy beyond membership of the Council on Foreign Relations in New York. Although the family had strong connections with France through their ownership of the legendary Château Haut-Brion, among the greatest and most storied wines in the world, Dillon himself knew the country's politics only moderately well. Even his French was passable at best. The *New York Times* reported rumblings in Paris, where "many French officials thought him too young and too inexperienced for the post." Benjamin Bradlee, later the editor of the *Washington Post*, remembers his misgivings as press attaché in the Paris embassy in 1953 on hearing of Dillon's appointment. "I was scared shitless as a matter of fact," Bradlee said bluntly, "because his father had bought him the job, really, by major contributions to Ike, and, as bright as he was, he was unproven in the world."[8]

What Dillon did have, however, was the ear of John Foster Dulles, the new secretary of state. Dulles came from a family steeped in public service. His brother Allen was to serve in the new government as director of the CIA. Their grandfather, John W. Foster, had been secretary of state under President Benjamin Harrison in the 1890s and their uncle, Robert Lansing, held the same post during the First World War and at the Paris peace conference. Foster Dulles was not always an easy man to like. His brusque, unclubbable manner often alienated friends and enemies alike. "The only bull who carried his own China closet with him," Winston Churchill would say in frustration (drawing on the secretary's well-known interest as a collector of fine china). He could also appear painfully boring. "His speech was slow," another British prime minister, Harold Macmillan, would write, "but it easily kept pace with his thoughts." Around Washington, the quip was "Dull, Duller, Dulles."[9] Yet Dulles's command of foreign policy was total. Many at the time would mistake command for domination of the president. The two men, in the words of diplomatic historian George C. Herring, "in fact formed an extraordinarily close partnership based on mutual respect" with Dulles often serving as "a lightning rod for his boss."[10]

Dulles's worldview and understanding of how foreign policy should be conducted was a good fit for a banker like Douglas Dillon. The new secretary of state was another figure drawn from the Wall Street world of Dillon Read. Dulles's public image was that of a Cold War hawk and anti-communist ideologue. In reality, he was more pragmatic and analytical, with an understanding of the world that was rooted in international finance more than "brinkmanship" and "massive retaliation." Successful foreign policy for him was as much about exchange rates as nuclear weapons. As a corporate lawyer at Sullivan & Cromwell, he had spent most of his career working for international banks, including clients of Dillon Read, and had come to associate the interests of Wall Street and the global economy with those of the United States. "His ideology was the defense of the two principles that he believed best served global commerce," his biographer Stephen Kinzer writes: "free enterprise and American-centered internationalism."[11]

It was during the 1940s, when Thomas E. Dewey, the forty-seventh governor of New York, made three bids for the presidency, that Dulles gave Dillon his first taste of national politics. "My father had been a good friend of Foster Dulles – used him as a lawyer [at] Sullivan & Cromwell – and so was aware of my interest in politics," Dillon recalled. Clarence always thought Dulles was "much more studious and cultivated than the run-of-the-[mill] lawyers that you meet downtown." He would help finance campaigns that Dulles was involved in and, when Dulles was in office, provide a sanctuary for him at his house in Jamaica. After the secretary's death in 1959, Clarence financed a memorial library of diplomatic history in his honor at Princeton.

It was this close relationship that provided Douglas with his entrée into politics. The younger Dillon helped Dulles raise money for Dewey's unsuccessful bid for the nomination in 1940 and, after missing the 1944 election on overseas duty with the navy, worked with Dulles on the nominating committee for Dewey in 1948. During the presidential campaign against President Harry Truman, Dillon helped write foreign policy speeches for Dewey. Although unsuccessful in 1948, Dillon became part of a team that would dominate American foreign policy throughout the next decade and beyond. "Foster Dulles had an office in the [New York] Roosevelt Hotel, and his chief assistant was his brother, Allen Dulles," Dillon recalled. "The next down the ladder was Christian Herter [a future secretary of state], and the next one was me [a future undersecretary of state and treasury secretary], and the youngest one was McGeorge Bundy [a future national security advisor], so we had quite the group."[12]

After Eisenhower's victory, Dillon received a phone call from Dulles asking him for lunch at the Commodore Hotel. Whether he was unaware of his father's previous conversation with the president-elect, or was simply being discreet, he expressed "surprise" and delight when Dulles tapped him for the Paris embassy. "My appointment as Ambassador to Paris was due entirely … to Mr. Dulles personally," Dillon would later say. "He had recommended me for this position, and the president had agreed to go along with it."

Still, there was a catch. In fact, there were several, the first of which was Dulles reminding him that he himself took a close interest in France. He had studied at the Sorbonne for a year and later attended the Paris Peace Conference as legal counsel for the United States delegation (headed by Woodrow Wilson, who had taught Dulles at Princeton). He had a real love and understanding of France, he told Dillon.

Dulles also revealed that the new ambassador was to have the indignity of a babysitter – and not just any babysitter, but David K. Bruce, a predecessor as envoy to France. The context was the Treaty of Paris, which in 1952 had established a European Coal and Steel Community (ECSC) and a European Defence Community (EDC) to reintegrate West Germany into the Western economy and defense architecture. Ironically, given that the idea had started with the French "Pleven Plan," the EDC element of the treaty was now in danger of being rejected by the French parliament. Bruce would be going to Paris as an "observer" to the interim EDC with the specific task of getting ratification. Known as much for his wealth and social connections – both of which he possessed in abundance – Bruce was in many ways an obvious choice to help schmooze the EDC past the French. Nevertheless, it was hardly a vote of confidence in Dillon that the most important item on his agenda had been handed off to someone else. He felt the snub keenly. "[Dulles] said we'd be able to get along fine," Dillon recalled drily, but it "didn't quite work out that way."[13]

Dillon would often find himself out of step with the State Department over the next few years, including with the other political appointees in the administration. In these bureaucratic disputes involving both personality and policy, his own relationship with Dulles was essential. "I must say, I found him more [sympathetic and understanding] than the other people in the State Department to whom the Ambassador ordinarily would report," he recalled, singling out Robert Murphy and Herbert Hoover Jr. for particular attention. In the end, Dillon would outmaneuver them both because, to their fury, "I found that I could get a hearing by going straight to Mr. Dulles." It was the relationship that would form the basis of his increasing influence throughout the decade.[14]

Dillon and his wife Phyllis set sail for France on Saturday, February 28, 1953, aboard the liner *America*. They took along an instructor to give them French lessons each day. Phyllis started more or less from scratch, but the quality of Dillon's own language skills was a matter of dispute. "I was rusty in speaking it myself," he would confess. "I had an accent, but I could get along [and] didn't have to do much special studying." He had the confidence to meet French politicians without a translator. "From day one, when I got to Paris, and I went to call on people at the Quai d'Orsay, or any other ministry, I never took a note-taker or an interpreter with me," he boasted. "I was always on my own." Others were less impressed. "His French was no good," Ben Bradlee said. "His French was really very poor." Perhaps sensing this himself, Dillon would soon hire "a failed actress of the Comédie-Française ... who spoke beautiful French" to visit the *résidence* each morning to help him improve.[15]

Arriving in Paris on March 7, the new ambassador seemed to *Le Monde* "very young in appearance [and] has all the features of the typical American: tall stature, blue eyes, a benevolent and tireless smile." Dillon quickly acknowledged "anti-American feeling in France" and did not try to hide that relations between the two countries were at a low ebb. He hoped it was "a question of mis-understanding," saying his principal task would be to "properly explain the United States to France." In fact, in his first meeting with the French prime minister, René Mayer, whose short-lived ministry survived only a few months, it became clear that the French government was as determined to enlist Dillon's help in properly explaining France to the United States as the other way round. Mayer spoke "very frankly" to him "about public opinion in the US."

All told, the new ambassador had arrived at a febrile time not just in Franco-American relations, but in French political culture. Raymond Aron, author of *The Opium of the Intellectuals* (1955), would call the period from January 1953 to August 1954 "the greatest ideological and political debate France has known since the Dreyfus affair." That was an overstatement, but French politics was in a state of chaos – Dillon would liaise with four prime ministers over the next two years.[16]

When Dillon arrived, the Eisenhower administration was still unsure about its tactics to get France to ratify the 1952 Paris Treaty. The EDC represented an attempt by France, Germany, Italy, Belgium, the Netherlands, and Luxembourg to create a common European Defence Force with a joint command structure and multinational military capability. The United States supported the proposal because it increased Europe's commitment – both military and financial – to its own defense, but did so within the framework of the US-dominated NATO alliance. The EDC also provided a way forward on the tricky question of how to reintegrate West Germany into the defense structures of the Western alliance.

Despite France having been in the vanguard of the original declaration, French public opinion was resistant to the notion of a common European army. Many worried it violated the "sacred" powers reserved to the nation state on the control of military forces and decisions in war. Even more feared it was a gateway to a remilitarized Germany. The carrot the United States offered was substantial – an aid package for 1954 worth over a billion dollars. This figure represented a reversal of cuts that had been implemented in the last days of the Truman administration. But Eisenhower also gave a clear warning that such largesse could not and would not continue for much longer if anti-American rhetoric went unchecked and France continued to postpone ratification of the EDC.[17]

After a meeting with foreign minister Georges Bidault in late March, Dillon urged "great care" on Washington not to give the French the impression that "anyone doubts [their] sincerity." However, "This does not REPEAT NOT mean that [Bidault] and Mayer should not REPEAT NOT be pressed hard for answer[s] as to plans and timing re. EDC."[18]

Ultimately it made no difference. On May 21, 1953, the government fell and the French parliament was plunged into a month-long crisis. Eventually the conservative Joseph Laniel put together a broadly based administration. He was "in many respects much less of a dark horse" than his predecessors, Dillon told Dulles, but "while not weak, [he] cannot be described as inclining toward toughness." Taken together with the overall political crisis, which had "seriously disturbed [the] country and deeply shaken [the] Assembly," the prospects for a better relationship with the United States looked bleak. Although Laniel was himself a supporter of the EDC, he had included three center-right Gaullists in his cabinet, thus bringing anti-EDC deputies into the heart of government. A ratcheting up of anti-American sentiment seemed inevitable.[19]

General Charles de Gaulle, hero of the French resistance during the Second World War, had nominally retired from politics by 1953, but his influence over the party he had founded, Rassemblement du peuple français (RPF), remained profound. He was hostile to "how the Americans are using open and secret pressure to compel France to accept the EDC which can only condemn her to decay." Given the influence that de Gaulle exercised, Dillon was astonished that the embassy had no formal contact with him whatsoever. "I said to the people in our political division that I wanted to meet General de Gaulle," he recalled. But they told him that "the American ambassador just doesn't talk to General de Gaulle." Jefferson Caffery, the ambassador from 1944 to 1949, "had a fight with him," the staff informed an incredulous Dillon, and since then "no American ambassador has had any connection." They didn't even know "how we could get in touch with him."[20]

Dillon immediately set about correcting that self-inflicted wound. The maneuver provides an insight into an aspect of his character that would be crucial to his success over the coming years. There was a gentlemanly quality to Dillon, an ease of personality, that meant he was often prepared to set aside vanity or *amour propre* to get what he wanted. In contrast, de Gaulle's whole program, C.L. Sulzberger of the *New York Times* pointed out, was "A Policy of Amour Propre." Further enquiries revealed that no previous ambassador had seen de Gaulle because they had all insisted that the general call upon them at the chancery. "I thought that was nonsense," Dillon said, "so I went up and saw him during the summer of 1953 at the Hotel La Perouse." The two men had supper and talked frankly about "the future of France" and relations with the United States. The encounter was the first in a series of regular meetings; significantly, it green-lighted other Gaullists in parliament to strengthen contacts with the embassy. De Gaulle also offered Dillon a subtle allusion that provided insight into his disposition. During the war, he explained, he had been "a great burden" on President Roosevelt. "He felt very badly about that because Roosevelt was carrying all the burdens of the world on his shoulders," Dillon said, "but he, de Gaulle, was responsible for France, and he had to think of France first, and let Roosevelt think about the world." Putting France first and letting the United States think about the world would be a useful framework for understanding de Gaulle in the years to come.[21]

Another important call that Dillon paid early in his tenure was to the Soviet ambassador Aleksey Pavlov. The Soviet leader Joseph Stalin had died while Dillon was crossing the Atlantic Ocean to France. Foster Dulles at State and his brother Allen at the CIA both strongly advised Eisenhower against making any new overtures, predicting that the new Soviet leadership of Beria and Malenkov would be as hardline as Stalin. Beria, after all, had been second only to Stalin in his use of terror ("Our Himmler," Stalin had said approvingly.) At a meeting in Paris on March 27, the secretary of state warned his French counterpart Bidault that the West must maintain "a skeptical eye knowing that the doctrine of world domination remained the same." Yet when Malenkov stepped forward at Stalin's funeral to say that "peaceful" solutions could be found to all "contested issues" in the Cold War, it was just the encouragement Eisenhower needed. Overriding the Dulles brothers, he gave an address that became known as "The Chance for Peace." It took as a starting point the idea that Stalin's death represented "the greatest chance we have had in decades ... to move history in the right direction without war." The speech stressed the wasted resources of the arms race ("We pay for a single destroyer with new homes that could have housed more than 8,000 people") and announced, "We are ready, in short, to dedicate our strength to serving the needs rather than the fears of the world." Sherman Adams, the president's chief of staff, called it "the most effective speech of Eisenhower's public career."[22]

When Dillon called on Pavlov at the Soviet embassy shortly afterwards, he was received with "cordiality and treated to wine and fruit." Immediately he noticed that "there were no pictures of Stalin in sight," only a "head of Lenin" and, he noted whimsically, "a very small head of Malenkov painted on a small lampshade." Pavlov began by harking back to the "close cooperation with [the] US during the war years" and spoke of "the great esteem in which they held President Eisenhower." The president's "Chance for Peace" speech was welcomed as "an event of real importance." But "it appeared that Secretary Dulles did not agree with President Eisenhower and that this created [a] difficult situation." Dillon refuted the notion, telling Pavlov that "there was no disagreement whatsoever, that President Eisenhower's speech represented US policy, and that Secretary [Dulles] supported it fully." Pavlov countered that the fundamental question was whether the United States "accepted the possibility of coexistence." Dillon told him "There was no doubt on this subject and that we could clearly see the possibility of coexistence provided there was an end to aggressive tendencies." The two men parted agreeing that "personal contacts such as our talk were most useful" and hoping to "establish friendly relations" between the two embassies.[23]

Five days later, the chance for peace collapsed even before it began. Soviet tanks moved into East Berlin to suppress the widespread uprising against the communist regime of the German Democratic Republic (GDR). Pavlov was recalled on July 7 and Dillon had to begin again with a new Soviet envoy, Sergei Vinogradov. He would turn out to be a formidable opponent, with a wine cellar almost as good as Dillon's own. The whole encounter was an object lesson for Dillon about his new role: promoting a policy (the Chance for Peace) that he had played no part in crafting; disingenuously denying rumors of splits in Washington about that policy, and then seeing its entire premise swept away in the churn of events. Such was the life of an ambassador.[24]

The dramatic way in which events could turn was brought home to Dillon that spring with the controversy surrounding Julius and Ethel Rosenberg, convicted of spying on behalf of the Soviets. During the weeks leading up to their executions, Dillon dealt with a "flash-fire of anti-Americanism" as demonstrations ripped through France. In Paris, violent protests took place outside the American embassy on the northwest corner of the Place de la Concorde, forcing the police to put up a security cordon around the building. Dillon warned Washington not to mistake these events simply for the gripes of "intellectual circles in Paris" which believed "the American is an undisciplined barbarian." Instead, this was a wider expression of revulsion. Even President Vincent Auriol took the extraordinary step of conveying to Dillon "his emotion at the exceptional scale of the demonstrations in favor of the Rosenbergs."

For Dillon, the outbreak of anti-Americanism illustrated "the particular sensitivity of Frenchmen throughout the country and in all walks of life when political, moral and human issues are mixed." As the day of executions neared, Dillon made the case for delaying the death sentence in "the higher national interest." His advice could not have been clearer: "I feel bound to bring to your attention," he warned Dulles, "that if [the] death sentence is carried out this will have a most harmful effect on the opinion and attitude of the French people toward the United States." His plea went unheard. When the

Rosenbergs were executed on June 19, 1953, French police advised Dillon to leave Paris for the countryside.[25]

When Foster Dulles wrote to the American ambassadors in eleven NATO countries that summer asking for their frank estimate of how the United States was viewed overseas, Dillon did not hold back. He met regularly with his staff for several weeks to put together a twelve-page, single-spaced memorandum from Paris that he boldly entitled "The Decline of French Confidence in US Leadership." He sent it to Dulles on August 4 with a four-page summary over his own name, employing the convention of using "I" rather than "We" to indicate that it was the ambassador speaking directly rather than embassy officials. Clearly angered by recent events, Dillon offered a stinging indictment of America abroad.[26]

"French confidence in US leadership has indeed declined in the last six months," Dillon reported. He set out the basic causes for this turn of events, including the most important – that the administration had not made any direct public denunciation of McCarthyism and the widespread smearing of prominent individuals as communists or communist sympathizers: "This is the greatest single cause of the decline of French confidence in our leadership. Behavior which the French associate with dictatorship cannot be indulged in any instance by the world's leading democracy and leave the confidence in that country as a leader of the free world intact in France."

Dillon did not shy away from saying where blame lay for this turn of events. There were "doubts as to whether the president has a firm grasp" on his party and administration. That weak hand on the national tiller was also matched by another that was too firm on the international one. The administration often acted without adequate consultation with allies. What kind of reaction did Washington expect when it insisted that allies adopt its policies even when the US is "in a minority of one"? No wonder there was "doubt, mistrust, and resentment" about American policy abroad. Eisenhower's wartime history as the Supreme Allied Commander in Europe and the savior of France gave him a unique position. "France looks to the president himself," Dillon urged, "not only to set the tone of American foreign policy, but also for the reaffirmation of the basic tenets of American democracy."[27]

Dillon's covering letter and the memorandum were remarkable for a new ambassador speaking in such frank terms within documents meant for wide distribution. But they were also important because they represented Douglas Dillon's first real statement of a political philosophy.

The State Department, however, barely noticed. That same day the Soviets sent a note responding to the Western proposal for a meeting of the "Big Four" foreign ministers. Dillon predicted a "'battle of notes' which may last many months." So it turned out, with four further exchanges until agreement was finally reached for a conference in Berlin in January. By then Dillon was in New York, flat on his back, and in considerable pain.[28]

While the notes flew back and forth, the ambassador had been playing tennis in extreme heat ("hot as hell") when something in his back ripped apart, leaving him in agony. Over the following months, the pain only intensified. His French doctors tried confining him to bed for a week lying on a board. When this approach failed to alleviate the problem, Dillon wrote to Dulles asking for permission to fly home for tests. "This has become steadily worse," he reported, "so that now I can put no weight on the [right] leg at all." Doctors at New York Presbyterian Hospital diagnosed multiple ruptured spinal discs. They operated on November 24, with Dillon undergoing spinal fusion surgery. As it turned out, the American doctors were no better than the French. The estimated recovery time was three weeks, but it quickly became clear that the operation had not been a success. In addition to continuing back pain, Dillon added inflammation of the shoulder girdle nerve to such an extent that "I actually couldn't move my arm anymore." He was pumped full of strong painkillers until the inflammation went down, but then required lengthy rehabilitation to break the adhesions.

Concentration of any kind was near impossible when the physical effort of working was so painful. Eventually he would have a special desk designed that allowed him to sit straighter. He used it throughout the rest of his government career. Only slowly was he able to return to light ambassadorial duties between treatments. Dillon was out of action for the best part of four months, only resuming active duty in March 1954. What he found when he returned to Paris was a country still in a state of crisis, as France spiraled into one of the greatest humiliations of its history. It would bring Dillon from the periphery of events to the center for the first time in his government career.[29]

By the spring of 1954, French efforts to hold onto its imperial possessions in Indochina depended on the outcome of a siege at the tiny fortress of Dien Bien Phu, where 12,000 French troops were being attacked by the communist-inspired Viet Minh. Ironically, it was the French themselves who had chosen this remote site as a test of strength, in order "to oblige the enemy to recognize the impossibility of achieving a decisive military outcome." In fact, Dien Bien Phu would prove the opposite. The general on the ground, Henri Eugène Navarre, a veteran of the First World War, had picked the site with little intelligence about the strength of the enemy. The Viet Minh had hoped to engage French troops as far away as possible from their bases. The choice of

Dien Bien Phu, in isolated northwestern Vietnam near the border with Laos, was beyond even their wildest hopes. By the beginning of April 1954, French troops faced certain defeat.[30]

At eleven o'clock on the night of April 5, Dillon received an unexpected call to see the prime minister immediately at his Hôtel de Matignon *résidence*. Courteous French officials had hesitated about summoning the American ambassador so late on a Sunday night, but when Dillon arrived, he soon discovered why there was so much urgency.

"Bidault received me in Laniel's office and was joined in a few minutes by Laniel," Dillon wrote. "They said that immediate armed intervention of US carrier aircraft at Dien Bien Phu is now necessary to save the situation." General Navarre had reported that "without help" the "fate of Dien Bien Phu will probably be sealed." Bidault sent Dillon back to the embassy "saying that for good or evil the fate of Southeast Asia now rested on Dien Bien Phu."[31]

Dillon fired off an urgent telegram at 1 a.m. Paris time. Just after eight o'clock the following morning in Washington, Dulles transmitted the news to a clearly irritated Eisenhower. In part, the annoyance was at Admiral Arthur Radford, the chairman of the joint chiefs of staff, who had implied to his French opposite number just days earlier that the United States might be prepared to act. "He should never have told a foreign country he would do his best," Ike snapped, "because they then start putting pressure on us." But the president's vexation also came because he thought "such a move is impossible"; worse, to move without the support of Congress would be "completely unconstitutional and indefensible." Take "a look to see if anything else can be done," Eisenhower told Dulles, "but we cannot engage in active war."[32]

Within the hour, Dulles had cabled those instructions to Dillon, telling him to inform the French government that the request for intervention was "impossible," although the United States would "do everything short of belligerency." The secretary added that the United States might change its position on military action if France could achieve "active British Commonwealth participation" and what he soon termed United Action (a notion the French would later throw back in Dulles's face during the Suez Crisis). But Britain was unwilling.[33] Summoned to see Bidault, Dillon found that the French cabinet had taken the news "better than he had expected," but that the request had become one for intervention by air power. Ten to twenty B-29 aircraft, Bidault told him, "might save the day" at Dien Bien Phu.[34]

In 1972, in the context of the Vietnam War, Dillon would recall the French request for B-29 bombers with scorn. "They seemed to have the idea that if we sent these planes over and had one mission, we'd blow up all the guns around there and their troubles would be over," he said. "I thought it was very unlikely." In 1954, however, his advice was more ambivalent. Like most members of the foreign policy establishment, he had a thin understanding of circumstances in Indochina. His eyes were focused on Paris and US-French relations. Given what he had written about the frayed relationship the previous August, he was concerned the current crisis might bring about a new low. "If we cannot find a way to comply with their alternative suggestion [B-29s] and if Dien Bien Phu should fall, the French Government will inevitably lay a major share of blame on our inability or unwillingness to help," he warned Dulles, adding, "I sincerely hope that it will prove possible to grant in one form or another, the latest French request for assistance."[35]

Dulles flew to Paris twice that month for further talks with the French. On April 22, Dillon accompanied him to a dismal meeting with Bidault on the margins of a NATO conference. The French foreign minister told Dulles that the situation in Dien Bien Phu was now "virtually hopeless." He spelled out the implications: "If Dien Bien Phu fell, the French would want to pull out entirely from southeast Asia and assume no continuing commitments and the rest of us would have to get along without France." Dillon was astonished, as Bidault had only recently told him that France would go on fighting "as a matter of honor." The reversal explained why the prime minister, Laniel, had refused Bidault's pleas to attend the meeting – the mortification was too much. Dulles was not without sympathy for Bidault, who he recognized was "a man close to the breaking point." But of the French government more generally the secretary could barely conceal his contempt. "The situation here is tragic," he wrote directly to Eisenhower. "France is almost visibly collapsing under our eyes."[36]

It was in this context that Dillon made his own position clear. As with his August 1953 memorandum on "The Decline of French Confidence in US Leadership," his cable to Washington was expressed with both clarity and force. The decision at hand may have been about whether the United States should intervene to save the French garrison at Dien Bien Phu, but the implications, he believed, were far greater. With American assistance, the French would continue to fight in Indochina regardless of the result at Dien Bien Phu. However, an American refusal to give armed support would "inevitably become public knowledge" and "I feel the inevitable result will be the prompt overthrow of the Laniel government which has done its best to carry on in Indochina and its replacement by a government pledged to negotiate with Ho Chi-Minh and to withdraw French Forces." Even if armed aid was offered to that new government, "I do not think that such a government would accept

[it]." The situation in Paris had come into sharp focus. "Military intervention by US Forces," he advised, was "the only way to keep the French Union Forces fighting in Indochina and so to save Indochina from Communist control."[37]

Where did this ability come from to speak his mind? It was not a quality that many had seen in Dillon on Wall Street, where he had so often seemed in his father's shadow. Nitze, we know, thought Dillon himself worried that he lacked the "inner drive" for "slaying rivals." Yet here he was, an inexperienced diplomat, confidently contradicting, among others, the chairman of the Joint Chiefs, Admiral Radford, with a call to action to Dulles and Secretary of Defense Charles Wilson in the middle of a Cold War crisis.[38]

In some ways, it is easy to overstate the distinction between Dillon the banker and Dillon the diplomat. He had a naturally diffident personal style that often masked the clarity of his thought. The nature of diplomatic cables stripped away the reserve, leaving only the tersely expressed advice. Yet there was also a marked and perhaps unexpected confidence in his own judgments. In part, that came down to finding that he had an affinity with the work. It was also a question of upbringing and training. Having been responsible for managing assets of up to $250 million at US&FS (Nitze's "big chunk of money") and knowing that making the wrong decision could cost millions, Dillon already understood the pressure involved in making margin calls. But the confidence must also have come, surely, from an instinctive awareness that being rich meant he could speak his mind without fear of losing his job. If politics did not work out, there was always Dillon Read and a personal fortune to live off. That was not an outcome he would have welcomed – far from it. But independent means afforded him the luxury of an independent mind. Dillon was never part of the professional political class, so he had more willingness to expose his flanks to criticism, if he was convinced he was in the right.[39]

Eisenhower, however, was resolutely opposed to unilateral military intervention. Without it, Dien Bien Phu fell on May 7, followed by the French government on June 18. A new government headed by Pierre Mendès France would eventually come to power, making clear its commitment to ending the war in Indochina, exactly as Dillon had predicted.[40]

But what of his wider strategic point that the United States should provide military aid to France? Years later, amid the nightmare of the Vietnam War, Clark Clifford, secretary of defense in the Johnson administration, would pen a famous *mea culpa* about the war and the misguided reasons for the United States being in southeast Asia. "The forces we now have deployed," he concluded, "and the human and material costs we are now incurring have become, in my opinion, out of all proportion to our purpose." In 1954, Dillon had suggested American military aid for the explicit purpose of keeping the French in Vietnam. Such action, he argued, would make the difference between retaining or not the presence of an ally and traditional great power in an important region of the world. Clifford would point out later that those strategic aims somehow got flipped in the 1960s, so that Vietnam came to be the end rather than the means in Cold War strategy. It ended up outweighing any strategic significance it might have had. Dillon in 1954 had recognized that the decision on American support was not about propping up Vietnam. The real question he asked and answered was about the United States propping up its ally, France.[41]

The atmosphere in Paris in the weeks after the fall of Dien Bien Phu was toxic. "You'd run into people that wouldn't talk to you and so forth," Dillon said, "because the French were very emotional about defeat." Disconcertingly, he found himself booed when dining out and the occupants of elevators turned their backs on him. "It was at times unpleasant," he reflected. "There were many in France who felt that they had been let down, that we'd had it in our power to very easily prevent this humiliating occurrence. It was just that France felt terribly humiliated."[42]

With talks already underway in Geneva between France, the Viet Minh, and the great powers on the future French Indochina, Dillon continued to impress upon Washington "the disastrous effect on French public opinion" of doing nothing to help. Rightly or wrongly, the United States was being blamed for "having built up French hopes of intervention and then for having failed in the crisis." The result could well be a neutralist government that would "reduce French military commitments to NATO," be "completely intransigent" on the question of German rearmament, and "in all probability" cozy up to the Soviets to prevent German rearmament. "We risk the very existence of the North Atlantic Alliance," Dillon warned.[43]

Dulles dismissed this analysis. The French "probably" did not even really want intervention but only "wanted to have the possibility as a card to play." Dillon, who had been listed as an advisor at the Geneva peace talks, now found his services were no longer required. On June 17, Dulles confirmed to the National Security Council his view that the French wanted "out" of Indochina and "it was probably best to let them quit." Mendès France became prime minister the same day, promising a cease-fire in Indochina by July 20. The Geneva Accords would bring the war in Vietnam to an end and agree to divide the country temporarily until elections in 1956.[44]

With Indochina lost, Mendès France turned his attention to the other great point of contention with the United States: the rearmament of West Germany. At the beginning of July, the prime minister told Dillon that the European Defence Treaty would need to be amended again. That news brought Dulles racing to Paris, where he berated Mendès France, in the presence of Anthony Eden, about the realities of life on the world stage. This drew a laconic apology from Mendès France for being "a complete neophyte." Any sarcasm was lost on Dulles, whose frustrations of recent months now came pouring out. Even the minutes of the meeting noted that he spoke "with complete frankness." How could the United States work in harmony with France, he wanted to know, in the face of so much "French vacillation and backing out on commitments"?[45]

Dulles had the tough words, but he wavered when Dillon, ever the banker, proposed hitting the French where it hurts – in the wallet. American aid flowed into France through the offshore procurement program (OSP) that gave the French contracts to build military equipment and then purchased that equipment from them. As Lord Ismay, the secretary-general of NATO, pointed out in a report that year, "This scheme is beginning to show significant results." By April 1954, American contracts in European NATO countries amounted to $1.727 billion (not including $388 million of Special Military Support for France).[46]

Dillon urged Dulles to turn off the taps. "I assume there is no intention of placing any further OSP contracts, 'follow-on' or otherwise, in France in the near future," he wrote, with no question mark at the end of the sentence. He was genuinely affronted that the anti-EDC campaign was being financed by the directors and shareholders of French heavy industry, "including those of some plants working on OSP orders." No new offshore procurement contracts should be given to France until after the outcome of the EDC debate had been determined. "If any urgent cases should arise," Dillon told Dulles with familiar forthrightness, "I should appreciate it if no action is taken until cleared with me."[47]

Dulles was hesitant. Such a provocative act "was almost certain [to] leak to industrials and government." Could Dillon clarify whether the intention was "only to prevent encouraging opposition" or actively to generate the "suspicion that US in fact is deliberately withholding contracts." Dillon's reply was clear. The French armaments industry "cannot expect [to] go on profiting from OSP contracts if there is no EDC," he told Dulles on July 26. "The withholding of OSP contracts in [the] present critical period is obviously necessary to implement this policy objective." Dulles took the point and approved the recommendation.

Two days later he informed Dillon that the Department of Defense had cabled General Gruenther, Supreme Allied commander (Europe) and commander in chief of US European Command, "to carry out OSP policy."[48]

It was Dillon's most significant contribution to policy to date, but the EDC was a lost cause. When the foreign ministers of the six EDC nations met in Brussels on August 19, the talks broke down almost immediately. Dillon saw Mendès France in Paris days later and found him "very serious and somewhat depressed." The prime minister informed him that the treaty would be coming before the French parliament for a vote on August 30. Although the PM "expected that the Parliament would vote against EDC," there was "no possibility" of making it a "question of confidence" – in other words Mendès France would not stake his own future on the result of the vote.[49]

In meetings with Mendès France, Dillon as ambassador was often taciturn and deferential. On this occasion, however, he allowed himself a lengthy, impassioned assessment of the situation. He too had been "very depressed and distressed" during the Brussels Conference to see France so isolated. For months he had been warning that the French had to choose between the EDC or a German national army. "The spectacle of France, which three years ago had been the intellectual and moral leader in Europe, finding herself in complete isolation had been very upsetting to me," he said, adding that "because of my affection for France and for the good of the West and world, I hoped that this would not continue." But rejecting the treaty would "only increase the distrust and suspicion" that other powers had for France.

Telling Mendès France that he was speaking "personally" and not for the secretary, he warned him that current events "would naturally strengthen the feelings of that section of American opinion which was beginning to lose confidence in Europe." That could only weaken the Western alliance, he said, and "increase the danger of an eventual collision between the East and the West." Mendès France ruefully admitted that "this was true." But when Dillon asked him what he would do after the EDC debate, the prime minister shrugged it off, scandalizing the American by saying that he "intended to take a vacation of a week or two in the south of France."[50]

One of the oddities of the meeting was the observation by Mendès France about being "very much upset and distressed by certain misunderstandings between himself and the Secretary." He complained that advice being passed back to Washington was "erroneous and may have caused serious misunderstanding of the French position." But the complaint was not about Dillon. It was directed at the other senior American diplomat in Paris: David K. Bruce, United States observer to the EDC.[51]

Dillon had been perplexed by Bruce's appointment, not welcoming the fact that a predecessor was going to be in Paris. Bruce's haughty manner did not help. He may not have formally been an ambassador but he behaved like one, with a retreat at La Lanterne in the grounds of Versailles. More pertinently, as befitted the former head of oss in Europe, he was conspiratorial by nature – a tendency aided and abetted by his wife, Evangeline, who was one the great purveyors of Washington gossip and now served as DC's informal Paris correspondent.

While Dillon did on occasion complain to Dulles that Bruce's initiatives were "counterproductive," in truth the fault lines were as much about the failure of the arrangement as they were in the personal relationship between the two men. Bruce dismissed any disagreements as "tempests in a teapot." Yet the differences in approach and on the question of Europe itself did show the kind of uncertainty and confusion that Mendès France complained about to Dillon. It was "no secret" in either Paris or Washington, noted Henri Pierre, the US correspondent of *Le Monde*, that there were "two opposing conceptions" with regard to France: Bruce wanted "to put the French up against the wall" while Dillon "tries to create a better understanding between the Mendès government and that of Washington."[52]

Bruce was an enthusiast for European integration, supported by his No. 2, Tommy Tomlinson, whom Dillon thought "very aggressive" and "a Euro fanatic." Communication with the embassy was almost nonexistent because Bruce confidently expected to get the job of ratifying the EDC done by himself. "He operated so separately," Dillon recalled, "that until the final part of the EDC push in the summer of 1954, we never really had any contact." But as his earlier failure as ambassador to contact de Gaulle illustrates, Bruce did not always talk to the right people. Dillon thought him under the thumb of Jean Monnet, one of the leading lights of European integration. Bruce's contacts were out of date, and he lacked the reach of the embassy staff in talking to unions, business, the media, and politicians outside his orbit. Only once it became clear that the treaty would not pass did he belatedly recognize that Dillon had been right about leveraging aid. "We have tried reason, persuasion, generosity, understanding, sympathy, patience," he conceded. "All have failed, and I see no alternative but to deal with the French as cold bloodedly as they deal with us."[53]

The conversion came too late. When the EDC treaty went before the French National Assembly on August 30, it was defeated on a procedural matter by 319 votes to 264. As Bruce prepared to exit Paris, disillusioned and personally distraught at the sudden death of his aide Tomlinson, Dillon was left with the task of picking up the pieces of the relationship with America's oldest ally. "In past history the French state and even the French as a people have appeared to have been finished but there have been successive revivals," he told Dulles. "This we should do everything to encourage."[54]

Chapter Two

Shock Treatment
Paris, 1954–1955

Part of the allure of being United States ambassador in Paris – but also one of its irritations – was that the City of Lights always attracted rich and famous Americans as expats and tourists. Douglas Dillon, like his predecessors, enjoyed and endured this phenomenon, but was unusual in having a glittering socialite and political hostesses as part of the Embassy team. Susan Mary Patten was married to an attaché to the embassy, Bill Patten, but had never seen any "future in being an ordinary person." As a direct descendent of John Jay, the first chief justice of the United States, her political instincts went back to the founding of the American republic itself – something she rarely let anyone forget. She was, her future husband, the columnist Joseph Alsop, would say, part of "the ever-diminishing group of survivors of the WASP ascendancy." Couturiers, including Christian Dior, dressed her and the Rothschilds socialized with her. Personal friendships ranged from Greta Garbo to Churchill.[1]

Later, she would tell her children that they would find it difficult to understand why the European Defence Community (EDC) seemed to represent "the last, best hope for the United States and Europe," but in August 1954 Susan Mary was uncharacteristically flustered. "The last week in Paris was extremely tense," she wrote to her friend and fellow socialite Marietta Tree shortly before the parliamentary vote. Stopping off in Hohenlohe, near Heidelberg, on her way to Bayreuth, she was "greeted at the drawbridge" by Prince Constantin Hohenlohe and his housekeeper, "who had been crying, she told us apologetically, because the news had just come over the radio from Paris that the Chamber of Deputies had turned down the treaty." Everyone was in "despair" about the "bitter disappointment" and "overcome by "bone-chilling apprehension about the future." By the time Susan Mary returned to Paris, she feared the worst. "I don't want to want to give you the impression that as I went to fit a ballgown at Balmain's I wondered as the fitter stuck the pins in whether I would have a chance to dance in my new dress," she told Marietta, "but now and then that sort of thing did cross one's mind."[2]

With Susan Mary Patten's connections in Washington and Paris, perhaps her alarm was occasioned not so much by what her dressmaker said as by knowing that John Foster Dulles was furious. Nine months earlier, Dulles had threatened "an agonizing reappraisal" of the American commitment to European security should the treaty be rejected, even threatening to withdraw American troops from Europe. Writing now to the Paris Embassy with a draft of the long, angry statement he planned to make the next day, Dulles made clear that he intended to deliver on that reappraisal.[3] The United States, he said, could no longer "identify our destiny" with such a "self-defeating" nation.[4]

Dillon was shocked at the vehemence. He had thought the earlier "agonizing reappraisal" speech "a mistake." Although more recently he had been urging Dulles to stand up to the French by freezing offshore procurement, now he touched the brakes and recommended caution. Yes, the French had put "selfish, short-range, interest and narrow nationalism above patriotism." But Dulles should proceed with care when meting out punishments. France was sick, he told Dulles. "Shock treatment is indicated, merited and sound therapy," he advised, "but the voltage must be carefully controlled so as not to kill off the patient." A quick glance at the map of Europe and North Africa was enough to show "why we must in our own interests continue to exercise almost superhuman patience and forbearance during the next few months."[5]

Others in the State Department, including Undersecretary Walter Bedell Smith and Assistant Secretary Livingston T. Merchant, weighed in to support Dillon. Crucially, they also had the president on their side. "We cannot sit down in black despair and admit defeat," Eisenhower privately told Dulles, urging him to "remove the tone of bitterness." It was enough to ensure that the final statement was more measured and recognized that "foundations should not be shaken by any abrupt or any ill-considered action of our own." A nine-power conference in London was called for late September.[6]

"Be under no illusions as to the strength of the feeling on the subject in Washington," Dillon warned Mendès France during a long walk in the parkland at Château de Marly on the outskirts of Paris. When the prime minister learnt that Dulles was flying to Europe for talks without bothering to stop off in Paris, he would admit to Dillon feeling "deeply hurt" by the rebuff.[7]

Hurt feelings were only the half of it. When Dillon met Georges Bidault later that month, the former foreign minister urged the United States to be tough on Mendès France and "not to help him too much." He spoke with "extreme bitterness," Dillon reported, and thought the "only real solution" was one that "forced Mendès out of office." Next came Maurice Schumann, a Gaullist loyalist but also a committed European, urging a similar course of action: Washington should refuse to deal with Mendès France altogether and thereby make his position untenable.[8]

It was a reckless notion for the United States even to consider interfering in the domestic politics of a Western ally. Yet such was the anger in Washington that the idea was briefly considered. Undersecretary of state "Beetle" Smith had served as director of Central Intelligence at the CIA in the early fifties – a time when internal meddling in European affairs was central to CIA activities. Now he wanted to know if a scheme to get rid of Mendès France could work. Dillon was skeptical. "Whether we like it or not, Mendès is [the] man we will have to deal with on the German rearmament issue," he counseled. The premier's majority may well have been "incoherent" and his "stock declined," but he still enjoyed "considerable credit and cannot be easily brought down." In the end, Washington backtracked and stuck with Dillon's tactic of putting economic pressure on France, including with offshore procurement. The political dark arts were better left to the French politicians of the Fourth Republic, where governments were short-lived at the best of times.[9]

Yet even consideration of the move had been self-defeating. The French press began reporting that Dulles and the embassy were involved in trying to overthrow the government. Dillon believed the rumors came directly from Mendès France "to rally chauvinistic and nationalistic feeling to his side" in advance of the London conference. It was a "Mendès tactic [that] must be borne constantly in mind," Dillon warned Dulles. In London, "no opportunity should be given him [Mendès France] to imply that the US or its representatives have treated France with anything other than correct politeness."[10]

For all the earlier talk of putting pressure on France and an "agonizing reappraisal" of the American commitment to Europe, in the end it was in Britain where Dulles's words had the most dramatic effect. "The danger was believed to be very real," the historian Kevin Ruane notes. Eden now took the lead in finding an alternative to the EDC treaty and showing the Americans that Europeans could work together effectively. From September 28 to October 3, Eden steered the nine powers towards a new structure – the Western

European Union – that stripped away the supranational elements the French had so disliked and replaced them with an intergovernmental alternative that included rearming West Germany and admitting it to NATO in a way that did not alarm France. A bonus for the French was that Britain, unlike in the EDC, committed itself to playing a leading role in the new structures.[11]

Attention then shifted back to Paris, where the foreign ministers met between October 3 and October 20 to finalize the formal text of the agreement. Dillon was part of the official American delegation, where his role was essentially to look for signs that Mendès France might try to wriggle out of the deal he had made in London. On occasion it was touch and go, but in the end the "Paris Accords" were signed amid much gilt and chinoiserie at the Quai d'Orsay on October 23. A test of nerve was still to come as Mendès France prepared to ratify the treaty in the French parliament. It would probably pass, the prime minister told Dillon, but would only do so "in a spirit of resignation to preserve the Atlantic alliance" and "with no enthusiasm whatsoever." In private, Dillon let French officials know that "this is the 'last chance' to maintain close US relations." Dillon cautioned Washington against "overconfidence" about the treaty passing.[12]

The ambassador was right to be concerned. When the treaty came before the lower chamber of the French parliament just before Christmas, it immediately got into trouble. In the early hours of December 24, the national assembly did the unthinkable and voted against parts of the Western European Union. Dillon met his British counterpart, Sir Gladwyn Jebb, with whom he had a good personal rapport. They agreed that Eisenhower and Churchill should use their prestige to issue a joint statement. "To be effective such reaction must be prompt and clear cut," Dillon urgently cabled Dulles. "Everyone in Paris" expected an Anglo-American intervention "so severe as to bring Parliament to their senses."[13]

Certainly, there was a severe reaction in the "little White House" at Augusta National Golf Club, where the president was staying for the holiday. "Those damn French!" he exploded on being told the news. "What do they think they're trying to do?" Dulles gave him "the Dillon report" on events in Paris. "Well, Foster, they surely have gotten things in an awful mess," Eisenhower groused, even telling his golf coach that "the French have not only disturbed the whole free world but they're cutting in on my lessons!"[14]

In Paris, Dillon held frantic talks with Mendès France. The prime minister complained bitterly that "France today was clearly the main battlefront of the Cold War and that the US and UK had not given his government enough support." He "strongly urged" Dillon to stop the president from issuing a joint statement with Churchill that "would do more harm than good." Dillon rushed from the meeting to telephone Dulles, who in turn called the president in Augusta. With Churchill phoning the president himself to urge his old wartime colleague to issue a joint message, Eisenhower was left in an awkward position. In the end, he stuck by Dillon. A bland statement was issued saying nothing more than the president "cannot believe that this represents the final French decision in this matter."[15]

The forbearance paid off. On December 30, the French national assembly ratified the Paris Agreements. Dulles and Secretary of Defense Charles Wilson immediately agreed that the United States "should take off all holds we have on France (vis-à-vis offshore procurement, military aid, etc.)." It turned back on the tap that Dillon had turned off the previous summer. Many believed that it was his approach that had been instrumental in getting the French over the line. *This Week* magazine hailed Dillon with the headline "He Changed France's Mind." Mendès France telephoned Dillon the day after the debate to say that the "restraint" exercised by the American government had been of the "utmost help to him." He realized "the great pressures" the United States had been under to speak out and was "therefore doubly appreciative of our silence." Dulles appreciated Dillon's efforts too. He sent the ambassador a personal telegram of thanks for his efforts. It was a welcome boost, as the exhausted ambassador had taken to his bed with what turned out to be cancer.[16]

Once Dillon was well enough to travel, he flew back to the United States and his New York apartment at 960 Fifth Avenue (one of those "A-Plus" buildings," the *New York Times* noted, which signifies "that you are wealthy and social, that you have made it to the pinnacle of what many consider world society"). He wrote to Dulles to tell him that "the tumor turned out to be the bad type," while reassuring him that "it had not had time to spread." The doctors advised him he could not return to Paris until March. Keen to keep the news out of the public eye, he told Dulles that those "who may be curious about what has been done to me" were being told he had "prostate trouble." When Dulles suggested that "perhaps it would be convenient for you to let me drop in on you for a few minutes," Dillon wondered whether he was going to be asked to resign. Instead, Dulles wanted to "rejoice" because the cancer had not spread.[17]

These first months of 1955 were the beginning of a difficult period for Dillon and his family. In addition to Dillon's own recuperation, which took him "longer to get going again" than anticipated, his wife Phyllis contracted jaundice. At the same time, their twenty-year-old younger daughter Joan, in her own words "seriously over thin" and often "weeping with frustration and hopelessness," was going through a painful separation and divorce. When Dillon eventually flew back to Paris, Joan and his granddaughter Joanie would go with him to live at the ambassador's *résidence*.[18]

Shortly before his operation, Dillon had attended a White House reception to celebrate the forthcoming "Salute to France" exhibition. Now his return to work in the spring enabled him to deliver the project that was a passion for him. Dillon had always been an avid collector of French Impressionist paintings and since 1950 had been a trustee of the Metropolitan Museum of Art. In 1954, he had been exhilarated to preside over the inauguration in Aix-en-Provence of the Cézanne Museum that he had helped fund. Now in conjunction with Jacques Jaujard, the civil servant who had done so much to save French art during the Second World War, Dillon had planned a major exhibition in Paris for the spring of 1955. It would see some of the finest French paintings from American public and private collections (including Dillon's own) displayed in Paris. The exhibition also included the largest display of American art ever to be shown outside the United States. Abstract expressionists such as Jackson Pollock, Willem de Kooning, and Mark Rothko dominated the American collection. These exhibitions were part of the grand exposition Dillon had organized to feature not just paintings but ballet, theater, shows, and classical music, with the title a nod toward the eponymous wartime film directed by Jean Renoir and Garson Kanin.

"Salute to France" was a major exercise in American soft power, with much made of the fact that it was privately funded, with no monies coming from public finances. In truth, it received CIA funding as part of efforts to use cultural propaganda to win hearts and minds during the Cold War. Dillon as ambassador would have been aware of this CIA involvement, not least because James Hunt Jr., the CIA's senior representative in Paris, was another friend from Wall Street. Dillon himself had been involved with OSS during the Second World War. His choice for exhibition joint chair was the soon-to-be president of the Museum of Modern Art in New York, William Armistead Moale Burden Jr. – a Vanderbilt and a member of Dillon's Wall Street circle – who was part of the "intricate linkages" between the CIA and the world of arts foundations and organizations. Attendance at the two art shows broke all records for visiting exhibitions in the French capital. One Paris correspondent remarked that the "Salute" succeeded "completely in negating the often-heard cliché of anti-American propaganda that the United States is nothing more than a materialistic, culturally barren nation of oversized motor cars and well-functioning planning." Another called it "an excellent way to win friends and influence people." The CIA could hardly have put it any better itself.[19]

"Salute to France" was a triumph for American cultural diplomacy in general and for Dillon in particular. "It was avenue Montaigne where the heart of Paris beat last night," *Le Monde* purred at the gala opening of the musical *Oklahoma!* on June 21, "in honor of America, its folklore and its ambassador."[20] Yet this success came as the United States and France embarked on one of the most difficult and dangerous periods in their complicated relationship. Having just played his part in helping the French government navigate the debates on European defense and German rearmament, Dillon now had to deal with the crisis that quickly engulfed French politics and would come to define the Fourth Republic. As Dillon wrote to Dulles that spring, the issue had become "both France's number one problem and [the] number one sore spot in Franco-American relations." Compared to this new problem of war in Algeria, the EDC shenanigans of the previous year would look like a walk in the Tuileries Garden.[21]

The Algerian war, which would claim as many as a million lives in 1954–1962, had started on November 1, 1954, although as Frank Giles, *The Times*'s Paris correspondent, pointed out, "few people saw it like that at the time." The National Liberation Front (FLN) hit military and civilian targets throughout Algeria and called on all Muslims to join the struggle for "the restoration of the sovereign, democratic and social, Algerian state within the framework of Islamic principles." Reaction in Paris was swift. "L'Algérie c'est la France" ("Algeria, it is France"), Mendès France and the interior minister (later president) François Mitterrand declared. Parachute battalions and a new governor-general were dispatched to Algeria under the injunction that "the only negotiation is war." Even this bullish response was not enough at home. Coming after the humiliation of Dien Bien Phu and unrest in other parts of France's empire, including Morocco and Tunisia, commentators now began talking about "the domino theory translated into French." When Georges Bidault demanded of Mendès France, "What do you want? Where are you going?" they were questions to which no one seemed to have an answer other than "the nineteenth century."[22]

Mendès France's grip on power had been tenuous at the best of times – the result of the inherently unstable constitution, the febrile politics of the day, and the fact that he himself was personally distrusted (an attitude often mingled with barely concealed antisemitism). Algeria finished Mendès France off. At four in the morning on February 23, 1955, he lost a confidence vote in the National Assembly. Breaking with all tradition, Mendès France sprang up onto the rostrum and launched a virulent attack on deputies for "kicking a man when he is down" and for the "sorry spectacle" France now presented to the world. He had to be physically dragged away from the dais, microphone still in hand. It was a characteristically defiant and unconventional end for one of the few memorable prime ministers of the Fourth Republic. Soon afterwards, he called on Dillon at the embassy, where Joan served him tea. "Mendès wept openly," she recalled. "He could not fathom why people now booed when they saw him in the news films. He was a broken man."[23]

Algeria dwarfed all other issues in Paris, not only due to "the scale, brutality, and proximity of the combat," writes Herrick Chapman, but because it was "an imperial territory uniquely integrated – administratively, legally, politically – into France itself." The war and the politics in Paris presented several conundrums for American foreign policy that would bedevil Dillon throughout the rest of his term as ambassador. The United States was itself a nation born out of a war of independence. For emotional as well as historical reasons, it saw itself as an anticolonial power; Americans liked to imagine they were on the side of the underdog. However, the Cold War complicated this calculation. Objections to colonialism were regularly toned down if independence shifted the balance of power towards the Soviets or undermined Cold War allies such as France and Britain. After all, as Jeffrey James Byrne points out, "American, British, and French diplomats had obvious reasons to dislike strident, open criticism of their imperial policies, military activities in the Southern Hemisphere, and, indeed, the simple suggestion that the Cold War between the United States and Soviet Union was not the most important issue in world affairs for all people."

Yet fostering better relationships in the Middle East and the developing world had been part of the Eisenhower administration's strategy from the outset. Forward deployment of nuclear weapons for pre- and post-strike options required air bases overseas, particularly in North Africa, Spain, Saudi Arabia, Greenland, Japan, and Britain. Eisenhower gave authority to deploy complete nuclear weapons in April 1954. The first overseas Strategic Air Command (SAC) bases with full nuclear weapons capacity were established in Morocco in May 1954. They enabled the United States to retaliate from the Mediterranean if the Soviets launched an attack into western Europe. In return, under an amended Mutual Security Act, Morocco got "military assistance."

French involvement in nuclear programs and the deployment of nuclear weapons was murky at best. French citizens had been involved in the Manhattan Project during the Second World War. Even after France was excluded by the Atomic Energy Act of 1946 (the McMahon Act), French scientists continued to be present as observers at Los Alamos National Laboratory while the thermonuclear H-bomb was developed. In 1954, when nuclear weapons were deployed in French Morocco, Dillon recalled the quiet, almost casual way in which the French gave the go ahead. At a meeting with Maurice Schumann at which the deputy foreign minister "had some request for us," Dillon used the opportunity to say, "Fine, but how about you helping us out? As you know, we'd like to get atomic bombs into our bases in Morocco." Schumann thought about it for a moment and then gave consent. Dillon immediately called General Lauris Norstad, air deputy to the supreme allied commander, Europe, and commander in chief of the United States Air Forces in Europe, who was headquartered in Fontainebleau, southeast of Paris. "How quick can you do it?" Dillon had asked Norstad. "We can do it today," Norstad replied. "Go ahead," Dillon told him. "You have French permission."

As Dillon himself noted, the French government "must have talked about it before," but he considered whatever role he played through his quick thinking to be his most important specific accomplishment as ambassador. "It did show," he judged, how "at that time an ambassador could do some things that would [now] be inconceivable." The State Department thought it should have been inconceivable too, upbraiding him for exceeding his authority. "They blew up all over – everywhere," he noted ruefully. "They said I had no authority to do this, even though it was what they wanted!"[24]

Given the strategic importance of Morocco and the need to maintain good relations in the region, the United States had a tricky balance to preserve. While its nuclear strategy was to some degree dependent on French cooperation in North Africa, it could only provide lukewarm support for French authority in Algeria. French hypocrisy about the United States, particularly from Paris intellectuals, did not encourage a more positive frame of mind. While many of those intellectuals roundly denounced American imperialism, they themselves, Odd Arne Westad points out, "found it hard to abandon France's own colonialism, which – by strange twists of terminology – was supposed to be more moral, involved, committed, and 'authentic' than any other. France knew Africa; the Americans did not."[25]

The first indication that all was not well in the relationship with Washington came in the spring of 1955. On May 25, Antoine Pinay, the former prime minister who, in the musical chairs of French politics, was now foreign minister, had made a formal request through Dillon. Could American helicopters lent to the French in Indochina be redeployed to Algeria? Not only did Foster Dulles answer in the negative, but he also made clear his concern about the "growing use of US furnished weapons and equipment" by French troops heading from Asia to North Africa. If France wanted American support, it needed to "restore peace and create [a] basis for enduring cooperation with North African peoples." There was "no time for France to lose."[26]

Dillon had been among the first to warn that Algeria had the potential to be the "number one sore spot" in the relationship. He feared Dulles was missing an opportunity. "The need for the helicopters is now," he implored him. The move could "offset the impression still generally prevalent that the US is acting in a way to make things as difficult as possible for the French in Algeria." Dulles took the point and recommended to the Defense Department that eight helicopters be made available to France on a priority basis.[27]

This small policy victory for Dillon seemed to work. In late July the Algerian question was debated in the French National Assembly. Beforehand, Dillon worked closely with Ambassador Jebb to offer public and private reassurance that the United States and Britain were not trying to undermine France's position in Algeria. The helicopters had led to "excellent repercussions in government circles." In the debate on July 25 and 26, not only did the government win a satisfactory majority, but Prime Minister Edgar Faure spoke in positive terms about the Atlantic alliance and the matériel provided by the United States. "It was not overoptimistic in that hot summer of 1955," recalled Frank Giles, "to think that France was at last emerging from the dark trough of the postwar years on to the sunlit plateau of peace and prosperity."[28]

In fact, the nightmare was just beginning. On August 20, twin terrorist attacks in Morocco and Algeria that included scores of children among the dead initiated a new period of violence and military reprisals in French North Africa. Dillon's perceptive deputy, Thomas Achilles, had characterized Washington's approach as a "middle-of-the-road policy in North Africa" that involved trying "not to take a line overtly or covertly against the continuance of the French presence there." But it was an attitude that was increasingly unsustainable.[29]

The contradictions were painfully exposed on September 30, when the United Nations agreed by one vote to place the "question of Algeria" on the agenda, thus threatening to internationalize what the French considered a strictly domestic dispute. Afterwards, Dillon was summoned to see Pinay and Hervé Alphand, France's permanent representative to NATO. It was, Dillon reported to Dulles, a meeting more painful for having been conducted with a "heightened dignity and restraint stemming from badly hurt feelings." Pinay was "extremely frank" that American support for France had "not been what he would have expected or hoped for." Not only had the United States failed to use its weight to lean on other countries, but the US ambassador to the United Nations, Henry Cabot Lodge Jr., had "only arrived a few minutes before the meeting" and "apparently had not felt it necessary or advisable to be available for consultations with other delegations prior to the vote." To rub salt into the wound, the French had "not received any word from the Secretary or any other American representative after the vote." This final indignity, Dillon judged, was a "main reason for Pinay's hurt feelings."[30]

These points clearly nettled Lodge, who was a cabinet member and an important transatlantic figure himself. In 1945 he had served as attaché to the First French Army Commander, General de Lattre de Tassigny, and was relatively sympathetic to France and its predicament in Indochina. As such, Lodge did not take kindly to being criticized by the French foreign minister and especially by a neophyte ambassador. "Dear Doug," he wrote, "I believe you should have in mind the following facts concerning United States support of the French on the Algerian issue," before launching into an eleven-point rebuttal that ended with the defensive "I did everything that the French asked me to do – and more." Dillon might remind them that "in this, as in all other occupations in life, the old saying that 'God helps those who help themselves' is pertinent."[31]

Lodge made clear in his letter that he expected Dillon to convey the point-by-point defense to the French, including the invocation of the Almighty. But the intemperate tone of the communication coming from one of America's most senior diplomats raised a red flag for the courteous and measured Dillon. He was always tactful, even during times of crisis and conflict. As with the Western European Union question, his constant refrain to Washington on the Algerian war was that the United States should do everything possible to avoid cutting the ground out from underneath moderates. If the United States was going to overcome this "most sensitive and troublesome single element in Franco-American relations," he advised, it had to give "every encouragement" to moderate and liberal opinion as the best way to "strongly oppose extremist elements."[32]

That task was not made any easier by a French political system that produced an ever-changing cast of characters in government. After Faure lost a vote of confidence on November 2, prompting a general election two months later, the socialist Guy Mollet became the next cab off the rank as prime minister of France. Dillon took the opportunity to ram home a familiar message in Washington. "For a long time to come France will be a difficult and often unsatisfactory partner to deal with but one whose intrinsic, as distinct from its former imagined, importance to the free world cannot be ignored," he wrote in a long dispatch. "Patience, tolerance and encouragement on the part of France's allies, particularly the United States, will be both necessary and fruitful." In fact, France in 1956 would test that patience up to and beyond its breaking point.[33]

Chapter Three

First Lesson
Paris, 1956

In March 1956 Ben Bradlee, now of *Newsweek*, landed Dillon with an international incident. Returning to Paris from an interview with the FLN, Bradlee was seized by the French security forces, who claimed he was in league with the Algerian rebels. Dillon heard of the arrest from François Mitterrand, the justice minister. "Won't you just let him go and kick him out of France?" the ambassador asked. Mitterrand consented, but Dillon sent his deputy Thomas Achilles to the French foreign ministry to get even the expulsion order annulled. Bradlee was released within a few hours and was ready to make the most of his newfound celebrity. "To our amazement," wrote Susan Mary Alsop, "he showed up right on time for lunch, with a policeman." For Dillon the affair was typical of a year when US-French misunderstanding reached new lows.[1]

A few weeks after the Bradlee incident, Dillon set about trying to move the needle on French attitudes. He suggested to Washington that he might make a highly publicized speech in Paris. It was an idea accepted more in hope than expectation. "We are continually casting about for ways to alleviate French suspicion and resentment of our role and intentions," Undersecretary of State Herbert Hoover Jr. confessed to Dillon.[2]

Dillon gave his speech at a luncheon hosted by the Diplomatic Press Association. The date, March 20, coincided with the French signing a protocol that ended its seventy-five-year protectorate over Tunisia. The tone was one of calmness, reasonableness, and courtesy, all of which were in keeping with Dillon's personal style of diplomacy. Yet for all his emollience, there was also a toughness. "France can and should be proud of her efforts in North Africa," he observed. However, "It would be helpful if she were to make a greater effort to spread the knowledge of these good works throughout the world." Very specifically, he offered American support for the idea of free elections in

Algeria that Guy Mollet's government was considering, but which was already proving controversial.[3]

The impact in France of Dillon's overture was immediate. "The French took [it] to be very supportive," he recalled. *Le Monde* noted that "we can easily imagine the resistance he had to overcome in Washington to be able to give this speech," adding that it was "a great personal success for the Ambassador, and a victory for the European and pro-French side of the State Department over the champions of uninhibited anti-colonialism and 'appeasement' towards the Arabs." The speech was splashed across the front pages of the evening and next-morning editions in France, with "universally favorable" analysis. Mollet, who had been given an advance copy of the speech, responded by thanking Eisenhower and Dillon as "great friends of France," and added that it was "an irreplaceable encouragement" for France to have them at its side. "France has never had any doubts," he said, with tactful memory loss.[4]

The speech bolstered Dillon's personal authority and reputation in Paris and Washington. Eisenhower reiterated the central message of the speech in his own remarks to the press. Dillon had spoken "with my approval," he told journalists the following day, and the speech had expressed "our hope that there can be an equitable and fair, just settlement" in French North Africa. The State Department briefing reinforced the same message, telling journalists how the speech had been "carefully prepared" to "clear the air of French suspicions" about the US wanting to "supplant" France in North Africa. It prompted headlines such as "Eisenhower Backs Dillon on Africa" in the *New York Times*. That same week, the Senate Foreign Relations Committee adopted a motion welcoming Dillon's success in encouraging the French toward a "policy of Franco-Muslim coexistence in North Africa" in accordance with "their common ideals of freedom and justice." The speech had been an "affirmation" of Dillon's "struggle to find liberal solutions" to the problems in North Africa. An editorial in *Le Monde* went even further by commending Dillon's intervention as "one more act of a great ambassador in improving Franco-American relations."[5]

Perhaps the most significant review for Dillon came in private: Foster Dulles wanted to bring him back to Washington to work alongside him at the State Department. Livingston T. Merchant, a career diplomat serving as assistant secretary of state for European affairs, would be leaving in May to become ambassador to Canada. Dulles wanted a political appointee to replace him. Would Dillon take the job? he asked on April 2. "There are no problems that are more important, and I need someone with whom I can talk with intimacy and confidence and on a statesmanlike basis," Dulles told him, adding that he had "discussed this matter with the president and he heartily joins in my judgment."

Unspoken was the fact of Dulles's worsening colon cancer. He needed Dillon at the State Department as a polished performer to carry on his work. The secretary suggested that Dillon fly back to Washington to discuss the matter, because "I cannot by letter adequately express to you how ardent is my hope that you will feel able to take on this new responsibility which is one of the most important that there is."[6]

Given the fulsome nature of the request, and the fact that Dillon's own political influence was so intrinsically linked to his relationship with Dulles, it is extraordinary that he said no. Yet although the post would have brought him closer to Dulles, it was at best a sideways move. Worse, because Dulles was himself an expert on Europe and always intimately involved in decision-making about the continent, there would be little room for Dillon to carve out an independent role. On a more personal level, his daughter Joan – newly divorced – was just starting to put her life back together. She had a job working for Robert Silvers at *The Paris Review*. Her father understood that his own presence gave her status, reassurance, and stability. So he politely declined. This was another example of his independence.

Reaction to Dillon's press club speech had been positive in Paris and Washington. It was a different matter in the Middle East. Even moderate nationalist figures such as Messali Hadj accused Dillon of encouraging "total war" in Algeria. The speech also drew a sharp rebuke from the Arab League, which passed a resolution of "support for the Algerian people and the deprecation of France's aggression" at its meeting in Cairo on March 29. Kamil Abul Rahim, a former Egyptian ambassador to the United States, issued an ominous statement saying that there would be "far-reaching repercussions in the Arab and Muslim world" after Dillon's declaration of support for the French policy in Algeria.[7]

French leaders in the Middle East seemed almost as hostile. Robert Lacoste, resident minister and governor general of Algeria, continued to denounce both American officials and private citizens living in Algiers, eventually forcing Dillon to complain directly to Mollet. When Lacoste was in Paris in July, he was dispatched to apologize formally to Dillon. The French throughout North Africa, Lacoste explained, had been "in a very sensitive state of mind during the past months" and so he "reacted violently." He "had been wrong" and would in future "be very careful" to make clear that the United

States was "not in any way acting contrary to French interests in Algeria." That Lacoste meant all this seems unlikely, but there were at least some limits to French criticism of the American position. Those limits, however, would shortly be tested to destruction.[8]

On July 26, the day after Dillon's meeting with Lacoste, the Egyptian leader Gamal Abdel Nasser nationalized the Suez Canal Company – the British-French entity that had owned and operated the Suez Canal since the nineteenth century. The crisis that followed seemed to bring out all the worst elements of the French fourth republic. Decision-making was chaotic and oblique, with political, bureaucratic, and military infighting overwhelming strategic thinking. To the French, the threat seemed existential. When Dillon saw Mollet days after the crisis began, he found the prime minister "in a highly emotional state" and "convinced that if Nasser is successful all Western positions in the Middle East and North Africa will be lost within the next 12 months." From the outset, the French government seemed determined to crush the Egyptian leader. "Senior figures in government, in the military, in the security services," Martin Thomas and Richard Toye note, were "predisposed to seize the opportunity for a killer blow."[9]

That French objective, shared by the British, put the Eisenhower administration in a strategic quandary. As the National Security Council briefing on the Suez Canal summed up, the crisis was likely to "widen the gap between the West and Egypt as well as other Arab and Asian states," to "strain relations between Western Powers," and to risk the Soviet Union "expanding its influence in the area." It was a potentially disastrous trifecta. Eisenhower made it clear that he would not countenance military intervention. "We are not going to war over it," he told Dulles bluntly, before writing to Eden and Mollet in similar terms. Nevertheless, Dulles admitted to his brother, Allen, that he hadn't the first idea about what the French and the British were up to. "They are deliberately keeping us in the dark," he complained.[10]

Dillon's position in Paris was a difficult one during the diplomatic crisis. He reported to Washington a "wave of anti-American sentiment in France over Suez" and the hostility about what was perceived as "Washington's preference for friendship of new Arab countries as opposed to her old European friends and allies." In regular meetings with Mollet, he found the prime minister "very disturbed at the apparent lack of unity" and still "prepared to impose [a] solution by military action." Dillon's own view in early October was that force would "only be used if there is further provocation, probably of a violent nature from Egypt" (while noting presciently that "it is well within the power of the British and French to provoke such an incident should they so desire"). That assessment precisely matched the US National Intelligence estimate, which concluded "military action is likely only in the event of some new and violent provocation."[11]

But Dillon soon became the fall guy in an elaborate deception by the French government. On October 19, 1956, the ambassador had lunch with Jacques Chaban-Delmas, a minister of state. The messenger was deftly chosen. Dillon already had a relationship with Chaban-Delmas through Château Haut-Brion in Bordeaux, where the French politician was an iconic figure. What the American heard at lunch that day astonished him. It was "absolutely necessary that Nasser lose face or go in the coming weeks," Chaban-Delmas said. Seeing the alarm on the ambassador's face, he reassured him that he understood the sensitivities surrounding the presidential election on November 6. Although the problem of Nasser could not remain "unsolved beyond Christmas at the latest," France was "prepared to meet the United States requirements for peace prior to early November." After that date, however, France and Britain "would be required to act."[12]

Dillon rushed back to the embassy and sought out James Hunt Jr., the CIA's senior representative. This intelligence was something that had to be reported back "on a very private basis," Dillon would recall. He used Hunt as a back channel to circumvent the State Department and communicate directly with Foster Dulles. "I feel that Chaban's views are [an] accurate description of French Government policy in Suez affairs as of today," Dillon said. Chaban, who was "privy to [the] closest held thinking in French Government circles," had sought him out on "a basis of personal friendship." Dillon's summary emphasized two points: first, the likelihood of "military intervention by France and the UK," and, second, the "assurance" that it would not come "prior to approximately Nov. 10." A meeting the next day with Maurice Faure, a junior minister at Foreign Affairs, confirmed that "France considered Nasser to be a mortal danger to her existence" and that he would be dealt with "immediately after [the] American elections." Unfortunately for Dillon, the second statement in both cases was an outright lie.[13]

A week earlier General Maurice Challe, chief of the French defense staff (who would later lead an attempted coup against the Fifth Republic), had flown to England to see Eden at his Chequers country retreat. There he had briefed the British prime minister on what later became known as the "Challe scenario" in which Israel would attack Egypt, prompting the British and French to send their own forces to "protect" the Suez Canal Zone. On the day that Dillon met Chaban, French forces had begun to load ships at Algiers and to airlift three parachute regiments to Cyprus in preparation for war. On October 22, three days after Dillon's meeting, Mollet and the Israeli prime minister, David Ben-Gurion, met for three days at Sèvres with the British foreign secretary, Selwyn Lloyd, to sign a secret protocol. Israel would launch its attack on Egypt on October 29, exactly ten days after Dillon had been assured that no such action would take place.[14]

Later, Dillon was defensive about his error, believing that the intelligence he passed along, though incorrect, should still have alerted Washington to the fact that the French and British were considering imminent military action. "We did have that one warning," he judged, "which should have prepared us a little more."[15]

In fact, Dillon's advice had been detrimental. In a meeting with Eisenhower at the White House on October 21, Dulles told the president that he now "felt confident that the British and the French would not resort to any of these measures before the election as they did not want to make it an election issue." The president should invite Eden and Mollet to Washington for "a frank exchange of views" after the election, he suggested, but there was no urgency. Ike would need "some vacation." Dulles was about to undergo surgery for colon cancer. They could return to the problem of Suez in "the latter part of November."

Dillon was in the south of France on October 29 when he heard the news that Israel had invaded the Sinai Peninsula in Egypt and advanced to within ten miles of the Suez Canal. Shocked that he had been deceived, the ambassador rushed back to Paris. The full extent of the subterfuge was revealed two days later, when it became known that British and French troops were on their way to the Canal Zone. The French foreign minister, Christian Pineau, summoned Dillon and "fully admitted" that the operation was a "long planned Franco-British-Israeli affair." He warned the United States to "exercise care and moderation in public utterances." If Eisenhower did anything to undermine the operation, he risked "a unilateral military intervention by the Soviet Union" and even a "generalized world war." Dillon acknowledged the minister's "frank exposé" and hurried back to the embassy to cable Dulles. "Cold" was Dulles's judgement of Pineau.[16]

Events now unfolded at speed. Although Dulles's illness complicated the American response, Eisenhower was so personally enraged at being lied to by his allies, he took a decisive stance against Britain and France. The president instructed Henry Cabot Lodge Jr. to vote in favor of UN resolutions condemning the invasion. He then applied all available diplomatic and economic pressure on Britain and France to accept a ceasefire. It did not take long for Britain, fearing a catastrophic run on the pound, to cave in to the pressure. That decision left France with nowhere to go. By November 6 the crisis was over, with the added indignity for France and Britain that the United States compelled them to accept the creation of a UN peacekeeping force in Egypt.

With Washington and the United Nations at the center of heated diplomacy during the crisis, Dillon was often a spectator and occasionally an emissary as events unfolded. He did, however, see first-hand what the intensity of Cold War politics really looked like. On November 5, the Soviets, eager to deflect attention away from their brutal suppression of the Hungarian Revolution that fall, told Britain and France that they had twelve hours to agree a ceasefire in the Canal Zone or be hit with a nuclear strike. Dillon was asleep at the *résidence* when he received a call from Mollet telling him to come immediately to the Hôtel de Matignon. Dillon found the place in a panic. The inner cabinet was still debating whether to accept the proposal for a ceasefire. Mollet came out, demanding to know what the Americans would do in the event of a Soviet strike. Dillon coolly replied that "of course" the United States "would be at your side." It did not matter whether Suez was technically outside the NATO treaty area. The United States would "live up to" its alliance obligations. A relieved Mollet immediately reported Dillon's comments to the cabinet. Paul Nitze later reflected that Dillon had shown real courage in taking matters into his own hands at a moment of crisis. "Douglas was fully right about this," Nitze said. "He had the guts to step up to that ball and right away take responsibility for it, without saying, 'I have to consult with Washington.'"[17]

If Dillon had shown courage and judgment on the issue of the Soviet nuclear threat, the political aftermath of the crisis led to personal humiliation. On November 29, he caught the "red eye" flight from Paris to Washington for talks about oil supplies to France. The United States had imposed de facto sanctions during the crisis. "The oil embargo hit very hard," Dillon said later, recalling his visits to the Quai d'Orsay where Pineau would welcome him to his office dressed pointedly in a heavy overcoat.[18]

Dillon had urged Washington to drop the informal sanctions. To do otherwise could only degrade an already "decreased and less effective role" for France as an ally. But he did not have his usual line to the top. "Unfortunately, at the time, Secretary Dulles had taken to his bed for his first cancer operation, and so he was not functioning," Dillon recalled. "The State Department was being run by Herbert Hoover Jr., and I don't think he had the same judgment." So the ambassador did what he had never done throughout his tenure: he asked to see Eisenhower in person.[19]

Dillon left for Washington with the stakes raised by the very public nature of his mission. "French Pin Hopes on Dillon's trip," the *New York Times* reported, noting that the ambassador had met the French prime minister and the finance minister hours before leaving. The results were immediate. On the day Dillon arrived home, the White House announced an oil assistance program that would supply western Europe with 500,000 barrels a day. "I don't know if my coming back" did the trick, Dillon reflected, "but I've always felt it did." After a debriefing at the State Department and pre-recording a radio interview with CBS's *Capitol Cloakroom*, he headed back to Paris in a confident mood, knowing that Dulles would be following shortly afterwards for a NATO summit meeting.[20]

Dulles arrived late on Sunday, December 9, and went straight to the *résidence* at the Avenue d'Iéna where he would stay with the Dillons. When he awoke the next morning, the secretary was given breakfast and a copy of the *Paris Herald*. The paper led with Dillon saying Soviet nuclear pressure had ended the Suez crisis.[21]

"Why did you talk like that!" Dulles shouted at Dillon.

"Oh, was he mad," the ambassador recalled. "I'd never had anyone quite so mad at me in my life!"

Dulles's wrath seemed to know no bounds. "[He] wouldn't speak to me," Dillon recalled of the awkward days that followed. Dillon even found the State Department briefing against him, expressing what the *New York Times* reported as "forthright exasperation with the Ambassador" for undermining the "moral force" of Washington's foreign policy. The embarrassing headline to the *Times* story was "Dillon's Remarks Irk U.S. Officials." On December 12, he was forced to issue a chastening statement to the effect that "I had no intention of minimizing the effect of moral pressure exercised by all nations through the UN."[22]

Even this humiliation was not the worst of it. At the end of the NATO ministerial meeting, Dillon hosted a large formal dinner in honor of Dulles, with all the conventional toasts and speeches. When Dulles himself came to speak, he uttered not one word of acknowledgment, let alone thanks, to Dillon. That would have been rude at the best of times but given that the ambassador was coming to the end of his tenure, the lack of any encomium represented a snub. "It was terrible," Dillon said, "and most embarrassing for everyone at the dinner." He just about managed to maintain his characteristic sangfroid, but his daughter did not. The next morning, with Dulles about to leave for Washington, the secretary of state asked her for help in purchasing a bag by Hermès for Mrs. Dulles. "I looked him square in the eye," Joan recalled, "and said, 'Mr. Dulles, I would not even buy you a toothbrush after the way you treated my parents.' Then I left him standing with his mouth open and went off to work."[23]

Dillon's humiliation was an introduction to the realities of politics. "I had no excuse," he reflected. "I shouldn't have said it. It was the truth, but I shouldn't have said it. At times, it's best not to talk to the media but just say you don't know anything – I learned that later, but this was my first lesson, and a very rough one."[24]

Dillon's misstep could have ended his political career, but the personal relationship with Dulles ran deeper. "I guess he didn't hold it against me too long," Dillon recalled, "because about two weeks later he sent me a telegram asking me if I would come back and be Deputy Under Secretary for Economic Affairs." In a move designed to reshape American foreign policy, Eisenhower and Dulles wanted to emphasize financial and economic matters. These were the areas in which Dillon was most skilled. The ambassador would not be going back to Wall Street. Instead, he was heading to Washington for Eisenhower's second term.[25]

Chapter Four

Dulles's Cool Economist
Washington, 1957

Despite any lingering embarrassment over the Suez interview on "Capitol Cloakroom," Douglas Dillon returned from Paris at the end of January 1957 with his reputation broadly enhanced. "He is generally considered here to be one of the most successful of non-career diplomats, among whom success has not been invariable," reported the Paris correspondent of the *New York Times*, adding that Dillon's "coolly realistic judgements … often expressed with a smile" had contributed to "the balance and sense of proportion that distinguished his judgments as a diplomat." The French press was similarly positive about the ambassador, with glowing reports of his farewell in *Le Monde* and a long profile on "An American in Paris" in *L'Express* which concluded that "he had excelled" in the post. "I never saw so much attention given to a departing ambassador," wrote Seymour Weller, nephew of Clarence Dillon and manager of Château Haut-Brion, to the paterfamilias after both chambers of the French parliament gave Douglas the rare honor of a joint reception. "My feeling is his departure is deeply regretted by all," he reported, "and that everything is much more a tribute to Douglas personally than to the USA."[1]

A political appointee, Dillon had been given his plum role at the Paris embassy not so much for his abilities as for his connections and his father's contributions to the Eisenhower campaign. But he had often shown an aptitude for the nuances of diplomacy and a grace under fire that had won admirers in Paris and Washington. There had been gaffes and moments of political naiveté, not least during the Suez crisis. But given the anti-Americanism of the times and the dramatic series of international crises that had put Paris at the center of world attention, Dillon left France with his political account in credit. Now he was returning to Washington for a post that, unlike an ambassadorial appointment, gave him the opportunity to shape policymaking. But it also came with all the attendant scrutiny that accompanied such a position. In the famous distinction made by Aristotle in *Nicomachean Ethics*, Dillon was moving from being a political "handyman" – a figure involved in making sure the plumbing of American foreign policy worked – to that of "statesman" or "architect" – someone who would play a role in shaping the "architectonic" structures of policy.[2]

Dillon himself seemed to grasp the difference between the two. He had intuitively understood that the job he turned down in April 1956 as assistant secretary of state for European affairs would have been more of the same – in essence, looking after the plumbing of grand strategy for Dulles. Moving to Washington in 1957 as the new deputy undersecretary for economic affairs gave him a position of much greater scope and importance. "Mr. Dulles told me to go in there and get this done, and he would pretty much back me up with whatever I felt was the right thing to do," Dillon recalled. The secretary had "no interest in this economic business at all ... but he did understand that it would be very important, and it would be increasingly important as the years went on." For such an enterprise, Dulles needed someone with the capacity to reimagine American foreign policy through an economic and financial lens.[3]

Putting Dillon into the role was not accidental. As Eisenhower prepared to enter his second term, he was at the height of his political powers. Not only had he won a landslide victory over Adlai Stevenson, but his reputation on the world stage was also at its zenith. His biographer Jean Edward Smith goes as far to claim that "never in the postwar era was American prestige higher than in the aftermath of Suez." Ike's action in rebuffing the Europeans had electrified postcolonial countries. The idea that the United States would back Egypt against colonial powers Britain and France, and a Muslim country against Israel to boot, was a genuinely empowering moment for non-aligned countries establishing their legitimacy. Eisenhower seemed to understand better than most that the Age of Empire was over. He had taken a personal lead during the Dien Bien Phu and Suez crises to push his European allies to give up the imperial ghost. Now he sought to revitalize the West with a strategy that might harness the "tempest of change and turmoil" blowing around the world.[4]

Part of that change was the new environment in the Cold War that both pushed and pulled the United States. The "pull" factor was the overall atmosphere in the conflict, which had thawed somewhat after the death of Stalin in 1953. Following the Geneva summit in 1955, Eisenhower had genuine hopes that a new spirit might prevail in East-West relations, including better economic relations and relaxed trade restrictions. The "push" factor was the active attempt by the Soviet Union to use economic aid to the developing world to find a strategic edge in the Cold War. By January 1957, however, as his first term came to an end, Eisenhower's policy had neither cohesion nor clarity. "The administration seemed to lack an effective and coherent policy at all," writes historian Burton I. Kaufman. "In this respect the White House had reached an impasse in the development of its foreign economic policy."[5]

To address that impasse, Eisenhower laid out his broad thinking in a major speech to Congress that soon became known as the "Eisenhower Doctrine." Communism, he warned, aimed for world domination, and currently had its sights set on the Middle East, which was at "a new and critical stage" in its history. A new Soviet sphere of influence would "gravely endanger all the free world." With the Soviets already making "superficially attractive offers" of military and economic assistance, it was vital that the United States follow suit. The doctrine also broadened Dulles's strategy of "peaceful evolution," set out in January 1953 and augmented in speeches by the secretary of state in 1957–58. In essence, Dulles sought to undermine the values of socialism through political, economic, and cultural penetration. "This penetration," Richard Ong points out, "often derives from Western economic assistance" – exactly the area that Dulles wanted Dillon to develop at the State Department.[6]

The request to Congress to authorize an unspecified sum in discretionary aid over the next two years aroused immediate hostility. Even though the estimated sum was a relatively modest $200 million for 1958 and 1959, the chair of the Senate Foreign Relations Committee, William J. Fulbright, accused the president of looking for "a blank grant of power, to be used in a blank way, for a blank length of time, under blank conditions with respect to blank nations in a blank area." Eisenhower dispatched a newly invigorated Dulles to speak before the committee. He delivered a hair-raising warning about how postcolonial countries such as Egypt "will almost certainly be taken over by Soviet communism" unless the United States did "something" involving hardcore economic and military assistance.[7]

Confounded by the hostility to his policy, the president used his inaugural speech on January 21 to pivot toward a higher moral rhetoric about the "winds of change" blowing through global politics. More than a "third of all mankind" was engaged in "an historic struggle for a new freedom; freedom from grinding poverty." America the bountiful must not "turn our backs to them" – for their sake and for that of the West. "For one truth must rule all we think and all we do," Eisenhower urged. "The economic need of all nations – in mutual dependence – makes isolation an impossibility; not even America's prosperity could long survive if other nations did not also prosper."[8]

No one could doubt that Eisenhower was personally committed to the policy, which represented the most ambitious strategic rethinking in overseas aid policy since the Marshall Plan ten years earlier. His official biographer, Stephen Ambrose, judged that it would be "one of the most frustrating experiences of his life" as Ike attempted "every form of persuasion at his command to demonstrate to his countrymen the importance of the Third World to the United States." In his first term, he had pushed a $5.15 billion request for mutual security programs through Congress, telling them that it was "the way best to defend successfully ourselves and the cause of freedom." The emphasis then had been on the hard link to American defense. Now, as he began his second term, Eisenhower put his full weight behind the idea that it was government-to-government foreign aid that would lead to self-sustaining growth and politically stable democratic societies in developing countries.[9]

The new emphasis put Eisenhower into direct conflict with those in his own party who wanted "retrenchment in aid," arguing that "American taxpayers were [being] fleeced to placate ungrateful nations." The principal opponent of the president's new approach was George M. Humphrey, his own treasury secretary, who, the authors of the *Biographical Dictionary of United States Treasury Secretaries* tartly noted, was "possessed of the righteousness and self-confidence that comes from being pampered and provided for" since birth. As treasury secretary, Humphrey was a fiscal conservative committed to tax cuts, balancing the budget, reducing government waste, and scaling back overseas and even defense spending. He was certainly no fan of foreign aid and regularly locked horns with Dulles on the issue. In a wide-ranging speech the previous year on "Incentives to Industry" he had argued strongly against any further expansion of foreign aid. In January 1957, between the president's speech to Congress and the inauguration, he gave an incendiary press conference at which he publicly criticized the proposed budget for the fiscal year 1958, arguing that expanding government expenditure, including foreign aid, would have consequences to "curl your hair."[10]

The move was a desperate rearguard action. In December, the president had effectively forced the resignation of Undersecretary of State Herbert Hoover Jr. to start a maneuver that was more ideological than a simple change in personnel. Hoover had been part of the "4-H Club" (so named for the "H" in the names of its four members – Humphrey, Hoover, Budget Director

Rowland Hughes, and Director of the International Cooperation Administration John Hollister). The group had worked in a coordinated fashion in the first term to resist the expansion of American overseas spending and aid. By February 1957, Hughes and Hoover had already left government service, and Hollister would follow soon afterwards. Humphrey himself would eventually resign in July 1957.

Eisenhower did his best to cajole the treasury secretary into accepting that the global situation demanded a new approach. The United States, the soldier Eisenhower told him in a call to arms, must "face up to the critical phase through which the world is passing and do our duty like men." That was the way to harness the "fierce pride" of independence movements to "whip" communism. Not so, Humphrey countered. The United States should be supporting the former colonial powers such as France in Algeria, not those seeking independence. The imperial powers were a better bet to use aid money wisely.[11]

This standoff was the context for Dillon's appointment. Unable to cajole his treasury secretary, Eisenhower went around him by boosting the role of the State Department in foreign economic policy. Christian Herter replaced the recalcitrant Hoover as undersecretary of state and Dulles's No. 2 in the department. Dulles needed another lieutenant with economic and financial expertise to devise and execute the new approach to foreign aid. That's where Dillon came in. "Dulles wanted someone in the Department who he felt compatible with," he recalled, "who would run the economic side the way that he liked without bothering him with the details." With a new economic and financial front opening in the Cold War, the *New York Times* reported that in Dillon, "the government for the first time has a 'captain' to run the whole show."[12]

Charged with helping some of the poorest countries in the world, Dillon began his tenure with a faux pas. The tabloid *New York Daily Mirror* was soon reporting that each day Dillon parked a fifteen-thousand-dollar Bentley in his reserved spot at the State Department's executive lot. Because Wiley Buchanan, chief of protocol and husband to a Dow Chemicals heiress, parked the same exclusive British marque in a nearby spot, the two men were quickly dubbed ("affectionately" noted the *Mirror* archly) "The Bentley Boys." The jab stung and Dillon quickly switched to a Ford, but the Bentley Boy tag stuck. It was particularly unfortunate, because it chimed with an existing image problem for an Eisenhower cabinet dubbed "nine millionaires and a plumber." (The plumber had been the short-lived secretary of labor, Martin P. Durkin, a Democrat and president of the Plumbers and Steamfitters Union.)[13]

The Bentley story was a rare misstep for a man who usually took care to avoid ostentatiousness. What Dillon could not hide, however, was that he was one of the richest men in the United States and heir to one of the country's fifty largest family fortunes worth ("on the conservative side," the *New York Times* noted) between a hundred and two hundred million dollars – approximately one to two billion dollars in today's money. After moving into 2584 Belmont Road NW in the Kalorama neighborhood of Washington, DC, Dillon regularly found his house profiled by society page writers. Betty Beale in the *Evening Star* gushed about the "lovely" Chinoiserie paneling, Louis XV furnishings, Aubusson carpets, black and white marble entrance hall, and the "marvelous" French paintings, including "a $92,000 Manet canvas" bought at auction in Paris before he left. Another cloying profile noted the "small and cozy" garden room to which Dillon would retreat to read, with its "two lovely French paintings, 'Lady in a Garden' by Monet and a pastoral scene by Pissarro." More egalitarian was his decision to keep his name and address in the Washington, DC, phone book – a practice he would later maintain even as a cabinet member. It was a gesture that perfectly captured the paradox of Dillon's life in Washington: how his wealth and privilege might stand alongside a personal sense of public service. But the paradox also impinged on public policymaking. The question loomed over the Eisenhower administration, as it had a generation earlier with "wise men" Dean Acheson and Robert Lovett, and would later over Jack Kennedy, about the extent to which economic debates within the administration and the definition of core American values were affected by a mindset that was more millionaire than plumber – a worldview some historians, particularly albeit not exclusively on the left, would term "corporatist."[14]

Dillon was never a man of the people, but on a personal level his fortune allowed him to be his own man in doing what he believed served the public good. For many it would have been an uncomfortable juxtaposition, but now installed in a job that drew on his specific abilities, he seemed liberated. Colleagues noted his sense of vitality and purpose. "To have a man like Dillon come in," recalled his State Department special assistant, the trade expert John Leddy, "and pick stuff up immediately with as broad a background that he obviously did have on international affairs in general, and a positiveness and constructiveness and a willingness to take charge: this was just a joy."[15]

First on the agenda for Dillon was not a new problem but the more familiar one of Suez. A few weeks before he was sworn in, Dulles wrote to "request you to take primary responsibility for the negotiations which will relate to the Suez Canal, i.e., the matter of payment of tolls and the matter of the future status of the Canal and its operations." It was a tricky assignment, not least because the department was also trying to find a solution to the territorial dispute between Egypt and Israel over the Gaza Strip. The secretary warned Dillon about the balancing act that would be required. While it was "important to try to preserve unity with the British and the French," he also needed to remember that "they are not the only users of the Canal and not the only nations concerned, and that a great many of our friends would not be as rigid as they are disposed to be." To add to the complication, Dillon would be pulling the strings on behalf of the United States while "the actual negotiations with the Egyptians will be conducted by and through [UN secretary general Dag] Hammarskjold."[16]

Although the immediate Suez crisis was over, important issues persisted – not least, that the canal itself remained shut. Ironically, given how they had opposed colonialism in November, it was now the Americans who found themselves worrying about the implications of nationalization and Egyptian control of the Suez Canal and its tolls. At a meeting of the National Security Council in February, Treasury Secretary Humphrey, who had been an arch dove the previous November, now reprimanded his colleagues for not taking the issue seriously enough. They had heard Allen Dulles's report that clearance of the canal was almost complete. A provisional reopening date had been set for March 15. Simultaneously, his brother Foster bemoaned Hammarskjold's involvement in the negotiating process with Egypt. Humphrey insisted that it was up to the United States to secure a deal if Nasser was not to have unrestricted control of the canal and its revenues in perpetuity.[17]

That task now became Dillon's. The president reinforced how delicate the task would be. A plan had already been on the table for the World Bank to play the role of honest broker by collecting and distributing canal dues. But when the British government leaked the scheme to the press, Egypt angrily rejected it as an unwarranted ultimatum. Eisenhower had been furious, but grudgingly accepted the advice of Jock Whitney, his ambassador in London, that British public opinion was "likely to explode if the Egyptians required tolls to be paid to them directly for Suez passage." Caught between a British rock and an Egyptian hard place, Eisenhower urged Dillon to find a solution. The US had been "compromised by the premature British release" and there was a fear that "anything we try to do now may result in the British saying that we are 'reneging' on them." It was time to use "our influence" to get "Egypt to make a proposal."[18]

Dillon quickly put in place a structure to meet that demand, establishing a senior advisory group and a working group "to coordinate and initiate action."

It was the first example of the freedom for maneuvering that his new post afforded. To confirm the point, when the new British prime minister, Harold Macmillan, expressed his "concern" about the "Suez tolls situation," Dulles told him that Dillon was dealing with the matter in Washington and not to "risk crossing wires."[19]

Dillon also warned the UN's Dag Hammarskjöld, telling him not to "attempt to negotiate any compromise himself." Instead, he utilized his Wall Street connections with John McCloy, "Wise Man" and the past president of the World Bank, who was acting as an adviser to the United Nations. Dillon sent him to Cairo with a message for Nasser that if he "did not act like a responsible person, then there would be no money for him and no business to be gotten." It was grist to the mill for a political fixer like McCloy. In the Egyptian capital on April 1, he spent five hours with Nasser. Speaking with "the utmost bluntness," he reminded the Egyptian leader that he would get the best deal from the United States by recognizing the international character of the waterway. McCloy told Dillon he detected "a little light through the clouds."[20]

In the end, practicalities on the ground took over. On April 24, the government in Cairo announced that the Suez Canal was now "open for normal traffic." That same day the first American flagship, the *President Jackson*, transited the canal. Washington advised that payments by American flagships should be made "under protest" to avoid double jeopardy, but that they were paid at all was recognition that *de facto* had superseded *de jure* on the matter. Dillon dispatched a telegram over Dulles's signature, effectively bringing the matter to a close. "With the Canal open for traffic and vessels from nearly thirty nations already using the Canal," he wrote tersely, "the US doubts whether principal maritime countries would wish to assume cost and economic impact of a policy of non-use."[21]

The American decision to drop its active opposition on the Suez payments caused bad feelings in London and Paris, where the governments wanted to force the issue with Egypt. It was not the only point on which Dillon had to navigate a falling out with important allies. He also took the lead as the West fretted about how to trade with the People's Republic of China, which would more than double its GNP/GDP between 1950 and 1959. In 1953, Eisenhower had identified containing China as a crucial element of his Cold War strategy. Part of this containment policy was to boost sympathetic regional partners through economic and military aid while trying to throttle Chinese economic development. Welcome as American largesse was in the region, the overall strategy pushed against the natural forces of trade in East Asia. Japan was an obvious example. Before the Second World War, 40 percent of its exports went to China and Korea; 70 percent of its imported soya beans came from China, as did 40 percent of its imported coal; by 1957 it was buying 75 percent of its coal and 90 percent of the soya beans from the United States. As one economic historian puts it, "Dollars linked to the expansion of the American military machine could not be expected to cover these requirements indefinitely; Japan needed a trade network that would allow it to earn them." Even beyond Asia, European powers, particularly France and Britain, which had traditional economic relationships in the region from the days of empire, were desperate to trade with China. Vast export markets and labor resources looked too good to miss out on. Western powers began to demand that the United States loosen its trade restrictions. The danger, however, the historian Xin-zhu J. Chen notes, was that "their eagerness to trade with China, in turn, gave Beijing an opportunity to resort to its old trick of playing 'one barbarian against another.'"[22]

On May 16, Dulles wrote to the president to lay out the dilemma. Britain and Japan wanted "to gain greater freedom in respect to China trade and do so quickly." Dillon ("who is handling this matter for us") had advised that reaching agreement with these countries would only come "if we agree to a substantial reduction of the present differential between China trade and Soviet trade." So, what to do? The United States could let Britain and Japan "go it alone," with the consequence that other countries in the region would see this as "foreshadowing a policy of lessening opposition to the Chinese Communists which might precipitate widespread efforts by Asian countries to seek an accommodation." However, to split with Britain and Japan would also have unwelcome consequences for the United States, not least that "if they start 'going it alone' we cannot be sure that they will stop with the present measures." There was a real danger that such a move would "constitute a precedent which, if pursued, could lead to a breakdown of the basic strategic controls which apply both to the Soviet Union and to China." It was a delicate situation and one that required a flexibility of approach. "My suggestion," Dulles advised Eisenhower, was to "give Douglas Dillon, who is directing negotiations, discretionary authority." The president agreed, telling Macmillan that he was "giving some new discretion to our representatives."[23]

The next three weeks would be complex and frustrating for Dillon as he oversaw the technical talks going on in Paris as part of the China Committee (CHINCOM) – the international working group on embargoing trade with China and North Korea. After Britain rejected the modified proposals made by the United States, Dillon summoned the UK ambassador, Sir Harold Caccia, to a meeting at the State Department to read him if not the riot act, then the

Battle Act – although in this case the two were effectively the same. Drawing Caccia's attention to the terms of the 1951 legislation, he reminded the ambassador that the president was bound by law to withdraw economic and military aid from countries that were not "effectively cooperating" in East-West trade controls. He emphasized that he was "in no way threatening the UK with this possibility" but simply wanted the British to "be aware of this statute" because "the president had no discretion" whatsoever in the matter.[24]

Unmoved by the threat, Macmillan informed Eisenhower on May 21 that he intended "to stick to the line" on UK-China trade. Foreign office officials briefed their American counterparts that the UK would hold its position "even if isolated" and forced to "go it alone." That line anticipated Dillon's next move, which was to start "pushing the French very hard ... [to] reverse their position." He summoned Hervé Alphand, the French ambassador, to express the "desirability" of France shifting its position. "Maintenance of the French position will inevitably affect Franco-American relations in other fields during the coming months," he warned. With the Mollet government teetering on the edge of collapse, both men understood exactly that those other fields included the Algerian question. "We had hit it awfully hard," Dillon told Dulles afterwards.[25]

France began to seek a compromise, but still Britain refused to relent. It was "No Dice," Dillon told Dulles on May 25. The secretary was livid, saying to Dillon that he was "going out and he [Dillon] need not bother" to bring the British note round or even to reply. On May 27, Britain publicly announced that it was going to eliminate the China differential. Privately, Macmillan urged Eisenhower that "we must try to play down this difference of view between us and do all we can to prevent the misconception that we have different policies on strategic controls, or on the great issues that lie beneath all this." Ultimately Eisenhower agreed to let the matter drop. He had already seen Macmillan abase himself over the Suez fiasco at a bilateral summit in Bermuda that March. (Macmillan christened the meeting "Operation Canossa" after the Holy Roman Emperor Henry IV who did penance there in 1077, standing barefoot in the snow for three days to get his papal excommunication revoked.) Briefing diplomats, Dillon explained that he knew the president had "attached great importance to reaching an agreement if at all possible" but since that had not been the case, he "naturally attaches importance to maintaining a united front" and to emphasizing "the continued unity on controls towards the Sino-Soviet bloc as a whole."[26]

As with the negotiations with Egypt over the Suez Canal, the China trade-control talks had been a frustrating experience for Dillon. More worryingly in the bitterly contested arena of Washington politics, it meant he was batting "0 for 2" on issues where he had been Dulles's designated hitter. Now he sat down to write a memorandum to Clarence B. Randall to analyze how and why the United States had been outmaneuvered by its principal allies. It was an interesting choice of recipient. Randall was not a State Department insider, but chairman of the Council on Foreign Economic Policy and a special assistant to the president. There was an element of covering his own back in taking the message outside the State Department, because its basic point was simple enough: the issue should have been sorted by the previous person in the job. Dillon could claim some measure of success by aligning most of the negotiating countries with the United States, but the fact remained that the permanent representatives on CHINCOM – Canada, France, Japan, and the United Kingdom – had all opposed the American proposals, or in the case of Canada, remained neutral. The irony, Dillon suggested, was that the United States had shown itself to be "flexible and cooperative." So why hadn't that been enough? Timidity, slowness to act, and a failure to seize the initiative earlier seemed to be the answer. "If we had been able to accept something like the proposed compromise about six months or a year ago, we might have been able to retain a significant differential," he judged, pointing to a time when he was not in Washington. "Our failure to consider a modified position at an earlier date apparently led the British to conclude that our concessions would never be enough to suit them." Although the British "recognized that we had gone a long way to accommodate ourselves to their problem," the reality was that "they were apparently so firmly committed that they could not consider our position on its merits."[27]

If Dillon was already showing himself adept at deflecting blame, he also began to find his feet in other areas. On May 2, he traveled to the beautiful surroundings of Arden – an estate forty miles north of Manhattan that Averell Harriman had gifted to Columbia when Eisenhower was university president – to announce a new economic aid plan. The audience of academics, business leaders, and public officials at the conference on "International Stability and Progress" made a tough but knowledgeable crowd for a detailed, technical speech. Participants included Truman appointees Eric Johnston (chairman of the International Development Advisory Board), Philip C. Jessup (the distinguished Columbia law professor who had served as ambassador-at-large), and Dillon's friend and sometime mentor, Paul Nitze.

The speech represented a decisive contribution to what the economist Walt Rostow would describe as "one of the most dramatic and illuminating strands in the Eisenhower Administration." The aid program Dillon outlined had the ambitious strategic objective of providing a bulwark against the advancement of Soviet communism in Asia and Africa. At its center was a new development fund to finance projects for "underdeveloped" countries that did not have capital available.

The proposed fund would work through the government's International Cooperation Administration (ICA), which ran foreign assistance and "nonmilitary security" programs. Crucially though, it would have quasi-independence and its own flexible authority like that of the Export-Import Bank (the federal government's official export credit agency). Proposals for funding would not be initiated in Washington but would be developed by interested countries themselves based on their own national and regional priorities. The initial request to Congress would be for half a billion dollars for the first year, rising to three quarters of a billion the following year, and would form part of Eisenhower's $4 billion Mutual Security Program for military and economic assistance.

Dillon made clear that the stakes in this new enterprise were high. Seven hundred million people lived in the nineteen new nations established after the Second World War. Most of them enjoyed only rudimentary economic conditions. If the people of these countries were unable to meet "the fulfillment of economic aspirations under free and democratic conditions," he warned, "there is a real danger of their falling into some form of totalitarianism."[28]

It was an assured performance and one that provided clarity amid widespread divisions. There had been no shortage of takers over the previous year or so to define what foreign aid policy might look like. Both houses of Congress initiated their own studies on the question, as did the International Development Advisory Board (IDAB) and the president's Citizen Advisors on the Mutual Security Program (the "Fairless Report"). The administration itself had seemed paralyzed. The problem, Rostow summed up after he and Millikan submitted a paper to the National Security Council, was the standoff between "a conservative phalanx ... that did not believe in development aid; and a liberal cohort ... that believed this new dimension of policy was urgently required."[29]

Some of the critics of foreign aid were mindlessly dismissive: John H. Ohly, deputy director for programs and planning at the International Cooperation Administration, wrote of the Fairless report that "Seldom have the taxpayers of a country been asked to pay $10,000 a page for 19 pages of such trash and trivia." Humphrey, on the other hand, was more principled and thoughtful in articulating his philosophical opposition to a radical expansion of aid.[30] "It is all well and good to talk about helping to stabilize the world, etc.," he told Council on Foreign Economic Policy (CFEP) chairman Randall, anticipating arguments that some modern critics of international aid would also use, "but it seems to me that we are in a great contest between two almost opposite ideologies: one based on freedom of the individual in the development of individual initiative for his own benefit … the other based on the all-powerful state directing the activities of the individual for the benefit of the state [and …] the politicians who then happen to be in control of a country." This outcome, Humphrey argued, was "exactly the opposite of the ideology which we are spending so much money to defend and of which we are so proud."[31]

Matters came to a head at a National Security Council (NSC) meeting that April when Eisenhower "warned" Humphrey that "we could not weigh our assistance programs solely in terms of the U.S. budget. We must weigh these programs against the objectives which the United States was seeking in the world – such as peace, security, the development of international trade." When Humphrey protested that they had to "solve the problem of the costs," Eisenhower cut him off. There would always be a problem with cost "until some real settlement with Russia had been reached." A Cold War problem required a Cold War solution, no matter what the cost.[32]

Dillon was not on the National Security Council, but he and Dulles had successfully lobbied the president in advance of the meeting. "We conceived the idea of changing the foreign aid program, creating a thing called the Development Loan Fund," he recalled. "We got the president to agree to it, even though Mr. Humphrey didn't agree with it." Eisenhower had personally given Dillon the green light for his Arden speech.[33]

The president formally launched the administration's campaign with an address to the nation on May 21 that emphasized the need for mutual security. "At this critical moment of their economic growth," he said of the Global South, "a relatively small amount of outside capital can fatefully decide the difference between success and failure. What is critical now is to start and to maintain momentum."[34]

That injunction "to start and to maintain momentum" became the over-riding priority for the administration in the coming weeks as Eisenhower's mutual security scheme, including the Development Loan Fund, ground its way through Congress. At the beginning of June, Dillon appeared before the Senate Foreign Relations Committee, treading the delicate line between emphasizing how vital the development loans were for nineteen developing nations in Asia and Africa while at the same time indicating that the commitment "will not be unending." Money was to be extended on a loan basis. "The obligation to repay would be unequivocal," he reassured senators.

The day after Dillon gave evidence, the Foreign Affairs Committee approved Eisenhower's mutual security proposals, as did the full Senate. While there were cuts in many areas, Dillon's signature loans fund was approved in full – $500 million for 1958 and $750 million for the following year. The House of Representatives frustrated him by pegging back the figure for 1959 to $600 million. Still, all told Dillon had delivered exactly the kind of measured, expert performance Dulles had anticipated. His competence and assurance when discussing the intricacy of financial details had instilled a widespread confidence about the Development Loan Fund. He had engendered some bipartisan support for the plan, including from John F. Kennedy on the Senate Foreign Relations Committee.

Dillon had also executed a deft political maneuver within the administration itself. By the time the Development Loan Fund emerged from the legislative process, it did so with Dillon at the head of an advisory loan committee, which had new and unexpected authority over the International Cooperation Administration. It was too much for Hollister, who announced that he would be joining Humphrey in leaving the administration that summer. As the *New York Times* noted, it was Dillon who was now at "the heart of the [president's] program."[35]

Chapter Five

The Dillon Plan
Washington, 1957–1958

By the summer of 1957, with the departure of conservatives Humphrey and Hollister, a new kind of republicanism seemed ascendant within the Eisenhower administration. These so-called "Modern Republicans" had more centrist attitudes at home and abroad, including on global trade and foreign aid. "These trends were noticeable before Christian A. Herter, undersecretary of state, and Douglas Dillon, deputy undersecretary, entered the State Department this year," James "Scotty" Reston, Washington bureau chief of the *New York Times*, wrote in June, "but the feeling of well-informed men here is that these officials have contributed to the new and more relaxed attitude that now prevails in that department." For others it was also a question of competence. "He was reasonable," the economist Walt Rostow recalled of meeting Dillon for the first time in 1957, "very bright, quick to understand the complexity and viability of an issue, and flexible, unlike many in the administration." If policy was shifting towards a more modern outlook, plenty in Washington were coming to see Douglas Dillon as representative of that change.[1]

Over the months that followed, Dillon grew in confidence and authority as he came to define economic foreign policy. With Humphrey gone, Dillon found himself in effective charge of the American delegation at the Economic Conference of the Organization of American States held in Argentina from August 15 to September 4. The new treasury secretary, Robert Anderson, would attend the first couple of sessions as a courtesy, but Dillon ran the preparations and got "full proxy for the Treasury" once Anderson flew home. John Foster Dulles had cunningly tapped up the president. "In effect it would mean the State Department would be running this instead of the Treasury Department," Dillon noted, "and that it would be a much more [forthcoming] policy."[2]

Getting the administration to that more "forthcoming" position, however, was no easy task. Dillon was shocked at the lack of imagination he found. McCarthyism had recently driven many of the best career foreign-service personnel out of State. Those who remained seemed "consistently negative." Whatever he looked at – commodity agreements, an Inter-American bank, development assistance – the briefing papers seemed to offer only problems, not solutions. "The positions which had been prepared were not fully tenable," he complained, especially "in view of the strong pressures that were coming from Latin America for … more equal treatment with the rest of the world."[3] Although Dillon doubted it would be possible to reach an accord on a General Inter-American Economic Agreement, it was imperative to avoid "Latin Americans getting the erroneous impression that we do not intend seriously to negotiate for a General Agreement."[4]

Dillon had inherited a complex economic relationship. During the Second World War, keen to get its hands on raw materials for the war effort, the United States had made several trade agreements in Latin America that included both technical and financial aid. But by 1957, with American industry complaining about cheap imports of minerals and the military expressing concerns about the quality of those imports for sophisticated weaponry, the United States raised taxes on key regional exports such as lead and zinc and imposed restrictive quotas on woolens just weeks ahead of the conference. State Department officials ruefully admitted the timing could hardly have been worse. Those steps blatantly reneged on commitments made at the 1954 Rio economic conference, when the United States had undertaken to keep its markets open. Moreover, despite promising to set up an international finance corporation to help with economic development in the region, not a single loan had been made.[5]

These elements contrived to promise a stormy welcome for Dillon in Buenos Aires that summer, but behind the practical difficulties lay a philosophical divide with Latin America. As Laurence Roy Robottom, assistant secretary of state for Inter-American Affairs, pointed out during the preparatory talks, the US position was essentially "a strong presentation of the benefits of private investment and free private enterprise." That free-market approach stood in contrast to the statist approach adopted in most of the region. Dominated by the theorists at the Economic Commission for Latin America (ECLA) – a UN agency based in Chile – Latin American countries mostly held to a "dependency theory" in which, Edwin Williamson notes, "countries were incapable of breaking their own economic dependency and achieving balanced growth on their own." Instead, governments and ECLA economists wanted international agreements that would keep commodity prices high and direct foreign loans and aid to and from governments rather than private companies.[6]

Illness compounded the problems Dillon faced, although his deputy, Thorsten Kalijarvi, reported that his boss always knew "what was transpiring and issued instructions." Neither did Robert Anderson's presence at the beginning of the conference ease tensions with other delegations. There were sharp protests, particularly from Peru, Mexico, and Chile, over the new tariffs on zinc and lead. There was equal dismay, including privately by Dillon, at the vehemence of the treasury secretary's opposition to the idea of an Inter-American Bank and his continued insistence that "loans and existing mechanisms should be used." Anderson left Dillon behind to clear up the mess and afterwards complained to Eisenhower that the Latin American countries were like ungrateful "stepchildren."[7]

Over the remaining weeks of the conference, there were constant briefings against the United States as part of what Ambassador Willard Beaulac called "the continual barrage of extreme ideas" that framed the debate. Once it became obvious that an economic treaty was impossible to negotiate, the focus shifted to finding agreement for a declaration of basic principles of economic cooperation and a Latin American regional market. After these were agreed to on September 3, Dillon told the press that he was "highly pleased about the constructive results" of the conference. "Another important block has been added to the Pan-American structure," he declared. Eisenhower, on holiday in Newport, Rhode Island, issued a statement praising Dillon for "reaching a large measure of agreement on the important economic problems confronting the American States."[8]

In private, Dillon was less sanguine. He found officials in Washington congratulating themselves on the emptiness of the conference outcomes. William Snow, deputy assistant secretary of state for inter-American affairs, gleefully told Dulles that the economic declaration was "without specific commitments, time limits or details of implementation." Jack Corbett from the department's office of international finance and development affairs announced to a staff meeting that all the conferences were a waste of time and should be avoided. "These countries have hobby horses they ride and things they want from us, and they have nothing we want," he groused. "It is hard to come to terms when we have nothing to bargain for." Dillon, who found such arguments fatuous, was determined to strengthen American policy. "We had been much too restrictive," he explained. The United States had abdicated its duty to the region, off-loading too much responsibility onto the World Bank. Everything that would follow in Latin America – from convincing Eisenhower the next year to throw his weight behind the idea of an Inter-American Bank to the creation of the Alliance for Progress as treasury secretary under John F. Kennedy in 1961 – was rooted in Dillon's experience in Buenos Aires that summer. "All these [developments]," he reflected, "flowed out of this change that began there."[9]

The problem for Dillon was the familiar one of internal politics within the administration. That point was brought home to him within weeks of arriving back from Buenos Aires as he scrambled to prevent another own goal over the establishment of a Special United Nations Fund for Economic Development (SUNFED). UN Ambassador Henry Cabot Lodge Jr. had been an enthusiastic supporter of the scheme, arguing that it would be a great propaganda coup for the United States to be seen to fund aid for developing countries through the UN. Humphrey and his ally in the State Department, Hoover, had vehemently opposed the measure – the whole scheme was a pointless "token," Hoover had argued. But Dillon, like Lodge, understood that gestures mattered.[10]

By September 1957, the issue had reached a critical phase, with the UN General Assembly about to vote to establish SUNFED. The United States was set to be isolated in opposition, with western European countries, the Soviet Bloc, non-aligned countries, and even the UK, its closest ally, all lining up to participate in one form or another. The problem, Dillon complained to Dulles on September 26, was "the absence of a constructive alternative" – so now he presented the secretary with one: a proposal to throw money at the UN Technical Assistance program. The program was already "doing a useful job well," but was "strapped for funds." The United States should offer to support "a doubling or tripling" of its funding. Such a move would give countries "that would like to vote with the U.S." an escape hatch. Even some diehard supporters of SUNFED "might be prepared to settle, for the time being, for something that promised additional resources."[11]

It was a clever plan, replacing hostility with money on the table. Dulles approved the proposal on October 1, but almost immediately ran into opposition from Anderson. "It became quite clear," Walter Kotschnig, a State Department official, reported to Dillon "that what has happened is that the same people who advised Mr. Humphrey against any kind of U.S. participation in any kind of an International Development Fund have prevailed upon Mr. Anderson to oppose our proposal." Treasury officials even kept referring to "Mr. Humphrey's position" rather than "Mr. Anderson's."[12]

In personal talks, Dillon convinced a reluctant Anderson to go along with the proposal provided it made clear that there would be no "blueprinting or engineering projects" involved, as these would need "immediate large capital investments and thus potentially increase pressures for the early establishment of an International Development Fund." Once the proposal got to the United Nations and was incorporated into a compromise proposal on SUNFED, Anderson backtracked and again tried to stop it. As Dillon had predicted to Dulles the previous month, "I doubt that Secretary Anderson's reservations could be met by further tinkering with the language." This time it would require the secretary of state himself to face down his cabinet colleague. "As Sputnik has taught us," Dulles told him, alluding to the Soviets launching the first artificial Earth satellite, "we cannot safely avoid the propaganda aspects of what we do." Surely Anderson could see that "to be a minority of practically one on the SUNFED resolution would be extremely bad at this juncture." Either way, he informed Anderson that he had authorized Lodge to vote in favor. "There are other than purely fiscal factors involved," he said.[13]

The outcome completed a diplomatic triumph for Dillon. As the Mission at the United Nations reported back afterwards, Dillon's proposal for enlarging the scope of UN technical assistance programs caused the seventy or so countries wanting an immediate establishment of SUNFED to reverse course. There was general acceptance that there was "no chance" of SUNFED going ahead until the United States and other industrial countries were prepared to fund it. "This," pointed out Congressman Walter H. Judd, who had participated in the UN negotiations, "gives us practically complete control over the time and conditions where such a fund could be established." All told, the agreement was being "widely hailed" as a "major" achievement. It was clear that Dillon was shifting the tone and practice of the United States as a participant in multilateral foreign trade. The following year, at the IMF/World Bank annual meeting in New Delhi, India, he would propose negotiations to found an International Development Association as an affiliate of the World Bank.[14]

Growing in confidence and increasingly mastering Washington insider politics, Dillon now maneuvered to consolidate his ascendancy in economic foreign policy. With Dulles more than ever convinced about the centrality of "the whole economic business" and furious with the fiscal conservatives at the Treasury, Dillon presented a plan to give himself "top control of the foreign aid program" within the department. "I spoke to Mr. Dulles about it," he recalled, "and he agreed completely. He gave me the authority, which I had for the rest of my time in the State Department." In fact, the two men agreed to take it one step further: that Dillon should have authority to coordinate aid policy within the entire administration. Dulles took the idea to Eisenhower, who signed off on it. On November 15, newspapers began reporting that Dillon was "slated" to be in charge of foreign aid programs. The *New York Times* described him as "a kind of chief of staff for foreign economic affairs," noting that the decision to centralize stemmed from "the growing realization that they have often operated at cross purposes, to the detriment of an effective foreign policy." Dillon was "well equipped by training and sympathies for his new job." The paper also reported that Vice President Richard Nixon had vigorously promoted him for the role – a sign of things to come as Modern Republicans began to look towards the election in 1960.[15]

A few days later, Dillon delivered a keynote speech on foreign aid to the National Foreign Trade Convention. He boldly declared that the United States should adopt long-term, well-financed programs on foreign aid and loans, and give stability to trade through a five-year extension of the Reciprocal Trade Agreements Act. Such moves were vital in a Cold War context to outmatch Soviet efforts to use economic assistance to gain influence in the developing world. "Unless the free nations, acting together, succeed in building strong and healthy economies which answer the aspirations of their people," he warned, "we may be sure that we will not stay the course of Soviet world domination, no matter what our military power may be." Eisenhower then signed the executive order to put Dillon in effective command of foreign aid programs. His job was "to achieve even greater efficiency and economy or more effective coordination of mutual security activities with related foreign policies and programs." It was a technical way of saying that the Cold War, as much as any humanitarian purpose, would define the program. It also meant that on foreign economic policy he was the top dog. "Dulles didn't want to do it himself," Dillon reflected, "so he created this job for me."[16]

Eisenhower's executive order put Dillon center-stage as the administration attempted to push increased funding for foreign aid through Congress. He was given the principal coordinating responsibility for the foreign aid bill, which would test both his patience and his skill over the next nine months. In January 1958, he set the scene for the battle to come with another keynote speech in Philadelphia that once again put foreign aid into the broader context of the Cold War. The Soviet economic challenge was "too serious and menacing" to be kicked to the curb, he cautioned. The "free world" had to meet the threat head-on "if our way of life is to remain the continuing choice of the great mass of the world's population." Millions were trying to lift themselves out of poverty, disease, and illiteracy. The United States had to identify with these aspirations and support them with aid and technology. If they did not, then the Soviets were ready to take advantage. "The Soviet leaders have shown that they are fully aware of this situation," he warned, raising the stakes. "Today the Soviet challenge to our way of life in this economic area is perhaps even more real and active than it is in the sphere of military and scientific technology."[17]

On February 18, the $3 billion foreign aid bill started its tortuous progress through Congress with hearings before the House Foreign Affairs Committee. Congressional correspondents predicted that Dillon would "doubtless meet a barrage" on aid and trade from those congressmen who "harbor a distaste for the State Department." He gave as good as he got. When his turn came to testify, Dillon was bullish, telling Congress specifically that on development loans, they were getting off cheap. The $625 million requested for the Development Loan Fund (DLF) was "the barest minimum" needed to make the program work. Monies appropriated the previous year had proved inadequate to meet demand. If he had his way, the figure would be a billion dollars a year. The State Department was looking into a multilateral fund to give "soft" loans to developing countries through the World Bank, but Congress should be in no doubt that it was the Development Loan Fund that was "the primary instrument of our government to meet this crying need." The consequences of withholding funding were unthinkable, he explained. If the countries of the developing world could not turn to the United States, then "the future will indeed be tragic for them and tragic for us."[18]

Dillon's testimony had staked out the public ground for the attritional process to follow. He publicly maintained the pressure with set-piece speeches about the Soviet Union's "large-scale economic offensive" and repeated his position that the Development Loan Fund be "something on the order of 1bn a year." In private, he began building consensus. He met regularly with small groups of legislators to discuss both aid and trade, telling them that the bill had been "drawn very tightly," but indicating where it "could stand a reduction." When in May the bill emerged first from the House Foreign Affairs Committee and then from the House itself with only modest cuts, it seemed as if the strategy had worked. The Senate even restored some of those cuts, and a Mutual Security Act totaling $3.069 billion passed after reconciliation on June 30. When it came to the appropriations process – actually getting hold of the money – Congress did take chunks out of the overall funds, but less than it had done in 1957. Crucially, funding for the economic assistance program was increased by $500 million, with an extra $100 million for Dillon's signature Development Loan Fund. It was nowhere near the $1 billion he thought was really needed, but it was another step in making foreign aid an essential part of Cold War strategy. "Present signs point to a loss of heart by the budget cutters," wrote long-time Capitol Hill reporter John D. Morris, who noted how opinion both in Congress and in the country had "shifted toward the Administration's viewpoint" after "months" of work by "C. Douglas Dillon, Undersecretary of State for Economic Affairs."[19]

The title Morris gave Dillon was a new one, reflecting his promoted status as the second undersecretary of state in the department and No. 3 in its hierarchy after Dulles and Christian A. Herter – "an upgrading of the whole thing," Dillon said. Congress had authorized the appointment (which had existed only once before) by including it in the Mutual Security Act. That legislators did so without a murmur was the best indicator that Dillon had conducted a tough negotiation without creating many enemies. Where the position would thereafter be subject to Senate approval, now that august body gave him a tip of the hat. "The President may initially fill the position of undersecretary of state for economic affairs," the act noted, "by appointing, without further advice and consent of the Senate, the officer who, on the date of the enactment of this subsection, held the position of deputy undersecretary of state for economic affairs." This gracious gesture indicated the personal esteem in which Dillon was held on Capitol Hill.[20]

The new undersecretary of state used his increased authority to ramp up efforts for the next stage of what both the Administration and the press now referred to as "The Dillon Plan." He understood that an expansion to the $1 billion a year figure he had in mind would require a massive effort in persuading Congress. Yet there were good reasons to believe that opinion on the Hill was breaking his way. During the committee hearings the previous spring, senators of both parties had asked him leading questions about whether the Development Loan Fund should be put on a long-term basis. A bipartisan group of senators from the Foreign Relations Committee had written to the president asking for more emphasis on aid the following year. During the debates on the mutual security bill in the full Senate, some of the most vociferous speeches had been those given in opposition to cuts to the DLF budget. Over that summer, Dillon convinced first Dulles and then Eisenhower that a "Presidential level" commitment would get any proposal over the line. Eisenhower duly informed the cabinet in July that the issue had become his "priority."

When Dulles spoke at the United Nations General Assembly in early September, he urged all nations to "dedicate the year 1959 to these purposes" and committed the United States to "development financing programs on a vigorous and effective basis." Background briefings to the press confirmed that it was "fairly certain" the president would "give the idea the initial push" and then ask Congress early in the new year to fund a multiannual borrowing authority for the development fund. As to the explanation for the new energy and strategic clarity, the *New York Times* reported, "officials here [in Washington] said that one of the reasons behind the decision to go ahead with the Dillon Plan was the high respect in which Mr. Dillon is held on Capitol Hill."[21]

Dillon's new authority gave him the opportunity to push through another idea that he had been supporting since the economic conference of the Organization of American States in Argentina the previous year. During that conference, he had become ever more convinced that in treating Latin America as the unloved "stepchild" of its Cold War strategy, the United States was buying trouble for itself in the region. The Development Loan Fund had focused on Asia and Africa, but Latin America needed its own pipeline for soft loans and technical assistance. Dillon broadly favored a regional development bank but had been irked by the unimaginative responses within the State Department and Treasury. Even after enlisting Dulles's support to initiate an inter-bureau task force to reexamine the "too negative" approach to Latin America, he was frustrated by the ultra-cautious results that emerged. These had suggested some tinkering with policy, but no new initiatives. Yet if all politics is local, then the arrival of Latin America on the front pages of American newspapers and the cover of *Life* magazine a few weeks later soon helped move the barometer of opinion in Dillon's favor.[22]

At the end of April, Vice President Richard Nixon left Washington for a routine goodwill tour of Latin America, during which his motorcade came under violent attack in Peru and Venezuela. In Caracas, writes his biographer John Farrell, "demonstrators rushed the car, some shouting 'Muera [die] Nixon!'" Protesters spat and threw stones and glass. "The hate on their faces was unbelievable," recalled Nixon's military aide, Don Hughes, who had flown 101 combat missions during the Korean war: "They were out to kill us." When the crowd started to rock the trapped car, the secret service pulled out their weapons, saying they would have to start firing, but Nixon forbade them. Only the quick thinking of his driver in bumping the car to the other side of the road and speeding back to the embassy saved the day. While Nixon would be praised for his coolness under fire (Eisenhower cabled to salute his "courage, patience, and calmness"), the tour left an impression on the vice president. Yes, there were "case-hardened Communists operatives," he said, but most "were clearly teenagers" And they "all had a look of unadulterated hatred."[23]

Something had to be done to repair the rapidly deteriorating relationship with the region. Nixon's assessment chimed with that of the earlier inter-bureau task force report which saw the problem as more about presentation than substance. "Our policies and actions were generally correct," Nixon told a meeting of the National Security Council on his return, so "we must join the battle in Latin America on the field of propaganda." Otherwise "the Communists would ultimately win out." Further pressure to do something – anything – kept mounting. A few weeks after the Nixon visit, the president of Brazil, Juscelino Kubitschek de Oliveira, renewed demands for a development bank for the Americas. He pointed to how the United States had helped reconstruct European economies after the Second World War but lamented that Washington did not show "equal interest in the serious problem of development in countries still with rudimentary economies." Latin America was now "the vulnerable point within the Western coalition," he warned, adding that "the Western cause will inevitably suffer if no help comes in its own hemisphere." Eisenhower reassured Kubitschek that he was "delighted" by the initiative and determined to find a way forward. That summer he sent his brother, Milton Eisenhower, on a fact-finding mission to Latin America. But it was to Dillon that the president turned for a remedial boost for the worsening relationship with southern neighbors.[24]

On August 12, 1958, speaking before the Economic and Social Council of the Organization of American States, Dillon announced that after extensive "coordinated studies of the economic problems of the area," the administration was "prepared to consider the establishment of an Inter-American regional development institution." Foreign ministers of twenty-one countries were invited to Washington for informal talks and a meeting with the president following the UN General Assembly in September. Technical talks would follow over the winter. It was, noted the *New York Times*, "a reversal of long-established policy."[25]

Throughout the technical discussions that followed, the treasury secretary would cut the US contributions and claw back voting stock to give Latin American countries as little influence over American foreign expenditure as possible. The eventual headline compromise figure of $1 billion was less than the $5 billion that Kubitschek had requested, but Dillon behind the scenes, as with the Development Loan Fund in Congress, kept emphasizing that greater resources could come later: the important goal now was to get the bank up and running. Anderson gave Eisenhower an ultimatum, saying he would resign rather than release more funds. In the end, all the American republics (minus revolutionary Cuba) agreed in April 1959 to take the offer on the table and establish the Inter-American Development Bank (IAD). It did not fully realize what Dillon, let alone the countries of South America, had wanted from the initiative. He would remain convinced that a spectacular opportunity to create even greater goodwill in the region had been missed. Still, as Thomas Zoumaras, who worked closely with Dillon after he left office, notes, "establishing the IAD in 1959 was a seminal development in United States-Latin American relations."[26]

Dillon by now had become a figure of public note in Washington. In a glowing double- page profile with photographs, the *New York Times* described how he was running foreign economic policy "with a zest not seen since the days of the Marshall Plan." Officials attested to his "knowledge of detail," his ability to read "every line of every paper and every figure in the appendix," and "his innate political orientation," which meant that he "instinctively places his political foot at least as far forward as his economic." This political instinct was matched by "the most striking aspects of Douglas Dillon's captaincy of foreign economic policy," namely his "imaginativeness and flexibility." He was brave in making sure that "fear of Congressional reaction" was "never enough per se to kill a plan before its birth." And although he might look like "the 'striped pants' type of diplomat," he had shown himself to be adept at working with "the 'small folks' congress." Written by Edwin L. Dale, the Washington bureau correspondent who covered economics, the profile included a long analysis of Dillon's policy initiatives, whose influence in changing the climate of opinion in Washington he thought "impossible to exaggerate." Perhaps sensing a skepticism in his readers that the "Captain of Our Economic Campaign" was perhaps a bit too good to be true, Dale ended with a quotation from an off-the-record official at the State Department.

"Quite frankly, we like him very much," the official observed, "and I think you'll have a hard time finding anyone around here with a different view."[27]

Chapter Six

Dillon Is Coming
Washington and Paris, 1959–1960

In the spring of 1959, as Douglas Dillon shepherded the Inter-American Development Bank bill through Congress, a major era in American foreign policy closed. On March 30, John Foster Dulles, his abdominal cancer inoperable, dictated a letter of resignation to his brother Allen and asked him to deliver it in person to the president. He was too weak to do it himself. A distraught Eisenhower refused to accept it for more than two weeks, only finally agreeing to do so on the understanding that Dulles would remain as a special adviser with full cabinet rank. Six weeks later Dulles was dead. He was, Eisenhower said in his tribute, "one of the truly great men of our time."[1]

The two men formed one of the closest partnerships that has existed between a president and a secretary of state, perhaps only rivaled in modern times by the ties between George H.W. Bush and James Baker. "Hardly a day passed when the president did not call Dulles at least once to ask about some problem they were working on or about something that had caught his attention in the daily cable traffic," Dillon recalled, "and Dulles had no hesitancy in calling the president." He judged it "the single most important relationship" of the administration.[2]

Dulles had also been Dillon's own most important political connection. Even when they disagreed, or when Dillon erred, as he did during the Suez crisis, the relationship between the two men had avoided any lasting recriminations. Their closeness had been evident at the end of Dulles's life when he recuperated with the Dillons at La Lanterne in Hobe Sound, Florida. "He was a close friend," Dillon reflected. "I was lucky to have known and worked with him."[3]

Given their close association, the end of this friendship might have signaled a loss of influence and even position. Instead, it furthered Dillon's ascent. That continued rise reflected both skill and luck. The skill was evident in Dillon's reputation as "the Captain of Our Economic Campaign" and a "modern republican" who was able to get important work done in Washing-ton. The *Wall Street Journal* even touted him as a successor to Dulles "if Ike wants a [comer]."

The luck lay in his closeness to the new secretary of state, Christian A. Herter, that made unnecessary the deference he had always shown Dulles. His familiar use of "Chris" in State Department memos would have been unthinkable with his former boss. The bond between the two men formed when both joined Dulles's team in 1948. They remained close, so that when Dulles brought both to the State Department as number two and number three in 1957, they worked easily and well together. Eisenhower appointed Herter as secretary, but he also nominated Dillon to become his number two as undersecretary of State.[4]

Herter today is usually remembered as an undistinguished manager of foreign policy during the last years of the Eisenhower administration. How-ever, it is worth remembering that when Eisenhower suffered a heart attack in 1955, Herter, the popular then governor of Massachusetts, received serious mention as Ike's successor for the 1956 election. When Eisenhower recovered, a campaign to replace Nixon with Herter as the vice-presidential candidate gathered steam. The president squelched the move because he did not intend to switch horses mid-race (Herter subsequently nominated Nixon at the convention). But while Herter had been seen as a major player, circumstances conspired against him by 1959. Although most observers assumed Eisenhower would immediately appoint Herter to replace Dulles, the president told reporters that he had several candidates to consider. He then asked Herter for a report on his osteoarthritis, which required him to use crutches or a wheelchair. Would this affect his ability to do the job, the president wanted to know. The appointment finally came after what Herter's biographer calls "several days of embarrassing delay." The Senate Foreign Relations Committee and the full Senate tried to redress the balance by confirming the appointment in just over four hours. But the impression that Herter did not command the confidence of the president dogged him for his entire term at the State Department. The media saw him more as a caretaker of the Dulles's legacy than a true successor. Dillon's own nomination got delayed behind a vicious and ultimately unsuccessful confirmation of a new commerce secretary, Lewis L. Strauss, who had played a controversial role in the political defenestration of Robert Oppenheimer, the former head of the Manhattan Project. By contrast, Dillon had widespread support and was finally sworn in as under-secretary of state on June 12. Eisenhower himself attended the ceremony – a mark of esteem for a man that *Time* described as having "nailed down a top place in Ike's regard."[5]

This remarkable moment for Dillon came ten weeks before he celebrated his fiftieth birthday. He had established a name as someone who commanded both the technical detail and a strategy for a coherent Cold War economic foreign policy. He had a reputation, said *Time*, as "the most popular of all State Department officials on Capitol Hill." The satisfaction Dillon felt was personal as well as professional. Seven years earlier he had been restless and unhappy. Now his change of direction from banking to diplomacy had proved a sound choice.[6]

Part of Dillon's political success was built on doing things his own way. Although he showed increasing skill at the game in Washington, he did not play dirty. He worked diligently, usually putting in twelve to fifteen hours each day at the State Department (also adding, to his chagrin, a stone in weight to a six-one frame, hitting 190 pounds by 1959). He was rarely sick. His quiet, courteous demeanor and mastery of material won the loyalty of his staff. Among his political colleagues, he did not often maneuver against them even when, as with Humphrey and Anderson at the Treasury, they disagreed – and as such, did not make many enemies. He cultivated relationships across the aisle, playing golf every Saturday with his friend and neighbor, J. William Fulbright (by then chair of the Senate Foreign Relations Committee), and earning plaudits from Democrats such as Senator Mike Monroney of Oklahoma, an ally on development funding, who described him as "the brightest light in the State Department." And of course, as one of the richest men in the country, he was practiced at extending hospitality in an understated way that smoothed relationships and engendered goodwill.

Only a few nervous habits hinted at the anxieties of high political office. A reporter profiling him for the *Cleveland Plain Dealer* noted how "he clicks-clicks the clip of his ball point pen or bends and unbends the bows of his glasses" throughout an interview. Yet while these tics made him appear "shy, earnest and sincere," there was none of what his friend August Belmont IV had described as the "beaten down nervousness" of his youth. In short, on the cusp of his sixth decade, Douglas Dillon seemed, indeed almost certainly was, a happy man.[7]

Weeks after his confirmation, Herter left for a conference of foreign ministers in Geneva that would last on and off the whole summer. Six months earlier, the Soviet leader, Nikita Khrushchev, had given the Western allies until the end of May to get out of Berlin or else risk a military conflict. A "hail Mary" trip to the USSR in February 1959 by the British prime minister, Harold Macmillan, had lifted the threat of the six-month deadline and led Khrushchev to agree to a four-power foreign ministers conference as a precursor to a potential leaders' summit. But the foreign ministers conference turned out to be a bust, making little or no progress, other than an agreement about the shape (lozenged) of the negotiating table.[8]

With Herter away in Geneva, Dillon ran the State Department as acting secretary. That allowed him to brief Eisenhower on a wide range of foreign policy matters and attend cabinet meetings with his trademark quiet authority. But with Herter less accomplished than his predecessor and often exhausted by shuttling across the Atlantic, even the fastidious Dillon missed details in a way that angered the president. On July 10, Herter, Dillon, and Deputy Undersecretary Robert Murphy had met Eisenhower in the Oval Office to discuss how to move the Geneva talks forward. The president told them that he planned to offer Khrushchev the prospect of a visit to Washington to winkle out a compromise from the Soviets at Geneva. Given general enthusiasm, the group agreed that Murphy would deliver an informal invitation via Soviet deputy prime minister Frol Kozlov, who was visiting the United Nations that week. The letter was hand-delivered on July 12 and Khrushchev accepted the offer ten days later. But to Eisenhower's alarm, the Soviet premier's reply made no mention of the need for progress at Geneva. Once it dawned on him that none had been requested, he immediately summoned Dillon and Murphy to the White House.[9]

At an uncomfortable meeting in the Oval Office, Murphy had to admit to a visibly "disturbed" president that "in fact what had been conveyed to Khrushchev was an unqualified invitation." In his memoirs, Eisenhower later admitted to his own errors in the matter. "After a bit of cool reflection, I realized the cause of the difficulty lay more in my own failure to make myself unmistakably clear than in the failure of others to understand me," he noted. "After all, here were some of the most capable men I knew in their field, and apparently all had failed to comprehend the idea in my mind." He was less magnanimous at the time and vented his anger at Murphy about having "to pay the penalty and hold a meeting he despised." What would the allies say, he demanded to know? Once he had finished with Murphy, the president turned on Dillon for a systemic failure. It would not have happened in Dulles's day, he informed him. "He and Mr. Dulles had always talked from ideas or topics and not from papers," he said, releasing pent up grief as well as anger. "Mr. Dulles would then put on paper the idea upon which they had agreed," he fumed, "and send it to the president to correct and confirm." The humiliated

Dillon could only remain silent. It was not his State Department, not his system, but he was the man who held the ball that day.[10]

The Eisenhower meeting alerted Dillon to some harsh realities of his new position. In his previous position, dealing with economic matters and having a powerful protector in Dulles, he had hitherto avoided much of the rough side of political life. But as undersecretary of state and No. 2, his brief now involved dealing with higher profile issues and personalities. At times when he was acting secretary, there was nowhere to hide. The transition required Dillon to reconfigure his character and public persona, not least in showing that he had the strength to be more than just technically accomplished. He needed to manifest the toughness demanded to represent a global superpower on the world stage.

At no time was this more the case than during Khrushchev's visit to the United States in September. The thirteen-day trip created a media frenzy as the Soviet leader, escorted by the smooth-talking Henry Cabot Lodge Jr., toured the country. Towards the end of the trip, Eisenhower and Khrushchev met for three days of talks (and watching Westerns) at Camp David. Dillon shadowed some of these talks, but when Khrushchev rebuffed Eisenhower's invitation to attend church near the president's own Gettysburg Farm, Ike asked Dillon to hold the fort by hosting Khrushchev for talks on trade and the repayment of wartime loans. So it was that on Sunday, September 27, at 9:35 a.m., while the president went to church, Dillon found himself hosting talks with Khrushchev and the flinty Soviet foreign minister, Andrei Gromyko. It would be one of the most remarkable meetings of his political career.

After the usual opening courtesies, Khrushchev began by saying that the United States had to decide whether it would open or close for trade with the Soviet Union. Dillon replied in his usual technical, mild-mannered way, pointing out that "peaceful trade" had been increasing in recent times, including in areas such as machinery and equipment for the manufacture of shoes and synthetic fabrics. Indeed, he observed pleasantly, "he had looked at the records and that at least five different processes in the synthetic textile field had been made available to the Soviet Union during the past year."[11]

Whether Dillon had failed to take the measure of the man opposite, or the man opposite had taken what he thought was the measure of him, the meeting turned in a way that even the usually bland official minutes described as happening "rather violently."

Khrushchev retorted that he had "not come to the United States to learn how to make shoes or sausage." Did Dillon think he was some lowly trade minister? He was there to discuss "the general principles of trade between the

USSR and the US" and whether the United States would "rescind its discriminatory practices in trade with the USSR." If they were talking about shoes, he continued, then "any offer to the USSR of such items as shoe lasts, etc., was insulting to the people of the Soviet Union. They knew how to make shoes, perhaps even better than the Americans."

Astonishingly, Khrushchev then took off his shoe and waved it in Dillon's face, shouting at him to "look at his shoes and see that for himself."[12]

It was a trademark Khrushchev maneuver. As Michael Beschloss points out, the "miner from Kalinovka was excruciatingly sensitive to his treatment" by Western diplomats and politicians. He was quick to take umbrage at any perceived disrespect and, if he sensed weakness in opponents, usually attempted to brutalize or embarrass them with an attack on diplomatic decorum. He would do so again, successfully, with President Kennedy at their first meeting. He would even deploy the shoe trick again, banging the heel on the desk at the UN General Assembly in 1960 to interrupt several speeches.[13]

As the son of Clarence Dillon, Douglas fully understood the behavior of a bully. At Camp David instinct kicked in, as he refused to be steamrolled by the Soviet leader. Dillon told Khrushchev that he "didn't intend to discuss specifics either," and that he agreed that the whole question of trade was "more of a political nature than economic." But if they were going to "create a better atmosphere" for trade, the Soviet Union would need to stop stealing American proprietary technology and agree on a schedule to repay its wartime debts. By law, the United States could not extend credits to countries that did not repay old debts. Khrushchev tried the steamroller again. Dillon was being "highhanded" and his approach "amounted to a policy of Diktat and of Cold War," he bellowed, seriously losing his temper. The Soviet Union had paid its "contribution in blood during the last war." No wonder Dillon had acquired a reputation "as being a conservative and aggressive man." He would "repeat Mr. Dillon's remarks word for word" at a mass rally in Moscow the next day. Of course, "if Mr. Dillon were to help" the Soviet Union then his bad reputation would "disappear." Indeed, Khrushchev promised ("facetiously" adds the notetaker), on the "day when the proletariats took over, he would put in a good word for Mr. Dillon and say that he had helped the proletariat."

Dillon "expressed his appreciation" for the intercession when the revolution came. But the only way to make progress on trade and the extension of credit, he told Khrushchev, would be if the Soviets "took steps to reduce the tensions existing between the two countries." Finally, just as the meeting was concluding, Khrushchev moved on the substantive issue of lend-lease debt. Grumbling that "insistence on its settlement could be compared to catching fleas in a dog's hair," he nevertheless agreed that "the Soviet Union would be willing to appoint representatives to start negotiations." Dillon smiled at him. "This would be very helpful," he said.[14]

It had been a notable encounter. "I didn't react the way he wanted, I guess," Dillon recalled. "I stood up to him ... to the horror of my advisors who were sitting behind me." At a reception in Washington at the beginning of the visit, photographers had snapped Khrushchev waving his finger aggressively in Dillon's face, saying loudly, "So you're the one who's blocking trade between our two countries!" An accompanying report in the *New York Herald Tribune* noted that the confrontation had come about because the Soviet leader was going to "ignore Mr. Dillon's argument" that the Soviets should "pay up the $11bn or so bad debt." Now, after talks, Khrushchev had conceded the point. By the time he came to write his memoirs in the late sixties, the recollection of the meeting with Dillon – "my chief opponent on questions of trade" – clearly still rankled. "Dillon's attitude toward us was very hostile," he wrote. "He simply could not tolerate us. He was a typical front man for the big capitalist monopolies, who held the keys to economic relations with the USSR and dictated conditions."[15]

The most important outcome of the visit was Khrushchev's removal of a deadline on the Berlin question. That guarantee gave Eisenhower the necessary "progress" required to agree to a four-power summit in Paris in May 1960. Events surrounding that meeting would involve Dillon in another of the more baffling moments of his career. First, however, he had to deal with an economic issue that would preoccupy him for the rest of his time in government.

Throughout the second half of 1959, the depletion of US gold and dollar reserves alarmed the Eisenhower administration. That summer Dillon and his team drafted a wide-ranging position paper that showed that between 1950 and 1957, the annual US balance of payments deficit had been less than $2 billion. Since then, however, the situation had escalated sharply, with the overall deficit for 1959 projected at $5 billion. The United States had lost $3.4 billion in gold and liquid dollar assets the previous year, while western Europe had gained $3.7 billion. Of western Europe's gain, $1.6 billion was attributable to direct transactions with the United States – an increase in the capacity of Europe to earn gold and dollars that was "markedly influenced by a shift in the terms of trade in favor of Europe." Clearly, the international monetary system no longer favored the United States. What, then, could or should the Americans do about it?

Dillon outlined the options in a way that favored his own preferences. "Efforts to adjust the U.S. balance of payments over the years ahead can be either expansive or restrictive," he noted. Restrictive or discriminatory methods would only serve "to suppress and conceal the symptoms of imbalance" and would "not promote, and usually impede, sound adjustments in the balance of payments." It would be pointless, for example, to tie Development Loan Fund loans to procuring goods and services in the United States. Only the "pressures of competitive market forces operating within a framework of sound fiscal and monetary policy" could bring about the necessary adjustment to the US balance of payments.[16]

Dillon's State Department paper kicked off an immediate turf war. At a cabinet meeting on August 7, treasury secretary Robert Anderson argued that it was "necessary to re-examine the kinds of things we are doing, including the problems we generate for ourselves." These entailed "military expenditures overseas" and, exactly as Dillon had predicted, "a rigid review of Development Loan Fund activities, including attention to ensuring that government loans are utilized in such a way as to increase procurement from the United States." Dillon, who was present in the room, must have been dumbfounded when his boss Herter said nothing to contradict the treasury secretary. After the meeting, Eisenhower approved the measure to restrict DLF financing "to the purchase of U.S. goods and services." A spokesperson for the Development Loan Fund announced the policy on October 20, 1959. "This is not a turn-around, a reversal, or going in another direction," Eisenhower said at a press conference two days later. "It is simply to point out that when we are making this money available, it's dollars that's being made available; and where it is feasible and reasonable, we want that money to be spent here."[17]

The move was a serious setback for Dillon. Washington insiders immediately identified a shift in the power dynamic within the administration, with Anderson taking over from Dulles as the president's most trusted adviser. "Anderson has emerged as the most powerful figure in the president's official family," columnist James "Scotty" Reston wrote. "His influence is being felt in a major review of the nation's economic foreign policy and in this … he has the solid support of the president" to whom he was closer than "anybody else in the Administration." The State Department and Dillon saw their roles diminished. Anderson was a skillful enough politician not to rub his ascendancy in their faces. He paid Herter and Dillon the immediate courtesy of going in person to the State Department to say that he had "given orders" in the Treasury that no statements should be made that might "indicate any friction" over decisions related to the Development Loan Fund, and he "hoped very much" that Herter and Dillon would do the same at the State Department. If difficulties arose, "We ought to work them out by discussion among ourselves."[18]

It was a shrewd play on Anderson's part and one that Dillon recognized as giving him some room to maneuver. "Secretary Anderson [was] far easier to deal with and more understanding of foreign policy than George Humphrey," he recalled. Although the two men "quite often had differences," he respected how Anderson would always attempt "to settle these." Dillon was astute enough to understand how to apply his own political pressure, not least in mobilizing his close friend William Fulbright to ask awkward questions at hearings of the Senate Foreign Relations Committee. Similarly, he used a GATT conference in Japan to warn, "Either we move ahead to get rid of outmoded trade restrictions, or we can expect a resurgence of protectionism and restrictive action." But essentially, he tried to work with Anderson to push American policy in the expansive, as opposed to restrictive, direction he had proposed over the summer. When Dillon dispatched a strategy paper to the president (sent over Herter's signature) on November 24 entitled "Proposed United States Initiative to Mobilize Free World Resources for Development and to Strengthen Trade Relations," he was able to note that the "outlines of this proposal have been discussed with Secretary Anderson, who concurs."[19]

Dillon acknowledged the "great – even startling – changes in the international economic situation" that had occurred over the past two years and which had created "new problems of major dimensions for our foreign policy." The first problem was the question of how the United States could "mobilize the energies and resources of the other industrialized countries to assist the development of Asia, Africa, the Near East and other development-hungry parts of the Free World?" The United States could not "provide the needed capital alone." Western Europe and Japan were now "financially capable of mounting a sizable effort which could powerfully assist our own, thereby greatly adding to the overall strength and cohesion of the Free World." The second problem was how to "redirect the emerging trade rivalries within Western Europe" into "constructive channels" that might "reinforce rather than weaken world-wide trade" and "avoid the present risk of serious harm to our exports and those of other friendly countries outside Europe."[20]

So what steps, Dillon asked, could the United States take "to enlist the full cooperation of Western Europe and Japan in making this effort?" His own prescription was that the United States had to "abandon its present passive role and exercise determined leadership." The United States should initiate "the reorganization and revitalization of the Organization for European

Economic Cooperation (OEEC)," he urged, and announce its willingness to join this revitalized institution (the renamed Organisation for Economic Co-operation and Development) as a full member. Such a move would increase the American ability both to push other nations toward "greater" development efforts and to settle "trade quarrels on a basis consistent with sound world trade relations." In both development and trade, Dillon concluded, this action "would constitute an act of creative United States leadership."[21]

Eisenhower gave Dillon the green light and the next day announced that he was dispatching him to European capitals to begin the process. "Probably the hottest news item during last week's session here of the parliament of the European common market," one American correspondent in Strasbourg noted breathlessly, "was the word from Washington that 'Dillon is coming.'"[22]

That Europe found itself quite literally at "sixes and sevens" was one of the many complications facing the undersecretary as he crossed the Atlantic. In one camp were the European Economic Community "six" (Belgium, France, Italy, Luxembourg, the Netherlands, and West Germany) that had been established by the Treaty of Rome in 1957. Britain had declined to join the EEC but instead, just weeks before Dillon's arrival, it had facilitated a European Free Trade Area (EFTA) "seven" (Austria, Denmark, Norway, Portugal, Sweden, Switzerland, and the UK) to rival the six. Dillon saw EFTA as an unwelcome distraction from the EEC political integration project which the United States broadly supported. How, then, to strike the difficult balance between expressing American alarm at Europe's divisions while also warning that any accommodation between the two rival blocs that was disadvantageous to American trade would have consequences? Dillon hoped his plan for a newly configured OECD might square the circle.

Beginning on December 7, he spent a week touring the major European capitals, with talks in London, Brussels, Bonn, and Paris. That tour revealed his confidence and authority. Almost six years earlier, he had arrived in Paris as a neophyte political appointee with a pleasant personal manner but no experience of international diplomacy. When he returned in late 1959, his assurance and command of detail were those of someone operating at the highest levels of policymaking. At a two-hour meeting on December 10 with the EEC Commission, led by its president, Walter Hallstein, the breadth of issues that Dillon covered – sixes and sevens, liberal trade policy, tariffs, Greece and Turkey, EEC relations in Europe, aid to developing countries, cooperation on business-cycle policy, commercial policy, free- and state-trading economies – was striking not just for its scope and sophistication, but for his command of detail and understanding of the political nuances. He wielded the stick on "the vital need for a liberal trade policy on the part of the Six" and warned of "increasing antagonism in the United States." But he also offered the carrot indicating "that we were opposed to anything which would impair the integration of the Six" – an unambiguous signal that in the contest of the sixes and sevens, he preferred the even number to the odd. It was a performance that made a deep impression on Hallstein and led to him recognizing Dillon as both a figure of substance and an ally. The relationship between the two would become crucial in the coming months.[23]

On December 13, Dillon reported back to Herter, who was in Paris for a foreign ministers meeting, that he had fulfilled the principal objective of getting support for reorganizing the OECD. The British, Germans and Dutch "strongly favored" the idea and even France, which had "some worry about modalities," broadly favored it. "I have come to the conclusion that it is best to act now," Dillon advised. Eisenhower would soon be arriving in Paris for a Western summit with the leaders of France, Britain, and West Germany. Dillon advised that he should take the matter to the heads of government and have them announce the creation of a group to construct a successor organization to the OEEC in the final communique. While Herter concurred, Anderson did not. Dillon surmised that the opposition was more tactical than substantive, being "largely" based on fears that the Department of State would benefit at the expense of the Treasury. Convinced that he had the best of the argument, Dillon took the matter directly to Eisenhower. "We quite often had differences that had to go to the president for resolution," Dillon recalled. "Secretary Anderson for the Treasury and me for the State Department." On this occasion, Dillon told Eisenhower that he was "more than ever convinced" about the need for a new initiative that would "find a constructive solution to the growing trade rivalries in Western Europe" and "mobilize the energies of the industrialized countries in a concerted effort to help the less developed areas." It was a forceful case and one that overcame Anderson's objections. The treasury secretary pivoted, urging Eisenhower to get a commitment from the other leaders on long-term lending for developing nations. Eisenhower successfully made both cases at the Western summit. The result was an announcement in the communiqué about an "informal" meeting in the "near future" to discuss the future of the OEEC.[24]

That informal meeting – the Special Economic Committee – took place in Paris on January 12–13, 1960, immediately before a full meeting of the eighteen OEEC governments (plus the United States and Canada). Dillon, who led the American delegation at both meetings, made clear from the outset that "the long-range plan was to propose the reorganization of the OEEC in such a way as to allow the U.S. to participate as a full member." The new organization would have a dramatic impact on the Cold War by allowing the United States, Japan, and the two European trading blocs to coordinate their overseas economic aid in the developing world. In the early hours of January 14, "after a long and tedious session," he wrote to Eisenhower to report success from the Special Economic Committee. "Agreement was obtained," he noted, "on all the objectives sought by the United States." These included a "workable procedure" for the reorganization of the OEEC, a "working committee" on sixes and sevens, and another group "to better coordinate procedures for assistance to less developed countries." Later that same day, a full meeting of the OEEC rubber-stamped the recommendations of the special committee. An expert group of four would draft a report on the new organization by April. It was known on both sides of the Atlantic as the Dillon Plan.[25]

The EEC president, Walter Hallstein, went even further. The plan, he declared, had initiated "The Dillon Era." The *New York Times* picked up the quote and ran an editorial under a headline using the same phrase. The newspaper's "Foreign Affairs" editorial columnist Cy Sulzberger – part of the dynasty that owned the paper – could hardly contain his pleasure. "Fortunately," he wrote of Dillon, "the United States has again begun to assert positive diplomatic leadership."[26]

Chapter Seven

Get the Ticker
Washington and Bogotá, 1960

Commodore Hotel, New York, April 20, 1959. As Douglas Dillon rose to address the AFL-CIO international labor unions conference on world affairs, loud applause greeted him. Walter Reuther, the head of the United Auto Workers, had joked that Dillon was so good at his job that he had recently been promoted "not by the president ... not by the secretary of state, it was done by act of the United States Congress!" Dressed in a black suit, with dark spectacles and hair swept back from his high domed forehead, Dillon looked every inch the Wall Street banker and international diplomat that he now was. And yet, Reuther had said, "we in the Labor movement have been greatly encouraged" by what Dillon's vision "represents to the free world." It was exactly the kind of welcome that the undersecretary of state needed, for this speech on "American Foreign Policy Today" was the most significant of his career to date.[1]

That Dillon was giving a speech of such importance was itself an indication of how high his stock had risen within the administration. The press had been briefed beforehand that this occasion was more than just a routine conference appearance. Dillon would make a statement on the fundamentals of American policy before the upcoming Paris summit between Eisenhower, Khrushchev, Macmillan, and de Gaulle.

Dillon began in uncharacteristically demonstrative style by setting out the stakes as "nothing less than the survival of free men in a free civilization." However, when he turned to "the central issue" at the summit, he struck a new and surprisingly hostile tone. There was "no issue on earth today" more important than Berlin. "It represents a critical test of integrity and dependability of the free world's collective security systems," he declared through noisy applause, "because no nation could preserve its faith in collective security if we permitted the courageous people of West Berlin to be sold into slavery." Dillon's long speech, lasting more than an hour, outlined complex proposals for arms control and his own ideas about how the United States "must continue to carry the message of freedom and share its rewards with less-privileged peoples ... everywhere." But the press already had their headline: "Dillon Says West Rejects 'Slavery' for West Berlin."[2]

The speech provoked a direct response from Khrushchev. On April 25, three weeks to the day before the summit was due to begin in Paris, Khrushchev addressed a rally that was broadcast live on Soviet national television and radio. Of course, he hoped that "common sense will prevail [and] that when the summit closes and the leaders leave Paris, relations between the countries at the talks will be better than before." But would the United States bring the same spirit of common sense? He doubted it. "Take the recent speech of the American undersecretary of state, Douglas Dillon," Khrushchev fumed. "That speech just reeks of the spirit of the Cold War ... Why did Dillon have to make a statement so clearly out of keeping with relations between the Soviet Union and the United States since my talks with President Eisenhower at Camp David?" It had been enough to make him "sit up with a start." If the summit failed, he would ignore Dillon's empty threats and sign a separate peace treaty with East Germany that would end the Western presence in Berlin. "Our might is indomitable!" he declared.[3]

What the Paris summit needed was a fair wind; instead, it got a crisis that found Dillon struggling to avert the worst humiliation of Eisenhower's presidency and his own career.

At dawn on May 1, 1960, CIA pilot Francis Gary Powers took off from Peshawar airfield in Pakistan in a U-2 reconnaissance aircraft. Within the hour he was inside Soviet air space. The titanium plane could fly at more than 70,000 feet for 4,000 miles and was so light that pilots dubbed it the world's first disposable airplane. The CIA had been flying U-2 missions to take surveillance photographs over the Soviet Union since 1956. Soviet air defense forces had always failed to shoot one down, but today their luck changed with a surface-to-air missile. "The rocket was armed with a detonator that exploded some 10 meters from the plane," recalled Georgi Aleksandrovitch Mikhailov, a colonel on duty that day at the Air Defense Department's central headquarters. "When Powers finally got out, he had lost height from 22,000m to 6,000m. He jumped with a parachute and a few seconds later a second rocket hit the plane."[4]

Eisenhower was told about the missing plane a few hours later by staff secretary Andrew Goodpaster. At the time, it did not seem like a big deal. It was not that Ike was insensitive to the political implications of the U-2 missions. In fact, he had stopped them before Khrushchev's visit to Camp David and only agreed to their resumption in 1960 because CIA director Allen Dulles told him it was essential to get photographs of Soviet intercontinental ballistic missile (ICBM) launch sites. As undersecretary of state, Dillon was a member of the three-man committee (with Dulles and Deputy Secretary of Defense James H. Douglas Jr.) that made the recommendation to the president to allow the flights, in order, he recalled, to get "pictures of the missile launching complex, with missiles standing on the launch pads." Eisenhower consented but, understanding that it might be "prejudicial to the kind of improvement we were working toward with the Soviets," he gave instructions that "no operation is to be carried out after May 1."

The gamble failed to work out by a matter of hours. For everyone but the pilot, the missing aircraft seemed at first more snafu than major embarrassment. The CIA's Richard Bissell thought the plane was so fragile that there might only be "one chance in a million" it would survive a missile attack. Even if the pilot had ejected, an explosive device would have been triggered to destroy the plane. The law had prevented the CIA from ordering Powers to kill himself to avoid capture, but every U-2 pilot knew what was expected when they were handed a hollow silver dollar containing a poison pin before takeoff. As for the Soviets, Khrushchev might be expected to turn a blind eye, just as he had in early April when the CIA had flown a similar U-2 mission. On May 3, NASA (the National Aeronautics and Space Administration, founded in July 1958) put out a standard statement reporting a plane missing after the pilot suffered oxygen failure during a routine weather research flight over Turkey. It was barely an inside page story.[5]

The situation began to deteriorate on May 5. Early that morning, Dillon flew by helicopter with the president and other members of the National Security Council to High Point Special Facility. This operations center, located fifty miles south of Washington in the Blue Ridge Mountains, was the "nuclear bunker" where the government would continue to operate in the event of a thermonuclear strike. ("In those days it was still thought you could get away from it," Dillon noted.) That day was a practice drill combined with a real meeting of the NSC. During the meeting, Goodpaster warned the president that Khrushchev had given a virulent speech denouncing the United States and saying a U-2 had been shot out of the sky. With Herter away in Turkey, Dillon as acting secretary of state joined a huddle that included the president along with CIA director Allen Dulles and Secretary of Defense Thomas Gates. The problem, Dillon later admitted, was that "We didn't know what to do."[6]

Dillon now commanded such confidence that Eisenhower asked him to take the lead in coordinating the administration's response to the U-2 incident. Ike gave clear instructions that only the State Department was allowed to speak on the issue. Around 11 a.m., Dillon flew back to Washington with the president. Back at the State Department, Dillon sat down with advisors to craft a response to Khrushchev's speech. Lincoln White, chief spokesman for the State Department, rushed in with a Teletype page of a new statement from NASA. Dillon could not believe what the NASA spokesperson had told the press. The release contained paragraph after paragraph of false or misleading information about the Powers flight. The hapless director of public information, Walter T. Bonney, was apparently still taking questions from reporters.

"God, get the ticker!" Dillon gasped.

"We couldn't understand how this had happened," he remembered, because Eisenhower had told everyone that "State and only State would handle all the publicity on this." To make matters worse, White had confirmed the NASA statement to reporters at his own State Department briefing. After the crisis was over, Dillon would ask Goodpaster how it had all gone so wrong. "It was terrible," the staff secretary told him. "I got back to the White House and told [White House press secretary] Jim Hagerty what the president had said, [but] he had to follow the cover story and send the reporters over to NASA."[7]

Dillon, though, was not entirely free of blame. On returning to the State Department, he had been so focused on his close advisers that he had neglected to bring White up to speed. "I was trying to get lines straight and we thought we had time to do that," Dillon remembered. "We were going to talk to him and get everything straightened out." When reporters had asked the press secretary about the NASA statement, he simply assumed the agency must be telling the truth. After the story unraveled, White was accused of misleading the press. "He was horribly upset, and naturally so," Dillon said. The result was that "we got our legs sawed off and it made us look very foolish." The *Washington Post*, under the title "State's Fabrication," reported how when "topmost officials" in the administration had met, "the State Department's representative wanted to fabricate the story that Powers had reported an oxygen failure" while the Defense Department argued that approach was "senseless." It was all "a desperate attempt" to make a "phony story stick." Although Dillon was not named, he was implicated, for it was only with the return of Herter, the paper reported, that it was decided "it would be better to confess the truth before matters got any worse."[8]

With political flak flying in all directions and recognizing the danger of reputational damage, Dillon was quick to blame anyone but himself. Whose fault was it? Hagerty who "didn't pay too much attention" to the president's orders, Goodpaster who had not "explained the seriousness of the situation" to the press secretary, NASA officials for issuing their story when "in five minutes they might have checked either with Allen Dulles or with me," Lincoln White for "a statement that was very unfortunate on his part," and even Allen Dulles, who was "aware" of the NASA cover story but "hadn't thought it necessary to say anything about it." Dillon himself meanwhile "was never informed" and "not aware of it." This duck and cover maneuver revealed a harder side to Dillon. Lower down the political food chain, he had seemed not to care about the cost of his mistakes. Closer now to reaching the top, he guarded his back.[9]

As the U-2 story unraveled, and with the Paris summit a week away, the central question became how far the president should go in admitting that he authorized the espionage flights. A fissure quickly opened within the administration on questions of honesty and transparency – with Dillon favoring neither. In a speech in Moscow, Khrushchev had left the diplomatic door open for Eisenhower by blaming "Pentagon militarists" for the flights. "I went out of my way not to accuse the president," he would write later. In a meeting with Herter and the assistant secretaries on May 7, Dillon argued that the president "should not take responsibility for this action, that it would cause international troubles, and that this was not the way that foreign policy was conducted." His designated scapegoat was the CIA director Allen Dulles. "I liked Allen Dulles, we all did," he recalled, "but I mean, this was the United States. It was a great big problem ... and a lot of people would have known underneath that he was just taking the rap for somebody higher and would have admired him for it." Foy Kohler, assistant secretary of state for European affairs, argued the opposite, saying it was "essential" not just to tell the truth but to own it by saying American espionage was "not only a right but a duty." Herter, while largely ineffective and vacillating, initially favored coming clean, saying they "couldn't go on lying forever," but in the end let Dillon push him into the half-truth of admitting the U-2 incursion while trying to "get the president off the hook." It was an approach that fooled no one, not least the press spokesman who had to deliver it. "W-wait, a minute," stammered an incredulous White when he saw the statement, "I've got to read this?"[10]

The fudge was a disaster, with Dillon and Herter delivering the worst impression of all: that Eisenhower was either asleep at the wheel or he was a liar.

On May 9, Ann Whitman, the president's personal secretary, recorded how "very depressed" Eisenhower was about "the matter of the spy in sky," even telling her, "I would like to resign."[11]

At that day's meeting of the National Security Council, Eisenhower was thoughtful, saying, "Well, we're just going to have to take a lot of beating on this – and I'm the one, rightly, who's going to have to take it." Vice President Richard Nixon served as his attack dog in the meeting. "Get away from this 'little boy in the cookie jar' posture!" Nixon barked at the unfortunate Herter, as Dillon looked on. He laid into the secretary of state for leaving "the president in the posture where he says he doesn't know anything about this," not least because "to give that impression would be to imply that war could start without the president's knowledge." No wonder that by the afternoon, Whitman was noting Ike had "bounced back with his characteristic ability to accept the bad news, not dwell on it, and so go ahead."[12]

At this point, Dillon finally decided that he should be one to carry the can for the fiasco. His daughter Phyllis recalls that Dillon went to see Eisenhower and pleaded with him to be fired. "But Ike wouldn't listen," he told her afterwards. "He was so stubborn and just summarily dismissed me from the room. The president wasn't going to let anyone think he didn't know what was going on."[13]

On May 11, Eisenhower went on the record about the U-2 incident, acknowledging without apology what most had already guessed: that "ever since the beginning of my administration, I have issued directives to gather, in every possible way, the information required to protect the Free World against surprise attack and to enable them to make effective preparations for defense." Such measures were "a distasteful but vital necessity," he admitted, but the alternative was unthinkable: "No-one wants another Pearl Harbor." If the Soviets did not like it, then they should end their own "fetish of secrecy and concealment."[14]

Historians, by and large, have praised Eisenhower for his integrity at this moment in the Cold War. One of his most recent biographers, Jean Edward Smith, even suggests the decision to take personal responsibility for the U-2 flights "may have been the finest hour of his presidency." Dillon would not have agreed with the assessment. He admired the president for "being the highly moral and wonderful person that he was," but he never hid his view that Eisenhower acted naively. "We all saw what happened because of his response that led to the breakdown in the Paris talks," he recalled. "I'm fully confident that if he had disowned responsibility, the Soviets would have acted differently."[15]

At a Republican leaders' breakfast on the morning of his press conference, Eisenhower had confidently predicted that "the United States would not be encumbered by the U-2 incident" and that Khrushchev was "much too smart" to crash the summit. When he touched down in Paris on May 15, Ike discovered that he had seriously misjudged the situation. The Soviet leader had arrived the previous day promising to "exert all efforts to make the conference a success," but in reality, he wrote years afterwards, "anger was building up inside me like an electric force which could be discharged in a great flash at any moment." At the first and only meeting between the two men in Paris on May 16, Khrushchev angrily demanded a personal apology in terms that British prime minister Harold Macmillan judged were "intended to be as offensive as possible to Eisenhower." The president sat impassively throughout the forty-five-minute tirade but passed a note to Herter that indicated his state of mind: "I am going to take up smoking again." By the time Khrushchev stopped speaking, it was clear the summit was over. The two leaders would never meet again. All Eisenhower's hopes of ending his presidency with a major step towards peace had collapsed.[16]

Back in the United States, Dillon denounced Khrushchev for his "calculated rudeness" at the summit, telling a gathering in New Jersey that the Soviet leader's attitude was "alien to our whole way of life and makes us wonder what pressures make him act in this unusual fashion." Privately, however, it was the president he found difficult to fathom. "He probably didn't realize that it would blow up the summit when he accepted responsibility," Dillon said, "although that was the advice he had gotten from the State Department." Yet, while in a narrow sense, Dillon may have been correct, he would have sacrificed much of the future credibility that Eisenhower had salvaged.[17]

The period after the failed summit was wretched for Dillon. The president could joke with congressional leaders that "as far as punishment was concerned the only way he could be punished would be by impeachment," but then he was not the one hauled in front of the Senate Foreign Relations Committee to explain the ignominy of the Paris summit. It was Dillon who faced the committee in closed session on May 27. Even with his friend Fulbright in the chair, he found it deeply uncomfortable. "We had a very difficult time," he recalled. Angry senators complained they had been treated with contempt by being kept in the dark. Senator Albert Gore, a Democrat from Tennessee, huffily pointed out that committee members "shall gladly abide by all security requirements" and chided Dillon for leaving the committee "to conjecture" on the U-2 flights. Caught in various binds – not revealing precise details of the flight, unable to lay out a precise chronology of the aftermath, not wishing to be seen to blame the president or the White House for "this thing having become public in the wrong way" – he ended up looking, according to senatorial tastes, either disingenuous or foolish. "While everything that was said was the truth, it was not the whole truth," he reflected afterwards. "So, everybody was very uncertain, and there was a miasma about it that looked as if things were just very stupid in the Department of State." The session left Dillon shaken. Having built his reputation on competence and candor, "stupid" and "uncertain" were unwelcome new additions to his reputation in Washington.[18]

With his morale low, Dillon was fortunate that he had other issues and events on the calendar to help him rebuild his reputation. At the beginning of the summer, he returned to more familiar territory as the member nations of the General Agreement on Tariffs and Trade (GATT) took up his suggestion to establish a working group. Their goal was to cope with the abrupt flooding of markets by goods from countries with low production costs. This attempt to integrate Japan more fully into global trading arrangements was part of the broader initiative that came to be called the "Dillon Round" of tariff nego-tiations. In July, Dillon embarked on a five-nation European tour to discuss tariffs, economic aid, and "sixes and sevens." Yet the collapse of the Paris summit hovered over everything.[19]

Dillon found some measure of redemption in Vienna, where serendipity gave his trip an additional Cold War significance. He arrived immediately after a contentious ten-day visit by Khrushchev, who had used the opportunity to lambaste the United States and reiterate earlier threats about Berlin. The American ambassador in Vienna, H. Freeman Matthews, dithered about whether Dillon's trip should even go ahead, at first saying yes and then advising no. Dillon recognized that cancellation "might be useful" to indicate "our increasing annoyance" at the Austrian government for giving Khrushchev a platform, but understood that the "Commies might be able to use cancellation for propaganda attacks" – so he went ahead. In the event, the visit was a marked success. In a speech to the Austrian Foreign Policy Association on July 15, Dillon rebuked the Soviet leader for throwing away a chance to make peace. The audience gave him an ovation when he said neutral Austria was "well able" to decide its own future "without assistance from the outside." Matthews could barely contain his relief. "I wish the Department to know it was very successful from every point of view," he cabled back to Washington. Dillon spoke to "a packed house including Ambassadors of all prominent European countries and leaders of Austrian political and business communities and evoked much applause," as well as "excellent press reaction." His verdict that "all in all it was a very worthwhile visit" was the best review Dillon had enjoyed in months.[20]

By early September, a profile in the *New York Times* seemed to confirm that Dillon had repaired some of the damage that the U-2 crisis had done to his reputation in Washington. He was Eisenhower's "Outspoken Diplomat" – the man who "has been called a 'cool economist' and a soft selling, calm realist whose judgments have been severely tested." The profile was a boost for the "Man in the News" Dillon as he headed to Bogotá for a crucial economic conference – "the Committee of 21" – under the auspices of the Organization of American States (OAS).[21]

Earlier in the year, Eisenhower had toured South America to counter both anti-Americanism and the growing enthusiasm for the new Castro regime in Cuba. The region had not yet been a priority. As his biographer Stephen Ambrose notes, "About the best that could be said for the journey as a whole was that it got him out of Washington at a miserable time of the year and allowed him to enjoy the South American summer while seeing places he had always wanted to see." After the collapse of the Paris summit, the region came more sharply into focus as an area where Eisenhower could still make an impact. At a National Security Meeting on June 30, Ike exhorted officials to come up with new policy initiatives and upped the ante by writing to President Kubitschek of Brazil on July 8 to advise him that the United States planned on "participating more effectively toward our hemisphere objectives." At a news conference three days later in Newport, Rhode Island, he told reporters that he planned to extend "American cooperation in promoting social progress and economic growth in the Americas."[22]

Dillon urged Eisenhower to "press forward with a broad program for Latin America." The Inter-American Bank had already started giving "soft loans" for economic development projects, he told the president, but the region was desperate for more funds in "social overhead" projects, including improved land use, sanitation, education, and vocational training. He proposed to offer Latin America a Special Fund of $500 million for grants or loans via the Inter-American Development Bank. Time was pressing. "Unrest with violent political consequences is likely in a number of Latin American countries," he warned.[23]

Pushback came from Robert Anderson, who, one journalist reported, had "a strong suspicion that what some Latin American governments want is a 'pie to slice' without any controls or accountability." That Ike ignored Anderson reflected his wish not to be seen as a lame duck after Paris as much as it did his support for the policy. Eisenhower sent a message to Congress on August 5 asking them to authorize $500 million (plus $100 million Chilean earthquake relief) for a "social development program" that would "help our Latin American neighbors accelerate their efforts to strengthen the social and economic structure of their nations and to improve the status of their individual citizens." He requested "urgent enactment" so that Dillon could launch a detailed plan at the OAS economic conference in Bogotá beginning on September 5. The accelerated process drew much huffing and puffing from Congress, with Senator Fulbright expressing "a good deal of regret and soul searching" about the undue haste involved, but the measure still passed in time to give Dillon the opportunity to unveil it formally in Bogotá. With the administration having endured so much disappointment in 1960, Dillon needed to deliver a win for Eisenhower in the last few months of the administration. Yet, as the State Department briefed reporters days beforehand, no one really knew "what nations are willing to stand up and be counted" or "whether the OAS is after all a weak reed to lean on." The trick, recalled Thomas C. Mann, the new assistant secretary of state for inter-American affairs and a long-term Dillon ally, was that "we should lend money to Latin American governments if they could make good use of it and that we should not pour money down a rat hole."24

Sensitive to hemispheric pride, Dillon stopped off first in Quito, Ecuador, to visit the magnificent Jesuit church of la Compañía before touching down in Colombia on September 3 at the head of a twenty-six-member US delegation. "The Government and people of the United States," he declared at the airport, "recognize that free and democratic institutions in Latin America can be strengthened and preserved only to the degree that the individual citizen can live a life of dignity and is accorded an opportunity to improve his status through his own efforts."25

As Dillon began circulating among delegates at the conference, he worked assiduously to reassure those present about the extent of the United States commitment. Brazil and Argentina, for example, feared loans for roads, power stations, communication links and other development projects might have to be repayable in local currencies. Others worried about whether the plan would live beyond the outgoing Eisenhower administration. In these informal discussions, Dillon's personal authority and general likability were crucial. Spotting Augusto Federico Schmidt, the chief delegate of Brazil, Dillon strode across the Gold Room of the Military Club and embraced him in a bear hug that was perhaps more familiar to the Brazilian than the buttoned-up east coast American banker. Such personal courtesies mattered because they reinforced the idea that Dillon, along with the likes of Mann, were allies who had pushed for the Latin American development policy in Washington. It was a reputation that served Dillon well when he came under attack from the Cuban delegation in Bogotá.

"How can you speak of cooperation when there is an aggressor in our midst?" the Cuban diplomat Óscar Pino Santos demanded at one of the first formal sessions when putting forward a resolution condemning the "imperialistic" United States. Many delegates were sympathetic to Cuba's critique about "the structural disadvantage of the present situation and the realities of our relationship with North American imperialism." But such was the personal way in which the attack had been directed towards Dillon that he found others jumping to his defense as if affronted on his behalf. "Nothing could be more unfair or removed from reality!" concluded Misrael Pastrana Borrero, Colombia's development minister, dismissing the proposals of the Cuban delegation. Augusto Federico Schmidt went even further: Dillon was quite simply "a man of vision."[26]

On September 13, amid the gilt marble columns of the Gold Room and the hot TV lights, Dillon stepped forward to add his name to the leather-bound Act of Bogotá which formalized the essence of the plan that he had brought with him to the conference. Of the twenty American republics present, only Cuba refused to sign. In concluding remarks, the Colombian foreign minister Julio Cesar Turbay Ayala singled out Dillon for praise, recalling the many years of "vain effort" to get a hearing in the State Department. As to the man himself, Dillon admitted that his hopes for the conference had "been realized beyond my expectations."[27]

In 1961, a new US administration would popularize social and economic modernization in Latin America by launching the Alliance for Progress. Walt Rostow, the MIT economist who developed the "Rostow Doctrine" on foreign aid policy, would often speak dismissively of what had been done in the region previously, saying that the 1960s needed to be the "economic development decade." Yet as the preeminent historian of trade and aid, Burton I. Kaufman, points out, "Subsequent administrations merely built on the legacies that Eisenhower left them." Dillon would be the link between the two.[28]

By the fall of 1960, with the presidential election in full swing, talk in Washington began to turn to who might be the secretary of state in a Nixon administration. "Dillon seems to be the outstanding potential secretary with respect to ability and experience," C.L. Sulzberger, the influential *New York Times* columnist, speculated. "Tough, imaginative, hardworking, he has great knowledge of both economic and conventional diplomacy." His colleague

James Reston chimed in the same week, pointing out that even the Democratic candidate, John F. Kennedy, who was "more interested in ideas than parties," might take "Dillon into the State Department across party lines" if he won.[29]

Dillon had no conversations with Nixon about what position he might occupy in a new administration, which, he later recalled, "was perfectly natural, because I wouldn't think any presidential candidate would make a commitment prior to the election." His relationship with the vice president had always been cordial. Dillon's innate personal courtesy and good manners helped in dealing with a figure that many found thin-skinned and prickly. As a State Department official, convention decreed that Dillon could not campaign for Nixon and he even blocked as too political the candidate from joining Eisenhower for the announcement of a de facto trade embargo on Cuba for everything except essential supplies. But Dillon was one of Nixon's top donors in 1960 and provided a Dillon Read investment banker, Peter Flanigan, to run the national Volunteers-for-Nixon fundraising campaign.[30]

On Tuesday, November 8, Nixon lost to Kennedy. The defeated candidate went to lick his wounds in Key Biscayne, Florida, where Kennedy called him from Palm Beach to ask for a meeting. (Nixon graciously offered to come to Palm Beach; Kennedy, just as graciously, insisted on coming to Key Biscayne. It was a different age.) During their meeting, the president-elect talked about bringing Republicans into his administration, mentioning Dillon by name. Afterwards, Nixon told Dillon that the new president wanted him "to be ambassador to NATO or some such position." It was a blow. "I was not interested in that sort of position," he recalled. Friends urged him to run for governor of New Jersey in 1961, but Dillon had no appetite for that contest. After eight years away from Wall Street, it looked as if he would be heading home to Dillon Read. Then Phil Graham of the *Washington Post* phoned and everything changed.[31]

Chapter Eight

Difficult to Say No
Washington, 1960–1961

Georgetown, November 16, 1960. Arthur Schlesinger Jr. – Pulitzer Prize–winning historian and the Democratic party's resident intellectual – could hardly believe what he was hearing. "Dillon as secretary of the treasury!" he exclaimed in dismay, before getting into a "serious wrangle" with his host and JFK friend, Philip Graham. "If [Jack] must have a conservative in the cabinet," Schlesinger pleaded, put him anywhere but "not in Treasury or State." The position was too "critical" and the Republican too "orthodox." The balance of payments crisis would "reinforce all Dillon's natural inclinations," Schlesinger argued, and surely lead to the "jettisoning" of Kennedy's entire platform. Graham was having none of it – indeed he was "euphorically insistent on Dillon." No wonder the historian left the dinner "in a state of extreme irritation."[1]

Graham and his friend, the syndicated columnist Joseph Alsop – both leading lights of the "Georgetown Set" – had been pushing the president-elect (himself a member of the set) on Dillon for treasury secretary and David Bruce for secretary of state. Bruce was proving a heavy lift, but Kennedy was more open to the idea of Dillon. Over the course of the election campaign, JFK had become increasingly obsessed with the balance of payments crisis. He recognized his own limited experience in economic and financial policy. Whoever went to the Treasury would need to reassure markets and have clout with international institutions and finance ministers. The question was whether a Republican would be loyal to him. "Joe responded that it would be very hard to imagine a man less likely to be disloyal than Dillon," recalled Katharine Graham, Phil's wife and the daughter of the *Post*'s owner, Eugene Meyer. Kennedy agreed to put him on the shortlist. "Get the message to Doug," he instructed.[2]

Graham was tasked with making the approach. The execution was not straightforward. In Katharine Graham's telling, her husband phoned Dillon at home and told him he needed to see him urgently. Dillon suggested meeting the following day, saying he was about to host a dinner for Republican donors. Phil was insistent, however, promising to come round the back of the house. "Not wishing to be observed by the dinner guests," Katharine recalled, "Phil crawled in through a dressing room window." A member of staff – presumably briefed in advance – called Dillon out of the dining room to meet the unconventional visitor. "He asked me if I would not consider the possibility of accepting an offer by President Kennedy to serve in his cabinet as secretary of the treasury should such an offer be made," Dillon recalled. "This naturally came as a great shock to me, and I could not believe that it was anything serious." Once Graham had convinced him otherwise, Dillon said that he was going away to Jupiter Island (everyone of note was in Florida that November) and would think about it. A few days later, he called Graham to tell him that "if something like that was in the wind," then he "could not say no out of hand." It was as close to a yes as any politician careful of his reputation could make.[3]

Radio silence followed for several weeks. Robert Kennedy, the president's brother, later said that the first pick for treasury secretary had been Robert McNamara, but that the president of the Ford Motor Company – also a Republican – preferred the Department of Defense. The president-elect did offer the job to the former defense secretary in the Truman administration, Robert A. Lovett, who turned it down on the grounds of poor health. He told Kennedy he thought "Douglas Dillon ought to receive consideration." Another Republican, Wall Street banker Henry C. Alexander, remained in contention, although his vociferous support for Nixon during the campaign (unlike Dillon, who had been in purdah at the State Department) weakened his chances. Also in the frame was Eugene Black, who was due to retire from the World Bank. From the Democratic party came Albert Gore, the populist senator from Tennessee, who was the preferred candidate of the liberals. In fact, Gore's non-starter candidacy helped Dillon's not just because Kennedy had disliked Gore as a senatorial colleague but also, in Alsop's words, because "he's incompetent" and "and when he isn't talking your ear off, he'll be telling *The New York Times* all." Dillon's competence and innate discretion increasingly began to work in his favor as names swirled in and out of contention. Even Arthur Schlesinger reluctantly admitted that "Dillon, of course, shines by comparison with his colleagues in the Eisenhower administration." Still, in a meeting on November 30, Schlesinger continued to lobby against Dillon when Kennedy admitted that the Treasury was giving him "trouble." The historian, soon to join the administration himself as a special assistant, suggested his own mentor Averell Harriman for the job, only to see the former commerce secretary knocked back as "too old hat." When Schlesinger challenged the idea of appointing Dillon, saying it was "too bad to give a big cabinet post to a man who had been only a sub-cabinet level official in the defeated government and who had contributed generously to Nixon," Kennedy's response showed which way he was leaning. "Oh, I don't care about those things," he told Schlesinger. "All I want to know is: Is he able? And will he go along with the program?" Two days later JFK had Pierre Salinger, future White House press secretary, telephone Dillon at the State Department to request a meeting. Could the president-elect call up to the house in Kalorama to see him? To avoid undue attention, the meeting was set up for nine in the evening and it seems that Kennedy drove alone from his Georgetown house to Dillon's in Belmont Road, where he strolled unobserved through the front door.[4]

Although the two men moved in the same worlds, they did not know each other well. Dillon was, after all, eight years older than Kennedy. They first met four years earlier when staying at the Spee Club – the social club of which both had been members. They had done no more than run into each other and there had been no great meeting of minds. Later that year, as ambassador to Paris, Dillon had given his daughter Joan the unenviable task of finding Kennedy in the south of France to tell him in person that his wife Jackie had lost a baby. (Joan was deeply "upset" at how "callous" JFK was on hearing the news.) There were a few other social interactions but "beyond that," Dillon recalled, "the only times I saw the senator was in the course of our work." As a member of the Senate Foreign Relations Committee, Kennedy had often questioned Dillon on foreign aid. During the campaign, Dillon had met with Kennedy to ask for support on funding for Latin America, which the candidate did "graciously," even though Dillon "had the impression that our action might have prompted a point that he would have liked to have made in the campaign himself." In essence, the men had a friendly professional relationship.[5]

Kennedy immediately made it clear to Dillon that he was considering him for the Treasury job. The president-elect told him about his fears concerning the gold crisis and the balance of payments deficit. There was "a lack of confidence in the US," Kennedy said and, because Dillon was "known in Europe and was known to believe in the maintenance of the value of the dollar," he hoped Dillon might "render substantial assistance" to his country on the question. A general discussion followed about international policy as well as their shared desire to achieve a "rapid rate of growth in our economy." JFK reassured Dillon that he believed in a "sound dollar." Only towards the end did Dillon raise the political elephant in the room: the fact that he himself was a Republican. Kennedy did not wave this away, but rather showed that he had been thinking about the question systemically. Noting how the State Department was "divorced from politics" during elections, Kennedy said that he wanted the same principle to apply to both the Treasury and Defense departments. The growing international financial problems and the balance of payments crisis made these issues of national security every bit as much as those handled by the State Department. Should Kennedy ask Dillon to take the job, "it would be on a non-political basis." After the president-elect left, the reality of the situation hit Dillon as "I realized I would have to decide what I would do should he make the offer."[6]

The trickiest task was settling the matter with his own party. He spoke first to the vice president and defeated candidate, Richard Nixon, telling him that the balance of payments situation meant "it would be something that one could not consider lightly." Nixon was gracious, telling Dillon that if Kennedy asked, "it would be difficult to say no." Yet behind Dillon's back his attitude was different. Nixon, reported to be "hopping mad," telephoned prominent Republicans to pressure Dillon into refusing any offer. Press reports told of how the "tacit repudiation" that Dillon's appointment would mean for Nixon would "anger and/or embarrass" him. It's a mystery why Nixon did not make this case to Dillon face-to-face, although also another sign of Dillon's steeliness that he did not make such a request easy. By framing the question as one of national rather than party interest, he left Nixon with limited room to maneuver.[7]

Dillon also enjoyed one piece of good luck. While speculation flashed around Washington, he was on the other side of the Atlantic at a ministerial meeting to sign the charter for the new Organisation for Economic Co-operation and Development (OECD). That meant he was out of reach to most of those who hoped to bring pressure to bear. The one person who had direct access and could have made a difference chose to do the opposite. Dillon had used the plane ride to Paris to have a frank conversation with Robert Anderson. The outgoing treasury secretary was reassuring about what he should do. The balance of payments crisis was "very severe," Anderson told him. There was a "lack of confidence" abroad in American financial policy. "If this offer should be forthcoming," the secretary said, "[you're] duty bound to accept it."[8]

Anderson inadvertently helped boost Dillon in other ways too, not least that his own unpopularity abroad contrasted so markedly with the man who perhaps might replace him. Anderson had always made "an inconceivably bad impression in Europe," the *New York Herald Tribune* reported, with his "pistol point" attitude to diplomacy. Dillon, on the other hand, was seen as "entirely free from blame" from such an approach, "which was just as well," the paper noted, "since Dillon needs to retain the respect of America's allies if he is to take a high post under President Kennedy." The OECD had been Dillon's project from start to finish, so while Anderson outranked him, he was the star of the show in Paris for this "major new era in free world economic cooperation."[9]

On December 15, Dillon and Anderson returned to Washington in a Lockheed Constellation government plane, flying through an electric storm. It was a terrible flight that Dillon feared at one point might go down. (The following day a TWA Lockheed Super Constellation would in fact be involved in the worst aviation disaster in the world to date, with 134 people killed; twenty-four hours later a US Air Force transport plane would also crash in fogbound Munich, killing fifty-two people.) Tired and somewhat shaken by the trip, Dillon arrived home to Belmont Road around 9 p.m. to find a phone message from Kennedy. In a wise but nonetheless cool move, the exhausted Dillon did not return the call, waiting until the next morning to get in touch. He was asked if he could go to the president-elect's house straight away. Measured again, Dillon said he had to go to the White House first to report to the president on the OECD meeting. It was agreed he would go to Georgetown immediately afterwards.[10]

The meeting at the White House promised to be an awkward affair. On returning from Paris, Dillon had found a letter from Eisenhower waiting for him about the offer of the Treasury job. "For whatever my opinion is worth," it said, "I would not favor your acceptance." In person at the White House, Dillon found the president cold and querulous. Ike pronounced himself "surprised" that Dillon was still thinking of taking the position. When Dillon spoke about the balance of payments crisis and the national interest, Eisenhower peevishly conceded that if "the president asks you to take on a particular job in the interest of the country," then he supposed it was "a very difficult thing to say no." But there was no blessing or expression of good luck. Although the two men continued to see each other in the final weeks of the administration, Dillon admitted that "I never talked to [him] at any length after President-elect Kennedy announced that I would accept this offer and serve as secretary of the treasury." Robert F. Kennedy recognized the price he had paid to accept the appointment. "When Dillon decided to take it, he [Eisenhower] was not pleasant about it," he recalled. George Humphrey, Christian Herter, and Richard Nixon "never spoke to him – or spoke to him in a rude fashion." It was "rather a tough time."[11]

Around 11 o'clock, the secret service drove Dillon the mile or so to the president-elect's house on N Street. Using the back door to avoid the crowd of reporters permanently stationed at the front steps, they found Kennedy upstairs. "He came very rapidly to the point," Dillon recalled. JFK repeated his deep concern about the balance of payments crisis and indicated that "no one could handle this in a better fashion." As he accepted the offer, Dillon did say he "assumed" he would have a "relatively free hand" in making appointments at the Treasury. Kennedy agreed, but then threw him a curveball. He wanted to appoint a liberal chair of the Council of Economic Advisers "in view of the fact that he was appointing me, a Republican and an investment banker with a Wall Street background." The person he had in mind was Walter Heller, a Keynesian professor at the University of Minnesota. Dillon agreed it was a "sound and reasonable idea," but it was a sign of the political deftness and self-confidence he now possessed that he asked Kennedy to confirm that it would be "clearly understood between us" that "my recommendations would be direct to him and that he would look to me" as his chief financial adviser. "Of course," Kennedy replied without missing a beat and suggested they go outside to announce the appointment right away.[12]

Getting to know Heller would have to wait for another day. First came an introduction to Bobby Kennedy – the choice for attorney general. The president-elect had previously told Ben Bradlee that he intended to announce his brother's nomination. "I'll open the door at 2:00 a.m., look up and down the street," he said, "and if there's no one there, I'll whisper 'It's Bobby.'" The two men had never met, but as they chatted, Bobby remarked that Dillon's appointment was unusual and asked what would happen if he found himself in disagreement with the president. Would he leave without a fuss? Dillon reassured him, saying that he would "quietly pack my bags and leave rather than to try and make a great political scene." Years afterwards, Bobby would ask Dillon, "Did you realize it was a put-up show?" The brothers had fixed in advance that Bobby would ask the question in an apparently casual way, but they were anxious to avoid risking having Dillon "quit in a huff." It had been one of the reasons that their father, Joseph Kennedy, had warned them off the appointment. JFK's decision to appoint Dillon had been animated at least in part by concerns that Republicans and the banking industry might embarrass him and undermine his presidency. But bringing Dillon inside the tent was not without its risks either, so they needed reassurance. "President Kennedy and his brother were close students of history," Dillon noted drily, "particularly political history."[13]

"Our next president doesn't take the old, easy way of making his announcements about new cabinet ministers, the fate of the new frontier, etc., from his office on Capitol Hill," Tom Wolfe wrote in the *Washington Post*, exuding the breeziness that would soon revolutionize journalism. "He just steps right out on the old front porch at 3307 N St. NW and starts talking." Shortly after noon on Friday, December 16, Kennedy did exactly that to explain that he wanted to appoint "the best people available in the United States regardless of their party" and that in Douglas Dillon, he had found someone "to see the United States move forward in the sixties, to see our strength increased." Dillon, in return, praised the president-elect for his bipartisan approach and added somewhat disingenuously that neither Eisenhower nor Nixon had objected "if I felt that this was something that would be in the national security interest."[14]

Press reaction to Dillon's appointment was broadly supportive. Newspapers everywhere returned to the idea of "The Dillon Era," which the *New York Herald Tribune* told readers "is now the phrase used by European economists." A leader in the *Chattanooga Daily Times* praised "an extraordinarily commendable nomination as secretary of the treasury," noting that Dillon had been the "leading probability" to be secretary of state under Nixon. The *Washington Post* reported that "Wall Street is reassured." The *New York Times* praised Dillon as an "outstandingly able" figure whose nomination would "reassure the business and financial community that [Kennedy] is not an irresponsible spender and fiscal experimenter." The "suave and sophisticated" Dillon, said the *Herald Tribune*, was "recognized as this nation's top economic strategist."[15]

White House press secretary Jim Hagerty, irritated by these positive headlines, began a dirty tricks campaign to suggest that Dillon had obtained written guarantees from Kennedy to stick to Eisenhower's economic and fiscal principles. Both Kennedy and Dillon were in Florida when these rumors started circulating and, after conferring, the president-elect gave a press conference in which he crisply pointed out that "Quite obviously Mr. Dillon has had sufficient experience in government to know that no such written commitments would be given by any President, and therefore it would not be asked of any president." Dillon followed up with an off-the-record briefing with the prominent syndicated columnist David Lawrence of *US News and World Report*. "Mr. Dillon is convinced that he and the president-elect are in basic agreement on treasury policy," Lawrence reported. "This was revealed officially in Mr. Kennedy's press conference a few days ago at Palm Beach. That's enough assurance for the new secretary and for the public unless otherwise advised." Republican attempts to divide the two had failed. By the time that Eisenhower accepted Dillon's resignation on January 4, 1961, the president seemed to recognize that he had come off worse from the situation by appearing to put party above country. His gracious letter to Dillon, praising his work at the State Department, allowed that "I look forward to a personal performance on your part fully as brilliant." In public at least, it was an elegant exit from an administration Dillon had served since 1953.[16]

Dillon began to assemble his team at Hobe Sound over the holiday. As his deputy, he picked Henry H. Fowler – a southern conservative Democrat known for his easy charm. "I was looking for a man as undersecretary who was a lawyer, which I was not, and who was close to the Democratic party," Dillon recalled, "because I knew there would have to be some relationship on a political basis." His closest ally, however, would be the undersecretary for monetary affairs and number three in the department. Dillon had a conversation with Robert Roosa from the Federal Reserve Bank of New York about the balance of payments crisis. "I was tremendously impressed," he said. After checking with friends in New York "who also had the highest opinion," he offered Roosa the job. Despite not having known each other, Roosa, along with Dillon's long-term aid, John Leddy, became his most important confidant within the department. To complete the team, Elizabeth Rudel Smith became treasurer of the United States, and it was her name that would appear alongside that of Dillon on United States currency.[17]

When Dillon appeared before the Senate Finance Committee in mid-January, he had been expecting a rough ride but instead, James Reston mocked, it was "soft fiddle music and soaring melody." Dillon's staff were exultant. "They don't do [bullyragging] with Secretary Dillon," one aide briefed. "He does his homework and knows what he's talking about so thoroughly that those who try to bait him quickly end up looking pretty foolish."[18]

Just after 10 o'clock on the morning of January 21, 1961, the Senate unanimously confirmed Dillon's nomination on a voice vote. Two hours later, in a ceremony in the East Room at the White House, Chief Justice Earl Warren swore him in as the fifty-seventh secretary of the treasury. Two days later, he watched as the first money bearing his signature rolled off the presses at the Bureau of Engraving and Printing, beginning with serial number A00000001A. Whatever political events lay ahead, these dollars and millions of others like them would make the name "C. Douglas Dillon" one of the most widely circulated throughout everyday American life. The real question, however, was whether he was a worthy successor to the likes of Alexander Hamilton, Salmon Chase, and Andrew Mellon to shape the American economy. "He is a liberal-minded man with a lingering commitment to the minor cliches of banking," John Kenneth Galbraith mused. "Banking may well be a career from which no man really recovers."[19]

Chapter Nine

Treasury Man
Washington, January–July 1961

Treasury Building, 1500 Pennsylvania Avenue. When Deane and David Heller, the Chicago reporters turned popular biographers, arrived at Douglas Dillon's office in early 1961 to interview him for their forthcoming book *The Kennedy Cabinet*, they found the new secretary of the treasury entirely at ease in his surroundings. Asked at his first public press conference how he was getting on being a Republican in a Democratic administration, Dillon had replied, "Highly congenial!" Now as he "peered benignly" at his questioners from behind horn-rimmed glasses, dressed in his habitual dark-blue Savile Row suit with navy tie, it seemed to them that it was "hard to imagine a sounder-looking man than Douglas Dillon." Just his presence at the Treasury was enough to reassure the international markets. His manner as he showed the journalists to leather armchairs was neither arrogant nor overbearing, but rather had about it "a quiet, almost shy air." The office itself seemed to reflect his political style. By the standards of other cabinet secretaries, at 600 square feet, it was modest – indeed only the Labor secretary had a smaller office. But along with a few personal *objets d'art,* the deep red Persian carpet, the high windows with old gold curtains, and a portrait above his desk of Albert Gallatin (the fourth and longest-serving treasury secretary), everything conveyed a sense of tradition and understated power. "C. Douglas Dillon is *the* man everybody likes," the impressed Hellers would write, but he was also someone who "commands virtually universal respect and admiration." For "perhaps more than any single man in Washington," they concluded, it was the fifty-seventh secretary of the treasury "in whose cool, dispassionate, slightly Olympian judgment all of Washington trusts."[1]

Not the least of those in Washington who hoped to trust in Dillon's judgment was the president himself. In part, this stemmed from Kennedy's recognition that he lacked authority in finance and economics. "Of all the problems [JFK] faced as President," wrote the historian Arthur Schlesinger Jr., "one had the impression that he felt least at home with this one." Kennedy's focus up to this point had been on foreign rather than economic affairs – from his Harvard thesis on British entry into the Second World War, through his early journalism at the San Francisco conference in 1945, to his membership of the Senate Foreign Relations Committee in the late fifties – his interests had always steered overseas. There was an element of self-deprecation involved too, with Kennedy often joking that he needed things explained simply because he had scored only a C grade for his Harvard freshman course in economics. (In fact, it was a B grade.) Kennedy's attitude also came from a clear-eyed understanding of the scale of the international threat that the United States faced, with the balance of payments crisis always in his sights. "He used to tell his advisers that the two things which scared him most were nuclear war and the payments deficit," Schlesinger wrote. Given that this would be the era of the Missile Crisis, it made for quite the pairing.[2]

For all Kennedy's self-deprecating attitude, he nevertheless placed himself at the center of economic decision-making. He would be in thrall to no one, including his new treasury secretary. The president wanted "to hear all sides of an important problem right from the beginning," Dillon recalled. Kennedy would often say "very little," but would listen and ask different people to speak and draw out of what had been said the essence of what was needed for him to make his final decision."[3]

Kennedy strengthened his connection with Dillon by giving him easy admission to the Oval Office. "I had instantaneous personal access to him at any time by calling his secretary, Evelyn Lincoln, who would tell me what his schedule was," Dillon recalled. "My office being so close, I could come over and wait in her room and then when someone went out, before the next appointment came in ... he'd hold off the next fellow." The speed and informality of these frequent interactions would only strike him later, when he saw the contrast in working with President Johnson, who, for Dillon at least, ran his schedule on a more formal basis. "It was harder for him to be as brief as President Kennedy," Dillon noted drily, because "when he did get someone in, he did like to talk." With Kennedy, it was an exclusive kind of relationship that allowed Dillon to make the two-minute walk through the underground connecting tunnel from the Treasury Building straight into the Oval Office. "I think there were a few other people," Dillon recalled, "of course the Attorney General [RFK]. The two of us may have been about the only ones this way." As Aurélie Basha i Novosejt notes, "What is remarkable is how much of this cooperation with President Kennedy remained secret to even senior members of the administration and how many internal debates Dillon won."[4]

The economic and financial team that the president put around himself followed a broader pattern. It was a feature of the administration that while Kennedy tended to put liberals such as Ted Sorensen, Schlesinger, and Richard Goodwin in positions where he wanted things *said*, he more often put conservatives like Dillon, McNamara, and McGeorge Bundy in positions where he needed things *done*. The Wall Street pragmatist Dillon was counterbalanced by the economics professor Walter Heller as chairman of the Council of Economic Advisers. "I want Doug Dillon to be my secretary of the treasury and my right bower," Kennedy told Heller, "and I want you to be my Chairman of the Council and my left bower."[5]

Heller was outside the usual run of Ivy League economists in Washington, but he was well regarded by his peers on taxation questions. "By 1960 Heller was not unknown in Washington, but he certainly was not well known," his profiler in the *Directory of the Council of Economic Advisers* notes. "[He] went to Washington as an outsider and, as he said, as a midwestern populist."[6]

Heller's relationship with the patrician east coast Dillon, by now a Washington insider, would provide one of the spikier policy elements of the Kennedy administration. Still, Dillon's reserve and good manners usually kept the relationship amiable. "Dillon was a gentleman," Heller would say, and "we always operated very compatibly." There was, "of course, continuous contention," but "no one should blink at that." Dillon, for his part, believed the differences were as much about presentation as they were personal. He thought Heller was "very public relations minded … talking to the press … in order to get people accustomed [to ideas]." In contrast, as the chief financial officer, Dillon himself "naturally had to be more conservative" in how he dealt with the press. When he spoke, markets around the world shifted.

Heller's ego and political inexperience often gave Dillon the edge in their internal tussles. Robert Kennedy would recall that while JFK admired Heller, "he always talked to the press too much [which] used to irritate the president." Only six days into the administration, the president summoned Heller to the White House to rebuke him for giving reporters a detailed background briefing on the state of the economy. "Never do that again!" Kennedy warned him. It was not a lesson Heller learned particularly well. The president, in contrast, quickly came to trust Dillon for his more discreet manner and judgment. "Douglas Dillon he liked very much," Robert Kennedy said.[7]

The other key figure who would join Dillon and Heller in the core financial team was Harvard professor David E. Bell. He became director of the Bureau of Budget, which prepared and executed the federal budget. Kennedy would describe him as "The man who says no," but the Second World War marine and ex-Truman staffer had a manner, Kennedy's brother-in-law Sargent Shriver wrote to the president, that was "low-key, well-informed, experienced, un-ideological, sensitive, quick, somewhat ironic and good humored." That attitude suited Dillon, who found him straightforward to deal with, and the two men quickly established a good working relationship. The so-called "troika" of Dillon, Heller, and Bell would often meet with the president to frame a final decision: Dillon's and Bell's congenial approach was a good match for Kennedy's personal style. "Well gentlemen, I guess we always have to have some fellow around with the job of shooting down the balloons," Kennedy said at the end of one meeting. "That apparently is the secretary of the treasury's task, so I guess that we will have to forget this wonderful idea. It is not really practical.'" As Dillon pointed out, "he said it in a very joking manner, and very pleasantly. He made everybody who had been working hard to get a different decision feel perfectly happy at having been overruled." That was an overstatement, as Heller rarely, if ever, was happy at being overruled. The three Harvard men shared a language that Heller did not.

Heller did recognize that "Dillon's idea" of the Troika was a genuine attempt to develop a coordinated approach to their three layers of responsibilities – namely, fiscal, financial, and tax at the Treasury; the budget at the Bureau; and economic forecasting at the council. "We really made that Troika work," Heller admitted. Bell agreed, saying in 1964 that "it was unprecedented, and it was very helpful and ... basically a sensible notion." On occasion, the three were joined by the fourth member of the economic and financial team, William McChesney Martin – the "boy wonder of Wall Street" and chair of the Federal Reserve since 1951 – together they became, with tongues very slightly in cheeks, the "Quadriad."[8]

In a remarkably balanced account, Raymond Saulnier, Heller's predecessor as chairman of the Council of Economic Advisers, pointed to the successes and failures that the Quadriad inherited from the Eisenhower administration. The minuses included three recessions, a growth rate below the historical norm, an increase in the structural element of unemployment, and a tepid approach to tax reduction and reform; on the plus side, he pointed to the balanced federal budget and a deficit that remained at or below 2.3 percent, personal incomes increasing, the size of the federal government stabilizing, historic improvements in infrastructure, and an economy left in generally good order. In short, "the record nets to a strong plus – a constructive presidency that was good for the nation." Certainly, there were "grounds for complaint," he conceded, but he also understood the basic unfairness of the political game in which it was "a standard in politics that when a new administration involves a change of party the newcomers complain of their legacy."[9]

"The American economy is in trouble," Kennedy declared in his first state of the union address on January 30, 1961. He lambasted the previous administration for "seven months of recession, three-and one-half years of slack, [and] seven years of diminished growth." Then there was the "knotty problem" of "the gap between the dollars we spend or invest abroad and the dollars returned to us here." As Dillon wrote to the president a few weeks afterwards, the speech on February 6 served notice "abroad in this country's recognition of what must be done."[10]

"When we took office in early 1961, we were in a period of crisis in our balance of payments," Dillon recalled in 1965. "One thing was perfectly obvious and that was that we had to create and carry out a new and different policy for the United States." The tussles within the Kennedy administration and abroad over that new policy would become a central focus of Dillon's entire tenure in the Treasury.[11]

The underpinnings of global economic management had been laid down in 1944 by John Maynard Keynes and others at the Bretton Woods conference, which created the International Monetary Fund and the World Bank, with the General Agreement on Tariffs and Trade (GATT) following in 1947. Under Bretton Woods, major industrialized nations could peg their currencies to the dollar, with overseas central banks able to convert US dollars into gold at $35 an ounce. "Unfortunately," writes Alan Greenspan, chair of the Federal Reserve from 1987 to 2006, "the system could only work if two conditions were fulfilled: if the United States maintained a large stockpile of gold and, second, if other countries refrained from hoarding dollars and then exchanging them for gold when the time seemed right." By 1961, with the price of gold regularly edging above $35, the time often seemed right to buy gold with dollars at the attractive fixed rate. In 1957, American gold holdings were 20,312 tonnes; by 1961 those holdings had reduced by a quarter to 15,060 tonnes. In 1971, the Nixon administration would take the United States off the gold standard and allow the value of the dollar to float downwards. But in 1961, with Kennedy already having given a guarantee during the election campaign to maintain the price fixed by Franklin D. Roosevelt in 1934, Dillon had one hand tied behind his back. The "gold window" was bad enough in terms of economic and financial stability, but when combined with the willingness of allies, particularly France, to use American weakness for political gain, it is not difficult to see why Kennedy focused on the issue. His favorite fiction writer, Ian Fleming, fed his neurosis with the 1959 novel *Goldfinger*, in which James Bond had to thwart a plot to hold the United States to ransom by stealing its entire gold reserves from Fort Knox. For Dillon, like Goldfinger, life in the Treasury would become a question of "Shall I proceed to the plan?"[12]

Even before Kennedy took the oath of office, Dillon had outlined his strategy to mitigate the balance of payments deficit. Seymour Harris, the Harvard professor who became his chief economic consultant at the Treasury, later recalled that it was Dillon's "remarkable memo of January 1961" that laid the groundwork for "so many of the important issues at the beginning." Dillon's own view was that because it was impossible to "cure the balance of payments deficits overnight," the United States had to get on the front foot from the outset. Foreign governments would be "encouraged" to prepay debts owed to the United States. Those same governments would also be made to feel an "intensification of pressure" to lift trade restrictions and discriminations. Foreign travel to the United States would be promoted. The activities of the Export-Import Bank would be reinvigorated so that American exporters would have access to export credit facilities every bit as good as those of their competitors. The United States would utilize its drawing rights at the International Monetary Fund (IMF) more effectively. Tax haven loopholes needed to be closed. International financial institutional arrangements, particularly GATT, needed to be strengthened to encourage the growth of global trade and investment. And from the beginning, there would be what Dillon described as the "intensification of efforts to maximize the contributions by other countries to the common military effort" – signaling Dillon's view that western European allies must be made to pay more towards their own defense costs, alongside his controversial willingness to use the American military presence in Europe as a bargaining tool with recalcitrant allies.[13]

Dillon's memo became the foundation for the president's special message to Congress on February 6 that presented more than a dozen specific measures. It was an early indication of how the relationship between Kennedy and Dillon would work. The president "didn't make any attempt to understand the details," Dillon judged, but "he understood the problem of the balance of payments extremely well in the broad." The crisis was always "on his mind" and was "the primary reason" that Kennedy had asked him to be treasury secretary in the first place. Dillon knew more about the problem and the people involved around the world than any other active political figure in Washington. That knowledge brought pressures with it too. For while other departments and agencies had to carry out policies which required complex negotiations with international partners and institutions, Kennedy made it clear to Dillon that the new secretary was "primarily responsible for overall balance of payments results." The January memo and subsequent special message to Congress demonstrated how Dillon was able to get on top of the issue "probably quicker than anyone." But it also confirmed that on one of the two issues the new president identified as his greatest concern, Dillon was the person in the hot seat.[14]

Since coming off the gold standard and letting the dollar float downwards were not options, Dillon and Roosa began the arduous process of defending the currency. Throughout 1961, their principal efforts were focused on what Dillon described as an attempt "to bring order out of chaos." In practice that meant an active policy of "close cooperation with all the other industrialized countries which had convertible currencies." Much of this cooperation was on a technical level. "Operation Twist" incentivized holding on to dollars by making short-term interest rates more attractive. Dillon intensified negotiations for a London "Gold Pool" that would see the Bank of England act as the broker for a consortium of seven other central banks in the United States, France, Germany, Italy, Switzerland, the Netherlands, and Belgium. The pool would buy gold when the price fell and sell when the price went up, sharing profits and losses according to fixed proportions – 50 percent in the case of the United States. Similarly, one of the first recommendations that Dillon made to the president was that the United States should participate in the monthly meetings in Basel of the Bank for International Settlements – a kind of central bank for national central banks – which provided a highly confidential way to make loans available to the major industrialized countries if their currencies came under threat from speculators or other national actors.[15]

International events gave another of Dillon's initiatives an unexpected boost. The Kennedy administration, like the Eisenhower administration before it, wanted to develop a system of "offsets" with West Germany, meaning that the Federal Republic (FRG) was expected to buy American military equipment with every US dollar it was given for its security. Neither administration had enjoyed much luck in persuading the Bonn government to agree to such a measure, but when East Germany erected a wall in Berlin in August 1961, intensifying West Germany's sense of vulnerability, Washington gained the upper hand in negotiations. Dillon told the president that the United States now had "the strongest bargaining position since the negotiations began" and urged him to use "our negotiation leverage" to "obtain a commitment from the FRG to completely offset our military expenditures in Germany affecting the balance of payments both for current forces and any additional deployments." Kennedy approved the measures, and by October a full offset agreement was agreed with a reluctantly compliant West Germany. The program would turn out to be a success: by 1963, the cost of the US presence in the country would be almost entirely offset.[16]

The offset agreement showed that Dillon was prepared to be tough when necessary to address the balance of payments crisis, but in general he preferred concerted effort. This course represented a general change of tone and approach by the United States. Dillon consistently emphasized "consultation and cooperation with key foreign countries" when making technical moves. By far his boldest maneuver was the creation within the International Monetary Fund of what became known as the G-10 group of nations (Belgium, Canada, France, West Germany, Italy, Japan, the Netherlands, Sweden, the UK, and the United States, with the non-IMF member Switzerland also involved). A longstanding American fear had been that the United States would need a far greater borrowing facility than the International Monetary Fund could provide in the event of a run on gold reserves. "There might be a sudden crisis arising from an unexpected kind of development," Roosa recalled, "one which would require immediate action, and where, in those circumstances, we ought to be able to show that there were massive resources available." That anxiety was one shared by other major powers, which recognized how a run on the dollar would destabilize the global financial system. The world's other major reserve currency – UK sterling – had already come under attack in 1960–61.

The idea of a similar situation involving the dollar was unthinkable. While the United States, which, like the British, had a veto, was prepared to pledge more funds to the IMF, European countries, particularly France, refused point blank to provide more funds to an organization over which they had no control. The idea of an elite group of major currency nations with its own decision-making mechanism was another matter. Dillon proposed a meeting to discuss a way forward on the so-called "General Agreement to Borrow" at the next meetings of the IMF and World Bank in Vienna in September. "Real progress there toward the plan for standby credit facilities in the International Monetary Fund should help to calm the financial markets," Dillon told Kennedy.[17]

Dillon still faced a major problem. Despite progress on building trust at a technical level between central banks, national politicians still feared that the United States and Britain were attempting to rig the system to maintain their economic dominance. "France is not alone," the *New York Times* warned as Dillon left for Europe. "Others are reported to share her suspicion that the plan will turn out to be dominated by the United States and Britain." The critical question was who would have access to the funds – all IMF members or just the G-10 nations. Dillon told Wilfrid Baumgartner, the French finance minister, in a sidebar, that the United States accepted that control would be "outside of the [IMF]." Its chief, Per Jacobsson, who wanted funds available to all IMF nations, was livid, but powerless to thwart the plan. This was high politics of the most elemental kind. "We came out of Vienna with the essence of the agreement," Dillon recalled, because "really it was made in the bilateral meeting with Mr. Baumgartner." Later in his tenure, Dillon would find himself in a high stakes conflict with France over the balance of payments crisis, but here the two countries worked in alignment. "At that time, we saw things very similarly," Dillon said.[18]

Dillon informed Kennedy that the General Agreement to Borrow was a major advance in dealing "with balance of payments pressures which impair or might impair [the] world monetary system." Others in the administration were not so sure. Almost as soon as Dillon returned from Vienna, Heller and the Council of Economic Advisers prepared a memo for the president on the balance of payments crisis that criticized Dillon for a short-term "dollar salvage" operation rather than recognizing that the entire international monetary structure was flawed. "Given the high regard with which the Bretton Woods system was generally held," Francis Gavin points out, "this was an extraordinary statement for the president's closest economic advisers to make."[19]

The CEA's radical plans, drawing on Robert Triffin's book *Gold and the Dollar Crisis*, argued for transatlantic negotiations to create a new monetary system. Robert Roosa was scornful of the intervention but Dillon was less dismissive, telling Kennedy that while "dissent by the CEA on the US side" did not find any favor with American allies, he thought it was important to keep "the long-range question," specifically any "Triffin-like" proposals, "on the agenda" if existing changes did not "turn out to be sufficient for the long-term future as well." The implication that he had no plan did irritate Dillon. Stung by the criticism that his policy was a series of reactive, temporary measures, he attached a covering letter to a rebuttal memo that Roosa produced. In it he laid out in a point-by-point fashion the strategy and operations that had been undertaken by the Treasury, including arrangements made in Basel, London, and Vienna. "All of these operations add up to a significant accomplishment," he told Kennedy, but because they were "highly technical and complex and to be successful must be confidential," it made it difficult to "fully appreciate the extent of our operations or their success." This was a political problem, he recognized, but where it mattered, among the central bankers of the leading industrial and financial nations, "their knowledge of, and confidence in our operations are a substantial element in the relative strength of the dollar in a time of speculative danger."

Kennedy deferred to Dillon in 1961 and throughout the first half of 1962, but the outflow of dollars continued to threaten American gold reserves. Both men recognized that quiet technical measures had been inadequate to address a problem that was more than simply financial. The relentless pressure on American gold, note Gordon Weil and Ian Davidson, "was seen in Washington as a drain on American prestige [and] became increasingly a political embarrassment to the administration." Dillon determined that the best means to ensure demand for the dollar surged around the world was to embark on major tax reform to supercharge economic growth. But first he had unfinished business to complete from the Eisenhower era.[20]

Chapter Ten

A Billion a Year
Punta del Este and Washington, 1961

Montevideo, Uruguay. Friday, August 4, 1961. The contrast could hardly have been more pronounced. As the United States military service jet touched down at Aeropuerto de Carrasco and taxied to the ramp, the crowd of thousands that had gathered in the airport gallery readied themselves to protest the visiting American. Douglas Dillon emerged from the aircraft into the cacophony of noise and backs turned in dissent. Dressed in a suit and gray herringbone coat, Dillon looked for all the world as if he were still on Wall Street. The crowd in the galley took up the chant of "Cuba, si! Yanquis, no!" as anxious Uruguayan troops looked on with tear gas and guns at the ready. Dillon's sangfroid deflected much of the anger. With a cheerful smile and hand extended in a friendly wave, he strolled down the steps to greet the US ambassador, Edward J. Sparks, and the Uruguayan foreign minister, Homero Martinez Montero. After a few platitudes about wanting to give "freedom full meaning by extending its benefits throughout every level of society," a limousine whisked Dillon away to the Atlantic coast resort of Punta del Este with only minutes to spare before another plane touched down.

That next arrival prompted an altogether different reaction. The bearded face that would soon adorn the walls of millions of student dorm rooms beamed while coming down the steps of the Bristol Britannia turboprop aircraft. The crowd that had only moments ago been so hostile now roared its approval in a frenzy of shouting and flag waving. Charging toward them, fists pumping, the Argentine-Cuban revolutionary leader, Ernesto "Che" Guevara de la Serna, pushed through the Uruguayan troops and grabbed at the many hands stretching out towards him. Dressed in army fatigues and trademark black military beret with silver star, he was the epitome of protean vigor. In short, Che Guevara, hero of the dispossessed across the Global South, was the antithesis of the Wall Street banker who preceded him. It was no wonder the *New York Times* worried the Cuban would end up "stealing the show."[1]

A special meeting of the Inter-American Economic and Social Council to discuss a new program of economic cooperation between the United States and Latin America brought both men to Uruguay. John F. Kennedy had called it the Alliance for Progress. Watching Guevara in action, Dillon quickly grasped what an impressive adversary he faced, writing to Kennedy that the Cuban was "masterful" as an advocate for the "Communist point of view." Yes, Guevara would attack "everything the conference is trying to do," which would probably make "little substantive impression" on the other delegates. But Dillon shrewdly recognized that the point of the meeting for Guevara was not to influence delegates. Instead, the Cuban minister was "aiming over their heads at people of Latin America."[2]

Countering Guevara's revolutionary appeal and scoring some kind of win against Cuba was an immediate priority for the Kennedy administration. Only four months earlier, the small island just ninety miles off the American coast had been the setting for an ignominious humiliation for the new president. On April 17, 1961, fourteen hundred Cuban exiles trained and sponsored by the CIA had landed on the beaches of the Bay of Pigs on the southern coast of Cuba. Operation "Bumpy Road" was a fiasco from the outset. Bad weather and poor planning meant that the Cuban émigrés struggled to get ashore, and when they finally did, Castro's forces were waiting to mow them down. The CIA and chief of naval operations asked Kennedy for permission to send in a destroyer, further American planes, or even ground troops, but the president, still thinking he could keep US involvement quiet, turned them down flat. "I can't get the United States into a war," he had said shortly beforehand, bluntly telling advisers that it could be "a fucking slaughter." Three days of fighting saw 140 killed and 1,189 taken prisoner. This fiasco made him a laughingstock around the world, while handing the Soviet bloc in general and the Castro government in particular a remarkable propaganda victory.

The reputational damage to JFK on the world stage was its own kind of disaster. "In view of the fact that God limited the intelligence of man," Dean Acheson, the godfather of American postwar foreign policy, noted (quoting a favorite aphorism of Chancellor Adenauer of West Germany), "it seems unfair that he did not also limit his stupidity." Kennedy echoed the same thought, asking, "How could I have been so stupid?"[3]

Even though Dillon had next to nothing to do with the failed Operation Zapata/Bumpy Road and walked away from the humiliation unscathed, his fingerprints were all over the original plan hatched by the Eisenhower administration. He was a member of the "Special Group" that recommended "an amphibious landing on the Cuban coast of 600–750 men equipped with weapons of extraordinarily heavy fire power" and supported by "air strikes as well as supply flights … to trigger a general uprising." That plan was the essence of the recommendation Eisenhower made to Kennedy a few days before he left office to push ahead.[4]

Given Dillon's institutional knowledge of Cuba, it was extraordinary that he was not brought into the planning for the invasion. Glossing over his own part in earlier plans, he saw the failure in 1961 as systemic. Policy under Eisenhower had been worked out in a highly structured way, with planning and technical groups vetting papers, considering the views of various departments so the proposals that came to the National Security Council for decision were presented in a formal manner. Eisenhower had always been "very interested in having a complete governmental position developed and certainly had the complete views of all sides of the government on any question before acting," Dillon said. In contrast, most policymaking under Kennedy was based on "decisions taken by the president himself," with the planning group structure abolished and "no long and complex papers written in advance."

The final blueprint for the Bay of Pigs had been cobbled together by Richard Bissell, CIA deputy director for plans, in just four days. Results spoke for themselves. Only "as time went on," Dillon judged, did Kennedy come to recognize "the necessity of being certain, more certain maybe than in the early days of his administration, that all those who should have a point of view were fully heard before he himself made up his mind." It was no coincidence that after the Bay of Pigs fiasco, Kennedy reinstituted the policy-planning-group structure under the chairmanship of General Maxwell Taylor, military representative to the president. By including Dillon along with Robert Kennedy, the new structure added two powerful and high-ranking members into the mix.

In the summer of 1961, as Dillon prepared to go head-to-head with Che Guevara in Punta del Este, he faced more immediate problems. Arthur Schlesinger had predicted in February that the Bay of Pigs operation would provoke a "wave of massive protest" and "fix a malevolent image of the new Administration in the minds of millions." Now Dillon found himself trying to repair that image in the region that the president had described as the Cold War's "most dangerous."[5]

The frustration was that shortly before the Bay of Pigs imbroglio, the United States had scored a public relations coup in Latin America with the announcement of the Alliance of Progress. Promising "a vast cooperative effort, unparalleled in magnitude and purpose," it attempted "to satisfy the basic needs of the American people for homes, work, and land, health and schools." The initiative was a natural extension of the principles Dillon had worked out in the Act of Bogotá the previous year, with some extra polish from the pen of Sorensen and his protégé, Richard Goodwin. "Supposedly begun by the Kennedy administration, the Alliance for Progress had its groundwork actually laid during the Eisenhower administration by Douglas Dillon and Milton Eisenhower," secretary of state Dean Rusk acknowledged in his memoirs. "The Kennedy administration put a new label on it and launched it with great fanfare."[6]

The initiative marked the opening of a new front in the Cold War to counter the threat of socialism and revolutionary Marxism inspired by the Cuban revolution of 1959. Havana demonstrated to populists in Latin America how foreign imperial forces could be overthrown through armed rebellion and the wave of a Romeo y Julieta cigar. After humiliating the United States in the Bay of Pigs, Castro now prepared to declare himself a Marxist. Revolutionary forces were on the march throughout this part of the hemisphere.[7]

A few weeks after stumbling on the Bumpy Road, Kennedy told Goodwin, "Let's get moving on the Alliance for Progress." "I can't even get the State Department to agree on a position," Goodwin complained. Even the name had been a source of recrimination, with State Department officials blaming the "totally ignorant" Goodwin for making the president a laughingstock by not being aware that "in Spanish you must use the definite article, making it 'Alianza para el Progreso' or in Portuguese 'Aliança para o Progresso.'"[8]

At the Department of State, under the muted leadership of Rusk, most officials were lukewarm about the Alliance for Progress. They dismissed it as little more than a rhetorical flourish. "What's the headache today? is their attitude," one Kennedy appointee complained of the staff at the bureau of inter-American affairs. There was "no purpose, no drive," only "a sullen resistance" to fresh ideas and approaches.[9]

Kennedy's initial attempt to overcome this lethargy produced only further chaos. Adolf A. Berle, a veteran Latin American expert from the FDR era, had headed a task force to coordinate policy in the region. That appointment led to a turf war with the State Department, which briefed the press about "the apparent lack of a firm hand" in policymaking and how "diplomats in the Latin American embassies cannot recall a time when it was so difficult for them to determine who was in charge of what."

Kennedy's response was to "talk to Dillon" and give him plenipotentiary powers for Punta del Este. "He asked me to do this as an individual," Dillon said, "and not as secretary of the treasury." A few days before the conference began, Chester A. Bowles, shortly to be fired as undersecretary of state, complained that Dillon had put too much emphasis on financial and technical measures. "The Alliance's success," he warned naively, would not be based on "the number of dollars that are made available by the USA."[10]

Dillon knew otherwise. Discussing strategy with members of the delegation in his hotel suite in Punta del Este, it became clear to him how spooked American officials were by the star power of Che Guevara. Dillon listened quietly, but when Goodwin asked how the United States could compete when "all we're giving them is words," the treasury secretary provided an answer that no one had been expecting.

"I'll pledge a billion dollars a year," he said.

"We can't do that," Ed Martin, the assistant secretary of state, spluttered in Goodwin's colorful account of events. "Nobody has approved it. It hasn't been cleared. At least we have to consult the secretary of state."

"What do you suggest?" Dillon asked him. "That we all sit on the beach in Uruguay for a month or two while the people in Washington discuss it?"

"We don't have the authority," Martin countered.

"Of course I have the authority," Dillon responded, effortlessly moving to the Olympian heights. "I am the personal representative of the president of the United States. Plenipotentiary. It says so on my credentials. *And I am going to give them a billion dollars.*"[11]

The next day, August 5, Dillon read a statement from the president to the restless, noisy audience in the airless auditorium of the Cantegril Country Club. "Only an effort similar to that which was needed to rebuild the economies of Western Europe can ensure the fulfillment of our Alliance for Progress," he said.

Then he pulled the rabbit out of his hat. "To that end, the United States will allocate at least one billion dollars in development assistance to Latin America in the first year of the Alliance."

Dillon's delivery had been measured to a fault – "flat, toneless," one magazine said – but now an audible ripple of excitement went around the room before everyone fell into complete silence to hear the rest of the statement. Dillon went on to pledge $20 billion over the next decade. When he was done, applause turned into an ovation, with only Guevara remaining impassive. "The sense of relief was palpable," Goodwin recalled. "This was not propaganda. This was dollars." It was easy to understand the excitement, notes George Herring, for this was "the Marshall Plan-like aid program hemispheric leaders had been asking for since the 1940s" and "seemed to epitomize the idealism of New Frontier foreign policy." Understated as ever, Dillon wrote to Kennedy to say that the opening day "went well."[12]

The conference broke up into working parties to draft the final text for the Charter of Punta del Este – the constitution for the Alliance for Progress. Dillon sent officials into action to hammer out a deal so that American money would be accompanied by verifiable commitments from the signatories to social, political, and economic reform. Dillon weighed in when negotiations got stuck. The trickiest customer turned out to be the host, President Eduardo Víctor Haedo of Uruguay, who felt "personal pique" at Kennedy's decision not to attend and tried "pure blackmail" to get an extra billion dollars for "emergency" projects. Dillon faced him down, but "this whole negotiation," he complained, was "disagreeable in the extreme."[13]

By August 17, the members of the Organization of American States had agreed on a final declaration. Dillon reported "enthusiasm from all sides," although he correctly observed that the "hard task" would be turning words into "concrete action." The lurking question was how Cuba would respond. Goodwin recalled that Guevara had been "unfailingly courteous, said little, his manner amiable" during the working party discussions. It was behavior that concerned Dillon, whose fear was not that Guevara would try to obstruct or disrupt the final proceedings for the treaty, but rather that he would sign it and "gain the right to be assisted."[14]

A joke going around the conference quipped that there were only two leftwing governments at the event – Cuba and the United States. Even John Leddy believed State Department officials "went overboard" in setting unattainable goals such as eliminating illiteracy in ten years. Historian María Josefina Saldaña-Portillo suggests the Kennedy and Castro governments shared genuine similarities in the way they spoke about modernization and transformation. Guevara himself noted "in all sincerity" that the charter could mean "a real improvement for Latin America in the standard of living of all its 200 million inhabitants." Somewhat cagily, he acknowledged a symbiotic relationship between the two regimes. "Cuba is the goose that lays the golden egg," he said. "While there is a Cuba, the United States will continue to give." He would even contrive a social meeting with Goodwin to explore the possibility for some kind of "modus vivendi" between the two countries. (As a gesture of goodwill, he gave Goodwin a box of Cuban cigars, which, oblivious to security and embargo concerns, the American later smoked with Kennedy in the White House.)

In the end, however, Guevara miscalculated and abstained, leaving Dillon free to taunt the Cuban representative that the United States would never recognize the legitimacy of the Castro regime. "The final result," Dillon reported to Kennedy, "is, I think, everything we could have hoped for."[15]

Kennedy had asked Dillon to get the job done and he had delivered – a fact the president warmly acknowledged when Dillon flew back to Washington on August 19. Arriving at Andrews Air Force Base just before eight o'clock, he was immediately taken by army helicopter to the White House. There waiting for him on the south lawn was the president, looking sleek and polished in a black suit, crisp white shirt, and black tie as he patted the secretary on the back. While the camera bulbs exploded, Dillon himself looked uncharacteristically crumpled in a tropical wool suit after the long flight, which had included a stopover in Venezuela. Exhausted and bedraggled though he may have been, the look of accomplishment on his face was impossible to miss. The two men moved to the microphones in the Rose Garden, where the president praised Dillon for leading "with the greatest distinction and the greatest credit." As the treasury secretary presented him with the signed leather-bound copy of the Charter, Kennedy leaned in and whispered, "Well Doug, I guess I'm going to have to find you your billion dollars!"[16]

Dillon was now attracting attention as he rode the crest of a wave. He had returned from Punta del Este with a charter for the Alliance for Progress. He had been publicly lauded by the president for his achievements and whisked inside the White House for a formal reception to celebrate his success. When Dillon finally returned home to Belmont Road in northwest Washington, waiting for him in the wood-paneled library amid French impressionist paintings and eighteenth-century furniture was another badge of esteem in American public life: the latest edition of *Time* magazine with his own image staring out from the front cover.

As the nation's widest-selling news magazine, *Time* appealed to elites and the middle class alike. The magazine took great care with its covers, commissioning artists to sketch an original for the main image. The one of "Treasury Secretary C. Douglas Dillon" for the August 18 edition had him looking tanned and blue-eyed, dressed in a trademark navy suit along with an uncharacteristically (indeed unlikely) bright tie. He stared off into the middle distance, his smile confident but not cocky. Looming behind him was an immense wall of gold bricks, with more waiting to be added. "U.S. Money & the Cold War," ran the tagline that cut diagonally through the *Time* masthead. Inside, the cover story gave further context. "The Economy – " ran the headline – "Man with the Purse."

Reading the unsigned profile today it is not difficult to see why these *Time* cover stories were so popular. Dillon was an enigma – a man of "enormous influence and responsibility" who was "virtually unknown, and even less understood, by the public he serves." The piece was not deferential. It drew attention to Dillon's "diffident professorial manner," his often "flat" delivery, and the fact that he was "notoriously demanding of subordinates." Neither did the piece fail to mention his wealth and privilege, and the fact that he "revels in tastes that few of his countrymen share," including "vintage wines, Savile Row suits, fine paintings and finer porcelain." In one particularly waspish aside, the profile noted that "Dillon is the only Cabinet member who can match homes with Millionaire Jack Kennedy. Besides his Washington residence, he has an apartment on Manhattan's Fifth Avenue, a winter retreat at Hobe Sound, Florida, called La Lanterne, a summer place in Dark Harbor, Maine, an estate in Far Hills, New Jersey, and a 'cottage' at Versailles, France."

Still, waspishness never turned to snark. In a world where "self-inflated egos and ruthless self-interest" were the norm, Dillon's "polite and unruffled demeanor," his aversion to making "memorable quotes," and "his careful homework" meant that he "accomplishes more by not drawing attention to himself" than most in Washington. It was also the reason that he had quickly become one of "Kennedy's most efficient cabinet operators" and "a trusted voice" in the White House. "There is no-one between Dillon and Kennedy," one insider was quoted as saying. As a result, "the staid U.S. Treasury" was "no longer just the government's check-cashing and revenue gathering arm." Instead, it had become an "active, shaping force" in policymaking.

Republicans in Congress, not knowing whether to be embittered or admiring, had even given this new influence a name. Washington, they said, had been taken over by the "Dilloncrats."[17]

Chapter Eleven

Always Supporting Dillon
Washington, Spring–Summer 1962

Towards the end of 1961, Dixon Donnelley, special assistant to the treasury secretary, ran into his counterpart, special assistant to the president Arthur Schlesinger Jr. As veterans of the failed Stevenson presidential campaign in 1956 the two men were friendly, although a certain frostiness had crept into their relationship once it became known that Schlesinger had opposed Dillon's appointment at the Treasury. Donnelley, who had worked for Dillon at the State Department and followed him across to the Treasury, greatly admired his boss. He was thus pleasantly surprised now to hear the historian speaking well of him. Gently chiding his colleague, Donnelley pointed out that he had been no friend of Dillon's. "Well, that was a year ago and my God was I wrong," Schlesinger replied effusively. "Now I am one of his big fans!"[1]

Schlesinger's enthusiasm reflected the view of the Kennedys themselves. At the turn of the year, Bobby – famously no soft-soaper ("hard as nails," his father said) – had written to Dillon to say "how much I have enjoyed working with you over the past year. I don't know anyone who has contributed more to the president – a contribution which he considers invaluable. It has made a major difference for him and thus for the country." The connection went beyond merely professional. When the First Lady reopened the elegantly refurbished White House Red Room ("the showpiece of Mrs. John F. Kennedy's work in decorating the mansion," the *New York Times* noted) to mark the president's first year in office, it was furnished with nineteenth-century American antiques donated almost entirely by Dillon. That was the kind of largesse rich friends showed each other.[2]

Among the many qualities Schlesinger admired in Dillon was the political adroitness with which he maneuvered through Washington. "He was [an] exceptionally skilled operator within the bureaucracy, ready to pull every stop and cut many corners to advance the Treasury view," Schlesinger wrote, "always (and justifiably) confident that his charm could heal any feelings hurt in the process." These sharp elbows combined with the gentle touch helped him thrive within an administration set up from the very beginning to be divided. Kennedy had made it clear when he appointed Dillon that he was bringing in liberal economist Walter Heller to act as a counterweight. It was a tactic, in part inspired by FDR, that the president applied in most areas of policymaking. It ensured that he remained the principal decider and did not get railroaded by advisers. Even in foreign policy, which had been a lifelong interest and where his comfort level was highest, serious missteps still tarnished Kennedy in his first year. In economic and financial policy, he was even more at the mercy of the economics professors who surrounded him. Heller was able to express his ideas with force and an eloquent, often witty style that Kennedy enjoyed. But the treasury secretary in return offered calm gravitas and the personal connection of a social equal. As exasperated White House officials observed, "The president always *agreed* with Heller but always *supported* Dillon."[3] "Kennedy had campaigned on a platform that suggested he would overturn Eisenhower's fiscal conservatism," Aurélie Basha i Novosejt writes. "However, much to the chagrin of his more liberal advisors, he was far more fiscally conservative than they had anticipated."[4]

By the time the new administration took office, the nation was amid "the great compression." The blatant wealth-gap from the late nineteenth century began to shrink during the Second World War and the 1950s. With Keynesians in the ascendant, a broad consensus emerged, which included pragmatic conservatives such as Dillon, that a progressive income tax system and income support measures could help reduce inequality and poverty. That basic premise would have prevailed irrespective of whether Nixon or Kennedy had won the election.

"Looking back at 1960 one cannot miss the presence of ... boredom," Herbert Stein, later chairman of the Council of Economic Advisers under Nixon, observed. "In such a mood it was easy to accept the idea that something unspecified was missing in the performance of the economy and that new interesting steps must be taken to fill the gap." But what exactly would those steps be? To answer that question, candidate Kennedy had commissioned two task forces on taxation and growth that ended up staking out the vital differences in philosophy and approach that would soon beset the administration itself.[5]

MIT professor Paul Samuelson, the godfather of neo-Keynesianism and later Nobel laureate, wrote one of the reports. His plan for supercharging the US economy was, in a nutshell, New Deal–style measures such as federal spending on big public projects for infrastructure, education, and slum clearance. He recommended a temporary tax cut up to 4 percent as a quick stimulus, but opposed a permanent cut, arguing "urgently" that to do so "might be tragic" in undermining any future government's ability to fight a recession. Keynes had famously observed that governments should tighten their belts during good times to have the means to let them out in leaner times. If this surplus-building approach had been followed during the 1950s, Samuelson argued, "the authorities might be facing the not unpleasant task of how to deal with such a surplus."[6]

The other task force, led by Harvard professor Stanley Surrey, the nation's foremost expert on tax law, argued the precise opposite. When he handed Kennedy his report on January 9, Surrey had urged the president-elect not only to make tax reform the central plank of his economic policy, but to put the full force of the presidential bully pulpit behind it. Surrey had spent his career demonstrating how what today we would call the top 1 percent (which included Dillon and Kennedy) escaped tax. With all the loopholes available, the top rates were "only paper rates" for those who understood how to play the system. Surrey argued for a fairer, more transparent, and above all simpler system, and one he believed had the potential to unleash the economy. Reform would, in turn, lead to tax cuts. While he did not make a recommendation on specific tax rates, the examples he gave sent their own message. A reduction in the top marginal rate of tax from 91 percent to 65 percent, he suggested, would result in only $300 million less revenue to the government. In contrast, a 1 percent drop to the bottom rate of 20 percent would mean $1.5 billion less revenue. The complexity of the task, the fact that a "program of tax reform necessarily arrays in opposition to it a variety of special interest groups," explained the need for the president to stake his own authority on reform. Surrey advised that he should plan during 1961 before sending legislation to Congress in 1962. Although it was a radical idea, Larry Kudlow, later director of the National Economic Council in the Trump Administration, points out that "all the positions [Surrey's] report laid out – how high tax rates redound to the benefit of the well-connected, do next to nothing to collect revenue, and lend dizzying complexity to the law, all necessitating rather brutal impositions on the little guy – were true to Democratic traditions."[7]

It would be an oversimplification to say that the reports offered two clear pathways for the incoming administration. For a start, even the supporters of each differed about the best approach to take. The ideas behind the Samuelson report, for example, would often come under assault from the economic independent voice in the administration, John Kenneth Galbraith, who pushed for more extensive regulation of the economy and greater redistribution of income than the more conventionally Keynesian Samuelson. Nevertheless, the two reports did represent important differences of approach and emphasis, and these differences became institutionalized in the organs of the administration. Samuelson turned down the chairmanship of the Council of Economic Advisers, but Walter Heller, as chair, and council members James Tobin and Kermit Gordon were all Keynesians. As for Stanley Surrey, he went to the Treasury, where he found a supporter in Dillon. "I read it and I had an opportunity to discuss it with Professor Surrey," the treasury secretary recalled. "My reactions were highly favorable." He created a new post for Surrey as assistant secretary for tax policy, recognizing that he was "probably the most knowledgeable man about the tax law in the United States." In this way the two task forces became parties in opposition – in other words, exactly what the president had wanted.[8]

With Surrey having advised that a move on tax reform should not come until 1962 and Dillon preoccupied with the balance of payments crisis, the CEA found itself with the initiative for the first year of the administration. Everything for them was predicated on achieving full employment (which they considered as being met when unemployment fell to 4 percent). To get there, the CEA, driven by Gordon and Tobin, committed to a policy of rapid fiscal expansion, with a preference for increasing expenditures over cutting taxes.

What followed in the spring of 1961 was an immediate spending boom with executive action to invest in new highways, federal facilities, technological systems, water and sewage plants, farm subsidies, small business loans, a pilot scheme for food stamps, and surplus food redistribution. Legislative action expanded Social Security, unemployment benefits, housing assistance, the minimum wage, home building and loans, slum clearance, emergency relief, and child benefits. Incentives for investment in areas of high unemployment and poverty rewarded state and local governments for spending federal funding quickly. The aim was "to restore momentum" by getting money into the American economy in the fastest possible time and creating a workforce that, through government investment, was healthier and better fed, better housed, and better educated.[9]

While the CEA spearheaded a federal stimulus, Dillon and the Treasury were left with the unglamorous and unpopular task of pioneering a tax credit for business investment. This reform proposed a 7 percent tax credit for investments in new machinery and modernized systems, as well as accelerating the timescale on depreciation so that businesses could write off old equipment for tax purposes. It was a fearsomely complex piece of legislation – one that had been abandoned by the Eisenhower administration – and was widely distrusted by business owners who could not figure out if there was a catch but were certain there must be one. Theodore Sorensen recalled a bemused Dillon telling him the story of explaining the bill's merits to the businessman in the next seat on a flight. "Wonderful!" the man said. "Now would you mind explaining to me again why I'm against it?" The bill would eventually pass in 1962, when it immediately became a popular and widely used credit, accounting for close to half of the $40 billion investment on new plants and equipment in the United States by the following year.[10]

Looking back two years later, Dillon thought the business credit had come to be understood as "more important as time wore on" and was part of a shift in which "a feeling has developed that the Democratic administration was truly in favor of promoting the economy through promoting private business." At the beginning of 1962, however, as the Kennedy administration ticked over into its second year, it was just one more disappointment for the administration. Hopes for a rebound in the economy, after an upbeat few months in the middle of 1961, had petered out. Economic growth was stuck at its 1960 figure of 2.6 percent. Unemployment refused to budge below 6 percent, in part thanks to growing automation, especially in the coal and steel heartlands. Behind the scenes, the economic advisers themselves were divided about what to do, with Heller losing faith in the growth school of Tobin and Gordon. "Kennedy wasn't getting anywhere with his expenditure programs," Heller recalled, so "there was a real difference of opinion among us." With the CEA strategy in shreds, the flailing Heller began looking around for an alternative. It did not take long for his eye to fall on the ambitious tax program being prepared by Surrey at the Treasury.[11]

"The Kennedy economists did not come to Washington in January 1961 with a program for a large permanent tax cut in their briefcases," Herbert Stein later mocked. "This became their program only a year and a half later and was their reaction to the developments, including the frustrations, of the intervening months." It was a point on which Heller himself became touchy. "Some amateur historians say we just folded under and decided to give to the conservative forces in the country and forgo the expenditure route," he complained in the 1970s. "Nothing could be further from the truth!" In a classic piece of *ex post facto* rationalization, Heller said that by May 1962 he simply felt "I had been right after all" in the "initial feeling that we couldn't struggle to full employment under this heavy over-burden of taxes." Having initially been opposed to Surrey's report (even convincing Kennedy not to publish it while allowing Samuelson's report into the public domain), Heller belatedly embraced its conclusion: taxation was the key to economic prosperity. In doing so, Heller would refashion the policy as his own and brazenly portray Dillon and the Treasury as opponents of tax cuts.[12]

By now, the Kennedy administration appeared to be lurching towards an economic and financial crisis, with economists and pundits alike predicting a "Kennedy recession." Politics had made matters worse. At the beginning of 1962, Kennedy had negotiated a non-inflationary deal in the steel industry, with the largest steelmakers agreeing not to raise prices in return for no wage increases for workers, only to see the steel companies renege on the deal by raising prices by 3.5 percent. Kennedy was incandescent ("They fucked us, and we've got to try to fuck them"). He unleashed Bobby to go to war with the executives of the steel companies, forcing them to back down. It ended in victory for the president, but the win came at a cost, judged Dillon, who had been on the periphery during the dispute, "scaring businesspeople that there would be over-regulation, or over-interference by government." On May 28, spooked by the threat of the FBI wiretapping steel executives, auditing their income tax returns, and stretching the boundaries of legality to the breaking point, Wall Street crashed to its worst one-day fall since 1929.[13]

The next day, Kennedy called Dillon, Heller, and chairman of the Federal Reserve Martin to the White House for an emergency meeting. It was a cheerless way for the president to spend his forty-fifth birthday. Dillon was astonished at how caught up Heller had become in the "psychological phenomena" of the crash and was baffled by his talk of "the economy going into a tailspin." Nightmarish comparisons to the 1929 stock market crash and the great depression seemed misplaced. "I particularly from the experience I had in business did not feel the 1962 drop was comparable to 1929 because there wasn't the same credit situation," Dillon recalled, pointing out that "four or five months" later "everyone looked back and wondered why they'd been so worried."[14]

The underlying problems with the economy were not so easy to dismiss. The weakness of the dollar, the rise of structural unemployment, a crisis of confidence in the markets, and anemic growth: few doubted that the recovery was not as fast or robust as had been anticipated. Heller chose this moment to pivot to tax cuts and "the discussion began to get a little hotter." The reason for the heated tempers was Heller's demand for a so-called "quickie" tax cut. He wanted a temporary across-the-board cut in personal income tax of 3 percent to begin in July or September 1962 and expire a year later. A matching 3 percent cut in corporate income tax would take effect in January 1963. "Their argument is essentially that a decline is cumulative," Seymour Harris wrote to Dillon, "and hence what one teaspoonful of medicine will do now will require a bottle a year from now." It was a good analogy, but one that was dependent on the notion that the economy was sick – a fact that Dillon disputed. In fact, he believed the short-termism – what Heller called "fine tuning" – would do the patient more harm than good.[15]

Dillon was broadly in favor of a permanent tax cut, but he argued that it had to come as part of a comprehensive revenue reform program to be effective. He allowed that there would be an economic benefit to the president announcing that a tax cut was on the way in 1963, but to act precipitously with a "quickie" tax cut risked destroying the systemic tax proposals that Surrey and the Treasury had been working on for over a year. "This requires a calm and confident attitude on the part of the government," he told Kennedy immediately after the meeting. "A temporary income tax reduction ... would constitute danger signals of a loss of control, discipline or nerve that might have a counterproductive effect on confidence in the economy at home and the dollar abroad."[16]

Kennedy had wanted a balance of conflicting opinions between his economic advisers and now he surely had it. Uncertain as to what to do, he hedged, announcing on June 7 a commitment to sending Dillon's comprehensive tax reform program to Congress in 1963. These measures would include an across-the-board cut in individual and corporate income taxes, but crucially, he also said he would not "stand helplessly by and watch a recovery run out of gas." He reserved the right to "make other judgments" if "new circumstances brought a new situation."[17]

The president's statement was a partial victory for Dillon, but it left Heller with his foot in the door. Over the course of the next two months, the CEA coordinated a relentless barrage of opinion both inside the administration and in the media to push for the "quickie" cut. New proponents of "fine tuning" such as Gardner Ackley were brought onto the Council as reinforcements. Even more important was the deployment of old faces. "I [was] called in as an ally by that time," recalled Paul Samuelson, author of Kennedy's other taskforce report in January 1961. On three separate occasions that summer, Heller used him to lobby the president in person for an immediate tax cut. Samuelson also applied pressure in public, writing in the influential *Financial Times* on July 11 that "the time has come for a sizable across-the-board reduction in tax rates ... if recession and stagnation are to be avoided." The Conference of Business Economists weighed in the next day with dire warnings about economic decline and loss of consumer confidence. At the same time, the Chamber of Commerce wrote directly to Kennedy recommending the "reduction and revision" of taxes for "the stimulation of investment at home and abroad." Non-economists were activated too. Sorensen slipped pro-cut phrases into the president's public remarks, with Heller understanding that if "I had Ted put in a little sentence … I don't think there was any question of the president being corrected on this by Dillon." Schlesinger provided cover from the liberal wing of the party, writing to Kennedy on July 17 that it was dangerous to let the public "think that we are abandoning the ancient Democratic faith in the support of demand and are instead trying to fight the stagnation on the old trickle-down theory." That argument was undermined by Schlesinger's friend and fellow liberal, J.K. Galbraith, telling the president that he surprisingly found himself in a "momentary alliance with my [conservative] friends" and urging him "to resist" the cut.[18]

The day after Samuelson's article in the *Financial Times*, Dillon spoke to Kennedy in quietly apocalyptic terms about a meeting of European central bankers in Basel at which US tax cuts had been discussed both formally and informally. "If there is to be a tax cut," he reported, it should be "of a permanent and reform character." The government could not risk "fiscally loose 'bread and circuses'" on the issue. An immediate tax cut, he warned, would leave European bankers facing "increasing internal pressures [to] take precautionary action by increasing their gold holdings." A tax cut could lead the European central banks to convert their dollars to gold, turning the persistent gold crisis into a full-blown emergency. Dillon also sent Kennedy a heavily marked copy of an article by Per Jacobsson, managing director of the IMF, about the dangers of weakening the dollar abroad. Two weeks later, Dillon sent another memo after a meeting with the big banks in New York. "None of the bankers present thought there was any need for a tax cut at this time," he reported. "All of them would strongly oppose such action."[19]

Both sides had laid out the stakes. At the end of July, the Troika submitted a monthly review of economic and budget estimates to the president which openly set out their differences. "Two different economic projections are showing the following tables, one reflecting the view of the Council of Economic Advisers and the other those of the Treasury," they told him, adding that the projections "diverge markedly" for 1963. "The CEA projections show a downturn around the turn of the year whereas the Treasury projections show a continued but moderate advance." Both projections assumed that "no tax legislation or changes in expenditure policy will be undertaken" beyond the administration's existing commitments. In a phrase that leaps from the page, the CEA noted that American business was "likely to hold firm to their conservatism with the economy slowing down." The cards had been dealt. The question for Kennedy was whether to hit or stick. In the days after the report was submitted, it looked as if the answer was hit. "The president has made up his mind for a tax cut," Bell reportedly told deputy national security adviser Carl Kaysen. Neither man realized that the treasury secretary had yet to play his ace.[20]

On August 6, Dillon took Congressman Wilbur Mills, the influential chair of the House Ways and Means Committee, into the Oval Office to talk to the president about the "quickie" tax cut. The relationship between Mills, an Arkansas Democrat, and the Republican Dillon had not always been an easy one. On one occasion, when Stanley Surrey rather than the treasury secretary turned up at a hearing, Mills stormed out, saying it was an affront to the dignity of Congress. Dillon subsequently courted him, so that by the time of this meeting in the Oval Office the two were allies of a kind. Mills told the president that the quickie tax "was a mistake." After holding private hearings with tax experts, he thought the temporary tax cut was half-baked and likely to face opposition in Congress. Moreover, Dillon had shown him the views of European central bankers. "Concern in these central banks" about an "illogical and unwise" move, he advised, playing to Kennedy's fears, would lead to an avalanche of overseas dollar holdings converted to gold. "I think that was the first thing, frankly, that swayed it," Mills said afterwards of the president. By the time the meeting was over, the debate had shifted in Dillon's favor. "Why don't we keep this to ourselves," Kennedy told the two men. "I'll be working on some satisfactory way of putting our case."[21]

That satisfactory way turned out to be a televised address to the nation. Heller and supporters of the "quickie" cut tried to make a last stand in the hours leading up to the broadcast. "The economic case for an immediate rate cut is strong," Samuelson implored the president. "*The boom is tapering off.*" Heller reinforced the point, with no attempt to bury the lede. "A 1962 tax cut: Our last chance," he wrote to Kennedy, adding that "Early action can break this vicious circle, visibly improve the economy in 1963–64 and shrink the Fiscal Year 1964 deficit." The alternative was "No Action now. Issue a reassuring statement." It was a bastardization of Dillon's view, but it made no difference: the president picked it anyway.

On August 13, while Dillon and Heller watched on, Kennedy went on national television, awkwardly surrounded by poster boards of economic data, to give a "report to the American people on the state of the national economy." Identifying "the right kind of tax cut at the right time" as "the most important fiscal weapon available to strengthen the national economy," he promised to present a bill to Congress in 1963 for a permanent "across the board, top to bottom cut in both corporate and personal incomes taxes." Crucially, the bill would include the "long-needed tax reform that logic and equity demand."[22]

Years later, Heller would present the broadcast as "the Council's big victory." Kennedy had "committed to a big tax cut in 1963." In reality, it was a bitter blow. The president had backed Dillon and the Treasury over Heller and the Council. Disappointed by all the clumsy movement between desk and charts, Kennedy graded his own TV performance as a "C minus," but it was also his judgment on Heller and the CEA. "I don't have any confidence in these fellas," he complained to Wilbur Mills in front of Dillon. It was the surest sign that the treasury secretary was winning the battle of economic and financial ideas within the administration. As James Tobin reflected, it was obvious by the middle of 1962 that US policy had become "a statement of what had long been in Dillon's mind."[23]

Chapter Twelve

War Hawk
Washington, Fall, 1962

Belmont Road, NW, October 16, 1962. Douglas Dillon, like John F. Kennedy, always liked to read the major newspapers over breakfast, although unlike the president he did not habitually do so in bed. That morning, whether in bed or at the breakfast table, the headlines did not make comfortable reading for either man. "Eisenhower Calls President Weak on Foreign Policy," the front page of the *New York Times* stated, adding the kicker that "He Sees Setback to U.S." The former president's speech had been delivered in his successor's heartland of Boston. Kennedy's "dreary" foreign policy record, Ike said, was "almost too sad to talk about." For the Republican Dillon, it was an embarrassing intervention. His only consolation was that Eisenhower had not tried to make too much mischief out of his presence in the administration, only referring to him obliquely as the "competent American."[1]

The break with convention as the former president reproved a sitting one was never going to be welcome. When a phone call summoned Dillon to an urgent meeting at the White House, he anticipated an awkward encounter. "I went over and found everybody looking very serious," he recalled. Then "there was described to us the intelligence … that showed that missiles were being planted in Cuba." Thus began the most famous crisis of the Cold War era. Not only would Dillon be involved in how the United States responded to the Soviet missiles, but he would also have to fight a rearguard action to ensure the crisis did not precipitate another uproar in the gold markets. The Missile Crisis brought together the two possibilities that kept Kennedy awake at night – a potential financial and military apocalypse.[2]

When Kennedy's advisers entered the Cabinet Room on October 16, they found him playing with his daughter, Caroline, and teasing her about eating candy. He gave no sign of the unfolding drama that was to come. After watching Caroline scamper away across the lawn, he settled into his seat and surreptitiously reached forward to hit a covert switch installed on the underside of the conference table. The president's brother may have noticed the action. Certainly, he knew about the taping system that would record all the key meetings during the crisis. Although he never confirmed it, the one other person in the room who must have known was Douglas Dillon. As the ultimate head of the secret service, the treasury secretary was given daily reports on matters concerning the president's security. On occasion this meant turning a blind eye to the private ins and outs at the White House that even involved Dillon's daughter, Joan. ("The good President then made the obvious pass which was immediately rebuffed but he did not seem to mind at all," Joan recalled of one such visit to the White House. "In the car, I wondered if CDD would see a report that one of his [secret service] cars had delivered his daughter home in the wee hours of the morning.")[3]

After the Bay of Pigs fiasco, Kennedy had been infuriated by the way his advisers claimed to have given him recommendations that were the opposite of what they said privately to him at the time. He asked Robert Bouck, the secret service agent whose job it was to protect him from electronic surveillance, to install microphones in the Oval Office and the Cabinet Room. "They were amplifying and discriminating microphones," Bouck said. "They contained noise frequency filters and they were particularly sensitive to voice. They also had a low-level built-in amplifier right in the microphone." Only the president could activate them. The recordings were made on a Tandberg system in a room in the basement.[4]

At regular Cabinet meetings, Dillon as treasury secretary sat in the chair immediately to the president's left; for most of the meetings during the Missile Crisis, he would sit directly opposite the president. Whether he knew it or not – and it would have been an astonishing breach of protocol if he had not – Dillon always occupied prime seats that the high-level equipment picked up. Later editors of the tapes, Ernest May and Philip Zelikow, in their review of participants at the meetings, note how Dillon's speaking style was like Kennedy's own, "though the accent is upper-class New York, faintly reminiscent of Franklin Roosevelt." Like Kennedy, Dillon "leaves his sentences unfinished if his meaning is clear; he does not use 10 words where 8 will do; [and] his customary lead-in has no trace of diffidence." His apparently self-deprecating "It seems to *me-e* ..." has about it the implication that it must also seem to be the case "for any rational person." In the days that followed, it was a voice that would ring clear in the debates about how the United States should respond to a crisis whose outcome threatened nuclear war.[5]

At the first meeting on October 16, staff from the National Photographic Interpretation Center (NPIC) and the CIA outlined how aerial photographs had identified what turned out to be sixty medium- and intermediate-range ballistic missiles on the island of Cuba, guarded by around 40,000 Soviet troops. "How long have we got?" Kennedy asked. "We can't tell, can we, how long before it can be fired?" The CIA thought two weeks. The working assumption was that the missiles had nuclear warheads. What remained unknown until decades afterwards was that ninety-eight Soviet tactical nuclear weapons were already in Cuba, with local commanders authorized to use these short-range weapons in the event of an American strike.[6]

After the technical briefing, the meeting turned to the critical question: How should the United States react? Secretary of State Rusk identified two possible courses of action: "One is the quick strike," he explained. The other involved a range of diplomatic actions to clarify for friend and foe alike that "we'll be facing a situation that could well lead to a general war" and "to do it in a way that gives everybody a chance to pull away from it before it gets too hard."

In setting out the terms of the debate, Rusk had anticipated the positions of what would later be termed "the hawks" and "the doves." Everyone in the cabinet room agreed that the missiles had to be removed from Cuba. The question was whether a diplomatic initiative should be tried before a military one. Defense Secretary McNamara said they had a week at most to make the decision before the story leaked.

From the outset, it was clear that Dillon was a hawk.

"Doug, do you have any ...?" Kennedy had asked him after hearing from Rusk and McNamara.

"The only thing I would say," he replied, "is that this alternative course of warning, getting public opinion, and OAS action, and telling people in NATO and everything like that, would appear to me to have the danger of getting us wide out in the open and forcing the Soviets to take a position that if anything was done, they would have to retaliate. Whereas a quick action, with a statement at the same time saying this is all there is to it, might give them a chance to back off and not do anything. Meanwhile, I think that the chance of getting through this thing without a Russian reaction is greater under a quick strike than building the whole thing up to a climax, then going through with what will be a lot of debate on it."

National security advisor McGeorge Bundy, an early hawk, immediately agreed. "I share the secretary of the treasury's feeling," he said, pointing to "the amount of noise we would get from our allies, saying that they can live with Soviet MRBMs, why can't we?" In taking this line, Dillon and Bundy flushed out Rusk, who, having delivered his two approaches in a measured, even-handed way, now panicked at the idea that the air strike option was gaining traction. "If we go with the quick strike," he pointed out, then "you have exposed all of your allies and ourselves to all these great dangers without the slightest consultation, or warning, or preparation."

Dillon doubled down on his hawkishness, asking Kennedy, "What if anything has to be done to be prepared for an eventuality of a Soviet action?" He then answered his own question, saying that it "might be helpful if we could maybe take some general war preparation type action that would show them that we're ready if they want to start anything."

By the end of the meeting, Dillon and the hawks, who included Bobby Kennedy, seemed to have had the better of the arguments. "Maybe we just have to take them out," JFK concluded. When Bundy asked the president "whether we have definitely decided *against* a political track," a rattled Rusk jumped in to say, "We'll develop both tracks." Still, as the members of the security council rose to leave, Kennedy left them in no doubt that the United States needed to be "prepared, almost any day, to take those [missiles] out."[7]

When the advisers gathered again in the cabinet room at 6:30 pm, Kennedy, still leaning toward a surgical strike, unexpectedly found Rusk and McNamara united in opposition to a surprise attack. Rusk still pushed for a diplomatic approach while McNamara outlined the options for a naval blockade as a prelude to negotiations with the Soviets. Dillon was intrigued by the idea of a blockade but scathing about Bundy's diplomatic path. "What is the advantage of the announcement earlier?" he wanted to know. "Because it's to build up sympathy or something for doing it?" A surgical strike would kill two birds with one stone. "You get the simultaneous announcement of what was there [the missiles], and why you struck, with pictures and all – I believe would serve the same purpose," he argued.

After the meeting, Dillon sent Kennedy a forceful memorandum – "hyperbolic," judges the historian, Martin J. Sherwin, who is critical of Dillon throughout the crisis – outlining why he opposed negotiations of any kind with the Soviets. He recommended a blockade if the military could show that it was feasible, but with a recommendation that it should be a prelude to a strike on Cuba. For him, negotiations remained a non-starter. Khrushchev had "initiated a test of our intentions that can determine the future course of world events for many years to come." Dillon was demonstrably not lowering the stakes. His firmly expressed belief was that "the survival of our nation demands the prompt elimination of the offensive weapons now in Cuba."[8]

Rusk and McNamara began to develop diplomatic and military plans for discussion at a special Saturday meeting of the National Security Council on October 20. The president would be making a televised address two days later. Dillon, meanwhile, had problems of his own. These included precautions against a run on the dollar, a sharp fall in the stock market, or heavy withdrawals of gold. Chillingly, they also included being "sure," he recalled, "that all the financial regulations and actions were ready for a real emergency if we should get into a nuclear exchange with the Soviet Union." The general counsel at the Treasury, Robert Knight, whom Dillon had known both as a Wall Street lawyer and as an official during the Eisenhower administration, had just returned to private practice a few weeks earlier. Paul Volcker, later chair of the Federal Reserve, who was working for Robert Roosa at the time, remembers Knight as someone who "exuded experience, calmness and good judgment" – in other words just the kind of person Dillon needed during a crisis of this magnitude. Dillon now quietly recalled him to the Treasury and ordered him to draw up "whatever controls might be necessary" in the event of a nuclear war.[9]

Dillon's second problem was logistical. On the very day that Kennedy was due to reveal to the world that there were missiles in Cuba, the treasury secretary would be in Mexico City for a conference of finance ministers from the Organization of American States. Urgent discussions took place at the White House about whether he should still attend. In the end, it was decided that he had to go "as part of the cover for the president's speech on Monday the 22nd so it wouldn't look as if anything unusual was taking place." However, it was agreed that Dillon would put off his departure until Sunday night to participate in the urgent discussions over the weekend, and then cut short his trip after Kennedy had made the TV address.[10]

Frustratingly for historians, the meeting of the National Security Council on October 20 took place not in the Cabinet Room, but in the more private Oval Room of the Executive Mansion. As a result, no microphones picked up what even the dry minutes made clear was an extraordinarily tense and contentious meeting.

"Gentlemen, today we're going to earn our pay," Kennedy told his assembled advisers. Over the next two hours and forty minutes everyone was expected to make their views plain. Kennedy "sharply rejected" some ideas, not least those of UN ambassador Adlai Stevenson who suggested that "we offer the

Russians a settlement" including evacuation from the US naval base at Guantanamo Bay in southeast Cuba. At the other extreme were General Maxwell Taylor, chairman of the joint chiefs of staff, and McGeorge Bundy, advocating for an airstrike the following Tuesday. Taylor did not rule out using nuclear weapons. "Now was the time to act," he warned, because "this would be the last chance we would have to destroy these missiles."

McNamara outlined what he called the "blockade route." Instituting a blockade ("quarantine," Rusk suggested) around the island would prevent the Soviets from getting any additional material into Cuba and allow time for the United States "to negotiate for the removal of the [American] strategic missiles from Turkey and Italy and possibly agreement to limit our use of Guantanamo to a specified limited time." He opposed as "too risky" the suggestion that "we should issue an ultimatum to the effect that we would order an air attack on Cuba if the missiles were not removed."[11]

"Afterward, McNamara recalled in some detail the arguments that he had made at this meeting for and against a blockade," May and Zelikow note, "but he appeared to have no recollection of taking this Stevenson-like position regarding possible negotiations with the Soviets."

Dillon, however, did notice. Speaking in coordinated fashion with Robert Kennedy and the director of central intelligence, John McCone, they eviscerated McNamara. Speaking last of the three, Dillon outlined how "the existence of strategic missiles in Cuba was, in his opinion, not negotiable." If the missiles were not removed or eliminated, the United States would "lose all of its friends in Latin America, who will become convinced that our fear is such that we cannot act." He admitted that the limited use of force involved in a blockade would make "the military task much harder and would involve the great danger of the launching of these missiles by the Cubans." Yet he remained adamant that "any effort to negotiate the removal of the missiles would involve a price so high that the United States could not accept it."[12]

A stunned silence fell over the room. "Awkward," Sorensen recalled. McNamara seemed momentarily unable to speak. It was left to his deputy Roswell Gilpatric, who rarely contributed to meetings when his boss was present, to emphasize the point of agreement between McNamara and Dillon. "Essentially, Mr. President," he said, "this is a choice between limited action and unlimited action; and most of us think it is better to begin with limited action." It enabled Kennedy to back the idea of a "quarantine" while demanding that the Soviets remove the missiles. Crucially, Kennedy indicated that it would be an air strike that was held in reserve, not negotiations on American missiles or bases – in other words, May and Zelikow note, "the option pressed by Dillon and McCone with backing from Robert Kennedy." Having won the point, the two advisers immediately encouraged Bobby to follow his brother out onto the Truman balcony to secure the advantage and make sure that it was articulated in the speech to the nation.[13]

Just as with the tax cut in August 1962, this meeting of the National Security Council illustrates how skillfully Dillon built and deployed his political alliances. On Cuba, he had been an early advocate of a preventative military strike, but then adapted his views sufficiently to jibe with McCone and Bobby Kennedy. He co-opted the quarantine idea while keeping the military option as his designated fallback.

This position was not simply tactical for Dillon. There was also an ethical aspect that he had found persuasive, remembering the moral revulsion that had swept the United States when Japan launched a surprise attack on Pearl Harbor in 1941. "I thought there was enough validity to that point of view, so I changed my mind," he recalled. But he did so without relinquishing his view about the need "for military action ... relatively rapidly if the missiles were not removed."[14]

On Sunday, October 21, having signed off on the final text of the president's speech, Dillon took a late flight on a military air transport jet to Mexico City for the one-year review of the Alliance for Progress. A delicate period followed during which Dillon had to keep what he knew to himself. After the president's televised address to the nation the next evening, he immediately began an intensive round of lobbying to win support for a resolution at the Organization of American States in Washington to authorize the quarantine around Cuba.[15]

The next day Dillon asked to speak first at the conference, rising to do so before even the introductory remarks had been made, explaining that having been recalled to Washington by the president, he had to leave promptly. Ashen-faced delegates listened in silence as he repeated Kennedy's warnings from the previous night that the buildup of offensive weapons in Cuba would not "be accepted by the United States." It was, he said, "a direct challenge to the entire Hemisphere and one that must be met and turned back."

An audible shifting and stirring crossed the room as Dillon observed that the Organization of American States was considering the invocation of Article 8 of the Rio treaty. Article 8 granted authority for hemispheric action just short of war. When the delegate from Brazil protested, Dillon dealt with him "bluntly," reported the New York Times, and the other delegates shouted the offender down. Dillon had "sought to put new heart" into the conference, the paper reported, and "he appeared to have succeeded." The State Department told Kennedy that Dillon provided "a tangible unifying effect."[16]

Immediately after his speech, Dillon returned to Washington. To his frustration, confusion about his departure time and the rapid deployment of air transport jets in the new crisis meant that the only available plane was a propeller-driven Lockheed Constellation, which took ten hours rather than the five hours on a jet. He would reach the capital only in the late hours. As Dillon's plane made its stately way across the Gulf of Mexico, it would have passed over US naval ships preparing to enforce the quarantine. For this brief period, Dillon was the most senior cabinet member in physical proximity to Cuba itself. The flight gave him time to clarify his thoughts on the crisis to come. "My own feeling was that the Soviets would eventually probably back down," he recalled. "Only I was never sure that this would happen short of the actual use of military force by the United States."[17]

By the time Dillon returned to the White House on Wednesday, October 24, he had become a member of the new executive committee of the National Security Council (ExCom) that Kennedy had secretly established in National Security Action Memorandum 196. Along with McCone, he figuratively represented the Eisenhower Republicans on a committee that the president had framed to give him the widest possible political support and advice. When they met at ten that morning, just as the quarantine officially came into effect, Dillon could take some satisfaction at having played his part in delivering the OAS vote that gave the United States a legal foundation for the action. "The official world reaction showed a generally favorable response to the US action, particularly in Latin America," McCone reported. The United States now stood at DEFCON2 – the second-highest alert state of defense readiness. "Never before had US strategic forces been put on that level of alert," Serhii Plokhy points out. "The fleet of 1,479 bombers and 182 ballistic missiles, with 2,962 nuclear warheads at their disposal, was getting ready to strike targets in the Soviet Union." Bobby Kennedy thought he had never seen the president so tense. "His hand went up to his face and covered his mouth and he closed his fist," Bobby recalled. "His eyes were tense, almost gray, and we just stared at each other across the table. Was the world on the brink of a holocaust?"[18]

Over the next twenty-five minutes, the executive committee debated what to do as Soviet ships, protected by Soviet submarines, moved inexorably towards the quarantine line. Before they debated options, Dillon raised an urgent point about homeland security. As treasury secretary, he was also head of the US Coast Guard. To facilitate naval intelligence on Soviet ships, the coast guard had "lifted up" surveillance black boxes for CIA use. "As a result, we're out of them," Dillon warned, "and we're not in a position to carry out our port security." Only after Kennedy had urged McCone to "do your part" to ensure there would be "enough for additional responsibility" did the conversation move back to the quarantine line. As the ExCom laid out military options, with McNamara pressing for an attack on Soviet submarines (not knowing some carried nuclear-tipped torpedoes), McCone received a note about ship movements. Baffled by its lack of clarity, he left the meeting to find out more. When he returned, he was uncharacteristically flustered and told officials to find him a map of Cuba. Where exactly was the quarantine line? he wanted to know. Kennedy pressed him to know what was happening. "What do they say they're doing with those [ships], John?" he demanded. "Well," McCone replied, "they either stopped them or reversed direction." Rusk then delivered his famous line: "We are eyeball to eyeball and I think the other fellow just blinked."[19]

Dillon reacted to this promising turn of events with quiet satisfaction. "Relief and a certain amount of pleasure," he recalled. "It was clear we didn't think this meant the end of anything. We thought it did mean that the Soviets had not foreseen the strength of our reaction and were confused as to what they should do. That indicated to us that they did not have any plan to push this incident, come what may, to the utmost. It strengthened the views of those of us, which I think was always the majority, that felt that a firm position by the United States, if maintained, would eventually bring about the removal of the missiles. So, we felt we were on the right track."[20]

The quarantine was working, but it did not solve the problem of removing the missiles already in Cuba. Attention moved to the United Nations, where Ambassador Stevenson confronted his Soviet counterpart, Valerian Zorin. Dillon faced another immediate problem. The president's national TV address had provoked a considerable run on the price of gold, with a three-day run on the London gold market that amounted to a $60 million loss. Crucially, Dillon told the ExCom, the "Gold Pool" system put in place the previous year ensured "an orderly market" to prevent a crisis for the dollar.

Even if the system was working, Dillon also had to report an alarming development involving the French. On October 24, while the superpowers were still "eyeball to eyeball," the governor of the Bank of France, Jacques Brunet, had phoned Alfred Hayes, the president of the New York Fed, to tell him that France intended pulling out of the gold consortium. The run on gold, Brunet said, was "clearly due to US action" over Cuba. Dillon was incandescent when informed, writing to Kennedy directly to ask for approval to read the French the riot act. "Withdrawal from the consortium under such circumstances would indicate a lack of solidarity in the face of the Soviet threat," he told the unfortunate Brunet. "The United States is surprised and seriously concerned that such a course of action would be seriously considered by the French Government." France quickly backed down. Dillon had successfully shelved the issue for the duration of the Missile Crisis, but the incident marked the beginning of a rapid deterioration of relations between the two nations on gold and the balance of payments crisis.[21]

Even with Dillon's interventions, the Missile Crisis had a destabilizing effect on the American economic position. For the month in which the crisis took place, the recorded outflow of gold from the Treasury stock was $90 million, which reduced the overall gold stock below $16 billion – its lowest rate since 1939. Problems with gold were compounded by what Dillon told Kennedy was "a difficult and dangerous situation" in the exchange markets, as funds hemorrhaged out of New York to London. Treasury ninety-day bill rates fell precipitously, forcing Dillon to announce the sale of an additional $1 billion in bills to increase the supply and force a mark-up. He also made informal overtures to the Bank of England "who are concerned at the situation and have told me that they think they can also be helpful on their side." It was an important piece of cooperation, because by reducing the spread between British and US Treasury bills "the danger of substantial outflows" was averted.[22]

With Dillon firefighting on the economy, he told the ExCom meeting on October 25 that the extreme disruptions in the markets "reflected the fear of the buyers." Bringing the crisis to a speedy conclusion was an imperative for economic stability.[23]

As the members of the executive committee gathered for the 10 a.m. daily meeting on Friday, October 26, they did so with a dawning recognition about the paradoxical nature of their strategy so far. That morning the United States had enforced the quarantine when crew from the USS *Joseph P. Kennedy Jr.* – a naval destroyer named for the president's late brother and on which Robert Kennedy had served in 1946 – boarded a freighter bound for Cuba and found nothing that contravened the blockade. The quarantine was working, but it had not solved the bigger problem of the missiles in Cuba that were "pointed," John McCone noted melodramatically, "at our heart."

By now Kennedy had concluded that he had only two days left to find a political solution. Rusk and the State Department, including Walt Rostow, laid out a case for bargaining followed by sanctions. The acting secretary-general of the United Nations, U Thant, was already engaged in peace efforts. "I think there would be some advantage in having a real shot at the U Thant talks for 24 hours," Rusk told the meeting, adding that if they failed, the United States would then move to expand the blockade to include petroleum, oil, and lubricants (POL). "The regime and the populace would be faced with the prospect of total economic collapse," he argued.[24]

Dillon intervened immediately to offer one of his longest ExCom statements of the entire crisis. The tapes reveal his voice as calm and controlled even as the substance of what he said was hair-raising. "If we follow this track, we'll be sort of caught up in events not of our own control," he argued, and "might wind up in some sort of naval encounter all around the world with the Soviet Union which would have *nothing* to do with the buildup of the missile bases in Cuba." The strategy increased the danger of a "confrontation directly with the Soviet Union at sea," he warned, and could even bring about "a possible general war." A hush came over the usually noisy room as he cautioned everyone not to lose sight of the real matter at hand. If there had to be "escalation," then the United States should be "preparing for air action to hit these bases" rather than "a confrontation of the US-USSR at sea." Rusk, Bundy, McNamara, and others all attempted to jump in, but Dillon waved them off, forcefully making the point that it was this choice that represented the "major decision" of the entire crisis. Bundy did concede the point at the end of the meeting: "We have a double choice, Mr. President, unless we propose to do nothing," he summed up. "One is to expand the blockade and the other is to remove the missiles by force." Kennedy agreed and asked for a presentation the next day on the pros and cons of air action. "I'd like to have us take a look," Kennedy said. A study group chaired by Dillon would prepare a paper for the meeting. Back at the State Department afterwards, a gloomy George Ball told aides, "Unless we can return to a political arrangement, we will all fry."[25]

That view was not one that Dillon accepted. In the first few hours of the crisis on October 16, he had been "frightened to death" at the prospect of a nuclear war. By day two, however, the National Security Council had seen a briefing that laid out the relative disposition of the nuclear forces available to the United States and the Soviet Union. Once Dillon had seen the figures – roughly 10 to 1, the State Department's Raymond Gartoff estimated – Dillon concluded that the Soviet could not go head-to-head with the United States because it would lose in any nuclear exchange. "Once they respond," he said, "they are going to face the nuclear quotient." His friend Paul Nitze, who as assistant secretary of the navy attended ExCom meetings, admired the detachment of Dillon's analysis. "That's when you get really rational," he recalled. "That's when you really get cold, when there is a real danger. And you can't let prejudices, stupid things get in your way. You've got to be cold, objective."

In essence, the Republican Dillon embraced the strategy of deterrence and "massive retaliation" that had been set down by Eisenhower and Dulles in the 1950s as part of the "New Look." That strategy had been established for essentially political purposes, Michael Mandelbaum notes, to answer "questions that the atomic age had pressed upon the [American government]: What political purposes would atomic weapons serve? And how should they be deployed to serve these purposes?" The answer was essentially "prevention by threat," or "the strategy of the hedgehog, who bares his bristles to keep other animals away." In 1962, Dillon pressed to apply those political calculations in this most dangerous of political situations. He determined that it would make the balance of danger worse if the Soviets had missiles with nuclear warheads in Cuba off the Southeastern United States. Rostow judged that Dillon "thought they represented, as I did, an attempt, undertaken by subterfuge, to change the nuclear balance of power in an instant in our own backyard. He thought we could not tolerate this." By Friday, October 26, Dillon and the more hawkish members of ExCom believed that Kennedy shared their analysis. "But then he [JFK] got flabby on it," Nitze said.[26]

The next morning – "the most important day, October 27," Bundy said afterwards – the executive committee gathered with Dillon's "Scenario for Airstrike against Offensive Missile Bases and Bombers in Cuba" paper on the table. It outlined advantages, leading with the statement that it "carries out the president's pledge to eliminate the offensive threat to the US and hemisphere from Cuba and avoids any erosion of US momentum and position. The pledge carried out shows that the US has the will to fight and to protect vital interests (of great importance vis-a-vis Berlin)." Additionally, a one-time action might carry fewer risks of escalation. Further, it signaled that the US was not prepared to bargain bases in Cuba for positions in other parts of the world. In this way, Khrushchev would be denied a "cheap victory." On the opposite side of the ledger, there was the possibility that the action might force Khrushchev to react, leading to war, that the use of force might seem disproportionate against a small country, and presciently, "the remote possibility that some local Soviet commander in Cuba may order firing of a missile."[27]

The context for this discussion of options changed almost minute by minute. Overnight, Khrushchev had sent the president a rambling, emotional private letter saying, "let us not quarrel now," and offering to withdraw the missiles from Cuba in exchange for a promise not to invade Cuba. Then, during the 10 a.m. ExCom meeting, another letter from Khrushchev was brought in that was more belligerent in tone and offered a swap – Soviet missiles in Cuba for American ones in Turkey. Right away, former ambassador to the Soviet Union, Llewellyn "Tommy" Thompson, identified the first letter as having been written by Khrushchev himself while the politburo generated the second letter.

Dillon was alert to the implications included in the second letter, which he believed threatened the basis of the entire Western alliance. "[There] might be a very dangerous sentence in this thing that no one has particularly mentioned, but it's a thing I've been afraid of all along in the Cuban trade," he said directly to the president. "Where he says: How are we to react when you have surrounded our country with bases about which your military speak 'demonstratively.' That will affect our whole base system." Kennedy tried to brush it off, saying it only meant Turkey, and believing Khrushchev had made "a pretty good play." Nitze (who always "spoke more directly than do most people when they talk to presidents," notes Kennedy biographer Richard Reeves) shook his head and came close to rebuking him. "That looks like a rationalization of our own confusion," he said. "I think we've got to take a firmer line than that."

Kennedy seemed less sure of himself than at any point in the crisis, but "the sense of the group," according to the formal minute of the meeting, "was that the door should be closed as quickly as possible on the idea of trading the U.S. position in Turkey for the Soviet position in Cuba." Kennedy remained despondent. "What we're going to be faced with is – because we wouldn't take the missiles out of Turkey – then maybe we'll have to invade or make a massive strike on Cuba," he complained. "Let's not kid ourselves. Today it sounds great to reject it, but it's not going to, after we do something."[28]

The pressing point came a few hours later. An afternoon meeting of ExCom was interrupted by news that an American U-2 reconnaissance plane had been shot down while photographing over Cuba. In a tragic irony, the dead pilot, Major Rudolf Anderson, was the very pilot who had taken the photographs that had revealed the missiles for the first time. Over the course of a three-and-a-half-hour marathon meeting, the president's advisers debated what to do next as Kennedy shuttled in and out of the cabinet room. Vice President Lyndon Johnson, who had been mostly silent throughout the crisis, asked why the United States was not prepared to trade the withdrawal of US missiles from Turkey for the withdrawal of the Soviet missiles from Cuba. George Ball urged accepting the Soviet offer and replacing the missiles in Turkey "by assigning Polaris submarines to the area."

Dillon remained resolute that the time had come for a military strike. At the end of the meeting, with support from Ambassador Thompson, he put the case in the clearest possible fashion. The two men had been aligned from the outset as the first advocates of linking a blockade to an ultimatum to remove the missiles. Now they took the strategy to the next level. "Instead of the ultimatum, a lot of talk about 'if you shoot any more of our unarmed planes,' [it] would probably be more effective, and make more impression on him [Khrushchev], if we did do what we said we were going to do before and go in and knock out just one SAM [surface-to-air missile] site," Dillon argued. "Don't say anything. Just do that." Still Kennedy demurred, talking of his fear of escalation and the cost in "toil and blood … when we could have gotten them [the missiles] out by making a deal on the same missiles in Turkey."[29]

What Dillon did not know was that the president was dissembling, as he had already begun secret diplomacy to strike a deal with the Soviets to exchange Cuban missiles for Turkish ones. At the end of the afternoon ExCom meeting, with another due at 9 p.m., Kennedy called some of his advisers, including his brother, Rusk, Bundy, and McNamara, into a huddle in the Oval Office to discuss how it could be done. The president wanted Bobby to speak directly to Soviet ambassador Anatoly Dobrynin to negotiate a missile swap. How to do it remained an open question. In the end, it was Rusk who came up with the proposal for a secret deal that would see American missiles coming out of Turkey a few months after the resolution of the Cuban crisis. As a backup plan, Kennedy instructed Rusk to pass a message to U Thant, asking him to call on the United States to withdraw the Jupiter missiles in Turkey. Everyone in the room understood the risk they were taking with a secret deal, relying as it did on Soviet discretion. "Concerned as we all were by the cost of a public bargain struck under pressure at the apparent expense of the Turks," Bundy recalled, "and aware as we were from the day's discussions that for some, even in our closest councils, even this unilateral private assurance might appear to betray an ally, we agreed without hesitation that none not in the room was to be informed of the additional message."[30]

Among those "not in the room" was Douglas Dillon, along with Vice President Johnson, CIA director McCone, and chairman of the joint chiefs Maxwell Taylor. "Shockingly, it would be kept secret from the rest of ExCom," Serhii Plokhy writes, judging that this was a "conspiracy." That assessment somewhat overstates the case. The members of the executive committee were advisers assembled by the president at a moment of international crisis. The committee was his to use as he saw fit. However, the political realities were more complex. After Robert Kennedy returned from conveying his message to Dobrynin, the executive committee gathered again to continue discussing options, with most still in the dark about the secret diplomacy that was taking place. Dillon had surely been excluded from the conversations because he had made clear his opposition to any bartering of weapons. By that Saturday evening, there was still no word on whether the Soviets would accept the missile swap deal. If it failed, an exchange between McNamara and Dillon made clear that the situation between the two superpowers could be expected to escalate quickly. McNamara said they needed to be "*damned* sure" the Soviets understood what they were letting themselves in for if they did not back down. "I would suggest that it will be an eye for an eye," McNamara said. "That's the mission," Dillon replied tersely. It was to be his last recorded comment during the crisis.[31]

The next morning, Sunday, October 28, just as Kennedy was preparing to leave for mass at Saint Stephen Martyr Catholic Church, word came from Khrushchev that he had accepted the deal. "I feel like a new man," Kennedy told his longtime body man Dave Powers. "Do you realize that we had an airstrike all arranged for Tuesday? Thank God it's over."

As the executive committee gathered at eleven o'clock that morning, there was a giddy excitement in the air. Rusk gave a general report on how the crisis had been averted. Bundy impatiently interrupted him to gloat that "everyone knows who were hawks and who were doves, but today is the doves' day." Kennedy, however, remained aloof. "Not once during this final meeting did the president join in the general spirit of triumph," Press Secretary Pierre Salinger remembered. Sorensen recalled someone in the room remarking Kennedy would be "ten feet tall" on the world stage now, but the president brushed it off, saying, "That will wear off in about a week." Perhaps most tellingly of all, Kennedy switched on the tapes when he entered the room but then thought better of it, turning them off once the compliments started flowing. Was it a guilty conscience? While he had just about been within his constitutional rights as commander in chief to conduct secret diplomacy with the Soviets, it had also involved deceiving many of those advisers in the room that morning, including Dillon.[32]

The treasury secretary was not caught on tape or mentioned in the minutes of the meeting that day, but he later described how he was "individually very relieved and pleased" at the resolution of the crisis. Despite the bumptious comment of McGeorge Bundy, the hawkish Dillon had every reason for believing that he had been right. The threat of overwhelming force had compelled the Soviets to remove the missiles from Cuba. "We had prevailed," he recalled, "and the missiles and other offensive arms were going to be removed from Cuba." Looking back two years later, he reflected on the most important turning point in the crisis. On Saturday, October 27, Khrushchev "took the impossible position of linking Cuban missiles to our bases in Turkey," he said. "This was obviously utterly unacceptable and I think the president was annoyed by the change, by the feeling that this looked like it might mean that, after all our efforts, the Russians were going to force us to use our military power to throw them out of Cuba. The President didn't want to have to do this, but I am sure he was prepared to do it if necessary." Asked why a missile swap was unacceptable and about reports that some on the ExCom had wanted to make the swap, Dillon doubled down. "If there were any that were in favor of this, they were such a small minority that it never was seriously debated or considered for a minute," he said, "because Turkey was part of NATO."

The lesson of the Missile Crisis for Dillon had been the efficacy of deterrence. "It was caused by Soviet provocation and the US very clearly stood up to it and said that if this is what you want, we are ready for you," Dillon concluded in 1964. "The Soviet Union, not being ready for that, pulled back, which is, of course, in accord with basic Communist doctrine which has always been to press as far ahead as they can and when they meet a stone wall to pull back for a while, regroup, and try again in some other way." Here was as simple a statement of the American strategy of containment as you could wish for from a major politician in the administration.[33]

Decades later, when the secret diplomacy with the Soviets about missiles in Turkey became public knowledge, many of the ExCom hawks were contemptuous of the action. Paul Nitze, who had agreed with Dillon that American nuclear superiority meant the Soviets would never dare go toe-to-toe during the crisis, was scathing about the likes of Robert Kennedy, McNamara, Sorensen, Ball, and Gilpatric "whose knees were knocking together with the greatest fear." Theirs was a reckless act that threatened the fabric of the NATO alliance. If it had leaked out that the missiles were removed "under threat," how would NATO members "have any confidence that we're going to stand by them if the Russians get cross with them?" They staked the Western alliance on a game of pitch and toss that the Soviets were "not supposed to blab."[34]

Dillon was more measured in his reassessment in the 1990s, but the essentials were the same. He had been used to receiving the annual presentation from the military during the Eisenhower administration about what a nuclear war would look like. When a similar presentation was made to the new administration, "it absolutely shocked the gizzards out of McNamara and also out of the president about how terrible [it was]." Dillon felt this badly affected McNamara's judgment during the Missile Crisis, "where I thought he was overly afraid." It was also why Dillon believed the president tipped the balance from the hawks to the doves during the crisis, leading to the Jupiter missile swap. "He was really afraid of nuclear war starting," Dillon concluded, "At the time of the Missile Crisis, it never occurred to me that it would start, that the Russians would initiate a nuclear exchange with this sort of difference [in nuclear weapons capability]. But I think the president was very much influenced by that and he was more afraid, more believed that they might."[35]

Given that Dillon had been a hawk during the crisis, he might have expected it to have an impact on his relationship with Kennedy and influence within the administration. In fact, the opposite occurred. Kennedy may not have discussed the Turkish missile swap with him, but once the crisis was over, the president drew Dillon even closer into his inner circle. Rostow believed this continued trust had to do with Dillon's essential integrity. "Doug Dillon is one of the few ExCom members (and I do not want to get into those who have not been consistent) who took a consistent line throughout the crisis and since the crisis," he judged. "He has not tried to cater his position and advice to the mood of the moment … He counseled, calmly and without any kind of militaristic eagerness, the necessity of removing the missiles from Cuba, by military intervention if necessary, before they became operational."

Understanding his proper role as an adviser, Rostow thought, was "one of the characteristics of Doug Dillon. He says what he thinks and does not package it based upon what is, or what he thinks, is popular." It meant that once the crisis was over, when as Kennedy wearily noted "everyone will get back to thinking of their own interests," Dillon retained his place as a key player.[36]

Chapter Thirteen

The Art of the Dillonbluster

Washington, Winter 1962 – Summer 1963

A week after the Missile Crisis ended, President Kennedy wrote to his treasury secretary to find out what the cost of the confrontation had been to the United States gold reserves – and more importantly, to see how much worse everything might have been. "What would have happened if the crisis had been more pronounced?" he wanted to know that November. Dillon replied quickly and positively. "It is my feeling that our present arrangements in international monetary policy met the test of the Cuban crisis with flying colors," he reported. "There were no crisis-induced withdrawals of gold whatsoever." The only visible effect had been a brief run on the London gold market after news of the missiles in Cuba broke, but this had been "entirely understandable in view of the serious situation." The United States had used Federal Reserve swaps and Treasury forward exchange operations to mop up excess dollars in the global markets and fend off any extra demand for gold, including from the French. Most Western countries, particularly the United Kingdom, had been "reasonably cooperative" during the crisis.

It was "more difficult to answer" what would have happened in the case of military action. Any confrontation, "even though nuclear weapons were not involved," still might have "necessitated worldwide action in the form of exchange controls such as might be expected in time of major war." Dillon was at pains to point out that "short of such a situation I think our present arrangements have proved out remarkably well."[1]

It was an upbeat answer born at least partly out of political necessity. Dillon had spent the previous eighteen months putting together these "present arrangements" on an issue that was a priority for the president. For Kennedy, solving the gold crisis was central to his entire project. "He knew that if this was not properly handled, everything else he wanted to do," Dillon noted,

"both abroad to make peace and to protect the peace and promote development, and at home in the way of reducing unemployment and helping
us to grow faster, could be brought to naught by a failure in this one area." It
was the reason Dillon had been put in the administration in the first place.
Now, he could claim some initial success. An offset agreement with Germany
to the tune of around $650 million a year helped ensure that US dollars spent
in West Germany on European defense would be "offset" by West German
spending on American military equipment. Robust new cooperative agreements with European central banks were in place to defend the dollar during
any aggressive run on gold. Increased presidential powers to negotiate reciprocal tariff reductions were about to come on track through the Trade
Expansion Act of 1962, which in turn would facilitate a sixth iteration – the
"Kennedy Round" to follow the "Dillon Round" – of ambitious multilateral
negotiations for the General Agreement on Tariffs and Trade (GATT). Even
tax policy had been sent into action, with Dillon's 7 percent investment credit
designed to give the United States better products to sell abroad and shore up
its competitive position in the world. "All of these operations add up to a
significant accomplishment," Dillon reassured Kennedy.[2]

However, this confidence was becoming increasingly difficult to sustain.
Since the summer of 1962, Dillon had been starting to look like the little boy
with his finger in the sea-dyke. "Gold kept flowing out," noted the financial
journalists Gordon L. Weil and Ian R. Davidson. "The disastrous drain of
American gold, which was seen in Washington as a drain on American prestige,
became increasingly embarrassing to the administration." The overall balance
of payments continued to deteriorate. Outflows of capital used for buying
overseas stocks and bonds escalated dramatically. The United States could
have tightened credit and driven up interest rates, but that action risked
bringing the economic recovery at home grinding to a halt. As the crisis
continued to build, Dillon found others in the administration muscling onto
his territory, not least the State Department's George Ball, who demanded "a
fresh approach to the Gold Problem."[3]

Ball was in many ways the mirror image of Dillon. Where Dillon was an
east coast patrician, outwardly cool and controlled, but in his own steely
fashion used to getting his way, the Midwesterner Ball was a gruff, argumentative iconoclast, often described by others as "imaginative" but "crazy as hell"
and by himself as the "champion of lost causes." Even the two men's choice of
Savile Row tailors (de rigueur, it seems, for members of the Kennedy administration) stood in contrast. While Dillon favored the conservative and

highly structured style of Henry Poole & Co, Ball sported the soft shoulders and slightly disheveled look of Anderson and Shepard. *Le style, c'est l'homme.*[4]

During the 1950s, Ball had worked for and been deeply influenced by Jean Monnet, the architect of the European Economic Community, and was as passionate an advocate of European integration as the "father of Europe" himself. He advised Kennedy on European policy during the 1960 campaign and, despite being a disciple of Adlai Stevenson, got his reward with an appointment as undersecretary of state. Thereafter, Ball said, Rusk designated him "the one who effectively made American policy with regard to Europe and the Common Market."[5]

By 1962, Ball had come to see Dillon and the Treasury as a roadblock to better relations with the countries of the European Community, particularly France. A series of caustic and destabilizing meetings with the government of Charles de Gaulle had taken place over the summer of 1962. These culminated at the White House when Kennedy bluntly informed French ministers that if France wanted a competitive rather than cooperative relationship, he would gladly pull American troops out of Europe, which would "just about meet our balance of payments deficit." When the finance minister Valéry Giscard d'Estaing obliquely hinted that the weak dollar would be helpless without French cooperation, Kennedy issued new threats. As even the unflappable Giscard told Ball afterwards, "the strong determination voiced to him by the president" was a shock.

An alarmed Ball called for a change of direction, accusing Dillon and the Treasury Department of failing to understand the crux of the issue was political. Ball believed Dillon worried too much about what European central bankers thought, without understanding that it was European politicians who held the key. He recalled being "unhappy about what seemed to me to be the very orthodox position that the treasury was taking" and criticized Dillon for "thinking in terms always of trying to satisfy the speculators and central bankers and not necessarily getting down to the hard problem we faced." Ball now advocated for a complete overhaul of the Bretton Woods system to facilitate a burden sharing – "multilateralizing" – of international liquidity to address the gold crisis. Negotiations would be conducted at the highest level to get "firm political commitments," interim at first, to achieve eventual equilibrium in the US balance of payments. Foreign allies would be asked to give the United States long-term loans to fund the payments deficit. Making this point, he reflected, meant "I got into a rather caustic series of exchanges with Dillon."[6]

If Ball thought that Dillon was not paying attention to the politics of the situation, he was wrong. Because Ball was only an undersecretary, Dillon had his deputy, Henry H. Fowler, write a rebuttal that took his opposite number at State's argument apart point by point. The language dispensed with the usual politesse of such memos. "Mr. Ball's proposed negotiating program deals with the symptom – outflow of US gold – rather than the disease – a continuing US imbalance of payments," Fowler wrote. "Moreover, the program suggested by Mr. Ball carries with it several grave risks, none of which the United States can afford to undertake." With a sideswipe at Ball's "firm political commitments" line, Fowler agreed that there should be high-level negotiations, but in an underlined passage etched with sarcasm, he added that there should be *"some firm political commitments ... having to do with actual substantive burden sharing."*

Dillon sent the note to Kennedy with a tart covering note. "I have some concern that the State Department interest," he wrote, "reflects a reluctance to squarely tackle the more difficult but fundamentally necessary job of obtaining a more adequate sharing of the burden by our European friends." In private, he thought Ball's plan was naive. "It did not really take account of the facts of the world today," he told Seymour Harris. "We simply could not give them the entire job of financing our balance of payments deficit more or less ad infinitum!"[7]

No disagreement about monetary or fiscal policy within the administration would have been complete without Walter Heller opposing Dillon. Two days after Dillon's memo to the president, Heller wrote to Kennedy in support of Ball's plan. "Our best efforts to reduce balance of payments deficits and gold losses have not succeeded in sustaining confidence," he told the president. Dillon had no strategy and had been proceeding on a "secret, day-to-day, piecemeal, ad hoc basis." The dollar and gold reserves had become subject to the "whims and prejudices of currency speculators and bankers." As a result, "the U.S. Government is not master in its own house."[8]

The conflict among his top advisers again left Kennedy without a clear path. On August 20, he called everyone together at the White House for a meeting that produced heat but little light. Unable to pick between the two sides, Kennedy played for time. He ordered a fact-finding mission, led by John Leddy from the Treasury and G. Griffith Johnson from State, to take "soundings with the French and others." That trip would be an embarrassment for the two institutional rivals, whose mistrust of each other was only outdone by that of French and British officials towards them. Leddy and Johnson reported back in September that the two countries seemed to be cooking up something between themselves, but what it was they had no clue. "The whole affair was mysterious," they noted lamely.[9]

The Missile Crisis the following month had put the issue on pause, but it did not remain there for long. As 1962 ticked over into 1963, the treasury secretary had the unwelcome task of writing to the president with figures for gold transactions the previous calendar year. They did not make for happy reading. "The total US gold stock declined by $890 million during 1962," Dillon told him, "as compared to a decline of approximately $857 million during 1961." Not only had the administration failed to reverse the outflow, but the situation had actually worsened. A week later, he sent a memo to Kennedy under the heading "Prospective Gold Losses" that was even bleaker. "We must expect further substantial gold losses over the next few months," he warned, pointing to the "certainty of such losses" and even the possibility that "any renewal of uncertainties and fears" could make things worse than predicted. "Meanwhile," he reported, "foreign countries that are gaining dollars over and above working balances or normal holdings are planning to take gold from us."[10]

For a president facing reelection in 1964, the memo could hardly have been worse. "I am concerned about the figures that you sent me on the gold drain for 1963," Kennedy wrote back. "Won't this bring us in January 1964 to a critically low point?" he asked. "What are the prospects that we could bring this under control by 1964?"[11]

In early 1963, a series of strategic plays by de Gaulle to move France out of the orbit of the Atlantic alliance introduced more complications. First, the French president rejected as "just words" Kennedy's offer (mangled in translation by George Ball) to supply the Polaris submarine-based nuclear weapon system to France, including for independent use if "supreme national interests" were at stake. To be dependent on American weapons technology, de Gaulle said, was to be an American client state. Second, he vetoed Britain's application to join the European Economic Community on the grounds that the UK was a Trojan Horse sent by the Americans to transform the EEC into "a colossal Atlantic community under American dependence and direction." Finally, de Gaulle signed a formal Franco-German treaty that, his biographer Julian Jackson notes, had "a potentially anti-American complexion." No wonder the French ambassador in Washington, Hervé Alphand, reported that "the Americans have the impression that the edifice of their foreign policy is collapsing."[12]

Kennedy was so concerned with the turn of events that he convened a meeting of ExCom to discuss the matter. "At present," he told them, "de Gaulle is cooperating with us in none of our policies." The French had moved to "lock the British out of Europe" and "may begin shortly trying to lock us out." Crucially, he identified the gold crisis as the greatest weakness for de Gaulle to exploit. "The French may suddenly decide to cash their dollar holdings," he warned.[13]

For the last ten minutes or so of the meeting, Kennedy turned on the tapes to record the conversation, thereby providing an example in real time of Dillon's political dexterity. As the cabinet official grappling with this area of vulnerability in national security, he might have been expected to be on the back foot. Instead, as the tape reels began to turn, we find the treasury secretary ramming home a point that he had been making since the summer. "Certainly in the long run, Mr. President, our policy has always been the hope that we'd be able to get our forces out of Europe," he drawled in familiar stentorian tones – "What's wrong with that?" Kennedy wavered. "I'm not suggesting that we should act on this presumption," he said. "I think" – he paused – "The only thing is, I think for the first time, at least as far as I am concerned, in the last week, I've really come to feel that this other policy [Dillon's] is very possible and that we ought to go."[14]

Six days later, an agitated Kennedy returned to the issue at another ExCom meeting (also caught on tape). "He's going to harass us," the president complained of de Gaulle. "He's going to try to lessen our influence and our prestige, and it's going to appear that we are in a sort of diminishing market." The gold drain and the balance of payments crisis were again forefront in his mind. "It's the financial where they've got us," he said. The United States had to "really stop this drain … The more I look at it, the more I see that's the one place we're awfully vulnerable."

Once again, Dillon embraced rather than backed away from the issue. Kennedy had put his "finger on the fact that our weakness here is in the financial area and that our strength is in the political and military area." So use that fact, he urged. French pressure on the dollar was nothing less than "a real attack" on the "whole world financial stability." The only way to match it was with pressure through "the political and military situation."

Here Ball jumped in. His lengthy contribution set out in laborious detail the case he had been making since the summer. Yes, he conceded, the United States "carrying all the responsibilities around the world [is] the reason for our balance of payments problem." But the answer was not to march American troops off the continent, as Dillon was suggesting. Instead, they should be "trying to lead the Europeans back into the world." This, Ball said, was "what really makes their eyes light up." What did this mean in practice? Nothing less than a full-scale review of the Atlantic Alliance to "work out a systematic way in which [they] would begin to have a share in the world."[15]

Ball had spoken for over ten minutes. Dillon's answer lasted ten seconds: "It costs us $750 million still in gold each year there in balance of payments costs, what we're doing in Europe with NATO."

"That's even after all the offsets?" Kennedy asked.

"After all the offsets," he confirmed.

When Kennedy came back to the figure in the meeting, Dillon reinforced his point with a dig at Ball's "A Fresh Approach to the Gold Problem" memo. Maybe it was time to "take a fresh look" at "all our forces in Europe."[16]

The ExCom exchanges left Kennedy flummoxed. Unsure as to how to proceed, he turned to a more experienced hand, the former secretary of state, Dean Acheson, to break the tie between his advisers. In many ways, it was an odd choice. The two men were temperamentally far apart, with Kennedy, notes his biographer, "put off by [Acheson's] bitterness and sarcasm." For his part, Acheson never bothered to hide his belief that the president was a lightweight. Still, admiring Acheson's ability to get to the heart of a question, Kennedy had brought him onto ExCom during the Missile Crisis. As an architect of the Bretton Woods financial system during the Truman administration and a Treasury official who had been fired by FDR for his unconventional views on the gold standard in the 1930s, he seemed well placed to help figure things out. Acheson recalled the president asking if "I could bring simplicity out of apparent complications and confusion ... and try to make a recommendation to him as to what to do."[17]

For almost the first time, Dillon was furious. The former secretary of state was close to Ball – the two men had been playing handball together since the 1930s – and even if Dillon and Acheson had been fellow "hawks" during the Missile Crisis, they shared little affinity. Dillon could not attack the scheme head on, but his mood was clear in a memo to the president that pulled no punches. Looking to those on the other side of the debate, notably Ball and his ally Walt Rostow, Dillon launched a broadside against the "philosophy ... of those who find their preferred policies threatened by balance of payment difficulties." All they wanted was "to make this very real problem go away without interfering with their own project." However, "such individuals are asking the impossible," he complained. The facts were simple enough: the

United States could not ignore "except at our peril" the disciplines of international monetary dealings by consistently running a large balance of payments deficit.[18]

When Acheson presented his own plan to the president on February 27, it was in essence a version of the Ball program, including an "updated, modernized" version of the international monetary system and loans to the United States where "most of the borrowing should be done in France and Germany." What was *not* needed, Acheson advised in a sly reference to Dillon, was "a cautious banking view about our balance of payments." At the end of the conversation, Acheson told Kennedy that he should call everyone concerned to a meeting to knock heads together and tell them what the line was. "He thought that was a good idea and we had such a meeting," Acheson remembered. "It just didn't turn out the way I thought it was going to."[19]

It was typical of the Olympian Acheson that he assumed the last word – so long as it was his – had been spoken on the subject, but he had underestimated Dillon's Machiavellian talents. Faced with what looked like a fait accompli by one of the most storied figures in American public life, the treasury secretary now pulled one of the oldest tricks in the political book. He talked Acheson's report to death.

"He conducted a filibuster," Acheson said after a meeting of all the principals to discuss his report. "This went on for an hour or more in which he pointed out all the problems and all the difficulties which came from taking action of any sort. He kept saying that the Treasury was having studies made and in one month or two months or three months they would have more data." In horror, Acheson watched as Dillon "began to weaken the president's will to tackle this problem." Uncharacteristically flustered, he fought back by pointing out that "no one would really ever know any more about this in six months than they knew then," and argued that they had to raise the whole matter from a Treasury and central bank problem to an inter-governmental one. If that were done, he urged, "we could really begin to make some progress." But as Dillon poured more and more fast-setting concrete over the proposals, Acheson recognized that he had lost the president. By the end of the meeting, Kennedy asked Dillon to complete his studies. "This allowed the matter to drop off the edge of decision," Acheson said.[20]

In a testy confrontation with Dillon after the meeting, he accused him of talking the report out, but he saved his real ire for the president who he thought not up to the job. "This was almost the last time that I had any direct contact with the president," he said unemotionally a year later. His ally George Ball was just as frustrated, but in his characteristically wry fashion, he was grudgingly admiring of the way this "extraordinary practitioner" of the political dark arts had outfoxed Acheson. "Doug [droned] on and on and on and on," he recalled. "By the time he had concluded, people had forgotten what he was addressing himself to. It was quite effective." Ball even came up with a name for the tactic. "Dillonblustering," he called it – "talking on and on and on about the minutiae of the issue and totally obfuscating what the argument was all about. And it used to be most frustrating to get into an argument with him for that very reason."[21]

His frustrations came to the fore at a difficult meeting of the cabinet committee on the balance of payments on April 18. At one stage Ball appeared to lose his composure, telling the president that "the policies advocated by the secretary of the treasury involved an unnecessarily large measure of risk." Dillon seized on the remark, retorting sharply that, on the contrary, it was he and the Treasury department who were measured and "Secretary Ball's proposal which was reckless." Kennedy, aware of Dillon's tactics, pointed out to him that he was "very skillful in shooting down, every three months or so, the balloons which other departments had floated." Dillon did not relent, observing that this only reflected the Treasury's "realism, its understanding that there were no panaceas and its cool assessment of the facts." Kennedy backed away, conceding the point that the Treasury "has done an excellent job to date."[22]

Dillon's position was made even more persuasive by having a powerful ally in Defense Secretary Robert McNamara. Although the two men had disagreed during the Missile Crisis, they had often found themselves in lockstep over troop withdrawals. McNamara's experience at the Ford Motor Company had interested him in the balance of payments question. His approach regarding the military was a quantitative one. He had consistently pushed for controls to limit overseas defense spending, including curbs on the expenditure by individual service personnel and their families. He had supported the "offset" payments from Germany, implemented "Buy American" policies at the Defense Department, rotated army divisions between Europe and the United States, and even had military equipment flown back to the United States for service and repair. Moreover, he had stepped away from his earlier strategy of "flexible response," which had put more emphasis on conventional forces and limited nuclear warfare than Eisenhower's strategy of "massive retaliation." McNamara made a formidable partner for Dillon, not least, writes his biographer Deborah Shapley, because when he briefed on "their quantitative progress at lowering the outflow of defense funds, with his hair slicked back and his straight-arrow part, he embodied the tough, number-crunching solutions the age admired." It was exactly this clarity that he brought to the April meeting of the cabinet committee on the balance of payments. "The only way to improve our position [is] to reduce troop deployments," he told Kennedy, while reassuring him that "this can be done without reducing our effective military strength."[23]

By the end of the meeting, it was clear that Dillon and McNamara had the initiative in the institutional fight with Ball and the State Department. The president remarked that they had all ended up in a place that was "screwy," but then he tipped his hand, directing that "we had to squeeze important public activities in the spheres of defense and aid." Afterwards, he told Dillon he wanted a special report on the balance of payments worked out by the beginning of July. McNamara would prepare a report on troop withdrawals on the same timescale.[24]

Dillon immediately set about to develop those plans. These included a controversial tax on foreign securities to discourage Americans from buying overseas stocks and bonds, and coordination with the Federal Reserve to introduce an increase on discount interest rates to stop the movement of short-term money overseas. He submitted his report to Kennedy in the middle of July, with an estimate that these two radical measures could reduce the balance of payments deficit by $2 billion within eighteen months. At the same time, McNamara submitted his own report, with the headline figure of a gross reduction in the annual rate of defense expenditures abroad of $300–$400 million. This reduction would be achieved through "our increased strategic missile capability" and the fact that "gradually increasing the capability of the Armed Forces to deploy rapidly will permit some reduction in other forces permanently in-place overseas." The chiefs of staff had accepted the proposals "if the contribution of these actions to the solution of the balance of payments problem is considered to outweigh the military risk involved."[25]

"There was a good deal of skittishness about this in the State Department," Dillon recalled. McNamara told Kennedy that Dean Rusk was imploring him not to present any cuts as a package "implying U.S. withdrawal from its commitment to maintain the integrity and freedom of the Free World." Rusk even asked him not to give allies any basis "for believing that the program is forced upon us by our balance of payments position." Dillon argued, to the contrary, that public clarity and a willingness to be seen to be taking firm action with allies was central to getting a grip on the crisis. There was a "lamentable lack of understanding" both at home and abroad on the issue, he told Kennedy, so it was vital to give a "new infusion of direction and confidence." Dillon advised him to make a presidential statement to "provide the dramatic emphasis that is needed to assure the world that we are on course." Kennedy agreed, and on July 18 sent a comprehensive message to Congress to announce the special tax on foreign securities, the hike in the discount rate, and a $300 million reduction in the annual rate of expenditures abroad by the Department of Defense "before the end of calendar year 1964." Controversy, noted the *New York Times* correspondent Eileen Shanahan, "began the instant they were announced and clearly will continue for months, and perhaps years."[26]

Dillon urged Kennedy to hold the line. "The balance of payments remains one of the most urgent problems confronting your administration and the country," he told him, so "it is imperative to keep our nerve." Kennedy seemed not to balk at the challenge, underscoring to European allies his seriousness of intent. Spanish leader Francisco Franco reported that the president had warned that "the question of the American balance of payments constituted one of his greatest concerns." He might be forced to "change his whole policy" in Europe and "dismantle the military support of Europe." Gerhard Schröder, the West German foreign minister, was told that the United States had no "wish to keep spending money to maintain forces which are not of real value." Peter Thorneycroft, the British defence secretary, feared that the president might just "haul out" of Europe altogether.[27]

Yet Kennedy could not shake his habit of always wanting just one more voice in the mix. Having tried Dean Acheson in the spring, he now turned to the Harvard economist and outgoing ambassador to India John Kenneth Galbraith. Again, things did not turn out quite as expected. Always an independent and unpredictable thinker, Galbraith impressed upon Kennedy that "it is much more important to our position to have a strong balance of payments than to have any given number of divisions in Europe." He urged the president to act quickly and to be tough. "The time for purely cosmetic action is past," Galbraith told him. "Hereafter, action must be considered and real. Anything that now smacks of toying with the problem will be damaging to confidence. Nor can we afford to waste more time." The president should not worry about bruised egos in the bureaucratic conflicts between the various departments. "Someone's ox must be gored," he advised.[28]

Galbraith reinforced the president's resolve to stick with Dillon and McNamara. In many ways, it was no surprise. "Not only were these two men among the most 'high powered' in the administration," Aurélie Basha I Novosejt writes, "they were also members of the cabinet who interacted with Kennedy socially and were friends whom he trusted." Shortly after Labor Day, Kennedy held a meeting with the two secretaries along with Ball, Heller, and

Bundy to give a new direction to policy. It was time for them to give "this problem our urgent attention." Again Ball overplayed his hand, "to the point," he recalled, "where I think the president thought I was quite a nuisance." The secretaries of the treasury and defense were now instructed to bring forward recommendations on slowing further outflow of capital and introducing more savings in overseas expenditures.[29]

Presidential policy was affirmed in National Security Action Memorandum No. 270. On November 18, McNamara introduced the policy in a speech before the Economic Club of New York. He pointed out that since the United States possessed a "strategic nuclear deterrent far superior to that of the Soviet Union," cuts in defense spending, including conventional forces overseas, were "in the works." This represented "a fundamental shift," the defense secretary said, "not just a temporary slash." As Francis Gavin notes, "The Dillon-McNamara approach seemed victorious in the domestic-political gold battle."[30]

Chapter Fourteen

Trading Places
Washington, 1963

The gold crisis was not the only front on which Dillon fought in the summer of 1963. At the height of that debate, the treasury secretary had urged Kennedy to use his bully pulpit to "[restore] the public image of an administration and a country determined to solve its balance of payments problems." But a presidential intervention could be vital for other reasons too. "Since your tax proposals will have reached a crucial stage in the House by the first week of July," he reminded Kennedy, "this could offer an unparalleled opportunity to combine another thrust in support of that program."[1]

After the drama of the previous summer, when the president had sided with Dillon over Heller on the "quickie" temporary tax cut, the issue laid fallow through most of the fall. The business investment tax credit meandered through Congress to become law on October 16 – the day the president learnt of the missiles in Cuba. That crisis had diverted most of the resources of the government for the rest of October. Even once the drama had ended, Kennedy seemed reluctant to back tax reform during the midterm elections in November. "The president himself did not pay a great deal of attention to taxation during the fall of 1962," Herbert Stein, CEA chair under Presidents Nixon and Ford, noted, "apparently not foreseeing the significance which historians – mainly members of his staff – would later find in the tax cut." Still, Dillon and the Treasury kept quietly working away on plans for a wholesale reform package to bring to Congress in the new year, all the time attempting to navigate around Heller and a president who did not always know his own mind.[2]

The first formidable obstacle facing Dillon in Congress was Wilbur Mills. As Kennedy ruefully admitted, "[Mills] knows that he was chairman of Ways and Means before I got here and that he'll still be chairman after I've gone – and he knows I know it. I don't have any hold over him." Mills had been an ally for Dillon in his battle with Heller that summer when they had averted the "quickie" tax cut. But Mills remained as skeptical about an immediate permanent tax cut as he had a temporary one.[3]

That November, Dillon had dispatched Henry H. Fowler to Arkansas to pay court and find out where Mills stood. The undersecretary spent three and a half hours with the lugubrious congressman, whom he did at least find "most cordial" and prepared to speak "openly and frankly" about his position. Mills apparently did "not see any evidence of a near-term recession as forecast by various economists this summer" – a dig at Heller. Besides conceding that existing tax rates were a "drag on the economy," Mills thought "the most important" way in which he could "promote a more rapid economic growth" was "to secure the legislative enactment of an orderly, permanent reduction of our income tax rate structure." The question of timing was the major stumbling block. Should any of this happen quickly? Mills thought not, warning that the president should publicly "close the door" on any such idea.[4]

Dillon briefed Kennedy and advised him to speak to Mills himself. With both sides essentially agreeing on the desirability of tax reform and a permanent tax cut, the subsequent meeting between Kennedy and Mills shifted from principles to raw politics. The president told Mills that of course, for appearances, he was happy to start from an unacceptable position to give the Ways and Means committee the opportunity "to scale us down some, because otherwise you can't get Congress."

It was not enough to placate Mills. "I'm not certain I could pass it," he told the president. Kennedy asked him to remember the election in 1964. Without the tax program, "we're liable to get … none of the advantage of the stimulus on the economy." Still Mills demurred, suggesting "maybe January 1, 1964." Larry O'Brien, congressional liaison representative for Kennedy, could not contain himself any longer. "It's a hell of a gamble, Walter, if you don't mind me saying so," he interjected, "to have a package that would ultimately be finalized in January 1965." They had to act sooner "so that we protect ourselves in '64." Again, Mills stalled, advising Kennedy not to set out a timetable that would back both men into a corner.[5]

In a major speech at the Economic Club of New York on December 14, Kennedy launched tax cuts and tax reform as the central goal for the remainder of his first term. The government, he told his audience of bankers and businessmen, had to "cut the fetters which hold back private spending" and "reduce the burden on private income and the deterrents to private initiative which are imposed by our present tax system." In a nod toward supply-side or "trickle down" economics and what would become known as "the Laffer curve" (the tax rate that maximizes government tax revenue), he pointed out that it was "a paradoxical truth that tax rates are too high today and tax revenues are too low and the soundest way to raise the revenues in the long run is to cut the rates now."

But while Kennedy promised a new tax bill that would "improve both the equity and the simplicity" of the tax system and "sufficiently large" rate cuts "to do the job required," he gave away next to nothing on timing. All the president could say was that a new tax bill "should reduce the net taxes by a sufficiently early date." To have said otherwise would have antagonized Mills, whom O'Brien called the "key player." They were all "aware of the absolute need for us to keep in total and constant communication with him – and probably more than that."[6]

The following weeks were fraught for Dillon as the president's economic advisers argued about how to get a tax program through Congress. Heller, urged on by Paul Samuelson, demanded that the president commit to a fast tax cut and ditch tax reform. Dillon argued that such a move was political madness, as Mills had specifically linked the two elements; to abandon either would be to condemn the president's tax plan to oblivion.

Dillon proposed a compromise that would satisfy Mills without sacrificing the Treasury's objective. He would prioritize the tax cuts in 1963 along with the simple elements of reform as the first stage; more cuts and the complicated reform elements would come the following year. Yet still Heller resisted. "We hate to pass up any opportunity for tax reform," he said, "but the important thing here is to get a big tax cut for economic stimulus purposes." Dillon retorted that he wanted reform *and* the tax cut. Heller would not budge, saying that "the excess baggage of the tax reform" would slow down the tax cut. It was a stalemate.[7]

With the legislative clock ticking, Kennedy summoned everyone to his house in Palm Beach, Florida, in the days between Christmas and New Year to resolve the impasse. The result was a walkover for Dillon. He persuaded the president, first, that they had to couple tax reform with the tax cut, and second, that they had to agree to split the bill into two or even three parts. Some in the administration jumped to conclusions about what had just happened. "If Wilbur wanted us to go down to Heber Springs and sing 'Down by the Old Mills Stream' we'd be glad to do it," one aide noted.[8]

Dillon had proved once again that he knew how to manipulate prevailing political circumstances to get what he wanted. Heller understood that reality only too well. "Dillon won an important victory when we went down to Florida for final decision making," he admitted. "The president still was not registering a complete understanding by any means of what he was in for on the reforms that he was signing on the dotted line for." Heller's colleague James Tobin resigned from the Council of Economic Advisers in protest.[9]

"There were a number of times like that," Dillon reflected, "and each time when [the president] made the decision, he simply decided that what he would do would be what we in the Treasury had recommended. I think that by the end of 1962, the Council became aware that this was the likely result of any controversy that might go to the president." Walt Rostow understood better than most this personal element in the relationship between the president and the treasury secretary. "They had reasons to be comfortable in each other's presence," he said, pointing out that "the Dillons were at the pinnacle of Washington society." That Christmas, however, decision-making involved more than a social friendship. These were the "Treasury's activities," Rostow said, "but they were the policies of the president."[10]

Kennedy sent his special message on tax reduction and reform to Congress on January 24, 1963. Signaling the victory for Dillon, it stated outright that the program had to be "promptly enacted as a single comprehensive bill." He proposed a reduction in personal income tax rates from the current levels of 20 and 91 percent to 14 and 65 percent. Corporate tax would be reduced less dramatically, from 52 to 47 percent. Reform would remove "certain inequities and hardships [… and] unwarranted special privileges, current defects in the tax law and provide more equal treatment of taxpayers." Rate reductions would cut tax liabilities by $13.6 billion – $11 billion for individuals and $2.6 billion for corporations. The tax program would become fully effective on January 1, 1965. "Now is the time to act," Kennedy urged. "We cannot afford to be timid or slow. For this is the most urgent task confronting the Congress in 1963."[11]

From the moment the message on tax had arrived on Capitol Hill, Dillon found himself on the back foot. Matters were not helped by Heller, who immediately stressed that it was the tax cut the president cared about most. "His economic advisers, headed by Walter W. Heller, have consistently put more stress on reduction than reform," the New York Times noted in a report that had the notoriously leaky Heller's fingerprints all over it. One legislator told the newspaper that he had been informed privately that the reform element of the tax message was "just window dressing." The president "doesn't care a bit whether tax reform comes this year or some other year," he reported. Only Mills's insistence that he would "do all he can" to combine cuts and reform into a single bill kept it alive.[12]

The hearings of the Ways and Means Committee began on February 6, when Dillon made the administration's case. Around four hundred people squeezed into the packed hearing room to watch as the treasury secretary forced his way through the melee, his left hand occasionally up to his eyes to shield them against the popping flashbulbs.

Once order had been restored, Dillon detailed the proposed program while referencing a vast dossier of technical supporting detail. He told the committee that tax cuts and tax reform were "inextricably tied," pointing out that dropping structural reform would "necessarily require an upward revision of the recommended tax rate." When he was questioned about the link between the two, Dillon noted in the same matter-of-fact fashion that he would likely recommend to the president that they abandon the entire program rather than cut taxes without reforming the system.

Dillon came under assault from Republicans, including John W. Byrnes of Wisconsin, who accused him of advocating reforms that "seek to favor the person who doesn't own his own home, who doesn't pay real estate taxes, who doesn't support his church, who doesn't give to the Community Chest." It was a topsy-turvy world, Herbert Stein points out, where congressional Republicans vehemently opposed tax reform that would directly reduce the budget deficit. "The conservatives were not less concerned about the size of the deficit or more anxious for a quick stimulus to the economy than the administration was," he writes. "The conservatives were willing to subordinate their traditional view about the deficit in order to avoid the tax reforms which they didn't like and get tax cuts which they did like." Democrats were not much more helpful to the administration, with the House majority whip Hale Boggs telling Dillon on the first day that Congress would likely pass the tax cuts but not the reform measures.[13]

Hearings lasted until the end of March, taking up twenty-seven long days of testimony, after which the committee still showed no sign of voting or reporting the bill out. As the process dragged on, Dillon increasingly found himself shoring up a wavering president. "He said he was getting quite a few letters," Evelyn Lincoln, the president's secretary, wrote to Dillon when passing along a message from Kennedy. That presidential anxiety became public knowledge just as the hearings ended. Sitting on the platform for a presidential speech at the American Bankers Association, Dillon had been stunned to hear Kennedy say during questions that "whatever is necessary to get that [tax] bill, I will do." Reporters immediately interpreted the remark as a willingness to abandon tax reform (and the treasury secretary), an interpretation that Kennedy did not immediately contradict. Even White House officials were forced to admit that Dillon was "shocked" and "could hardly believe what he was hearing." When Mills got wind of the president's remark, he was incandescent, briefing the press off the record that Kennedy had just "pulled the rug out" from under Dillon and himself.

Kennedy was forced into a quick retraction. Asked at his next news conference whether "if all else fails" he would accept the tax cut without the reform, he brazened it out, telling the reporter, "No, that isn't what I said," and reiterating that "my judgement is that they [Congress] will enact a tax reduction bill which will include important elements of the reforms that we sent up." Afterwards a "top tax official" at the White House admitted that "The president is just sick about what he did" in the first set of remarks, noting that "he didn't mean to say what the transcript indicates clearly that he did say." Walter Heller thought differently. Kennedy was "just amazed when he saw the barrage of criticism of the reform proposals," he judged. That was when in effect he said, "Who the hell sold me on these reforms?"[14]

Dillon had managed to walk Kennedy back from the remarks this time, but the treasury secretary took the trouble to save a cartoon from the *Philadelphia Inquirer* that caught his mood. It showed him rowing along a river, perspiration pouring down his face from all the exertion, while his boat sank under the weight of a passenger wearing a t-shirt labelled "Tax Reform."[15]

With the tax program stuck in committee and the president sliding back and forth, Dillon set out to make sure that the boat did not in fact sink. He quietly began making concessions on tax reform, dropping, for example, the highly unpopular measure that would have seen itemized deductions on income reduced by 5 percent. He also started addressing the concerns of deficit hawks by accepting a Republican proposal from Byrnes to reduce by around $5 billion the amount of the national debt set by Congress. An economy that had just hit its target of 5 percent GDP growth for the first time under Kennedy, Dillon pointed out, already meant that "if the improvement continues our estimated revenues for fiscal 1964 may well be more than we estimated in January – perhaps by as much as a billion dollars – thus reducing the deficit" – thereby offering further reassurance. He also founded a "Business and Finance Committee for Tax Reduction in 1963" to coordinate five hundred tax experts and business leaders to act as a lobby group for the program.[16]

That spring, Dillon began an intensive round of speeches and television interviews to sell the program. The most important of these was an address on April 30 to the US Chamber of Commerce at the Statler Hotel in Washington. Dillon took a forceful approach that night, demanding answers rather than complaints from his audience. "You have made it very clear that you strongly support the principle of tax reduction as vital to the continuation of a healthy free economy," he pointed out. "The practical question is: What can you actively do to make that goal a reality when you do not agree with all the means proposed to reach it?" Their effective support was urgently needed if the best was not to become the enemy of the good. The president's tax program offered "strong encouragement to ... every income group and to every sector of our economy," he told them. It met the "need to keep the budgetary deficit within a tolerable limit," and provided "the private economy the freedom it needs to draw upon its own inherent resources for growth, to create the job opportunities we will need in the years ahead, and to provide the revenues necessary to preserve our national security and answer our critical national needs." The tax program had to be implemented now, he concluded, because "action is vital if we are to meet today's economic realities."[17]

It was one of Dillon's best speeches as treasury secretary. Forceful without being strident, commanding without being overwhelmed by technical issues, it accepted differences of opinion while demanding others recognize the need for action. By emphasizing tax cuts, he played to the strengths of the overall program without backing away from the need for reform. "The trend of editorial comment on the president's tax proposals continues on the upgrade," an official in the Treasury Department wrote in a press analysis a few weeks later. "Secretary Dillon's speech before the US Chamber of Commerce generated a great deal of editorial comment," the official continued, with 10–1 in favor. Dillon sent the analysis to the president to highlight the growing support and success in "[placating] many fears."[18]

As the debate rumbled on at the House Ways and Means Committee throughout the spring and summer, Dillon continued his strategy of compromise and reassurance to keep conservative Democrats from the South in his column and even pull across a few Republicans. It was a delicate balance to maintain, because the administration had also begun its contentious push for a Civil Rights act.

Given the universal nature of civil rights, it is often forgotten that the focus of the administration and activists alike in 1963 was as much on labor law and opportunities in the workplace as it was on political freedom. The March on Washington for Jobs and Freedom that took place on August 28, at which Martin Luther King Jr. made his iconic "I have a dream" speech, had originally been conceived by A. Philip Randolph, president of the Brotherhood of Sleeping Car Porters, as a "march for jobs." The jailing of MLK in Birmingham, Alabama, in April had given a new impetus to the "freedom" agenda, but the demand for jobs and economic opportunities remained a critical element of the civil rights movement and still went first in the title of the march. It was one of the many ways in which Dillon's tax program was intertwined with the

Civil Rights bill, not just in terms of a legislative agenda, but also in being a key element of the broader economic objective of the civil rights movement to give "all Americans," said Bayard Rustin, deputy director of the march, "a decent standard of living."[19]

Dillon had a limited field of view on race matters. As the son of one of America's richest men, his experience of African Americans was more often than not as domestic servants, doormen, and drivers. On Wall Street, where the first Black-owned US brokerage firm (McGhee & Co.) was not formed until 1952 and Joseph Searles became the first Black floor member and floor broker in the New York Stock Exchange only in 1970, racial diversity was not part of the world of Dillon Read. In the US navy during the Second World War, Dillon had regularly interacted with Black sailors among the enlisted men. He would never have had the opportunity to salute a superior officer who was Black.[20]

Dillon's political attitude to race and civil rights was essentially carried over from the Eisenhower administration: conservative and gradualist, with a strong emphasis on promoting equality and fairness of opportunity in employment rights while eliminating the most egregious examples of discrimination in workplace practices. He appointed the Black economist Samuel Z. Westerfield as a senior official in the Treasury, where he was instrumental in negotiating the Alliance for Progress; later Dillon supported his move to the State Department as assistant secretary of the Bureau of Economic Affairs (and later ambassador to Liberia). Dillon also recognized there was a systemic problem in the department. "The difficulties are perfectly obvious," he said in 1964, using the language of the day. "They stemmed from the fact that not many Negroes had educational opportunities similar to those available to their white brothers – this [is] particularly true in the field of economics and finance." As treasury secretary, he began an immediate "campaign to try and train others and to encourage" Black economists, accountants, and financial analysts. And he ensured that the department, in the words of his special assistant, Dixon Donnelley, took the "leading role in [the president's] drive to extend civil rights" in the federal government as set out at a cabinet meeting on February 13, 1961. "We were in the forefront" over other government departments, Dillon said, noticeably the State Department, when it came to "hiring" and "opportunities to advance." The Internal Revenue Service (IRS) was the most controversial element of this process, "particularly in the South, where in the past they had had many segregated offices." Within weeks of taking office, he also ordered "positive action" be taken to enforce compliance "which prohibits recognition of employee recreational organizations practicing discrimination," which instead had "to be available to *all* employees."[21]

One of Dillon's responsibilities at the Treasury Department that attracted particular attention on race was the United States Coast Guard. Looking down from the reviewing stand on Inauguration Day 1961, Kennedy had been shocked to see that the honor guard of the US Coast Guard Academy contained not a single person of color. "Did you see the Coast Guard detachment?" he fumed. After the first cabinet meeting, Kennedy pulled Dillon aside. "He jumped me on it," Dillon recalled, "and said this was very noticeable and what was going on." Kennedy was crisp. "I want no discrimination," he instructed Dillon. "Get after them!" Following up, Dillon was shocked to discover that of the 893 candidates added to the eligibility list (from 4,393 applicants) in 1960, precisely zero were Black. In fact, the coast guard commandant wrote to Dillon that "the only known Negro cadet entered the Academy in June 1955 [and] while he acquitted himself well in academics, athletics, extracurricular activities and barracks life, he resigned in November 1957 due to a failure to meet physical standards."

As Dillon told Kennedy, it was clear "there has never been any positive effort to obtain the services of Negro officers, either through the Coast Guard Academy route or through entrance into the Coast Guard as reserve officers." He introduced new measures to find well-qualified Black candidates to stand alongside the 4,500 applicants who each year sought to become one of the 200 or so who were admitted. Dillon did not formally introduce affirmative action, but he made it clear to the commandant that he expected immediate change and was pleased when the academy "found ways" to improve. "We put on a great effort," he said, and "went around to different colleges … to persuade them to take the entrance exam." In 1962, the Coast Guard Academy admitted Merle James Smith Jr., who four years later became the first Black cadet to graduate, with cadets London Steverson and Kenneth D. Boyd graduating two years afterwards. These pathfinding graduates represented less than 1 percent of their entering class, but as Dillon would say in 1964, he hoped it was the first step in a process "to search out fine candidates so that the Coast Guard Academy would be a truly integrated institution as any government institution should be."[22]

Race also become a major factor in the passage of the tax bill, not least when it reached the Senate where segregationists held powerful committee positions. To get the legislation through the House, Dillon had asked the president to make a public intervention giving reassurances to Mills that the tax program would be accompanied by expenditure discipline in the 1965 budget. It was done "rather dramatically in the form of this letter to Mr. Mills," Dillon said, which then allowed the House Way and Means chair to include its sentiments in the preamble to the bill. On September 10, the committee finally voted 17–8 in favor of sending the bill to the floor of the House, with two Republicans, Howard H. Baker and Victor E. Knox, voting with the majority. The bill proposed $11 billion in tax cuts – "the biggest tax cut in history," proclaimed the *New York Herald Tribune*. Much of the original structural reform had fallen by the wayside during the committee process, but Dillon recognized that the pugnacious Mills had been more friend than foe. He had shown "fighting spirit," Dillon told Kennedy."[23]

The House bill passed comfortably on September 26 by 271 votes to 155. "A good many Republicans reversed themselves and voted for the bill," Dillon noted of the broad coalition he had assembled. He immediately announced that the administration would not be seeking any amendments in the Senate. "Although the bill rejected some of the president's original proposals and substantially modified others," he told the press, "we must subordinate differences to the broad consensus on basic principles and the need for prompt enactment of the bill." Above all, he wanted the bill passed by the end of the year, not just for economic reasons, but also because, as a Republican, he wanted to be out of the political spotlight in a presidential election year.[24]

To prepare for the forthcoming hearings in the upper house, Dillon quietly paid a side-door visit to the office of Senator Harry F. Byrd of Virginia, the Democratic chair of the Senate Finance Committee. The episode was a study in courtliness. Dillon – unassuming, gracious, and Northeastern rich – tentatively inquired of Byrd – genteel, quietly spoken, and Southern rich – whether they might come to some gentlemanly agreement about moving things along in an expeditious fashion. The Virginian imperceptibly shook his head. Regretfully, time was not on their side, he explained. The House had taken eight months to consider the matter. His colleagues on Senate Finance could not be hurried. There would have to be two weeks of briefings by experts. More than sixty witnesses were already slated to testify. Amendments had been tabled. Why, Senator Albert Gore of Tennessee had submitted twenty all by himself! It would be impossible, just impossible, he told Dillon sadly.

Still, he was open to that gentleman's agreement. He would give Dillon his "personal guarantee" that the tax bill would be passed, and the tax cut applied retroactively if the president might perhaps agree to delay until January and submit a reduced budget for the next fiscal year. Now it was Dillon's turn to shake his head. Alas, he told Byrd, such a delay might precipitate a recession, so he must reluctantly demur. Dillon knew there was no question of trying to push or prod Byrd, which his deputy Henry Fowler had warned "would be considered an affront to the Chairman." So, an outwardly cheerful Dillon took his leave of the cherubic senator, with both men aware that for all the elegance of the meeting they had just engaged in the opening skirmishes of the vicious political battle to come.[25]

Dillon knew exactly what Byrd was up to. "There is emerging in the Senate Finance Committee an incipient combination of the tactics of delay and expenditure control," Fowler had written to him shortly before the side-door meeting. Byrd and his allies were "attracted to this combination of tactics because they wish to defeat the tax bill completely." So why hadn't Dillon accepted Byrd's bargain, made it public, and then bided his time? Because he understood that it was a trap.[26]

In the fourth volume of his unfinished biography, *The Years of Lyndon Johnson*, Robert Caro disparages Dillon on this point, saying that he "did not seem to grasp the reality of what was happening," showed a "lack of understanding of Byrd's tactics," and underestimated the senator's rigid determination "to see the budget come in under $100 billion." Caro tied Dillon in with legislative aides in the administration who naively believed it was possible to go around Byrd. ("You *couldn't* go around Harry Byrd," he quotes Horace Busby Jr., a longtime Johnson confidant, saying.) Yet the documents contradict Caro's analysis. In a series of briefings for the president in September 1963 entitled "Tax bill strategy and tactics," Dillon and Fowler laid out an assessment of the opposition the tax bill would face in the Senate and their strategic plan to defeat it. That plan showed how precisely they understood Byrd. Moreover, it was a plan that would turn out to anticipate how the bill would pass almost to the letter.[27]

"We shall have to fight a determined opposition in the Senate," the first of these memos predicted. They could expect opposition to "rely primarily upon the tactics of delay" with "some specific measure of 'expenditure control' to be persistent." Whereas in the House Ways and Means committee they had been dealing with Mills, for whom tax reduction was "close to the heart," now they faced a Senate Finance chair in Byrd, supported by Gore, who represented "hardnosed Democratic opposition" to a bill he thought favored the rich. Having diagnosed the problem, a second memo outlined "a strategy for dealing with these efforts." The secretary and his deputy were more than ever convinced that Senate Finance would filibuster until the budget for 1965 was made public. Byrd would then use a growing federal budget either to "defeat the tax bill," or, at best, to win "a Presidential commitment by law" to "specific expenditure limits." No amount of "prodding," they warned Kennedy, was likely to prevent "a procedural motion at the conclusion of the public hearings that the Committee defer action on the tax bill until it has before it your Budget Message, scheduled now for mid-January."

So how to endplay Byrd and his allies? For Dillon, the answer was simply to take Byrd at his word. At a moment that it would "serve best to undercut" the finance committee, Kennedy should announce "an expenditure total for fiscal 1965 under $100 billion." The political logic was flawless. *Obviously*, you couldn't go around Harry Byrd, but perhaps you could outwit him. "I do not mean to infer that an expenditure estimate of less than $100 billion ... would still the opposition of those who think the 1964 totals were too high," the strategy memo pointed out, but it would "spell 'expenditure control' to reasonable people" – as well as meeting the specific demand made publicly by Byrd. It would mean hard choices within the administration, and a fight with Heller too, as the current projected budget was $102.1 billion – an increase of $5 billion on actual 1964 expenditure.

But this was not simply a matter of economics. At heart it was a "political judgement," a political judgement with real electoral consequences for Kennedy, because it was one that would "put you and the Democratic Party in a much stronger political position next fall."[28]

Aside from Byrd's antipathy to tax cuts of any kind and the inevitable fight to come with Heller over expenditure figures in the budget, another factor complicated the strategy Dillon planned: the fact that the tax bill was ineluctably tied to the civil rights legislation making its way through Congress right behind the tax bill. Byrd was an arch-segregationist who seemed likely to kill legislation that would end racial separation in schools, public places, and public employment in the United States. In 1960, he had refused to support Kennedy in the presidential election on the grounds that the candidate seemed likely to appoint Black federal judges. He privately helped draft the controversial public letter to Kennedy written by Virginia House of Delegates speaker E. Blackburn Moore that promised "chaos" in Virginia and throughout the South in the event any new administration attempted desegregation. By the fall of 1963, Byrd anticipated an interminable filibuster of the civil rights legislation the following year. If he slowed the Senate Finance hearings down for long enough, there was a strong chance that the tax bill would get choked off by the civil rights filibuster and both bills might die.[29]

When the hearings began in October, the awkward pair of Dillon and Byrd began their tortuous dance of quick-quick slow. "Treasury secretary Douglas Dillon marched into the Senate Finance Committee hearing room prepared to do battle – speedily, he hoped – for the Administration's tax cut bill," *Time* reported on October 25, "but the only person there who seemed to be in much of a rush was Doug Dillon." While the treasury secretary urged speed, "Chairman Byrd benignly regarded Dillon from behind blue-tinted glasses," asking laborious, tedious questions and, without enforcing time limits, allowing further laborious, tedious interventions from anyone on the committee who wanted to speak. "Things were going his way," *Time* reflected, "– slowly." With an apparently never-ending line of witnesses now scheduled to be heard – 170 at the last count – Dillon could only grimace and bear it, knowing that he had a strategy in play that required extreme patience. "All of this indicates that the bill, as presently drafted, is pretty squarely in the middle and subject to crossfire from extreme elements on both sides," Dillon warned Kennedy, adding that "it is for this reason that we feel it is the only type of bill that can be passed, and it is probably about right in its effects." To the committee itself, he continued politely but firmly to warn that "to delay its passage would incur serious economic risks." He thus urged members to heed "the national consensus that the bill is a necessary and proper measure that is vital to our economic progress."[30]

One problem for Dillon was stopping the political time-bomb that was Walter Heller from going off during the hearings. The CEA chair's testimony before the House Ways and Means Committee earlier that spring had been a disaster. Pointedly asked by Representative Martha Griffiths, the first woman to serve on Ways and Means, why he supposed it was that the administration was trying to hand this gift of a tax cut to the American people and "they don't seem to want it," Heller had rashly replied, "I suppose it's the Puritan ethic." Kermit Gordon, the budget director, who had used the phrase privately in a meeting with Heller shortly beforehand, reflected that he wished "I could have torn my tongue out." All hell had immediately broken out. Opponents of the tax program leapt on the remark, with the ranking Republican, John Burns, saying on the floor of the House that he would "rather be a Puritan than a Heller."

By early November, as the CEA chair prepared to go before the Senate committee, Dillon told the president that he was "working with Heller" to avoid a repeat performance. Kennedy reinforced the message. "If you can," he told Gordon and Heller, "just try to avoid using colorful language, colorful phrases." Gordon recalled that "he had a twinkle in his eye when he said it," but the instruction was heard and understood. Heller's testimony turned out to be exemplary – self-consciously so – and followed Dillon's line on expenditure discipline to the letter, even declaring that he was a "Puritan" too. "This is one of the things about the Kennedy administration that I keep coming back to," Heller would reflect. "Once you got everybody on board, we were really on board, and we were all out selling that policy."[31]

The seller-in-chief, of course, was the president himself. Just as he had been deployed in August to help Mills push the tax program through the House Ways and Means Committee with a television address from the White House, now Kennedy used a major set piece speech at the convention of the American Federation of Labor, Congress of Industrial Organization (AFL-CIO) to give what Fowler called a "gentlemanly prod" to the Finance Committee.

"Clearly no single step can now be more important in sustaining the economy of the United States than the passage of our tax bill," Kennedy told the labor delegates at the Americana Hotel in New York on November 15. "I cannot tell whether we are going to get this legislation before Christmas, but I can only say that I believe that this Congress will not go home next summer to the people of the United States without passing this bill. I think we should stay there until we do."[32]

Back in the Senate, Byrd, dismissing such efforts as "a publicity stunt," made a motion to curtail committee hearings on the tax bill. "The committee thus removed all hope for Senate passage of the measure this year," the *New York Times* noted, adding that "there is no possibility of bringing the bill to the Senate floor until sometime in next year's session, which convenes January 3." As Arthur Krock, the paper's Washington bureau chief and a longtime Kennedy family confidant, put it, this was a "first-let's-see-the-budget" strategy.[33]

But Dillon had his strategy too. As Byrd conducted what was in effect his own committee filibuster, the treasury secretary and his advisers recognized that the issue had little or nothing to do with the details of the tax bill. He had always understood that a political question, not a fiscal one, was at the heart of the matter. His entire strategy was built around that calculation. As Dillon and Fowler had reminded the president a few weeks earlier, safe passage of the bill would be inextricably linked to budget discipline. "The proponents of delay seem to have the initiative," they told him, but the bill would get out of committee and pass the Senate if they played the politics right. It was their judgment that committee members would "vote for a bill cutting taxes, but only after the budget has been submitted in January and they can claim some credit for the adoption of a policy of 'expenditure control' reflected in the budget." But "the other side of the coin is that, if the budget total is not compatible with a policy of 'expenditure control' (whatever that may be) they could justify their vote against the bill on that ground." As a result, the crucial recommendation, the recommendation on which Dillon's entire strategy depended, was that "the 1965 budget expenditure be under $100 billion" – the threshold set by Byrd.

Kennedy's speech to the AFL-CIO therefore achieved a double purpose. It had been what it appeared to be: an effort to build public support for the tax bill. But it had also been a feint: a request to the Senate for speed that everyone already knew would be rejected, but which came with a reward down the road. In a town where it almost always paid to leave something on the table for your opponents, it was the smart – perhaps the only – play.[34]

On Wednesday, November 20, five days after the speech, Dillon attended the annual judicial reception at the White House with other members of the cabinet and the justices of the Supreme Court. In the East Room, while the Marine band played show tunes from *Camelot* and *My Fair Lady*, Dillon found the president in good spirits. Kennedy "looked great," he said afterwards, and was "in wonderful form."

Dillon reminded his chief that he was about to leave for Tokyo with Rusk and other cabinet members.

"This is hello and goodbye," he said.

"I know!" Kennedy replied, laughing. "*You're* going off to Japan, *I've* got to go to Texas. God, how I wish we could trade places."[35]

Chapter Fifteen

Death and Taxes
November 1963–February 1964

Kalorama, Washington DC, November 23, 1963. After listening to Dean Rusk make his flat statement to the press at Andrews Air Base after returning from Honolulu, Douglas Dillon had hung back to avoid talking to reporters and then immediately headed home to Belmont Road. He conferred with his deputies, Fowler and Roosa, before trying to rest for the first time in more than twenty-four hours. Dillon would recall lying in bed unable to sleep amidst the shriek of sirens and in personal grief at the assassination of his friend.

That morning, he phoned Paris to speak to his daughter, Joan, who remembers him as being "very, very upset." Just before 10 o'clock, Dillon entered the White House for the first time since his return, arriving with his wife Phyllis at the East Gate as the rain came down. They were there to attend mass in the family dining room, where an altar had been hastily assembled. The service was just for family and close friends, but even though the Dillons were Episcopalians, William Manchester noted, "they were at the top of the list." It was another poignant sign of the friendship and affection between the Kennedys and the Dillons. For the older man it also spoke to the passing of something beyond friendship. As he would write of Kennedy many years later, "I found him to be a truly great man and have seen no reason to change my opinion in the years that have passed since November 1963."[1]

Amid the trauma of losing a friend and a commander-in-chief, Dillon remained treasury secretary during a national crisis that demanded the very best of him. Urgent issues required his immediate attention. Not the least of these was whether he would continue in office. When the new president phoned him that morning at the Treasury Building, Dillon had immediately offered his resignation. Johnson told him that he had to stay to pass the tax bill and Dillon agreed. "It would have been most indecent for someone in my position to leave the ship," said the former Second World War naval officer.

"My position was perfectly clear, which was that I would stay throughout the four-year term because that's what I'd told President Kennedy I'd do if I took the job. And under the circumstances, with the shock and the change of the administration, it became even more necessary."[2]

While Johnson wanted Dillon to stay on to emphasize continuity and confidence, the new president did not particularly know what he was getting with the treasury secretary he had inherited from Kennedy. In the short term, Johnson told national security advisor McGeorge Bundy that he was "a little worried" about Dillon and whether "the securities exchange, commodity markets, and so forth" would be handled correctly, remembering how they had dropped when President Eisenhower suffered a heart attack. He asked Bundy "if you wouldn't mind talking to Dillon," but the national security advisor assured him that he had already "talked in a general way to Doug yesterday and he [Dillon] was not worried." Still Johnson remained concerned. "They ought to be imaginative enough to find something that they think might stabilize it," he urged Bundy, who promised to follow up with Dillon.[3]

The reason Dillon had offered calm reassurance to Bundy was because he already had his plan in place to ensure that the markets did not go into meltdown when the stock exchange reopened after the assassination. In fact, it had been in place since 1961. On taking office that year, Dillon had been shocked to discover how unprepared the government was for what he described as "a situation so extreme as to represent virtually a 'disorderly situation.'" Dillon had been concerned that speculators and even foreign governments would exploit the US balance of payments weakness during any emergency. In the Second World War, the Federal Reserve had developed a program to make certain that there would always be ample reserves in the banking system. This program had fallen somewhat into abeyance during the postwar era, but Dillon demanded they prepare "new procedures made necessary by … a new and changing situation in the financial markets."

Over the first months of 1961, the United States had negotiated "swap" arrangements with major central banks, buying foreign currency that could be used in the event of an emergency to force the markets to exchange dollars for currency, not gold. Even as Kennedy's death was confirmed, Fowler had ordered the Federal Reserve to request an immediate shutdown of the New York Stock Exchange, thereby avoiding an instant crash. Dillon would also use his relationship with Nelson Rockefeller, the governor of New York and an old schoolfriend, to shut the Stock Exchange on Monday as a mark of respect for Kennedy. That gave the Treasury more time to instill confidence in the markets during the transition of power.

Yet the threat to the United States remained a real one. Over the next two-week period, the United States conducted a $30 million swap with the Bank for International Settlements "in which," Dillon later reported to Johnson, "we swapped our dollars for their gold." All told, it was a spectacularly successful rearguard action, providing what the *Boston Herald* called "the most elaborate defense arsenal for the U.S. dollar ever devised."[4]

These moves to help prevent American gold reserves, the markets, and the dollar from going into free fall saw Dillon operating under duress, but well within the areas of his strengths. The assassination of the president also brought him into other murkier areas over which he had notional but not operational oversight. As secretary of the treasury, Dillon was also the head of the US Secret Service, which was tasked with protecting the president. From the moment Kennedy was killed, urgent questions were raised about how the secret service had allowed the assassination to happen, whether it was part of some broader conspiracy (as Lincoln's had been in 1865), and whether the new president was adequately protected from the same fate.

Dillon would soon have to face the blue-ribbon President's Commission on the Assassination of President Kennedy, led by Chief Justice Earl Warren and unofficially bearing his name ("The Warren Commission"). In the immediate hours after the assassination, however, Dillon had no time to wait for formal inquiries. He had to act immediately to find out what had happened and assess the threat to President Johnson.

Half an hour before the mass in the White House, Dillon held his first debrief with the chief of the Secret Service, James Joseph Rowley. The chief was less than a year older than Dillon and, like him, grew up in New York. There the similarities ended. Rowley was the son of two Irish immigrants. He had worked his way up from the bottom of the Secret Service after joining in 1938, working on presidential protection teams for Roosevelt, Truman (when he thwarted a direct assassination attempt on the life of the president), and Eisenhower. Dillon, with Kennedy in attendance, had sworn him in as the Service's fourteenth chief in September 1961. Dillon liked and trusted Rowley, as had the late president, but now he needed answers fast. Amid grief, the treasury secretary reverted to type with a systematic and reasoned approach to a situation that seemed to allow for neither quality. He asked Rowley for two immediate reports: one on the assassination of the former president, the other on the threat to the new president.

The first would result in a forty-five-page account, "Report of the Secret Service on the Assassination of President Kennedy," that described in clear, unemotional prose the events that had taken place in Dallas, drawing on first-hand accounts from agents in the field, whom Rowley had instructed to write up their recollections of events in the immediate hours after the assassination. Considering that it represents the case for the defense for the Secret Service in how they protected the president, the report is striking for its lack of editorializing, finger-pointing, and self-protection. Rowley would have to defend himself publicly once the Warren Commission got underway. He would face a barrage of criticism from his own predecessor, U.E. Baughman, and the likes of editorial muckraker Drew Pearson, who stated publicly that he thought agents had behaved negligently, possibly even criminally, in the hours before the assassination. Even the new president would undermine him, telling the director of the FBI, J. Edgar Hoover, that he "had more confidence in your judgement" than Rowley's and asking him to "put down your thoughts" on the assassination.

The oral account from Rowley in the days after the assassination and the formal report that came shortly thereafter convinced Dillon that, despite some mistakes, he should stand by the service. "Everyone is watching me," Rowley had observed. "All the agents are going to look at me as a signal." Dillon understood that the same was true for him. To symbolize his confidence, and with Jacqueline Kennedy present, on December 3 he presented an ashen-faced Clint Hill, the agent who had been on the president's personal detail in Dallas, with a gold medal for exceptional bravery. Agent Hill, the secretary pointedly declared, had added luster to the "great tradition of courage and heroism" in the Secret Service.[5]

Dillon also focused on potential threats to the new president. "Number one," Rowley said, "because of the tragedy, we've found we had to have more personnel and resources." He already had the necessary upgrades to hand. In 1962, he had argued for ninety-six new agents and an additional "fourth shift" of the White House detail protecting the president, to rotate agents more regularly. Congress had refused to fund the measures, with lawmakers sniping that he wanted the extra agents to help lead Caroline Kennedy's pony around the paddock. As the contrite Republican congressman Silvio Conte told Rowley after the assassination, "I think we fell far short of the mark." Long-term upgrades with congressional funding would come in 1964 and 1965, but in the days immediately after the assassination Dillon authorized "Project Star." Rowley increased the president's detail from twenty-eight to fifty agents whenever Johnson left the White House, as well as borrowing more than 670 FBI agents, customs officers, and postal investigators for additional support services. Dillon met personally with Jerome B. Wiesner, special assistant to the president for science and technology, to discuss technological advances they could adopt.

The presidential limousine was immediately returned to the manufacturer for "quick stop bullet proofing" and "new research on Presidential automobiles valued at $500,000" was authorized. When the rebuilt Lincoln Continental was returned by the Ford Motor Company, Dillon even insisted on seeing and testing it himself before releasing it for the president's use. He also consulted Eugene Fubini, assistant defense secretary with responsibility for military research and development programs, about "more advanced ways of building protection" into presidential transport. In addition, Dillon, Weisner, and Fubini discussed "so-called 24-hours-a-day protection." They agreed on an immediate "expenditure of $1 million" for Project Star, with funding coming directly from the Defense and Treasury budgets. Dillon would eventually ask Congress for $12.6 million in additional funding for the Secret Service.

In his testimony to the Warren Commission, Dillon would submit a plan worked out with Rowley on "what has to be done." It seemed a flagrant breach of Washington protocol, because the president had not approved it, yet politically the approach served Johnson well. As Bundy pointed out to the president, after being instructed by him to form a small committee with Dillon and deputy-attorney general Nicholas Katzenbach to study the recommendations of the Warren Commission Report, their task would be "not to let this damn thing get in your hair." Dillon's initiative also spoke to the nervous times. "Dillon gave Justice Warren and Congress what they were both clamoring for," Carol Leonnig writes in her history of the Secret Service: "the comfort of a well-reasoned plan."

"Nothing can redress the tragedy of that day," Dillon would tell the House Appropriations Committee, "but we all bear an awesome responsibility both to the country and the entire free world to ensure that the protection now and hereafter provided our president, whoever he may be, is the most effective possible in our democratic society."[6]

The Kennedy assassination placed Dillon, as titular head of the Secret Service, in the foreground of events. That did not lessen his more conventional functions as treasury secretary. He also found himself at the center of the new president's ambitions for winning his own mandate in 1964. Half an hour before his first cabinet meeting on November 23, Johnson phoned one of his closest allies in the Senate, George Smathers of Florida, to find out what the state of the tax bill was in committee. A brilliant fixer, Smathers had already been working closely with Dillon and Fowler to reassure Byrd that the budget would come in under $100 billion. Now Smathers told Johnson that they had the votes to get the tax bill through the Senate, but that it would not happen in 1963. "I tell you Mr. President, I'd hate to see you make that a big issue," Smathers warned, "because I'm afraid we're not going to be able to do it." Byrd's tactics had been clear all along. "What Byrd was really trying to accomplish is to hold up the tax bill until he could see and prove that Kennedy was going to have a budget announcement of over a hundred billion dollars, see," Smathers reported. "So, he could then argue, you know, that we're financing this tax cut with deficits and so on" – hence Smathers's attempt, with "the approval of Dillon," to "try to make another deal with Byrd" whereby the Senate Finance chair would cooperate in return for a commitment on the budget.[7]

Caro wrongly suggests that Smathers's observation that "we're not going to be able to do it" referred to "the prospects for passing the tax cut bill" rather than the more prosaic chances of getting it out of the committee in 1963. In fact, Dillon had predicted all along that the bill would pass in 1964 if they accommodated Byrd's determination to link the tax cut to the budget. He had approved the Smathers approach to Byrd precisely because it matched the strategy that he and Fowler had agreed to with Kennedy in September and confirmed again with him only weeks before the assassination. Coming in under a hundred billion was essential, he advised, not because it "would still the opposition of those who think the 1964 totals were too high," but because it would "spell 'expenditure control' to reasonable people." More politics than economics was involved. The tax bill would only pass if "the 1965 budget expenditure be under $100 billion," Kennedy heard, but it also had to be done in a way that Byrd and the deficit hawks "can claim some credit for the adoption of a policy of 'expenditure control' reflected in the budget." It was why Kennedy had already overridden Heller and quietly directed that the budget should be around the $98 billion mark.[8]

Johnson knew little of these facts, because like most vice presidents before him, he had been kept almost entirely out of the policy loop. Anything he knew about the tax proposals, Johnson had bitterly complained a few months earlier, he "got it from the New York Times." Now the new president had to play catch up. On November 25, hours after Kennedy's funeral, he summoned the Troika of Dillon, Heller, and Gordon. "What about your tax bill?" he said directly to Dillon, although he did not wait for the treasury secretary to respond. Instead, recorded Gardner Ackley, who had accompanied Heller from the Council of Economic Advisers, "he answered his own question," telling the Troika that Byrd's $100 billion was not an estimate but "a magic number" and "a psychological barrier that should not be breached." The political facts were simple, Johnson told them: "We won't have the votes to get it to the floor unless we tell them the budget will be about one hundred billion. It's as simple as that."[9]

Heller and Gordon protested that the figure was too low – "this totally artificial administrative budget figure was just a will-o-the-wisp," Heller said, urging the president to adopt a figure nearer $108 billion. Johnson responded with characteristic earthiness (recorded surely euphemistically by Ackley) that "Unless you get that budget down around $100 billion, 'you won't pee one drop.'" To all this blustering but shrewd presidential analysis, Dillon gave quiet, understated agreement. He noted that indeed "you had to pay the price to get the tax bill, but it was worth it." What he did not do, however, was tell Johnson that the strategy the new president had outlined was identical to the one he had already agreed to with Kennedy, and which had been in play since September.

That shrewd evasion offers a telling insight into Dillon's deftness as a political operator. The new commander-in-chief – who had previously been on the margins of the administration – was clearly in "I'm in charge mode." He was determined to make sure that everyone understood, in his biographer's words, that "it was his administration now, and they heard what he was saying." So Dillon let him enjoy this moment in the saddle, not least because Johnson was doing the treasury secretary's work for him in laying down the $100 billion "magic number," while his counterpart Heller, who understood economics better than he understood politics, was arguing that they should face down Byrd with an unrealistic number.[10]

Heller would later say that Johnson "carried on a masterful charade saying he couldn't possibly get the budget below $110 billion, then, maybe he could get it to $105 billion, and finally, he actually brought it in at $98 billion or $97.8 billion – then Harry Byrd went along with it." It was a brilliant piece of political showmanship by Johnson – one that William Manchester notes "bewitched the financial community, creating the image of the most economical president since Coolidge." Even Robert Anderson, Dillon's predecessor as treasury secretary and a fiscal hawk, praised Johnson for reducing the deficit. He and Eisenhower "are going to have to vote for me now," Johnson remarked.

Yet the plan itself was the one Dillon outlined to Johnson in a memo entitled "Tax Bill – Strategy and Tactics," written with Fowler immediately following the Troika meeting. It made no reference to earlier memos or strategies developed with Kennedy. In fact, the entire document was framed as having been "prepared pursuant to the conference last Monday night" with "the conclusion confirmed [that] without a new initiative ... many months of potential delay" would ensue.[11]

"What is the best device to break the procedural impasse?" Dillon asked. This time it was the secretary who answered his own question. "The best device to break the procedural impasse," he wrote in advice sure to appeal to Johnson, "would seem to be a negotiated arrangement with Chairman Byrd undertaken directly or indirectly by the president." Was such an advance commitment "wise policy?" the memo asked rhetorically. "The answer," it confirmed, "is unequivocally affirmative." Dillon took aim at Heller's rival memo, written after the meeting, which argued that the lowest the budget could go was $102 billion. "This evaluation misses the main question," he wrote, pointing to the politics of the situation – "How do we overcome our present inability to secure the enactment of the tax bill ... and what are we prepared to give up for it?"

Dillon outlined tactics for negotiating with Byrd. He suggested the president tell the Finance chair that he would be willing to limit expenditure "to a figure not to exceed $100 billion," but with a clear understanding that delay beyond January would mean a higher figure of $101.5 billion. In this way, Byrd and supporters would "share with the president some of the responsibility for a budget increase well beyond the $100 billion level or the credit for holding the level below that figure." The tradeoff between reducing budget expenditures and delaying the tax bill clearly favored early enactment of the tax cuts. As Fowler quipped, "this is preferring a bird in the hand as being worth more than a bird in the bush."[12]

Some in the White House still tried to push back against the idea of slashing the budget under $100 billion. "I *know* you can get the tax bill without doing that," Theodore Sorensen told the president. Johnson knew better. "Our problem seems to [Dillon] is getting it out of the Finance Committee," he told Sorensen, noting that "They're not going to give us the tax bill unless we get our budget down to 100 billion." When Sorensen complained that "the fellows who told you that happen to be giving you a fact which justifies the conclusion with which they sympathize," Johnson swatted him away. "I want to keep it alive," he said. To do otherwise meant "they'll say the Kennedy program was defeated, and next, Johnson is repudiated."[13]

Doubtless Johnson, the former "Master of the Senate," needed no advice from his treasury secretary on how to handle Congress. All the same, he applied Dillon's approach with alacrity. Two weeks after taking up the presidency, he invited Byrd to lunch at the White House, where no lack of care was taken to flatter and sweet talk the intransigent but courtly senator. Jack

Valenti, one of Johnson's closest aides, who lived in the White House for the first few months, recalls that it was the only time he could remember LBJ using the small private room off the Oval Office for a luncheon. The menu included Byrd's favorite potato soup. There was a personal tour of the White House that even included the swimming pool with its famous mural of the US Virgin Islands painted for JFK by Bernard Lamotte. And while Byrd did not move one inch from his position that he wanted the budget cut under $100 billion and to see the full estimates before he would let the tax bill be reported out of the committee, he nevertheless made it clear that he appreciated the courtesies and was not an immovable object. "Senator Byrd was a gentleman of the old school," Dillon noted, "essentially a country gentleman." He certainly knew what was happening to him with all the soft soap being lathered on by Johnson. *Time* journalist Neil McNeil noted that there was a "twinkling" in the senator's eye and a "fond note" in his voice afterwards as he spoke of Johnson wanting "to work on me a little bit" at the White House lunch. It confirmed Dillon's own impression. "The big difference I noticed in Byrd," he told Johnson, "is that personally, whereas two or three months ago he was sort of bitter about the bill, he now gives the impression of being rather relaxed about it, and saying he's opposed to it, but indicating he believes it will pass."[14]

Despite the public expression of bonhomie between Johnson and Byrd, the president remained frustrated that for all his "mastery," he could not get the tax bill reported out of committee faster. This frustration boiled over in a phone call with Dillon in December. "You didn't make any progress today, did you?" Johnson asked testily, pointing out that the Civil Rights bill was due to "hit the Senate" on January 17. If it got ahead of the tax bill, then "you wait four months." When Dillon blandly stated, "that's what we don't want to do," Johnson let a flash of anger show. "Well, that's what's going to happen, though, the way you're moving," he grouched. "They just procrastinate, and put off, and shimmy around. I've never seen such an operation up there." He wanted more from his treasury secretary. "You've got to get them all in there, and get them organized, and say 'God Almighty, fellow, we can't stand this ... You're going to ruin us on our fiscal program.' I'd go and plead with Byrd."[15]

Dillon followed up the next day with a memo to Johnson that showed a defensiveness rarely seen in his correspondence with Kennedy. "Personally," he told the new president, "I am convinced the Treasury position ... was the best position we could have taken and that it has not caused any delays in the Committee beyond what would have occurred in any event." The telephone exchange the day before could be put down to a moment of White House irritation at the slow progress. Dillon sensed that it also showed Johnson did not particularly like or trust him as an adviser. Quite why or how this had happened is hard to document, but not difficult to imagine. Dillon was the cabinet member who had been closest to Kennedy personally and the new president remained highly suspicious – antagonistically so – of Kennedy people. He rightly believed most looked down on him as the Southern hick "Rufus CornPone." Dillon was above such behavior personally and was never part of the more abrasive elements of the Kennedy operation led by Bobby. But Dillon, the multimillionaire Wall Street banker with a character that blended complete self-assurance with a diffident sense of reserve and high moral purpose, could hardly have been more programmed to raise suspicions in someone who had grown up in poverty in rural Texas. On one occasion in December, Johnson shocked Kermit Gordon by telling him he didn't need to bother consulting Dillon, who was in Florida. "If he wants to have his rest or his leisure on Hobe Sound," Johnson groused, "he can have it."

Worse were the stories David Halberstam would recount in *The Best and the Brightest* – namely that Johnson humiliated an unnamed cabinet member believed to be Dillon by taking a meeting with him while "in the can" with the door open. When the book was published in 1972, Dillon refuted the story as false, writing to Tom Johnson, executive assistant to the former president, that the gossip was "gross and insulting" and "a slur on the president's sense of decency, invented out of whole cloth." He asked the aide to show the letter to Lyndon and Ladybird Johnson and requested that it be deposited at the Johnson Presidential Library so that "this falsehood is thoroughly discredited." Yet the reason such a story later seemed so plausible was precisely because of the vast gulf in upbringing and personal style between the two men. Johnson did similar things to many people and was notoriously both thin-skinned and overbearing. If there was ever someone he might look to put in his place by showing that raw political power outranked money and class, it was Douglas Dillon.[16]

Still, it was Dillon, a gentleman of the old school New York style, whom Johnson now sent to pay court to the old school Virginian Byrd. Dillon reported back on December 14 that slowly but surely, Byrd appeared to be moving. "He is willing to see faster action in the Committee," the secretary told Johnson on prospects for January, "but it is equally clear that he himself will do nothing to force a speed up." The key factor remained Byrd seeing and approving a budget under $100 billion. Dillon made four recommendations for action by the president. These were, first, to give personal time to "important individuals in the business world" who would have "very substantial influence" on the Republican members of the committee; second, to make overtures to the left-of-center Citizens Committee for Tax Reduction for reasons that would "be of little positive help but unless it is done the liberals would feel offended and could cause unnecessary difficulties"; third, to have the galley proofs of the budget made available to Senate Finance members and to speak to the Senate minority leader Everett Dirksen to "personally request his cooperation in moving the bill in Committee"; and finally to "continue personal attention to the Democratic members of the Finance Committee."[17]

Johnson worked the phones ceaselessly over the following weeks. "I worked as hard on the budget as I have ever worked on anything," he would say. He called members of the Senate Finance Committee personally to cajole and promise favors on projects that mattered to them. He used his good personal relationship with Dirksen, whose time as minority whip and minority leader had overlapped with Johnson's time as Senate majority leader, to find Republican support. "Every businessman in this country would have some confidence and you'd probably pick up a bunch of Senate seats," he laughed, "because you're running the Senate like I ran it [by] being pretty patriotic and you cooperate." The most crucial meeting came on January 7, 1964, when Johnson had Byrd back to the White House to report on the budget. "I have a surprise for you, Harry," the president told him. "I've got the damn thing down under one hundred billion – way under. It's only $97.9 billion, [so] now you can tell your friends that you forced the president of the United States to reduce the budget before you let him have his tax cut." Once outside, Byrd told reporters that he wanted to "congratulate the president" on reducing the federal budget. When the two men spoke again the next day, Byrd told Johnson that he had "made a good start." He could not vote for the tax cut himself – that was a step too far – but he would no longer block it "in any way" and neither would he encourage others to do so.[18]

The tax bill was almost over the line. Johnson told Dillon not to take anything for granted in getting it out of committee, urging him to "suck up" to tricky customers such as Russell B. Long of Louisiana, who was a Democratic floor leader of the bill. "Tell him the president called you and said that 'God Almighty, Russell sure did a good job,'" the president told him. It was good tactical advice, because it was Long who threw the final spanner into the congressional works. On January 23 he sprung a last-minute amendment that would see excise duties on luxury goods abolished. To Dillon's astonishment, the committee passed it. The potential cost to the Treasury in revenue was $400 million – a figure that blew a hole in the bill and the budget. With Dillon unwell, Fowler took the brunt of Johnson's fury in the Oval Office. "I've spent more damn time on this tax bill than I have on all bills put together," he raged at the undersecretary. "Y'all ought to have better relations with those Finance members than this. It's a damn shame."[19]

Johnson now conducted the kind of full court press for which he was famous. He flattered or browbeat the members of the committee into reversing the vote. "Now the great tragedy to me, Mr. President, and I want to be frank with you," Senator Abraham Ribicoff of Connecticut complained, "is that Dillon doesn't know the politics and the – If he was, well, he would –" Johnson cut him off. "I think that's right," he said, "and I don't know them either!" He gave the hapless Ribicoff the famous Johnson treatment. "You save my face this afternoon," he half-promised, half-threatened, "and I'll save your face tomorrow." It was pure politics and it worked. The amendment was overturned and the Finance Committee sent the tax bill to the Senate floor that same day.[20]

Finally, the logjam broke. The Senate passed the bill on February 7, and the reconciled House and Senate bills passed in both houses on February 26. Johnson signed the Revenue Act of 1964 into law at a ceremony that same evening. Immediately afterwards, the Civil Rights bill was introduced on the floor of the Senate. In a sad but touching gesture, Dillon went from the White House to Georgetown. There he presented four pens that the president had used to sign the act to Jacqueline Kennedy as gifts for herself, her two children, and the Kennedy Library. The late president now had a major legislative achievement as part of his legacy. For Dillon, the accomplishment was personal as much as it was political: he had delivered the Kennedy tax cut for his slain friend.

"How much did the tax program get changed from Mr. Kennedy's concept to the way Mr. Johnson got it passed?" an interviewer asked Dillon five years later.

"Well," he replied, "not at all."[21]

Chapter Sixteen

We've Got to Save the World
March 1964–April 1965

The Kennedy tax cut represented the high-water mark of Dillon's time at the Treasury. Now he yearned to leave the political stage as his lack of connection with the new president continued to manifest itself. "I had easier access to and much greater personal access to President Kennedy," Dillon said. "I saw him a great deal more than I saw President Johnson." As LBJ moved to his high-cost War on Poverty, he consulted Heller more regularly than Dillon. That move was a recalibration within the administration, although more galling was that Johnson spoke to Robert Anderson, treasury secretary in the Eisenhower administration and an old acquaintance, more frequently than he did to his own treasury secretary. The former secretary could hardly contain his glee at being consulted by a president who affectionately called him "Uncle Robert." To some degree this action was political, because Johnson knew that his support for the budget and the tax cuts gave the administration cover with conservatives. But the full and uninhibited range of their long, regular conversations, covering not just the budget but the balance of payments, the price of gold, and even Anderson personally blocking the appointment of Seymour Harris to the Fed, spoke to a closeness that did not exist with Dillon.[1]

Old Kennedy hands in the administration would urge Johnson to bring Dillon into the fold that spring. "I think that there's a lot of – and I had the same feeling with President Kennedy," Bobby Kennedy told Johnson when discussing Vietnam, "I think there's a lot of people around such as Douglas Dillon who frequently, based on experience and some judgment, have some good ideas on some of these matters." Johnson demurred, but Kennedy tried again a few weeks later. "The other person, Mr. President," he urged, "who has some sense on these matters is – you know, again, none of us are always right, but who has got some sense and has had a great deal of experience is

Douglas Dillon." Again, Johnson fobbed him off, saying that "I told them, I tell them every day" to involve Dillon. "Once again," writes Michael Beschloss, editor of the Johnson tapes, "Kennedy is pushing Dillon and once again Johnson is not buying. If LBJ had really told his people to include Dillon, they would have complied."[2]

Having informed Johnson of his intention to leave after the election and wishing to remain above the fray during the campaign, Dillon's activities began to assume a valedictory quality. During a keynote address at the Harvard Business School on June 6, Dillon made the bold claim of having crossed "a significant watershed" in the long history of American economic policy. Ranging across his three and half years in the Treasury (and perhaps enjoying the dig at Anderson), he pointed to policy changes that "have encompassed perhaps our most significant advance in decades." Although he drew attention to the record-breaking performance of the economy that was already underway, his main emphasis was on the change in philosophical mindset and the structural reform that supported it. He pointed to "the emergence of a national determination to use fiscal policy as a dynamic and affirmative agent in fostering economic growth." Government spending and taxation were no longer just about canceling each other out (another shot at Anderson); the key was to make them work together to spur on the economy. The period since 1961 had "demonstrated, not in theory but in actual practice, how our different instruments of economic policy – expenditure, tax, debt management and monetary policies – can be tuned in concert toward achieving different, even disparate economic goals."

A dynamic expansion of the economy at home could be undertaken without aggravating the balance of payments abroad. Where systemic problems remained, "the chief of these obstacles is the fact that within our constitutional system, a long lag typically intervenes between a request for a change in tax rates and legislative approval." This last dig was aimed at Byrd and Congress in general for the sclerotic passage of the Kennedy tax cut. "Unless and until some method is worked out, acceptable to the Congress and consistent with its prerogatives, whereby tax rates can be varied without undue delay," he admonished, "the purely countercyclical function of tax policy will remain outside our arsenal of economic tools."[3]

The speech was a landmark statement, not just for Dillon personally but for what it represented about fiscal policy in the United States. For this secretary of the treasury – a Republican in a Democratic administration – to talk about an aggressive deployment of both demand-side and supply-side policy working together for economic growth was something new in American politics and symbolized the political equivalent of Milton Friedman's oft-quoted aphorism the next year that "in one sense, we are all Keynesians now; in another, nobody is any longer a Keynesian." Dillon represented that equipoise as a conservative Keynesian. As the *New York Times* economics correspondent (and later budget spokesman for the Reagan Administration) Edwin L. Dale summed up in his report of the speech, "Economists by and large agree [with Dillon] that there have been such shifts. They also generally agree that the policy changes have been right."[4]

"I must confess that I was surprised at how successful tax reduction was," Wilbur Mills admitted. "While ready to concede that a massive tax cut would stimulate the economy to move closer to full employment, I did not expect the economy's reaction to be quite so prompt and quite so vigorous." That economic expansion was spectacular. The gross national product for 1965 exceeded Council of Economic Advisers' projections by $9 billion. Unemployment dropped to a record low of 4.1 percent. The deficit fell to 0.2 percent of GDP. Three million more people were in work in 1965 than in 1961. Corporate tax rates were slashed. Personal tax cuts were the biggest to that date in American history. Tax revenues were cut by around $11 billion, with top and bottom rates cut from 91 and 20 percent in 1963, to 77 and 16 percent in 1964, and to 70 and 14 percent in 1965. The average marginal rate for a moderate-income couple in 1965 was 25 percent. No wonder that when Lyndon Johnson returned from a campaign visit to Massachusetts in the summer of 1964, he reported that he had seen 200,000 employed married men and that every single one of them had been smiling.[5]

Johnson belatedly appreciated Dillon's achievement. That summer he told the secretary, "No man in my administration has my confidence more than you do. In my judgment, no man deserves it more." The praise was the start of the "Johnson treatment" that would have seemed remarkable only a few months earlier. "I'll follow," the president told Dillon as they headed into the election, while trying to convince him to stay. "Anything you want me to do, you just tell me."[6]

The election would be a triumph for Johnson – "the largest popular vote, the greatest margin, and the biggest percentage (61 percent) ever received by a President to that point in US history," his biographer notes. It was a success that would also reach a long way down the ballot to give him the biggest majority to work with in Congress for a president since the reelection of Johnson's hero, FDR, in 1936. Yet on election day itself – Tuesday, November

3, 1964 – LBJ felt out of sorts. For his whole political career, he had often found himself ill in bed and twice even in a hospital bed, on election day, worn down by the punishing physical exertion of campaigning and a sensibility that, for all its bravado, was highly strung and prone to nervous collapse. This day was no different, with Johnson complaining to anyone who would listen that he was laid low. "I've just got a sore back," he moaned to Dean Rusk that afternoon. "Sore hip been hurting me. And sore head. I've had a headache all day, and I've been in bed all day. I just kind of came off the mountain, you know. I've been kind of keyed up and I'm just kind of feeling punch-drunk."[7]

In the aftermath of the election, there would be plenty of hyperbole about what the result meant for the Republic. James Reston of the *New York Times* predicted a new "Era of good feelings" with the United States "on the fringe of a Golden Era." Perhaps "era" did not go far enough. The historian James MacGregor Burns, who had written a waspish biography of Kennedy in 1960, now proclaimed "this is as surely a liberal epoch as the late 19th century was a conservative one." Never one to be outdone, Johnson himself added his own twist. "These are the most hopeful times," he would say when turning on the lights of the National Christmas Tree, "in all the years since Christ was born in Bethlehem."[8]

Others were more skeptical. Arthur Schlesinger Jr. recognized the ascendancy of the 36th president. Soon after the election, he would dwell on "the ruthlessness of history and power which makes so many in Washington today act as if JFK never existed." He grudgingly acknowledged that Johnson "understands that to be a great president you must do great things – and he is determined to do them," yet was convinced "the test will come when he runs out of ideas – up to this point he has been living intellectually off the Kennedy years." Lying in bed, nursing his sore head and his aching back, the lachrymose Johnson came to a similar conclusion, already recognizing that he would still need to draw on at least some Kennedy people for his own first full term.[9]

While Johnson suffered, Douglas Dillon was in more relaxed form at Hobe Sound, Florida. Because Johnson had affirmed Kennedy's understanding that the heads of the Treasury, State, and Defense departments would not be politically active during the campaign, Dillon managed to sidestep its worst excesses and walk the narrow path between statesmanship and the conduct of everyday Treasury business. His more pressing difficulty – the fact that he was a Republican serving a Democratic president – turned out to be no difficulty at all. The nomination by the Republican party of the right-wing senator from Arizona, Barry Goldwater, as its presidential candidate let Dillon off the hook in a way that the nomination of a more philosophically compatible liberal Republican such as Henry Cabot Lodge Jr. or Nelson Rockefeller would not have done. Lodge might as well have spoken for Dillon that summer when Goldwater was nominated in Daly City, California. "This convention was run by people who have no understanding of the world we live in," he said, opting instead to "go out on my boat" rather than get involved. Dillon pledged his own support to Johnson, although he was scrupulous in the way that he did it. "I told him I was going to support him financially in the campaign," he recalled. "I told him that I felt strongly and that I wanted to support him, but I did not want him to misinterpret that and think that it had anything to do with the desire to stay in the government. At the end of the year, I'd have to leave; well, he heard about the support and didn't listen much to my future plans."[10]

In fact, Johnson had been listening closely, as became clear when the telephone in Hobe Sound rang on Election Day and the president came on the line. "I wanted to call you," Johnson told him, "I wanted you and Phyllis to know how much we loved you and how fine you were and you always did the right thing at the right time and how much comfort you gave us and how competent and courageous and solid you've been – and how much I think whatever vote we get is gonna be a vote of confidence in how you run your business."

Dillon, audibly in jovial form down in Florida, thanked Johnson warmly, reaffirming that the prospect of Goldwater becoming president had been anathema to him. "The country needed it and we've gotten it and you've really saved us from something that could have been awful," he told Johnson.

LBJ came back with more praise of his own. "You couldn't have been better," he said. "If I had looked the world over, I couldn't have found anybody who gave me more comfort and more competence and more strength and I just wanted you to know it!"[11]

The next day LBJ told Abe Fortas, one of his closest confidants and a soon-to-be Supreme Court nominee, that he knew "Dillon wants to leave," noting plaintively that "I sure don't want him to." He resolved to lay it on thick for Dillon.[12]

On Monday, November 9, after receiving a letter from Dillon saying that the "time had come" to plan his exit, Johnson telephoned him in Florida from the LBJ Ranch near Stonewall, Texas. After some pleasant chit-chat during which Dillon reported "getting a good rest here, it's nice and sunny," the president got down to business, asking him to come to the ranch to discuss the letter.

"Why don't I just send my plane," Johnson announced grandly. "I have a JetStar standing by. Come prepared to stay all night!"

Dillon agreed, saying he would like the chance to "explain my problem" – but LBJ, in avuncular fashion, cut across him.

"Don't you get in any argumentative mood now, because you know I can't do without you," he laughed. "I can't have a problem with you 'cause you're too solid."

"I've got to rely on you," he went on. "We've got to save the world! Tell Clarence to get someone else to run all that money. We want you right there at my side."[13]

Two days later Dillon left Palm Beach airport at 7 a.m. to fly to the LBJ Ranch to explain why he planned to leave the administration. "He says his daddy is worth a quarter of a billion dollars and nobody's handled it for ten or twelve years," Johnson complained, "and he's just got to do it and he can't stay after January."[14]

Dillon's own reaction to the visit was captured in a phone call that Johnson made that day to Sidney Weinberg, the head of Goldman Sachs, nicknamed "Mr. Wall Street." The president joked of Dillon that "he's a Republican, you know, but he and I agree once in a while!" before handing the phone over to the treasury secretary to say hello. "It's wonderful to talk to the president and he still has his sense of humor," Weinberg told his fellow banker. "He certainly does," Dillon replied, dragging out each word and unable to keep the weariness out of his voice. No doubt it had been a trying day. "He liked to visit with you and go on," Dillon later reflected on Johnson. "It was just his nature."

It was easy to see why Johnson might want Dillon to stay, telling aides that he "has the confidence of the country and the dollar." Dillon himself, however, was convinced that he could no longer operate at the top of his game. "I was just exhausted," he said. "I'd had eight years in Washington at top-level jobs and I just thought I was tired out and had enough and had to leave under any circumstances." Johnson pushed him to stay for another year, but Dillon firmly told him, "No, sir, that's too long!" In the end, Dillon agreed to stay at the Treasury until the spring, although tellingly, whenever he tried to pin Johnson down on a specific date, the president always remained vague or ignored the letters. In the end, Dillon simply wrote to him saying that he would be leaving on April 1. "That brought action," he said. "I finally got an answer."[15]

If Dillon was hoping for a quiet last few months, he would be disappointed. On February 4, 1965, without warning, Charles de Gaulle launched a blistering attack on the US dollar and the wider Bretton Woods international monetary system. By making the dollar the reserve currency in 1945, convertible into gold, the United States had been able to run vast postwar balance of payments deficits, knowing that its creditors would always hold their reserves in dollars and even lend them back to the United States. This arrangement had given Washington a financial and political advantage that the French president was no longer prepared to tolerate. "The gold exchange standard no longer corresponds to present realities and, in consequence, entails heavier and heavier inconveniences," he loftily declared, noting that gold was the only "unquestionable monetary basis which did not bear the mark of any individual country." In practical terms, this proposal meant that France would be looking to redeem most of its holdings of dollars – estimated at $300 million – for gold. "De Gaulle dramatized this decision," writes his biographer Julian Jackson, "by refusing to allow the Americans to move the newly converted gold to the vaults of the Federal Reserve Bank. Instead, he sent a special Air France plane to pick up the cargo from New York."[16]

"I will tell you one thing," the French president boasted to his closest aide, Jacques Foccart. "A press conference by de Gaulle is noticed by the entire world!"[17]

In response, Dillon authorized the kind of press briefing rarely seen during his tenure. It depicted de Gaulle as an out of touch, historically amnesic crank. The French plan was "drastic" and a "reversion to a long-gone yesteryear." The gold standard had "collapsed in 1931 and proved incapable of financing the huge increase of world trade that has marked the twentieth century." Any move to restore the system, "with all its rigidities and sharp deflationary consequences," would be "quite contrary to the mainstream of thinking" among the leading economies of the world. "If one member goes off in an abrupt departure," a Treasury spokesperson concluded, "the system can stand it." After all, "He doesn't have an awful lot of dollars to convert!"

When Dillon faced the Senate Foreign Relations Committee the next day, he made similar points, albeit in measured tones that spoke of puzzlement rather than anger. When looked at beside earlier statements by de Gaulle, this recent position represented "a seeming contradiction." As to the gold standard, well, that was obvious to any sensible person. "The collapse of the former was really the basis of the worldwide recession in the 1930s," Dillon reminded the senators. It was difficult to understand why anyone would wish to return to it.

America's allies, notably Britain and Germany, moved quickly to distance themselves from the French statement, making it clear that they would not support the return to a gold standard or engage in the large-scale redemption of dollars for gold. Despite de Gaulle's boasts, the markets barely rippled during the incident.[18]

Part of the reason for American resilience in the face of the French assault was that Dillon had successfully stopped the hemorrhage of gold from American coffers. Between 1958 and the first months of the Kennedy administration in 1961, the United States had lost $5.4 billion in gold. "[It was] a rate that would have completely depleted America's gold stocks within the decade, if not sooner," writes Francis Gavin, "but that is not what happened." Dillon stemmed the tide, and over the same timescale the United States lost less than $2 billion in gold.

The unshowy, behind-the-scenes initiatives that Dillon developed to intervene actively in the currency markets, particularly the gold pool agreement, dampened demand and provided mechanisms to deal with emergencies (as was shown in November 1963). It meant that despite still running large payments deficits, the United States was able to withstand hostile attacks on gold stocks such as de Gaulle's in 1965. This robustness had happened "just in the nick of time," Dillon told Johnson. "While it looks like we may be heading into a stormy period for the international monetary system in view of possible devaluation in the United Kingdom and the current French attitude, I feel confident that your program has given the dollar all the strength needed to weather the storm and more besides."[19]

On the question of the balance of payments, the outlook was hazier. Dillon had been grappling with the problem since his first day in office and had enjoyed some measure of success. A task force report written at the end of 1964 by Carl Kaysen, former deputy national security advisor in the Kennedy administration, pointed to "three important tasks [that] remain on the agenda of international financial policy for the new Administration." These were ending the deficit in the US balance of payments, protecting US gold reserves against conversion of outstanding dollars, and reforming the international monetary system. "Solid progress toward all three goals has been made in the past three and a half years," Kaysen wrote to Johnson, "But we are not yet out of the woods." It was a succinct summary of Dillon's record to date in addressing this intractable issue.[20]

The US balance of payments was better than it had been since the late 1950s. "A very significant part of the improvement in our balance of payments results from the actions we have taken to cut the outflow of dollars for Government spending abroad," Dillon told Johnson in the run up to the 1964 election, pointing to the retrenchment measures in aid and military spending that he and McNamara had introduced the previous year. "In that regard, we are well on our way toward reaching the target of a $1 billion reduction in Government spending from 1962 levels which was set in President Kennedy's Balance of Payments Message of July 18, 1963." The Vietnam war, already escalating by early 1965, would soon reverse the trend and make these figures look miniscule.[21]

In his last year in office, Dillon introduced the Interest Equalization Tax, which helped stem the outflow of dollars by making it more expensive for foreigners to raise money in the United States. He also engaged in diplomacy within the framework of the International Monetary Fund (IMF) to make the Bretton Woods system work better. He proposed a quota system whereby members would up their contributions to the IMF by 50 percent but crucially, they would also be able to increase what they took out, thereby expanding international liquidity. After much wrangling, with the French complaining that the United States and Britain would be the main beneficiaries, a deal was struck at the IMF meeting in Tokyo in the fall that saw lower increases of 25 percent introduced. "This should handle the international credits issue at least for the immediate future," Dillon told Johnson. It was another example of his gradualist approach, working within the existing system, to make it more efficient and effective.[22]

After his departure, the administration shifted from this approach to a more aggressive attempt to reconstruct the international monetary system based on a new form of international liquidity called "special drawing rights" (SDRs). In July 1965 it announced that "the United States now stands prepared to attend and participate in an international monetary conference which would consider what steps we might jointly take to secure substantial improvements in international monetary arrangements." The resulting negotiations were bitter and protracted. By the time the United States got its way in 1967, the ballooning costs of the domestic "Great Society" program and the disastrous war in Vietnam put unsustainable inflationary pressures on the dollar and the balance of payments deficit, making the new system irrelevant. In the end, it would take the 1971 "Nixon shock," when President Richard Nixon suspended the dollar's convertibility into gold, to call the last rites on the Bretton Woods system. It was, Nixon said in a statement that outraged allies, the only way "to create a new prosperity without war."[23]

Finding a successor to Dillon as treasury secretary proved harder than Johnson imagined. His first choice was Donald C. Cook, president of the American Electric Power Company – the largest privately owned American utility. Even today, business historians describe Cook, trained as a lawyer and accountant, as "an acknowledged 'legend' of American industry." Having served as chairman of the Securities and Exchange Commission in the Truman administration, he would have come into the Treasury with a comprehensive range of expertise from industry and finance. He also had a shadow hanging over him. Cook was a longstanding crony of Johnson's, which brought with it suspicions of corruption. Questions swirled around Cook for insider trading with another longtime Johnson sidekick, Bobby Baker. The toxic nature of those rumors became clear when LBJ telephoned Everett Dirksen, Republican Senate minority leader, to see whether nominating Cook would fly. "He is by far the best and the most qualified," Johnson told him. "He wants to come, he's a great expert and my man. McNamara said he's the smartest man in the country." Dirksen demurred. "Don't do it," he said, causing LBJ to interrupt himself. "And if – Huh?" he exclaimed. "Life's too short," Dirksen told him. Cook "can't live it down, no matter how long he serves."[24]

"Both the president and Donald Cook thought it was all set and he was supposed to take over about the first of March," Dillon recalled. "He came and spent a couple of hours in my office, and I talked to him about the details of taking over the Treasury … Well, something unknown occurred in between there and a couple of weeks later it was announced that he wasn't going to be the new Secretary."[25]

What was unclear was the extent to which Dillon was that "something" that occurred. In February, leaks appeared in the newspapers saying Johnson had tapped Cook as Dillon's successor, but that there were concerns in the Treasury about the appointment. LBJ phoned Dillon directly to express his fury, but he only managed to get hold of Dillon's unfortunate special assistant, Robert Carswell. "It has hurt us and more than that it has hurt my pride," he fumed. "Anybody over there who can't be loyal to us ought to leave … You tell the Secretary I want it stopped!" In more measured fashion, Johnson fell back on the former treasury secretary, Robert Anderson, to try to stop the leaks. "Any way in the world that you could use any influence with any of your financial friends or Doug himself," he pleaded, "to quit giving out interviews about when he's leaving and how he's leaving and why he's leaving and all this stuff would be greatly received!"[26]

Once his first and only choice was out of the running, Johnson seemed at a loss about whom he should pick. Rumors circulated that he was set to announce David Kennedy, who would later hold the job in the Nixon administration. In the end, when the president asked Dillon for his advice, the current incumbent recommended continuity. By that he meant Henry "Joe" Fowler, who had served as undersecretary from 1961 to 1964. "I couldn't think of anyone who would be better," Dillon recalled, "because he knew the ropes. He was extremely loyal, and I thought he could get on well with the president." On March 18, 1965, two days after their talk, Dillon received a message from the president asking him to phone the White House. "So, I called him and he said, 'Hi, Doug, I want you to talk to the new secretary of the treasury,'" Dillon remembered. "Here was Joe Fowler sitting in his office. So that was that." Right to the end, Dillon had quietly succeeded in getting his own way.[27]

Now it was all over bar the parties. Dillon's successor threw a farewell dinner for him with members of Congressional committees "with no hearings, executive sessions or conferences" to celebrate a relationship that had been "marked by fruitful cooperation." Rusk hosted a reception at the State Department, with speeches given beneath the magnificent French crystal chandeliers that Dillon himself had given to the Department when he was undersecretary of state. "Those who worked in the cabinets of presidents Kennedy and Johnson with Douglas Dillon shared a precious experience together and know what he means to the country," Rusk said in an uncharacteristically fulsome speech. "He can't escape from public service for long: I believe we'll be calling on his talents for service to the nation again."

Over at the Treasury Building, an emotional reception for 2,200 staff saw their departing boss showered with thousands of gifts and personal mementoes. Topping the bill – literally – was a new greenback issued by the Bureau of Engraving that "had gone into restricted circulation." At the bottom of the note, underneath a picture of Dillon and his signature, the words One Dillon appeared in large print. "Dillon's Bigger Than $," quipped the society page of the Washington Post the next day.[28]

The president hosted the most glamorous party of all. There had been some concern about whether it was appropriate to hold the farewell dinner-dance when only weeks beforehand the United States had started its ground war in Vietnam, but the White House briefed that "the honor and tribute due a man who had so long served his country through so many administrations" justified the decision to go ahead. Johnson gave a witty speech, praising Dillon to the skies, before joking to Dillon's wife (herself a noted DC society host at Belmont Road) that no one minded "Doug leaving Washington, but a president has many burdens, Phyllis, and I am going to have much explaining to do if I let you go at the same time."[29]

Writing officially to Dillon to accept his resignation, Johnson was more valedictory in tone. "Every American is in your debt for the outstanding contributions you have made to your country's welfare over the past twelve years," he told him. Dillon had been "a major force in bringing our economy out of recession into an economic upsurge" and he had delivered "the most comprehensive program of income tax reduction and reform in our nation's history." These "crowning achievements" were the mark of his "creative counsel and wise leadership."[30]

Even the economy threw a party for the departing Dillon. Entering the Treasury in 1961, the gloomy predictions had been for a deep recession. Figures released days before his departure in 1965 showed a boom entering its fiftieth month – equaling, and soon surpassing, the longest sustained upswing in American peacetime history. Industrial production, personal income, capital spending, corporate profits, average weekly earnings for production workers – all these and other leading economic indicators touched record levels. Employment stood at a new high, unemployment at new lows, and the average factory workweek was at the highest level since the Second World War. The steel and auto industries were surpassing previous records. "All of this," the New York Times noted approvingly, " – a characteristic of the entire 1961–65 surge – has been accomplished without any noticeable overheating of the economy." It was little wonder that an editorial in the Washington Post declared Dillon to be "by far the best secretary of the treasury of the postwar period."[31]

Dillon characteristically was more measured in his final speech and press conference as secretary. He ignored his own record, pointing instead to the issues that he felt remained unresolved. These included how, with unemployment expected to dip below the so-called "natural" rate of 4 percent the following year, the country might avoid inflation. He also returned to "the greatest and most difficult challenge facing the United States and the world's finance ministers in the next few years" – the unsolved problem of the balance of payments deficit and reform of the international monetary system – urging the leading economies of the world to engage in "meaningful discussions" on how to finance an expanding level of world trade.[32]

Dillon also had a political message to impart – one aimed not just at his successor but also at the political party to which he still belonged. Income tax hit the poorest one-fifth of American families disproportionately hard while the same metric for the top 5 percent had not changed. Those in public life, of all political and theoretical persuasions, should take up major tax reform to relieve the burden on the poorest in society. His comment represented a quiet cri de coeur for the difficult work of collective action from the center. For twelve years he had occupied the center ground of American politics under the Republican Eisenhower and the Democrats Kennedy and Johnson. Now, as he exited, Dillon willingly let public good rather than party interest define him. "I have always been what is called a moderate Republican," he said in his final remarks as secretary, but "I do not believe that there are great differences between that kind of Republican and the objectives of the last two Administrations."[33]

With that valedictory comment he was gone, although not before attending the swearing-in of Fowler at the White House on April 1. Dillon left town immediately afterwards, heading south to his Jupiter Island idyll and life as a private citizen.[34]

Epilogue
American Equipoise

When Douglas Dillon left office in the spring of 1965, it seemed reasonable to expect that he might return at some point to the frontline of American politics. President Johnson had said as much in his letter of farewell. "I fully intend to call upon you to serve your country again," LBJ told him. Dillon was that rare and valuable commodity in Washington – someone who was "a strong voice for sense and sanity, as well as for innovation." And yet, despite widespread admiration for these fine qualities, Douglas Dillon would never again serve in high public office.[1]

That situation did not arise from a want of offers. By the summer of 1966, with the Vietnam war at a tipping point, the need for sanity seemed more necessary than ever. Following LBJ's escalation in 1965, 385,000 Americans went to Vietnam. The cost of the war for 1966, which had been budgeted at $2 billion, became $15 billion – just shy (and rising) of 3 percent of US gross national product. Televised congressional hearings, led by Dillon's old friend Senator William Fulbright, raised questions not just about the administration's strategy but about the entire rationale for the war itself. Running alongside that gloomy prognosis, there also existed a more optimistic view, promoted by Henry Cabot Lodge Jr., now ambassador to South Vietnam. Lodge cabled Johnson at the beginning of August that there was "the smell of victory" in the air. "Never have things been going so well," he ventured. That same month Johnson appointed Averell Harriman as an "ambassador for peace," giving him the explicit task of finding a route to a negotiated end to the war.[2]

Looking for someone with the gravitas to navigate such a fraught situation, Johnson turned to Dillon and asked him to return to the State Department as undersecretary of state with a seat at cabinet. Inviting a former treasury secretary to take up a more junior position in the government, and one moreover that he had occupied during the Eisenhower administration, might almost have been seen as an insult. Yet Johnson made clear what the appointment meant. "In effect there will be two secretaries of state," he told Dillon in a phone call on August 8. Unspoken, but implicit, was the idea that he would eventually replace Rusk as secretary of state. "Nobody else can bring the unity that you can," Johnson pleaded with him. Dillon was "the best equipped to serve in this particular time as anyone else in the country." Never "in my 35 years in Washington" had there been a time, the president implored, "when we need any individual more than we need you."[3]

It was to no avail. Dillon begged off, saying it would cause "an awful lot of problems" with his family – for which read his father, Clarence, to whom he had given his word that he would run the family fund after leaving the Treasury. "I just don't see any way out of it," he told an audibly disappointed Johnson. As important, the limits of Dillon's personal distaste for Johnson's style had been exceeded. "He got along perfectly well with President Johnson," Dillon's daughter Phyllis recalled, "but my father didn't feel he was exactly a gentleman." Eventually Dillon would agree to serve as one of the so-called "Wise Men" who advised the president on Vietnam from late 1967 onwards. It was a distinguished, blue-chip group, made up of senior statesman and generals, coordinated by seasoned political adviser and Defense Secretary Clark Clifford, and included Dean Acheson, McGeorge Bundy, George Ball, Robert Murphy, Maxwell Taylor, Henry Cabot Lodge Jr., and John McCloy, the majority of whom – including the realist Dillon – would come to favor de-escalation of American involvement in Vietnam. But it was a kitchen cabinet, not the real cabinet.[4]

In 1967, he accepted Bobby Kennedy's personal request to join the inaugural board of the Bedford-Stuyvesant Development and Services Corporation (D&S) to tackle what its historian calls "the tangled web of poverty, disinvestment, and decay in 'America's largest ghetto.'" He chaired the board from 1967 to 1969 and initiated a program that would renovate and build homes on the ninety-six blocks, train thousands of residents in trades, and offer advice on housing, education, and employment.[5]

Other opportunities would come Dillon's way in the late sixties and early seventies. Hubert Humphrey unexpectedly sounded him out in 1968 about becoming his running mate on the Democratic ticket. "I remember he came to the house in Maine," recalls Phyllis, "but my father wasn't tempted at all." He gave the idea short shrift, telling Humphrey that he was "finished with politics" and that the political climate would not suit a cross-party ticket. (The advice did not stop Humphrey from then sounding out another Republican, Nelson Rockefeller, for the job.)

Few would doubt that Dillon made the right call. It is difficult to imagine the urbane Wall Street banker at the 1968 Chicago convention amid the violence of antiwar demonstrators in Grant Park and the heated scenes inside the convention hall. For Dillon, still a registered Republican who had never run for elected office, it would have been a baptism of fire bordering on self-immolation. Still, it was noticeable that Humphrey's final choice of Senator Ed Muskie – calm, tall, reticent, and popular with Republicans – bore some similarities with Dillon.[6]

Better suited to Dillon's temperament was another act of public service involving Rockefeller, by then vice president in the Ford administration. In late 1974, the American intelligence community found itself in the spotlight again, with accusations of spying at home and nefarious, even murderous, activities abroad. Some critics, notably the influential *New York Times* reporter Tom Wicker, even argued that it was time to "Destroy the Monster" by abolishing the CIA. In response to the public furor, President Gerald Ford formed a blue-ribbon commission in early 1975 to investigate the intelligence community. It was led by the vice president and would include seven other prominent public figures, including the future president, Ronald Reagan, and Lyman Lemnitzer, chairman of the Joint Chiefs of Staff during the Kennedy administration. It was a mark of Dillon's prestige that he was appointed vice chair of the committee.

The commission met weekly during its strict three-month mandate. Erwin Griswald, solicitor-general under Johnson and Nixon, argued that in a democratic society, civil liberty trumped secrecy. Dillon, supported by Lemnitzer, argued that democracy also required an alert intelligence capacity, not just for reasons of national security but also to protect against domestic threats. Interestingly, it would be Reagan who would bridge the divide once the committee got to the drafting stage, showing not just his experience as a Hollywood union negotiator, but also the same diplomatic skill that he would bring to discussions with the Soviets as president. With Rockefeller, Dillon, and Reagan taking the leading role at different times, it was no surprise that the conservative line held, yet even the more liberal Griswald expressed himself "very pleased" with the outcome.

Only in one regard did Dillon and other commissioners find themselves blocked. In May 1975, Dillon led the charge to include references to foreign assassination plots in the report, but in the final version these were dropped. David Belin, executive director for the commission, later explained what had happened. "The request came to Rockefeller directly through the president," he recalled. "The State Department – that meant [Henry] Kissinger – felt it would be 'inappropriate for a presidentially appointed commission' to report that the CIA had been involved in plans to assassinate leaders of foreign countries in peacetime." A larger investigation in the Senate, the Church Committee, would soon get to these questions that the White House forced the commission to exclude.[7]

The Rockefeller Commission would turn out to be Dillon's last major contribution to political life in Washington. He enjoyed his role as one of the "Wise Men" of American politics, called upon to advise at moments of national crisis, but he never showed any inclination to return to Washington full time. As his spell at the Treasury receded into the distance, so his official contributions to political life became fewer and fewer.

Instead of politics, most of Dillon's professional efforts focused on running the family investment trust, United States and Foreign Securities Corp (US&FS). His father's biographers write that here he showed "an incredible sense of investment value and timing as evidenced by his outstanding performance in managing the US&FS investment portfolio." Stepping back full time into the Wall Street world of Dillon Read, however, had no appeal. "I got into Wall Street after the glory days were over," he reflected. "There was very little work to be done and most of the business became more and more a question of whom you knew, played golf with, or took to dinner or to the theater. It was not because you had some brilliant idea." Given that Dillon pretty much knew everyone already, the prospect of that life bored him. "The opportunity to do different things that existed in the 1920s was gone," he admitted. In 1970, Dillon appointed Nicholas Brady to run Dillon Read so he could step back from day-to-day operations. It was a shrewd piece of business on his part in talent-spotting the man who would lead the Treasury in the Reagan and George H.W. Bush administrations.[8]

Dillon increasingly focused his efforts on cultural philanthropy. In 1970, a year after turning sixty, he became president of the Metropolitan Museum of Art, to which he could walk from his apartment on Fifth Avenue. He raised millions (in addition to $10 million of his own money) to create the Douglas Dillon Galleries for Chinese Painting and Calligraphy, which opened in 1981. That act typified Dillon's public ethic. Chinese art was not one of his own interests, which tended toward the French, but it represented a weakness in the holdings of the museum that needed addressing. "He was that kind of man," said Thomas Hoving, director of the Met in the seventies.[9]

Dillon's gradual withdrawal from political life reflected several points about his character and ambition. Most obviously, Dillon was never a professional politician in the same sense as, say, Lodge, who, while he came from a similar social class to Dillon, became a political "gun for hire" moving seamlessly from administration to administration and embassy to embassy. The conversation Dillon held with Paul Nitze back in 1952, when the author of NSC-68 told him that there was "more real excitement to be had working for the government than in Wall Street," had been like "opening a door" for the younger man. He had walked through that door when the opportunity presented itself in 1953, but twelve years later he exited just as happily with barely a look back over his shoulder. That decision showed an impeccable sense of historical as well as political timing. Dillon instinctively seemed to understand, as his near-namesake famously put it, that "The Times They Are A-Changin.'"[10]

The historian Rick Perlstein writes in *Nixonland* of "the rise, between the years 1965 [the year Dillon left office] and 1972, of a nation that had believed itself to be at consensus instead becoming one of incommensurate visions of apocalypse: two loosely defined congeries of Americans, each convinced that should the other triumph, everything decent and true and worth preserving would *end*. That was the 1960s." It may well have been the world of the sixties, but it was not Douglas Dillon's world.[11]

On a narrow level, Dillon's voluntary detachment was about the changing nature of conservatism. When the Republicans chose Barry Goldwater as their presidential candidate in 1964, the decision let Dillon – a Republican serving in a Democratic administration – justify his apostasy. In good conscience he could say that Johnson had "really saved us from something that could have been awful." To Dillon it seemed obvious that the Republican nominee had been an aberration for the party. Yet it was Dillon's brand of conservatism that turned out to be aberrant. The party gradually moved further to the right – first rhetorically under Nixon and later ideologically and in practice under Reagan and Newt Gingrich. As time went on, it was Goldwater's 1964 question – "What's happening to this country of ours?" – that seemed the relevant one for most conservatives. Centrists like Dillon found themselves increasingly beleaguered. In 1976 Dillon's friend, Vice President Nelson Rockefeller, suffered the indignity of being dumped from the Republican ticket by Ford because he was unpopular with the party's right-wing base. With the Democrats broadly moving to the left, the consensus in American politics that included Dillon in the fifties and early sixties began to disintegrate.[12]

For the historian Robert Dean, Dillon's generation was part of the "imperial brotherhood" that had always dominated American politics and foreign policy. In 1961, Kennedy had simply "'passed the torch to a new generation' of establishment recruits, [including] the patrician banker Douglas Dillon (Groton, Harvard, and the Spee Club)." They were bolstered from the outside by figures such as the likeminded Joseph Alsop, an influential columnist who, looking back to Roosevelt, proclaimed that the "country had at last found successors to Wise Men" in these "tough" figures like Dillon. But as Dean notes, they were all members of a "small but powerful social world rooted in a particular construction of class and gender." The way they spoke and dressed, the professional associations and social memberships they maintained, the worldview honed at elite schools, all contrived to bind these men together as a group. Perlstein criticizes them for complacency before 1965. "The crumbling of this myth of consensus, as the furies of the 1960s advanced, would not have been so rageful," he suggests, "would not have been so literally murderous, had the false rhetoric of American unity not been so glibly enforced in the years that preceded it: that some of the 1960s anger and violence was a return of what America had repressed." Had it been, in the famous put down by Daniel Bell, "a middle way for the middle aged"?[13]

It is undeniable that Dillon's generation can look blasé about the problems facing many Americans in the late fifties and early sixties. Dillon's specific frame of reference as one of the richest men in the United States left him out of touch with the vast majority in the country even as he sought to improve their lives. His interest in issues such as civil rights was never more than functional. It was the kind of blind spot that the generation that followed viewed with scorn. "WASPs lost their grip on power and were soon doing penance for having been in power at all," writes Michael Knox Beran, adding that instead "WASPs contented themselves with the cocktail party, ideally to be conducted on a patch of emerald lawn at Nantucket, with a glimpse of the sea, or on a promontory in Maine, with the wood thrush singing through the fog."[14]

Dillon aboard his sailboat at Dark Harbor, Maine, might seem to fit that bill precisely. Yet the appraisal also underestimates the nature of the period between 1952 (the election of Eisenhower) and 1964 (the Civil Rights Act and the Revenue Act). "In democratic countries you get things done by compromising your principles in order to form alliances with groups about whom you have grave doubts," the philosopher Richard Rorty pointed out in *Achieving Our Country*. Vital to those alliances were "people who have enough security, money, and power themselves," but who nevertheless understood that progress came only if they "lent a hand." Dillon was one of those doing the lending.[15]

In fact, the Eisenhower and Kennedy years were more about *balance* than they were about consensus. The historian W.L. Burn, writing in 1964, characterized the mid-nineteenth century in Britain as an "Age of Equipoise" – a time when "the old and the new, the elements of growth, survival and decay, achieved a balance which most contemporaries regarded as satisfactory" and when, "although [it] produced many critics and some rebels, scarcely any of them gave it up as a bad job." We might easily say the same of the American Age of Equipoise from 1952 to 1964. Eisenhower even made the point explicitly in his Farewell Address in 1961, when he revealed that "the only way to the road we wish to travel" was to weigh decisions "in the light of a broader consideration": "Balance between the private and the public economy, balance between cost and hoped for advantage; balance between the clearly necessary and the comfortably desirable; balance between our essential requirements as a nation and the duties imposed by the nation upon the individual; balance between action of the moment and the national welfare of the future. Good judgment seeks balance and progress; lack of it eventually finds imbalance and frustration."[16]

Douglas Dillon, who died in 2003 aged ninety-three, personified this balance of an American Age of Equipoise. As a Republican who served in a Democratic administration, he influenced the very nature of that administration. In economic and financial policy, his conservative outlook counterbalanced the liberal Keynesianism of the likes of Walter Heller. "Dillon was the major counterweight to the Council," Heller recalled, "and we were the major counterweight to the Treasury." Kennedy understood this point when he made the appointments.

Dillon not only recognized the president's approach, but he also embraced it. Dillon sat at the apex between Paul Samuelson's Keynesianism and Milton Friedman's monetarism, which is how he managed to be praised so effusively by Samuelson on leaving office while later being claimed by Reaganite conservatives in the 1980s. Economists refer to the period from the sixties to the eighties as a transition from "great volatility" to "great moderation." Other commentators extend the concept beyond economics. "By 1984, 49 states were voting the same way (for Ronald Reagan)," Janan Ganesh sums up. "The Great Moderation in economics and politics began." It was no coincidence that this transition should have seen a return to some of the priorities established by Dillon two decades earlier. In 1986, a bipartisan consensus was reached for the Tax Reform Act, the most ambitious taxation legislation since Dillon's Revenue Act of 1964. "We always used to cite the Kennedy tax cuts," says Buck Chapoton, assistant secretary of the Treasury for tax policy under Reagan. "In many ways we ended up achieving what Dillon had set out to do. In 1981 we lowered the rates and then, after some smaller bills, we came back in 1986 to undertake a broad tax reform that made the tax system simpler, fairer, and neutral."[17]

This sense of balance applied in other areas of Dillon's career too, including his activities on the world stage. His strategic vision in driving forward the Inter-American Development Bank, the Organisation for Economic Co-operation and Development (OECD), and the Alliance for Progress illustrated not just a desire to reform global financial and development systems, but also to put the world itself into better equilibrium. Time and again his speeches referred to helping the developing world as the most important step toward "the creation of a stable world order." It was a strategy that came partly from a genuine disquiet about global poverty, but also stemmed from a recognition that the United States had to help developing countries if it wanted to prevail in the Cold War. It is an important caveat, because it illustrates how Dillon's appreciation of what equipoise meant was underpinned by political realism.[18]

To this sense of equipoise Dillon brought a distinctively conservative sensibility that seemed entirely natural at the time but which by the 2020s often seems hardly to exist at all. That sensibility was not about being right wing, which the centrist Dillon never was, but it exemplified a certain way of seeing the world. It advocated evolution and reform over radicalism, bipartisanship above division, and the national interest as higher than the party interest. It was the essence of the Dillon Era.

Acknowledgments

For help in a variety of ways, I wish to thank the following: Daniel Akst, Nigel Ashton, Patricia Beard, Maurice Bric, Buck Chapoton, Nick Crowson, Susan Eisenhower, Alvin Felzenberg, Eileen Kane, Fredrik Logevall, Michael Mandelbaum, Damir Marusic, David Reynolds, Andrew Roberts, Declan Ryan, Mary Sarotte, Natalie Fell Spencer, Harry White, and David Woolner; the faculty, staff and students of Bard College, particularly the president, Leon Botstein, Ian Buruma, Deirdre d'Albertis, Omar Encarnación, Frederic Hof, Stephen Graham, Sean McMeekin, Walter Russell Mead, and Karen Sullivan; Jeff Gedmin, Michelle High, Laura Silverman, Carolyn Stewart, and everyone at American Purpose, where I host the *Bookstack* podcast; Chris Artis and Suzanne Williams at Shreve Williams; the archivists of National Archives II and the Eisenhower, Kennedy, and Johnson presidential libraries; Lucy Flamm (Bard '15), whose research assistance was pivotal to the early progress of the book; Simon Ball, Lawrence Haas, and Mark Lytle for their generosity and collegiality – not for the first time – in reading and improving my work.

I am also grateful to the two MQUP peer reviewers for the quality and collaborative spirit of their feedback; my excellent editor Richard Baggaley; and the entire team at MQUP, especially Kathleen Fraser, Jacqueline Davis, and Susan Glickman, as well as indexer JoAnne Burek.

I am again grateful to Simon Ball for introducing me to Richard Baggaley; the ever-supportive Georgina Capel of Georgina Capel Associates; my family, Kathryn Aldous, Elizabeth Aldous, and Patricia Aldous, for their encouragement, not least during the pandemic, and for much else besides – and to my late father, John Aldous, whose fascination with the Kennedy administration is reflected in the three books I've written on the period. Finally, I would like to express my gratitude to the Dillon family for their kindness in welcoming this project and making Douglas Dillon's private papers available to me without restriction. Special thanks go to Dillon's daughters, Phyllis Collins and Joan de Mouchy, and to his grandchildren, Frances Collins, Douglas Collins, Charlotte Cunningham, Joan Frost, Robert Luxembourg, and most particularly Mark Collins, my cheerful and insightful liaison with the family, who encouraged the book at every stage.

RICHARD ALDOUS
Annandale-on-Hudson, New York
March 2023

Notes

PROLOGUE

1   Account of SAM 86972: Henry Raymont, "6 Cabinet Members Turn Back after
    Getting News over Pacific," timesmachine.nytimes.com, November 23, 1963,
    https://nyti.ms/3xGtFT4. The events onboard SAM 86972 are described in
    William Manchester's classic account of the Kennedy assassination, *The Death
    of a President: November 20–November 25, 1963* (New York: Harper & Row,
    1967), 89, 139, 193, 245, and 356. See also Pierre Salinger, *With Kennedy* (New
    York: Doubleday, 1966), 1–10; Dean Rusk, *As I Saw It: A Secretary of State's
    Memoirs* (London: I.B. Tauris, 1991), 268–9. Joan (Dillon), Duchess of Mouchy,
    interview by Richard Aldous, July 10, 2018.
2   Robert F. Kennedy, *Robert Kennedy, in His Own Words: The Unpublished
    Recollections of the Kennedy Years*, ed. Edwin O. Guthman and Jeffrey Shulman
    (New York: Bantam Books, 1989), 420. Bobby Kennedy is quoted in Patricia
    Beard, *Douglas Dillon* (Cambridge, MA: Tidepool Press, 2018), 143. Jacqueline
    Kennedy Onassis and Arthur Schlesinger Jr., *Jacqueline Kennedy: Historic
    Conversations on Life with John F. Kennedy*, ed. Michael R. Beschloss (New
    York: Hyperion, 2011), 116–17. Dulles to Dillon, personal, April 2, 1956, Dillon
    Fund Archive. Editorial, "The 'Dillon Era,'" timesmachine.nytimes.com, March
    30, 1960, https://nyti.ms/3ukLK8x. Theodore H. White, *In Search of History:
    A Personal Adventure* (New York: Harper & Row, 1978), 504. Paul Samuelson,
    "A Word to the Wise: On Pitfalls for Secretaries of Treasury and Appreciation
    for Dillon's Work," *Washington Post*, April 25, 1965.

CHAPTER ONE

1   Robert C. Perez and Edward F. Willett, *Clarence Dillon: A Wall Street Enigma* (Lanham, MD: Madison Books, 1995), 149. In 1957, *Fortune* magazine put Dillon in the top fifty richest people in the United States, with estimated assets between $100 million and $200 million. Patricia Beard, *Douglas Dillon* (Cambridge, MA: Tidepool Press, 2018), 51. Stephen E. Ambrose, *Eisenhower, Vol. 2: The President: 1952–1969* (New York: Simon and Schuster, 1984). Clarence Dillon, interview by Richard Challener, Dulles Oral History Project, Princeton University Library, August 15, 1964.

2   August Belmont, interview by Thomas Zoumaras, June 2, 1991. Paul Nitze, interview by Thomas Zoumaras, November 13, 1990. Perez and Willett, *Clarence Dillon*, 134.

3   The summary of Dillon's early life is drawn from Perez and Willett, *Clarence Dillon*, xiv, 131–4; Nitze, interview by Zoumaras.

4   Douglas Dillon, interview by Robert Perez, October 29, 1991. Belmont, interview by Zoumaras. Nitze, interview by Zoumaras.

5   Douglas Dillon, interview by Perez.

6   "Eisenhower Faces Delays on Cabinet and Envoy to India," *New York Times*, January 18, 1953. "New Paris Envoy Aided Jersey GOP," *New York Times*, January 18, 1953. Randall Bennett Woods, *Fulbright: A Biography* (Cambridge; New York: Cambridge University Press, 2006), 238. James Reston, "Reaction in Capital Is Mixed on Conant Mission to Bonn," *New York Times*, January 13, 1953. William S. White, "Senate G.O.P. Acts to Ease Transfer," *New York Times*, January 10, 1953.

7   Douglas Dillon, interview by Colburn, January 22, 2002. "Mrs. Luce and Dillon, Ambassadors-Designate, Appear before Senators," *New York Times*, February 18, 1953.

8   Benjamin Bradlee, interview by Thomas Zoumaras, November 13, 1991. "An Outspoken Diplomat," *New York Times*, September 5, 1960.

9   George C. Herring, *From Colony to Superpower* (New York: Oxford University Press, 2017), 656–7. Stephen Kinzer, *The Brothers: John Foster Dulles, Allen Dulles, and Their Secret World War* (New York: St Martin's Griffin, 2014), 123–4.

10 Herring, *From Colony to Superpower*, 655–6. Richard H. Immerman, "Eisenhower and Dulles: Who Made the Decisions?," *Political Psychology* 1, no. 2 (1979): 21, https://doi.org/10.2307/3791100.

11 Herring, *From Colony to Superpower*, 657. Kinzer, *The Brothers*, 109. Richard D. Challener, "The Moralist as Pragmatist," in *The Diplomats, 1939–1979*, edited by Gordon A. Craig and Francis L. Loewenheim, 135–66, https://doi.org/10.2307

/j.ctv8pz9nc.10. John Foster Dulles, "Policy for Security and Peace," *Foreign Affairs* 32, no. 3 (1954): 353, https://doi.org/10.2307/20031035.

12 Douglas Dillon, interview by Robert Schulzinger, April 28, 1987. Clarence Dillon, interview by Challener.

13 Douglas Dillon, interview by Richard Challener, Dulles Oral History Project, Princeton University Library, June 24, 1965. Douglas Dillon, interview by Colburn. Clarence C. Walton, "Background for the European Defense Community," *Political Science Quarterly* 68, no. 1 (March 1953): 42, https://doi.org/10.2307/2145750. E.L. Kayser, "The European Defense Community," *World Affairs* 117, no. 3 (1954): 77–9, www.jstor.org/stable/20668930. Jack L. Hammersmith and Nelson D. Lankford, "The Last American Aristocrat: The Biography of David K.E. Bruce, 1898–1977," *The Journal of Southern History* 64, no. 1 (February 1998): 169, https://doi.org/10.2307/2588119. Gerhard Bebr, "The European Defence Community and the Western European Union: An Agonizing Dilemma," *Stanford Law Review* 7, no. 2 (March 1955): 169, https://doi.org/10.2307/1226391.

14 Douglas Dillon, interview by Challener.

15 "Dillon, New Envoy Departs for Paris," *New York Times*, March 1, 1953. Douglas Dillon, interview by Schulzinger. Bradlee, interview by Zoumaras.

16 "Dillon Reaches Paris," *New York Times*, March 8, 1953. Dillon to Department of State, March 16, 1953: RG 84, UD2453A, Box 173, National Archives at College Park, MD (henceforth NACP). Raymond Aron quoted in Frank Giles, *The Locust Years: The Story of the Fourth Republic, 1946–1958* (New York: Carroll & Graf, 1994), 179. "M. Dillon nouvel ambassadeur des États-Unis est arrivé à Paris ce matin," *Le Monde*, March 9, 1953, https://www.lemonde.fr/archives/article/1953/03/09/m-dillon-nouvel-ambassadeur-des-etats-unis-est-arrive-a-paris-ce-matin_1981632_1819218.html.

17 Bebr, "The European Defense Community and the Western European Union," 169, https://doi.org/10.2307/1226391. Brian R. Duchin, "The 'Agonizing Reappraisal': Eisenhower, Dulles, and the European Defense Community," *Diplomatic History* 16, no. 2 (April 1992): 201–22, https://doi.org/10.1111/j.1467-7709.1992.tb00496.x. Jorge Silva Paulo, "The European Defense Sector and EU Integration," *Connections* 8, no. 1 (2008): 11–57, https://www.jstor.org/stable/26326158.

18 Irwin M. Wall, *The United States and the Making of Postwar France, 1945–1954* (Cambridge: Cambridge University Press, 2002), 268. Dillon to Department of State, March 21, 1953: RG 84, UD2453A, Box 173, NACP.

19 Dillon to Department of State, June 25, 1953: RG 84, UD2453A, Box 173, NACP. Dillon to Department of State, June 26, 1953: RG 84, UD2453A, Box 179, NACP.

20 De Gaulle quoted in Giles, *The Locust Years*, 182. Douglas Dillon, interview by Schulzinger.

21 C.L. Sulzberger, "Foreign Affairs: De Gaulle: IV – A Policy of Amour Propre," *New York Times*, June 11, 1958, sec. Archives, https://nyti.ms/1kPI6yO.

22 US-French Political Talks, Minutes on Political and Military Subjects, March 27, 1953: RG 84, UD2453A, Box 173, NACP. William I. Hitchcock, *The Age of Eisenhower: America and the World in the 1950s* (Simon & Schuster, 2019), 96–100. Herring, *From Colony to Superpower*, 658–60. Odd Arne Westad, *The Cold War: A World History* (New York: Basic Books, 2019), 181–2. Miller Center, University of Virginia, "April 16, 1953: Chance for Peace," millercenter.org, October 20, 2016, https://millercenter.org/the-presidency/presidential-speeches/april-16-1953-chance-peace.

23 Dillon to Department of State, June 12, 1953: RG 84, UD2453A, Box 174, NACP.

24 "Sergei Vinogradov, 62, Dead; Soviet Envoy to Cairo and Paris," *New York Times*, August 28, 1970. "Les tentatives soviétiques pour exploiter les différends entre les puissances occidentales échoueront déclare M. Dillon à l'American Club," *Le Monde*, April 10, 1953, https://www.lemonde.fr/archives/article/1953/04/10/les-tentatives-sovietiques-pour-exploiter-les-differends-entre-les-puissances-occidentales-echoueront-declare-m-dillon-a-l-american-club_1974924_1819218.html.

25 Dillon to Department of State, Supplementary Memorandum on French Public Opinion, August 4, 1953: RG 84, UD2453A, Box 173, NACP. Dillon quoted in Wall, *The United States and the Making of Postwar France*, 269. Dillon to Department of State, "eyes only," May 15, 1953, Dillon Fund Archives. "Manifestation à la mutualité en faveur des Rosenberg," *Le Monde*, June 6, 1953, https://www.lemonde.fr/archives/article/1953/06/06/manifestation-a-la-mutualite-en-faveur-des-rosenberg_1969094_1819218.html. "M. Georges Bidault informe M. Dillon des sentiments de M. Vincent Auriol," *Le Monde*, June 18, 1953, https://www.lemonde.fr/archives/article/1953/06/18/m-georges-bidault-informe-m-dillon-des-sentiments-de-m-vincent-auriol_1969386_1819218.html.

26 Dillon to Department of State, "The Decline of French Confidence in US Leadership," August 4, 1953: RG 84, UD2453A, Box 173, NACP. Depcirtel 53, July 23, 1953, summarized in William Slany, David M. Baehler, and Department of State, *Foreign Relations of the United States*, 1952–1954, Western Europe and Canada, vol. 6 (Washington: U.S. Government Printing Office, 1986), 997. "Milestones," *Time*, August 10, 1953.

27 Dillon to Department of State, August 4, 1953: RG 84, UD2453A, Box 173, NACP.

28 Dillon to Department of State, August 6, 1953: RG 84, UD2453A, Box 175, NACP.

29 Dillon to Dulles, personal, November 9, 14, 22, 1953, Dillon Fund Archives. "Dillon Undergoes Operation," *New York Times*, November 25, 1953. Douglas Dillon, interview by Thomas Zoumaras, June 15, 1989. Douglas Dillon, interview by Thomas Zoumaras, October 19, 1989. Joan (Dillon) Duchess of Mouchy to Richard Aldous, Email, July 5, 2018. "M. Douglas Dillon ambassadeur en France va suivre un traitement médical en Amérique," *Le Monde*, November 16, 1953, https://www.lemonde.fr/archives/article/1953/11/16/m-douglas-dillon-ambassadeur-en-france-va-suivre-un-traitement-medical-en-amerique_1964087_1819218.html.

30 Max Hastings, *Vietnam: An Epic Tragedy 1945–1975* (New York: Harper Perennial, 2019), 37–9. Herring, *From Colony to Superpower*, 661–2.

31 Dillon to Department of State, April 5, 1954: https://history.state.gov/historical documents/frus1952-54v13p1/d691. Fredrik Logevall, *Embers of War: The Fall of an Empire and the Making of America's Vietnam* (New York: Random House Trade Paperbacks, 2013), 472. "Des bombardiers B 26 auraient déjà été envoyés en Indochine," *Le Monde*, April 6, 1954, https://www.lemonde.fr/archives/article/1954/04/06/des-bombardiers-b-26-auraient-deja-ete-envoyes-en-indochine_2013989_1819218.html.

32 Memorandum of Presidential Telephone Conversation, April 5, 1954: https://history.state.gov/historicaldocuments/frus1952-54v13p1/d694.

33 Aldrich to Department of State, April 6, 1954: https://history.state.gov/histor icaldocuments/frus1952-54v13p1/d704. Logevall, *Embers of War*, 475, 481–6, 489.

34 Secretary of State to Dillon, April 5, 1954: https://history.state.gov/historical documents/frus1952-54v13p1/pg_1242. Dillon to Department of State, April 6, 1954: https://history.state.gov/historicaldocuments/frus1952-54v13p1/d702.

35 Dillon to Department of State, April 6, 1954. Douglas Dillon, interview by John Luter, 1972.

36 Minutes of conversations held in Paris by the Secretary of State and Foreign Minister Bidault, April 21, 1954: https://history.state.gov/historicaldocuments/frus1952-54v13p1/d747. Secretary of State (Paris) to State Department, April 22, 1954: https://history.state.gov/historicaldocuments/frus1952-54v13p1/d769. Secretary of State (Paris) to State Department, April 23, 1954: https://history.state.gov/historicaldocuments/frus1952-54v13p1/d778. Secretary of State (Paris) to State Department, April 23, 1954: https://history.state.gov/historicaldocu ments/frus1952-54v13p1/d780. Secretary of State (Paris) to President, April 23, 1954: https://history.state.gov/historicaldocuments/frus1952-54v13p1/d779.

37 Dillon to Department of State, April 25, 1954: https://history.state.gov/his toricaldocuments/frus1952-54v13p1/d796.

38 Nitze, interview by Zoumaras.

39 Ibid. George C. Herring and Richard H. Immerman, "Eisenhower, Dulles, and Dienbienphu: 'The Day We Didn't Go to War' Revisited," *Journal of American History* 71, no. 2 (September 1984): 343–63, https://doi.org/10.2307/1901759.

40 Memorandum of Discussion, National Security Council, April 29, 1954: https://history.state.gov/historicaldocuments/frus1952-54v13p2/d818. Hitchcock, *The Age of Eisenhower*, 199. Logevall, *Embers of War*, 509.

41 Clark M. Clifford, "A Viet Nam Reappraisal: The Personal History of One Man's View and How It Evolved," *Foreign Affairs* 47, no. 4 (1969): 601, https://doi.org/10.2307/20039403.

42 Douglas Dillon, interview by Luter. Douglas Dillon, interview by Schulzinger.

43 Dillon to Department of State, June 14, 1954: https://history.state.gov/historical documents/frus1952-54v13p2/d968.

44 Secretary of State to Dillon, June 14, 1954: https://history.state.gov/historical documents/frus1952-54v13p2/d969. Douglas Dillon, interview by Schulzinger. Memorandum of Discussion, National Security Council, June 17, 1954: https://history.state.gov/historicaldocuments/frus1952-54v13p2/d980. Douglas Dillon, interview by Luter.

45 Memorandum of Conversation, July 13, 1954: https://history.state.gov/historical documents/frus1952-54v05p1/d553. Memorandum of Conversation, Hotel Matignon, July 14, 1954: RG 84, UD2453A, Box 206, NACP.

46 Lord Ismay, "NATO: The First Five Years" (Brussels: NATO, 1954), https://ar chives.nato.int/uploads/r/null/2/1/216977/NATO-The_first_5_years_1949-1954__by_Lord_Ismay_.pdf.

47 Dillon to Department of State, July 21, 1954: https://history.state.gov/historical documents/frus1952-54v06p2/d649.

48 Secretary of State to Dillon, July 23, 1954: https://history.state.gov/historical documents/frus1952-54v06p2/d650. Dillon to Department of State, July 26, 1954: https://history.state.gov/historicaldocuments/frus1952-54v06p2/d651. Secretary of State to Dillon, July 28, 1954: https://history.state.gov/historical documents/frus1952-54v06p2/d653.

49 Dillon to Department of State, August 15, 1954: https://history.state.gov/his toricaldocuments/frus1952-54v05p1/d562. Editorial note on Brussels meeting, August 19–22, 1954: https://history.state.gov/historicaldocuments/frus1952-54v05p1/d574. Dillon to Department of State, August 24, 1954: https://history.state.gov/historicaldocuments/frus1952-54v05p1/d590.

50 Dillon to Department of State, August 24, 1954. "La France a le choix: C.E.D. ou armée nationale allemande déclare M. Dillon," *Le Monde*, June 30, 1954, https://www.lemonde.fr/archives/article/1954/06/30/la-france-a-le-choix-c-e-d-ou-armee-nationale-allemande-declare-m-dillon_2019789_1819218.html.

51 Dillon to Department of State, August 24, 1954.

52 Dillon to Department of State, March 24, 1954:
https://history.state.gov/historicaldocuments/frus1952-54v05p1/d489, fn. 3.
Gregg Herken, *The Georgetown Set: Friends and Rivals in Cold War Washington*
(New York: Vintage Books, 2015), 187. Nelson D. Lankford, *The Last Aristocrat:
The Life of David K.E. Bruce, 1898–1977* (Boston, MA: Little, Brown, 1996).
Henri Pierre, "Deux conceptions s'opposent au département d'état sur la
politique à suivre à l'égard de La France," *Le Monde,* September 20, 1954,
https://www.lemonde.fr/archives/article/1954/09/20/deux-conceptions-s-
opposent-au-departement-d-etat-sur-la-politique-a-suivre-a-l-egard-de-la-
france_2022410_1819218.html.

53 Douglas Dillon, interview by Zoumaras. Giles, *The Locust Years*, fn, 173.
Lankford, *The Last Aristocrat*, 263. Bruce to Department of State, March 21,
1954: https://history.state.gov/historicaldocuments/frus1952-54v05p1/d484

54 Dillon to Department of State, August 31, 1954: https://history.state.gov/his
toricaldocuments/frus1952-54v06p2/d656.

CHAPTER TWO

1 Douglas Martin, "Susan Mary Alsop, 86, Washington Hostess and Author,"
New York Times, August 20, 2004, sec. Arts, https://www.nytimes.com/2004/08/
20/arts/susan-mary-alsop-86-washington-hostess-and-author.html. Susan
Mary Alsop, *To Marietta from Paris, 1945–1960* (London: Weidenfeld &
Nicolson, 1976).

2 Alsop, *To Marietta from Paris*, 253–5.

3 Brian R. Duchin, "The 'Agonizing Reappraisal': Eisenhower, Dulles, and the
European Defense Community," *Diplomatic History* 16, no. 2 (April 1992):
201–22, https://doi.org/10.1111/j.1467-7709.1992.tb00496.x. James Hershberg,
"'Explosion in the Offing': German Rearmament and American Diplomacy,
1953–1955," *Diplomatic History* 16, no. 4 (October 1992): 511–50, https://doi.org/
10.1111/j.1467-7709.1992.tb00630.x, 545.

4 Secretary of State to Dillon, August 31, 1954: https://history.state.gov/historical
documents/frus1952-54v05p2/d1.

5 Dillon to Department of State, August 31, 1954: https://history.state.gov/his
toricaldocuments/frus1952-54v06p2/d656. Douglas Dillon, interview by
Richard Challener, Dulles Oral History Project, Princeton University Library,
June 24, 1965.

6 Eisenhower is quoted in Richard H. Immerman, *John Foster Dulles: Piety,*

Pragmatism, and Power in U.S. Foreign Policy (Wilmington, DE: Scholarly Resources, 1999), 104ff. Statement by the Secretary of State, August 31, 1954: https://history.state.gov/historicaldocuments/frus1952-54v05p2/d5.

7   Dillon to Department of State, September 2, 1954: https://history.state.gov/historicaldocuments/frus1952-54v05p2/d12. Dillon to Department of State, September 15, 1954: https://history.state.gov/historicaldocuments/frus1952-54v05p2/d56.

8   Dillon to Secretary of State, September 7, 1954: RG 84, UD2453A, Box 207, NACP. On bringing down Mendès France: Irwin M. Wall, *The United States and the Making of Postwar France, 1945–1954* (Cambridge: Cambridge University Press, 2002), 287–90.

9   D.K.R. Crosswell, *Beetle: The Life of General Walter Bedell Smith* (Lexington: University Press of Kentucky, 2010), 35–7. Dillon to Department of State, September 11, 1954: https://history.state.gov/historicaldocuments/frus1952-54v05p2/d40. Wall, *The United States and the Making of Postwar France*, 287.

10 Dillon to Department of State, September 11, 1954. Wall, *The United States and the Making of Postwar France*, 287.

11 On Churchill, Eden, and British policy, see the persuasive revisionist article by Kevin Ruane, "Agonizing Reappraisals: Anthony Eden, John Foster Dulles and the Crisis of European Defence, 1953–54," *Diplomacy & Statecraft* 13, no. 4 (December 2002): 151–85, https://doi.org/10.1080/714000354. John W. Young, ed., *The Foreign Policy of Churchill's Peacetime Administration, 1951–1955* (Leicester, UK: Leicester University Press, 1988), 95–102.

12 Dillon to Department of State, October 13, 1954: https://history.state.gov/historicaldocuments/frus1952-54v05p2/pg_1387. Dillon to Department of State, October 16, 1954: https://history.state.gov/historicaldocuments/frus1952-54v05p2/pg_1394. Dillon to Department of State, October 20, 1954: https://history.state.gov/historicaldocuments/frus1952-54v05p2/pg_1402. Dillon to Secretary of State, October 13, 1954: RG 84, UD2453A, Box 207, NACP. Dillon to Department of State, October 29, 1954: https://history.state.gov/historicaldocuments/frus1952-54v06p2/d665.

13 Dillon to Department of State, December 23, 1954: https://history.state.gov/historicaldocuments/frus1952-54v05p2/pg_1517. Dillon to Secretary of State, December 24, 1954: https://history.state.gov/historicaldocuments/frus1952-54v05p2/pg_1519.

14 Diary entry by the president's press secretary (Haggerty), December 24, 1954: https://history.state.gov/historicaldocuments/frus1952-54v05p2/pg_1520 ff.

15 Ibid. Dillon to Secretary of State, December 24, 1954: https://history.state.gov/historicaldocuments/frus1952-54v05p2/pg_1524.

16 Memorandum by W.K. Scott, January 5, 1955: https://history.state.gov/his toricaldocuments/frus1952-54v06p2/d686. Barrett McGurn, "He Changed France's Mind," *This Week*, May 1, 1955, https://www.cia.gov/library/reading room/print/1281929.

17 Dillon to Dulles, January 28, 1955, Dillon Fund Archives. Dulles to Dillon, February 9, 1955, Dillon Fund Archives.

18 Joan (Dillon) Duchess of Mouchy to Richard Aldous, Email, July 5, 2018.

19 Monique P. Yazigi, "New Yorkers & Co., Big, Beautiful Numbers: 820, 834, 960," *New York Times*, November 23, 1997, sec. New York, https://www.nytimes.com/ 1997/11/23/nyregion/new-yorkers-co-big-beautiful-numbers-820-834-960.html. "M. Douglas Dillon, ambassadeur des États-Unis, inaugure Le Musée Cézanne," *Le Monde*, July 9, 1954, https://www.lemonde.fr/archives/article/ 1954/07/09/m-douglas-dillon-ambassadeur-des-etats-unis-inaugure-le-musee-cezanne_2037965_1819218.html. "Salute to France," *New Outlook* 8, no. 1 (July 1955): 31. Eric Pace, "C. Douglas Dillon Dies at 93; Was in Kennedy Cabinet," *New York Times*, January 12, 2003, sec. Business, https://www.nytimes.com/ 2003/01/12/business/c-douglas-dillon-dies-at-93-was-in-kennedy-cabinet.html. The Museum of Modern Art, "Largest American Modern Art Exhibition Ever Seen Abroad Opens in Paris," March 31, 1955, https://assets.moma.org/moma org/shared/pdfs/docs/press_archives/1924/releases/MOMA_1955_0039_24.pdf. On the cultural Cold War, see Frances Stonor Saunders, *Who Paid the Piper? The CIA and the Cultural Cold War* (London: Granta Books, 2000). Senate Committee on Appropriations, *The Supplemental Appropriation Bill, 1956: Hearings before the Committee on Appropriations, United States Senate, Eighty-Fourth Congress, First Session, on H.R. 7278, an Act Making Supplemental Appropriations for the Fiscal Year Ending June 30, 1956, and for Other Purposes*, [June 8, July 7, 8, 11, 15, 18, 20, 21, 22, 1955] (Washington, DC: United States Government Printing Office, 1955). "Proceedings in Washington," *New York Times*, January 20, 1955, sec. Archives, https://www.nytimes.com/1955/01/20/ archives/proceedings-in-washington.html?searchResultPosition=2. Renée Gesmar, "En marge de salut à La France," *Le Monde*, June 4, 1955, https://www. lemonde.fr/archives/article/1955/06/04/en-marge-de-salut-a-la-france_195 7478_1819218.html. Christine de Rivoyre, "Soirée de gala aux Champs-Élysées avec 'Oklahoma,'" *Le Monde*, June 22, 1955.

20 De Rivoyre, "Soirée de gala aux Champs-Élysées avec 'Oklahoma.'"

21 Dillon to Secretary of State, June 14, 1955: RG 84, UD2453A, Box 220, NACP.

22 French political reaction: Frank Giles, *The Locust Years: The Story of the Fourth Republic, 1946–1958* (New York: Carroll & Graf, 1994), 237–9. Hugh Roberts, "Sovereignty: The Algerian Case," *Diplomatic History* 28, no. 4 (September

2004): 595–8, https://doi.org/10.1111/j.1467-7709.2004.00439.x, 595. Jeffrey James Byrne, *Mecca of Revolution: Algeria, Decolonization, and the Third World Order* (New York: Oxford University Press, 2019), 42–67.

23 Giles, *The Locust Years*, 242–3. Joan (Dillon) Duchess of Mouchy to Richard Aldous.

24 L. Wainstein and Institute for Defense Analysis, *Evolution of U.S. Strategic Command and Control and Warning, 1945–1972* (Springfield, VA: U.S. Dept. of Commerce, 1975), 150–3. Douglas Dillon, interview by Robert Schulzinger, April 28, 1987. Matthew Fuhrmann and Todd S. Sechser, "Nuclear Strategy, Nonproliferation, and the Causes of Foreign Nuclear Deployments," *Journal of Conflict Resolution* 58, no. 3 (November 15, 2013): 463, https://doi.org/10.1177/0022002713509055. The decision of the French government in 2020 to reseal the archives has complicated research for scholars of French nuclear strategy; see Terrence Peterson, "The French Archives and the Coming Fight for Declassification," *War on the Rocks*, March 6, 2020, https://warontherocks.com/2020/03/the-french-archives-and-the-coming-fight-for-declassification/. Herter to Eisenhower, March 4, 1960, Mutual Security Act: https://history.state.gov/historicaldocuments/frus1958-60v13/d363. Schumann, Maurice, Interview with Maurice Schumann, 1986 [1], 1986, WGBH Media Library & Archives, http://openvault.wgbh.org/catalog/V_31B1CB3DDC7B4180BF4209CFD3BF384 E; Interview with Maurice Schumann, 1986 [2], 1986, WGBH Media Library & Archives, http://openvault.wgbh.org/catalog/V_68A96F02DD9D4CCB83 B00886A5F22441.

25 Herrick Chapman, *France's Long Reconstruction: In Search of the Modern Republic* (Cambridge, MA: Harvard University Press, 2018), 206. Odd Arne Westad, *The Cold War: A World History* (New York: Basic Books, 2019), 265, 275. Roberts, "Sovereignty: The Algerian Case," 596. Byrne, *Mecca of Revolution*, 10.1093/acprof:oso/9780199899142.001.0001. For American policy on the Algerian war more broadly, see Irwin M. Wall, *France, the United States, and the Algerian War* (Berkeley: University of California Press, 2001).

26 Secretary of State to Dillon, May 27, 1955: https://history.state.gov/historicaldocuments/frus1955-57v18/d58. Robert S. Norris, "Where They Were," *The Bulletin of the Atomic Scientists*, November 1999, 29, https://www.archives.gov/files/declassification/pidb/meetings/where-they-were.pdf.

27 Dillon to Secretary of State, June 28, 1955: RG 84, UD2453A, Box 217, NACP. Department of State to Embassy in France, June 17, 1955: https://history.state.gov/historicaldocuments/frus1955-57v18/d59.

28 Martin S. Alexander and J.F.V. Keiger, eds., *France and the Algerian War, 1954–*

62: *Strategy, Operations and Diplomacy* (London; Portland, OR: Frank Cass Publishers, 2002), 163–4. Giles, *The Locust Years*, 247. Dillon to Secretary of State, June 24, 1955; July 6, 1955: RG 84, UD2453A, Box 220, NACP.

29 Martin Thomas, "France Accused: French North Africa before the United Nations, 1952–1962," *Contemporary European History* 10, no. 1 (March 2001): 103–5, https://doi.org/10.1017/s0960777301001059. Wall, *France, the United States, and the Algerian War*, chapter 1.

30 Dillon to Department of State, October 4, 1955: https://history.state.gov/historicaldocuments/frus1955-57v18/d60.

31 Lodge to Dillon, October 6, 1955: https://history.state.gov/historicaldocuments/frus1955-57v18/d63. Luke A. Nichter, *The Last Brahmin: Henry Cabot Lodge Jr. and the Making of the Cold War* (New Haven, CT: Yale University Press, 2020), 69–70.

32 Dillon to Department of State, October 6, 1955: https://history.state.gov/historicaldocuments/frus1955-57v18/d62, fn. 1. Dillon to Secretary of State, December 9, 1955: RG 84, UD2453A, Box 219, NACP. Embassy in France to the Department of State, "Decline of French World Position and Local Reaction Thereto," https://history.state.gov/historicaldocuments/frus1955-57v27/d14.

33 Embassy in France to the Department of State, "Decline of French World Position and Local Reaction Thereto": https://history.state.gov/historicaldocuments/frus1955-57v27/d14.

CHAPTER THREE

1 Douglas Dillon, interview by Thomas Zoumaras, October 20, 1989. Benjamin Bradlee, interview by Thomas Zoumaras, November 13, 1991. Benjamin C. Bradlee, *A Good Life: Newspapering and Other Adventures* (New York: Simon & Schuster Paperbacks, 2017). Susan Mary Alsop, *To Marietta from Paris, 1945–1960* (London: Weidenfeld & Nicolson, 1976), 285.

2 Dillon to Dulles, March 7, 1956: https://history.state.gov/historicaldocuments/frus1955-57v18/d67, fn. 2. Dillon to Secretary of State, March 10, 1956: RG 84, UD2453A, Box 238, National Archives at College Park (NACP). Hoover to Dillon, March 17, 1956: https://history.state.gov/historicaldocuments/frus1955-57v27/d20.

3 Address to Diplomatic Press Association, March 20, 1956: Department of State, *American Foreign Policy: Current Documents, 1956-* (Washington, DC: U.S. G.P.O, 1959), 703–7. Dillon to Dulles, March 16, 1956: RG 84, UD2453A, Box 238,

NACP. "M. Douglas Dillon sera l'hôte d'honneur de la presse diplomatique française," *Le Monde*, March 15, 1956, https://www.lemonde.fr/archives/article/1956/03/15/m-douglas-dillon-sera-l-hote-d-honneur-de-la-presse-diploma tique-francaise_2239773_1819218.html. "La Politique française en Afrique du Nord 'a l'appui total des États-Unis' déclare M. Douglas Dillon devant la presse diplomatique," *Le Monde*, March 21, 1956, https://www.lemonde.fr/archives/article/1956/03/21/la-politique-francaise-en-afrique-du-nord-a-l-appui-total-des-etats-unis-declare-m-douglas-dillon-devant-la-presse-diplomatique_2238971_1819218.html.

4   Douglas Dillon, interview by Robert Schulzinger, April 28, 1987. Summary of press: Harold Callender, "U.S. Backs France on Liberal Plans in North Africa," *New York Times*, March 21, 1956, sec. Archives, https://www.nytimes.com/1956/03/21/archives/us-backs-france-on-liberal-plans-in-north-africa-dillon-says.html; Harold Callender, "U.S. Africa Stand Hailed by Mollet," *New York Times*, March 23, 1956, sec. Archives, https://www.nytimes.com/1956/03/23/archives/us-africa-stand-hailed-by-mollet-french-heartened-by-dillon-and.html. Dillon to Department of State, March 20, 1956: https://history.state.gov/historicaldocuments/frus1955-57v18/d70. "La Politique Française en Afrique du Nord 'a l'appui total des Etats-Unis.'" "Le discours de M. Dillon est accueilli avec faveur par la presse française," *Le Monde*, March 22, 1956, https://www.lemonde.fr/archives/article/1956/03/22/le-discours-de-m-dillon-est-accueilli-avec-faveur-par-la-presse-francaise_2239911_1819218.html. Dillon to Department of State, March 20, 1956: https://history.state.gov/historical documents/frus1955-57v18/d70.

5   Dana Adams Schmidt, "Eisenhower Backs Dillon on Africa," *New York Times*, March 22, 1956, sec. Archives, https://www.nytimes.com/1956/03/22/archives/eisenhower-backs-dillon-on-africa-says-he-approved-speech-by.html. Editorial, "Light on Algeria," *New York Times*, March 22, 1956, sec. Archives, https://www.nytimes.com/1956/03/22/archives/light-on-algeria.html. "La commission sénatoriale des affaires étrangères se félicite du discours de M. Dillon," *Le Monde*, March 23, 1956, https://www.lemonde.fr/archives/article/1956/03/23/la-commission-senatoriale-des-affaires-etrangeres-se-felicite-du-discours-de-m-dillon_2239736_1819218.html. "Le discours de M. Dillon est accueilli avec faveur par la presse française."

6   Dulles to Dillon, personal, April 2, 1956, Dillon Fund Archive. Theodore N. Pappas and Christopher G. Willett, "John Foster Dulles, His Medical History and Its Impact on Cold War Politics" in *Journal of Medical Biography* 28, no. 4 (November 2020): 213–20. https://doi.org/10.1177/0967772018771432.

7 Quoted in Callender, "U.S. Africa Stand Hailed by Mollet"; Callender, "U.S. Backs France on Liberal Plans in North Africa." "Le discours de M. Dillon est accueilli avec faveur par la presse française."

8 Dillon to Department of State, July 25, 1956: https://history.state.gov/historical documents/frus1955-57v18/d72.

9 Dillon to Department of State, July 31, 1956: https://history.state.gov/historical documents/frus1955-57v16/d38. On recent research on France during the Suez crisis, see Martin Thomas and Richard Toye, *Arguing about Empire: Imperial Rhetoric in Britain and France, 1882–1956* (Oxford: Oxford Scholarship Online, 2017), https://doi.org/10.1093/acprof:oso/9780198749196.001.0001, 212–29. Though older, Wm. Roger Louis and Roger Owen, eds., *Suez 1956: The Crisis and Its Consequences* (Oxford: Clarendon Press, 2011) remains indispensable.

10 Eisenhower and Dulles are quoted in William I. Hitchcock, *The Age of Eisenhower: America and the World in the 1950s* (New York: Simon & Schuster, 2019), 310, 313. CIA Freedom of Information Act Electronic Reading Room, "NSC Briefing on Suez," www.cia.gov, August 6, 1956, https://www.cia.gov/ library/readingroom/document/cia-rdp79r00890a000700080004-8.

11 Dillon to State Department, October 5, 1956: https://history.state.gov/his toricaldocuments/frus1955-57v27/d28#fn:1.5.4.2.10.88.12.4. Dillon to Department of State, July 31, 1956: https://history.state.gov/historical documents/frus1955-57v16/d38. Dillon to Department of State, October 6, 1956: https://history.state.gov/historicaldocuments/frus1955-57v16/d306. CIA Freedom of Information Act Electronic Reading Room, "The Likelihood of a British-French Resort to Military Action against Egypt in The Suez Crisis," www.cia.gov, September 19, 1956, https://www.cia.gov/library/readingroom/ document/cia-rdp79r01012a007400040001-7.

12 Dulles to Secretary of State, October 19, 1956: https://history.state.gov/his toricaldocuments/frus1955-57v16/d357. Douglas Dillon, interview by Richard Challener, Dulles Oral History Project, Princeton University Library, June 24, 1965.

13 Dillon to Secretary of State, October 19, 1956: https://history.state.gov/his toricaldocuments/frus1955-57v16/d357. Dillon to Department of State, October 20, 1956: https://history.state.gov/historicaldocuments/frus1955-57v16/d359. Douglas Dillon, interview by Schulzinger.

14 Avi Shlaim, "The Protocol of Sévres, 1956: Anatomy of a War Plot," *International Affairs* 73, no. 3 (July 1997): 509–30, https://doi.org/10.2307/2624270. Special to *New York Times*, "Gen. Maurice Challe Dead at 73; Led 1961 Coup against de Gaulle," *New York Times*, January 20, 1979, sec. Archives,

https://www.nytimes.com/1979/01/20/archives/gen-maurice-challe-dead-at-73-led-1961-coup-against-de-gaulle.htm. Challe quoted in Keith Kyle, *Suez* (London: Weidenfeld and Nicolson, 1992), 296–7; 310.

15 Douglas Dillon, interview by Schulzinger. Douglas Dillon, interview by Challener.

16 Embassy in France to State Department, October 30, 1956: https://history.state.gov/historicaldocuments/frus1955-57v16/pg_847. Dillon to Department of State, November 1, 1956: https://history.state.gov/historicaldocuments/frus1955-57v16/d459 and https://history.state.gov/historicaldocuments/frus1955-57v16/d453. W. Scott Lucas, *The Lion's Last Roar: Britain and the Suez Crisis* (Manchester, UK: Manchester University Press, 1996), 281. Thomas and Toye, *Arguing about Empire*, 224–5.

17 O.M. Smolansky, "Moscow and the Suez Crisis, 1956: A Reappraisal," *Political Science Quarterly* 80, no. 4 (December 1965): 589, https://doi.org/10.2307/2147000. Douglas Dillon, interview by Schulzinger. Paul Nitze, interview by Thomas Zoumaras, November 13, 1990. Dillon to Department of State, November 6, 1956: https://history.state.gov/historicaldocuments/frus1955-57v16/d515.

18 Douglas Dillon, interview by Schulzinger. Dillon to Department of State, November 27, 1956: https://history.state.gov/historicaldocuments/frus1955-57v27/d29. "M. Douglas Dillon: Les divergences d'opinions sur Suez n'altèrent pas le fait que la France et la Grande-Bretagne sont nos alliées naturelles," *Le Monde*, November 16, 1956, https://www.lemonde.fr/archives/article/1956/11/16/m-douglas-dillon-les-divergences-d-opinions-sur-suez-n-alterent-pas-le-fait-que-la-france-et-la-grande-bretagne-sont-nos-alliees-naturelles_2248983_1819218.html.

19 Douglas Dillon, interview by Schulzinger.

20 Harold Callender, "French Pin Hopes on Dillon's Trip," *New York Times*, November 30, 1956, sec. Archives, https://www.nytimes.com/1956/11/30/archives/french-pin-hopes-on-dillons-trip-paris-feels-envoy-may-spur.html. Douglas Dillon, interview by Schulzinger. "M. Dillon: Le peuple français reste aux côtés des États-Unis," *Le Monde*. Fr, December 8, 1956, https://www.lemonde.fr/archives/article/1956/12/08/m-dillon-le-peuple-francais-reste-aux-cotes-des-etats-unis_2243603_1819218.html. André Fontaine, "L'O.T.A.N. à l'heure des 'sages' [NATO in the era of the 'sages']," *Le Monde*.Fr, December 10, 1956, https://www.lemonde.fr/archives/article/1956/12/10/l-o-t-a-n-a-l-heure-des-sages_2242681_1819218.html.

21 Eugene Rabinowitch, "The First Year of Deterrence," *Bulletin of the Atomic Scientists* 13, no. 1 (January 1957): 2–8, https://doi.org/10.1080/00963402.1957.

11457499. "Mise au point sur les déclarations de M. Douglas Dillon [Update on Mr. Douglas Dillon's Statements]," *Le Monde*.Fr, December 14, 1956, https://www.lemonde.fr/archives/article/1956/12/14/mise-au-point-sur-les-declarations-de-m-douglas-dillon_2243579_1819218.html. Douglas Dillon, interview by Schulzinger.

22 Special to *New York Times*, "Dillon's Remarks Irk U.S. Officials," *New York Times*, December 13, 1956, sec. Archives, https://www.nytimes.com/1956/12/13/archives/dillons-remarks-irk-us-officials-state-department-regrets-his.html. "Mise au point sur les déclarations de M. Douglas Dillon," Patricia Beard, *Douglas Dillon* (Cambridge, MA: Tidepool Press, 2018), 87.

23 Joan (Dillon) Duchess of Mouchy to Richard Aldous, Email and unpublished memoir, July 5, 2018. Douglas Dillon, interview by Schulzinger.

24 Douglas Dillon, interview by Schulzinger.

25 Robert J. Donovan, "Herter to Replace Hoover Jr. in the State Dept. Feb. 1," *International Herald Tribune*, December 9, 1956. Douglas Dillon, interview by Schulzinger. Douglas Dillon, interview by Challener.

CHAPTER FOUR

1 Seymour Weller to Clarence Dillon, January 22, 1957: Dillon Fund Archives. "Dulles' Cool Economist," *New York Times*, January 15, 1957. "M. Dillon parle de progrès de l'économie française," *Le Monde*, January 25, 1957. "L'Homme de la semaine: Un Américain à Paris, Douglas Dillon," *L'Express*, January 4, 1957.

2 Marguerite Deslauriers and Pierre Destrée, *The Cambridge Companion to Aristotle's Politics* (Cambridge: Cambridge University Press, 2013), 18–19.

3 Dulles to Dillon, personal, April 2, 1956: Dillon Fund Archives. Edwin L. Dale Jr., "Captain of Our Economic Campaign," *New York Times*, August 31, 1958. Douglas Dillon, interview by Robert Schulzinger, April 28, 1987. Douglas Dillon, interview by Richard Challener, Dulles Oral History Project, Princeton University Library, June 24, 1965.

4 See Jean Edward Smith, *Eisenhower: In War and Peace* (New York: Random House, 2013), 703. Eisenhower's second Inaugural, January 21, 1957: https://www.eisenhowerlibrary.gov/sites/default/files/research/online-documents/inauguration-1957/inaugural-address-reading-copy.pdf.

5 Burton Ira Kaufman, *Trade and Aid: Eisenhower's Foreign Economic Policy, 1953–1961* (Baltimore, MD: Johns Hopkins University Press, 1982), 59, 95. Odd Arne Westad, *The Cold War: A World History* (New York: Basic Books, 2019), 228–9.

6   Eisenhower doctrine, January 5, 1957: *The Department of State Bulletin*, XXXVi,
    No. 917 (January 21, 1957). Russell Ong, "'Peaceful Evolution', 'Regime Change'
    and China's Political Security," *Journal of Contemporary China* 16, no. 53
    (November 2007): 717–18, https://doi.org/10.1080/10670560701562408. Extract
    from Bo Yibo, *Recollections* (1991): https://digitalarchive.wilsoncenter.org/
    document/memoirs-chinese-finance-minister-bo-yibo-excerpt-preventing-
    peaceful-evolution.

7   Richard H. Immerman, *John Foster Dulles: Piety, Pragmatism, and Power in
    U.S. Foreign Policy* (Wilmington, DE: Scholarly Resources, 1999), 157–8.

8   Eisenhower's second Inaugural, January 21, 1957: https://www.eisenhower
    library.gov/sites/default/files/research/online-documents/inauguration-1957/
    inaugural-address-reading-copy.pdf.

9   Stephen E. Ambrose, *Eisenhower, Volume 2: The President* (New York: Simon &
    Schuster, 1984), 377. Raymond J. Saulnier, *Constructive Years: The U.S. Economy
    under Eisenhower* (Lanham, MD: University Press of America, 1991), 207–9.
    Louis A. Picard and Terry F. Buss, *A Fragile Balance: Re-Examining the History
    of Foreign Aid, Security, and Diplomacy* (Sterling, VA: Kumarian Press, 2009),
    92–3.

10 Bernard S. Katz and C. Daniel Vencill, *Biographical Dictionary of the United
    States Secretaries of the Treasury, 1789–1995* (Westport, CT: Greenwood Press,
    1996), 205, 209–11. Ambrose, *Eisenhower, Volume 2: The President*, 377.

11 Dale, "Captain of Our Economic Campaign." Robert J. Donovan, "Herter to
    Replace Hoover Jr. in the State Dept. Feb. 1," *International Herald Tribune*,
    December 9, 1956. Eisenhower-Humphrey correspondence: Ambrose,
    Eisenhower, vol. 2, 378. James Reston, "New Sub-Cabinet Team – An Analysis
    of Major Shifts Carried Out among Operating Heads of Government,"
    timesmachine.nytimes.com, July 2, 1957, https://nyti.ms/3p6sBE1.

12 Dale, "Captain of Our Economic Campaign." Donovan, "Herter to Replace
    Hoover Jr. in the State Dept. Feb. 1." Douglas Dillon, interview by Schulzinger.
    Douglas Dillon, interview by Challener.

13 *New York Daily Mirror*, October 6, 1957. Judson MacLaury, *History of the
    Department of Labor, 1913–1988* (1988): https://www.dol.gov/general/aboutdol/
    history/dolchp05.

14 *Evening Star*, December 9, 1957. Unidentified clipping, December 18, 1960. "List
    of 76 Said to Hold above 75 Million: Preparing the Estimates," timesmachine.
    nytimes.com, October 28, 1957, https://nyti.ms/30I1Pkr. Melvyn P. Leffler,
    "National Security," *The Journal of American History* 77, no. 1 (June 1990):
    143–52.

15 Al Kamen and Colby Itkowitz, "In 1963 Washington, Most Everybody Was in

the Book," *Washington Post*, March 17, 2015. Patricia Beard, *Douglas Dillon* (Cambridge, MA: Tidepool Press, 2018), 90.

16 Dulles to Dillon, March 5, 1957: https://history.state.gov/historicaldocuments/frus1955-57v17/d192.

17 Keith Kyle, *Suez* (London: Weidenfeld and Nicolson, 1992), 534–5.

18 Dulles to Dillon, March 5, 1957. Memorandum of a Conference with the President, March 8, 1957: https://history.state.gov/historicaldocuments/frus 1955-57v17/d203.

19 Dillon to Senior Advisory Group, March 9, 1957: https://history.state.gov/his toricaldocuments/frus1955-57v17/d192. Dulles to Herter, March 12, 1957: https://history.state.gov/historicaldocuments/frus1955-57v17/d213.

20 Department of State to Mission at UN, March 15, 1957: https://history.state.gov/historicaldocuments/frus1955-57v17/d225. Mission at UN to Department of State, March 15, 1957: https://history.state.gov/historicaldocuments/frus1955-57v17/d228. Embassy in Egypt to the Department of State, March 17, 1957 & Secretary's Staff Meeting, March 18, 1957: https://history.state.gov/historical documents/frus1955-57v16/d664. James Reston, "Nasser's Terms on Canal Bared – Full Rule Asked – U.S. View Opposed," timesmachine.nytimes.com, March 28, 1957, https://nyti.ms/2N5zZBH. Harrison E. Salisbury, "U.S. Maps New Aid for Asia, Africa," *New York Times*, May 3, 1957, sec. Archives, https://nyti.ms/1ikNoBO. Richard Pearson, "Statesman and Banker John J. Mccloy, 93, Dies," *Washington Post*, March 12, 1989. Memorandum of Telephone Conversation by Dillon, March 25, 1957: https://history.state.gov/historicald ocuments/frus1955-57v17/d249. "John J. McCloy, Lawyer and Diplomat, Is Dead at 93," timesmachine.nytimes.com, March 12, 1989, https://nyti.ms/2XHmZ7m. Kyle, Suez, 544–5. Tentative Notes of the Secretary's Staff Meeting, April 5, 1957: https://history.state.gov/historicaldocuments/frus1955-57v17/d267. Telephone Conversation Dulles and McCloy, April 4, 1957: https://history.state.gov/his toricaldocuments/frus1955-57v17/d267. Department of State to the Embassy in Egypt, April 18, 1957: https://history.state.gov/historicaldocuments/frus1955-57v17/d291.

21 Tentative Notes of the Secretary of State's Staff Meeting, April 26, 1957: https://history.state.gov/historicaldocuments/frus1955-57v17/d302. Department of State to All Diplomatic Missions, April 27, 1957: https://history.state.gov/his toricaldocuments/frus1955-57v17/d303. Tentative Notes of the Secretary of State's Staff Meeting, April 29, 1957; Department of State to the UK Embassy, April 29, 1957: https://history.state.gov/historicaldocuments/frus1955-57v17/d306. Department of State to UK Embassy in the United Kingdom. Dillon to Dulles, October 14, 1957: Dillon Personal Papers, CDDPP-011-007, JFK Library.

22 "Multilateral Export Control Policy: The Coordinating Committee (CoCom),"
    Congressional Office of Technology Assessment (1979): https://www.princeton.
    edu/~ota/disk3/1979/7918/791810.PDF. Hitchcock, *The Age of Eisenhower*, 177–8.
    Japanese figures taken from Scott Newton, *The Global Economy, 1944–2000:
    The Limits of Ideology* (London: Arnold; New York, 2004), 74–5, and Xin-zhu J.
    Chen, "China and the US Trade Embargo, 1950–1972," *American Journal of
    Chinese Studies* 13, no. 2 (2006): 173–4. https://www.jstor.org/stable/44288827.

23 Dulles to Eisenhower, May 16, 1957: https://history.state.gov/historicaldocu
    ments/frus1955-57v10/d163. Eisenhower to Macmillan, May 17, 1957:
    https://history.state.gov/historicaldocuments/frus1955-57v10/d164.

24 Memorandum of a Conversation, Department of State, May 20, 1957:
    https://history.state.gov/historicaldocuments/frus1955-57v10/d167. Frank Cain,
    "The US led Trade Embargo on China: The Origins of CHINCOM, 1947–52,"
    Journal of Strategic Studies, 18:4, 33–54, DOI: 10.1080/01402399508437618.

25 Macmillan to Eisenhower, May 21, 1957: https://history.state.gov/historical
    documents/frus1955-57v10/d168. Department of State to the Embassy in
    France, May 24, 1957: https://history.state.gov/historicaldocuments/frus1955-
    57v10/d170. Embassy in London to State Department, May 14, 1957: https://
    history.state.gov/historicaldocuments/frus1955-57v10/d160. "Mollet Defeated in
    French Crisis – Cabinet Resigns," timesmachine.nytimes.com, May 22, 1957,
    https://nyti.ms/3bT9olz.

26 Memorandum of a Telephone Conversation between Dulles and Dillon, May
    25, 1957, 5:40 p.m.: https://history.state.gov/historicaldocuments/frus1955-
    57v10/d172. Editorial note: https://history.state.gov/historicaldocuments/
    frus1955-57v10/d173. Macmillan to Eisenhower, May 29, 1957: https://history.
    state.gov/historicaldocuments/frus1955-57v10/d174. "Transcript of the
    President's News Conference on Foreign and Domestic Matters," times
    machine.nytimes.com, June 6, 1957, https://nyti.ms/3sI9BOo. William White,
    "President Opens Door to Renewal of Peiping Trade," timesmachine.nytimes.
    com, June 6, 1957, https://nyti.ms/2KyAcwm. Memorandum of a Conversation,
    Department of State, June 6, 1957: https://history.state.gov/historicaldocu
    ments/frus1955-57v10/d180. Ball, *The Guardsmen*, 331.

27 Memorandum by the Under Secretary of State for Economic Affairs (Dillon),
    June 4, 1957: https://history.state.gov/historicaldocuments/frus1955-57v10/d175.

28 Kimber Charles Pearce, *Rostow, Kennedy, and the Rhetoric of Foreign Aid* (East
    Lansing: Michigan State University Press, 2001), 14–15. Summary of speech:
    Salisbury, "U.S. Maps New Aid for Asia, Africa." This account of the debate that
    follows also draws on the groundbreaking study by Burton Ira Kaufman, *Trade
    and Aid: Eisenhower's Foreign Economic Policy, 1953–1961* (Baltimore, MD: Johns

Hopkins University Press, 1982). Kaufman, *Trade and Aid*, 96–9. Minutes of a Meeting of the Subcommittee on Soviet Economic Penetration, March 26, 1957: https://history.state.gov/historicaldocuments/frus1955-57v09/d11. "Johnston Urges More Foreign Aid," timesmachine.nytimes.com, May 4, 1957, https://nyti.ms/30idcQ9.

29 Pearce, *Rostow, Kennedy, and the Rhetoric of Foreign Aid*, 15.

30 Memorandum from the Deputy Director for Program and Planning, International Cooperation Administration (ICA), to the Director (Hollister), March 7, 1957: https://history.state.gov/historicaldocuments/frus1955-57v10/d29.

31 Secretary of the treasury (Humphrey) to the Chairman of the Council on Foreign Economic Policy (Randall), March 20, 1957: https://history.state.gov/historicaldocuments/frus1955-57v10/d36.

32 Memorandum of Discussion at the 320th Meeting of the National Security Council, April 17, 1957: https://history.state.gov/historicaldocuments/frus1955-57v10/d38.

33 Douglas Dillon, interview by Challener. Dillon would later write of how Eisenhower ran his National Security Council: "The National Security Council worked effectively through a whole series of working level groups which developed papers which eventually came to the surface and were presented in formal manner to the National Security Council for approval or modification or rejection. The National Security Council met regularly once a week and these papers had previously been vetted by what was called the Planning Group, which was a group consisting of either Under Secretaries or in some cases Assistant Secretaries. They had, in vetting these papers, given the views of their own departments so the papers were thoroughly representative of combined views of the various departments. Often those views could not be reconciled … [so] a good deal of the time in the National Security Council meetings themselves was devoted to reaching agreement on compromise language to cover the various subjects that were under discussion." (C. Douglas Dillon, interview by Elspeth Rostow, August 4, 1964, John F. Kennedy Library Oral History Program.) Memorandum of a Conversation (Dillon, Ambassador Mehta), May 13, 1957: https://history.state.gov/historicaldocuments/frus1955-57v08/d165.

34 Public Papers of the presidents of the United States: Dwight D. Eisenhower, 1957, 392, reprinted in https://history.state.gov/historicaldocuments/frus1955-57v08/d165.

35 Allen Drury, "Aid Backer Cites Soviet Expansion," timesmachine.nytimes.com, June 6, 1957, https://nyti.ms/36egwW3. William S. White, "Eisenhower Plan for

2 Billion Aid Wins Senate Test," timesmachine.nytimes.com, June 7, 1957, https://nyti.ms/305iiih. Allen Drury, "Rebellious House Cuts 747 Million from Foreign Aid," timesmachine.nytimes.com, July 20, 1957, https://nyti.ms/3a2qni. L. Kaufman, *Trade and Aid*, 106–8. Papers of John F. Kennedy. Pre-Presidential Papers. Senate Files. Speeches and the Press. Speech Files, 1953–1960. First General Session of the 45th annual meeting of the National Chamber of Commerce, Washington, D.C., 29 April 1957. JFKSEN-0897-005, John F. Kennedy Presidential Library.

CHAPTER FIVE

1 James Reston, "Shifting World Conditions Alter Washington Outlook," timesmachine.nytimes.com, June 24, 1957, https://nyti.ms/3pc81Cf.
2 Douglas Dillon, interview by Richard Challener, Dulles Oral History Project, Princeton University Library, June 25, 1965. Ambassador in Argentina (Beaulac) to the Department of State, August 21, 1957: https://history.state.gov/historicaldocuments/frus1955-57v06/d149.
3 "Champion of Foreign Aid," unidentified, Dillon Fund Archives.
4 Memorandum of Discussion at a Bipartisan Congressional Meeting, White House, Washington, May 9, 1957: https://history.state.gov/historicaldocuments/frus1955-57v06/d141.
5 Dillon to Dulles, May 15, 1957: Dillon Personal Papers, CDDPP-011-09, JFK Library.
6 Summary of economic relations: Edwin Williamson, *The Penguin History of Latin America* (London; New York: Penguin, 2009), 332–4. Summary Notes of a Meeting of the Subcommittee on the Buenos Aires Economic Conference, May 28, 1957: https://history.state.gov/historicaldocuments/frus1955-57v06/d138.
7 Minutes of a Staff Meeting, Bureau of Economic Affairs, September 11, 1957: https://history.state.gov/historicaldocuments/frus1955-57v06/d167. Minutes of a Cabinet Meeting, The White House, Washington, August 23, 1957: https://history.state.gov/historicaldocuments/frus1955-57v06/d152.
8 *Current Economic Developments*, No. 528, September 17, 1957: https://history.state.gov/historicaldocuments/frus1955-57v06/d168. Special to *New York Times*, "Americas Parley Hailed by Dillon," timesmachine.nytimes.com, September 4, 1957, https://nyti.ms/3ai6PqO. Statement by the President, Department of State Bulletin, September 30, 1957: https://history.state.gov/historicaldocuments/frus1955-57v06/d165.

9 Deputy Assistant Secretary of State for Inter-American Affairs (Snow) to the Secretary of State, September 4, 1957: https://history.state.gov/historicaldocuments/frus1955-57v06/d166. Minutes of a Staff Meeting, Bureau of Economic Affairs, September 11, 1957: https://history.state.gov/historicaldocuments/frus1955-57v06/d167. Douglas Dillon, interview by Challener.

10 David Ekbladh, *The Great American Mission: Modernization and the Construction of an American World Order*, Princeton University Press, 2010), https://www.jstor.org/stable/j.ctt7sg53.11, 156–7. Kaufman, *Trade and Aid*, 100–1. Luke A. Nichter, *The Last Brahmin: Henry Cabot Lodge Jr. and the Making of the Cold War* (New Haven, CT: Yale University Press, 2020).

11 Dillon to Dulles, September 26, 1957: https://history.state.gov/historicaldocuments/frus1955-57v09/d162.

12 Director of the Office of International Economic and Social Affairs (Kotschnig) to the Deputy Assistant Secretary of State for International Organization Affairs (Hanes), October 26, 1957: https://history.state.gov/historicaldocuments/frus1955-57v09/d163.

13 Dillon to Dulles, September 13, 1957: Dillon Personal Papers, CDDPP-01-010, JFK Library. Dillon to Dulles, October 31, 1957: https://history.state.gov/historicaldocuments/frus1955-57v09/d164. Dulles to Anderson, December 7, 1957: https://history.state.gov/historicaldocuments/frus1955-57v09/d166.

14 Mission at the United Nations to the Department of State, December 20, 1957: https://history.state.gov/historicaldocuments/frus1955-57v09/d169.

15 Douglas Dillon, Dulles Oral History Project, Princeton University Library, interview by Richard Challener, June 25, 1965. E.W. Kenworthy, "Dillon Slated to Coordinate All Foreign Aid Programs," timesmachine.nytimes.com, November 15, 1957, https://nyti.ms/3ja2dXK.

16 Brendan Jones, "Dillon Proposes Long Foreign Aid," timesmachine.nytimes.com, November 19, 1957, https://nyti.ms/2MOVuql. Special to *New York Times*, "Eisenhower Clears the Way for Dillon," timesmachine.nytimes.com, December 1, 1957, https://nyti.ms/3pUUAHa. Douglas Dillon, interview by Challener.

17 Special to *New York Times*, "Russians Called Economic Threat," timesmachine.nytimes.com, January 9, 1958, https://nyti.ms/3rpJMBz.

18 On the intricate stage-by-stage process of the foreign aid bill, see Kaufman, *Trade and Aid*, 136–41. Special to *New York Times*, "Aid Loan Request Called Minimum – Officials Insist 625 Million Is Needed to Spur Plans for Poor Countries," timesmachine.nytimes.com, March 12, 1958, https://nyti.ms/3ar7nL8. E.W. Kenworthy, "750 million Urged for Needy Lands," timesmachine.ny

times.com, March 20, 1958, https://nyti.ms/3jgbMEK. Special to *New York Times*, "Trade Hearings Near Conclusion," timesmachine.nytimes.com, March 23, 1958, https://nyti.ms/3pMuaHM.

19 Notes on Legislative Leadership Meeting, April 22, 1958: https://history.state.gov/historicaldocuments/frus1958-60v04/d217. John D. Morris, "Congress Softens on Aid but Trade Faces a Fight," timesmachine.nytimes.com, May 18, 1958, https://nyti.ms/3trIjMy. Will Lissner, "Dillon Warns U.S. of Soviet Moves, Economic Adviser to Dulles Says Kremlin Is Planning 'Economic Offensive,'" timesmachine.nytimes.com, May 22, 1958, https://nyti.ms/3rkR9Kg. Appropriations in Kaufman, *Trade and Aid*, 139–41. Raymond J. Saulnier, *Constructive Years: The U.S. Economy under Eisenhower* (Lanham, MD: University Press of America, 1991), 209–10.

20 "Under Secretaries for Economic Growth": https://history.state.gov/department history/people/principalofficers/under-secretary-for-econ-business-ag. Mutual Security Act, 1958 (P.L. 85-477; 72 Stat. 274): https://uscode.house.gov/statutes/pl/85/477.pdf. Douglas Dillon, interview by Challener.

21 E.L. Kenworthy, "President Plans Loans to Combat Soviet Aid Drive," timesmachine.nytimes.com, September 21, 1958, https://nyti.ms/3aHjljI. Saulnier, *Constructive Years*, 209–10. Minutes of the Cabinet Meeting, July 25, 1958: https://history.state.gov/historicaldocuments/frus1958-60v04/d222.

22 Interbureau task force on Latin America:https://history.state.gov/historicaldocuments/frus1958-60v05/d41.

23 John A Farrell, *Richard Nixon: The Life* (New York: Doubleday, 2017), 264–7. Conrad Black, *The Invincible Quest: The Life of Richard Milhous Nixon* (Toronto: McClelland & Stewart, 2007), 359.

24 Memorandum of Discussion at the 366th Meeting of the National Security Council, May 22, 1958: https://history.state.gov/historicaldocuments/frus1958-60v05/d56.

25 "Operation Pan America," *Time*, June 30, 1958. Embassy in Brazil to the Department of State, May 23, 1958: https://history.state.gov/historicaldocuments/frus1958-60v05/d243. E.W. Kenworthy, "U.S. Backs Move in Latin America for a Loan Bank – Step Is a Reversal of Policy," timesmachine.nytimes.com, August 13, 1958, https://nyti.ms/3cM9Z9o.

26 See the excellent essay by Thomas Zoumaras, "Eisenhower's Foreign Economic Policy: The Case of Latin America," in Richard A. Melanson and David Allan Mayers, *Reevaluating Eisenhower: American Foreign Policy in the 1950s*, 155–91 (Urbana: University of Illinois Press, 1989). Zoumaras worked with Dillon on historical projects and undertook oral history interviews with him. Felipe Herrera, "The Inter-American Development Bank," *Social Science* 35, no. 4

(1960): 216–21, http://www.jstor.org/stable/23907312. Editorial Note, on US regional economic policies with relation to Latin America, see: https://history. state.gov/historicaldocuments/frus1958-60v05/d41. Louis A. Picard and Terry F. Buss, *A Fragile Balance: Re-Examining the History of Foreign Aid, Security, and Diplomacy* (Sterling, va: Kumarian Press, 2009), 72. Rosemary Thorp, *Progress, Poverty and Exclusion: An Economic History of Latin America in the 20th Century* (Washington, DC: Inter-American Development Bank; Baltimore, MD, 1998), 145.

27 Edwin L. Dale, "Captain of Our Economic Campaign," *New York Times*, August 31, 1958, https://timesmachine.nytimes.com/timesmachine/1958/08/31/8186 6439.html. Dale later served as spokesperson for the Office of Management and Budget during the Reagan Administration.

CHAPTER SIX

1 Richard H. Immerman, *John Foster Dulles: Piety, Pragmatism, and Power in U.S. Foreign Policy* (Wilmington, DE: Scholarly Resources, 1999), 196. Dana Adams Schmidt, "John Foster Dulles Dies – Special Funeral Decreed – Geneva Talks to Suspend," timesmachine.nytimes.com, May 25, 1959, https://nyti.ms/3a S6CLo.

2 Peter Baker and Susan Glasser, *The Man Who Ran Washington: The Life and Times of James A. Baker III* (New York: Doubleday, 2020). Douglas Dillon, "Remarks on Eisenhower and Dulles" (February 25, 1988).

3 Joan (Dillon) Duchess of Mouchy to Richard Aldous, Email and unpublished memoir, July 5, 2018. "Man on Jupiter Island," *Time*, April 13, 1959. Gerald Clarke, "Ralph Lauren's Two-House Retreat in Jamaica," *Architectural Digest*, October 3, 2016, https://www.architecturaldigest.com/story/ralph-lauren-jamaica-home-article.

4 E.W. Kenworthy, "Dillon Is Slated for Higher Post – To Be No. 2 Man in State Department," timesmachine.nytimes.com, April 24, 1959, https://nyti.ms/2LHbfiJ. "Dillon Is Nominated as Top Herter Aide," timesmachine.nytimes.com, May 1, 1959, https://nyti.ms/3rJHk8V. *Wall Street Journal*, December 10, 1958: Clippings file, Dillon Fund Archives. For Dillon and Herter addressing each other as "Chris" and "Doug," see, for example, Dillon to Herter and Herter to Dillon, July 1, 1960: Dillon Personal Papers, CDDPP-011-017.

5 George Bernard Noble, *Christian A. Herter* (New York: Cooper Square, 1970), 34. Arthur Krock, "In the Nation; Importance of No Answer to Some Questions," timesmachine.nytimes.com, April 17, 1959, https://nyti.ms/3a9n9LB.

"Dillon Takes Oath – President Attends Ceremony for State Department Aide," timesmachine.nytimes.com, June 13, 1959, https://nyti.ms/3tNAwsM. "Top Hands at State," *Time*, February 23, 1959. John P. Leacocos, "Dillon's Home Coach of the Herter Team," *Cleveland Plain Dealer*, June 21, 1959.

6   Paul Nitze, interview by Thomas Zoumaras, November 13, 1990: Dillon Fund Archives.

7   Joan (Dillon) Duchess of Mouchy to Richard Aldous, Email and unpublished memoir, July 5, 2018. Phyllis (Dillon) Collins, interview by author, November 3, 2021. "Top Hands at State," Time, February 23, 1959. Leacocos, "Dillon's Home Coach of the Herter Team." August Belmont, interview by Thomas Zoumaras, June 2, 1991: Dillon Fund Archives.

8   Richard Aldous, *Macmillan, Eisenhower and the Cold War* (Dublin: Four Courts Press, 2005), 62, 75, 78–90. E. Bruce Geelhoed and Anthony O. Edmonds, *Eisenhower, Macmillan, and Allied Unity, 1957–1961* (Houndmills, Basingstoke, Hampshire; New York: Palgrave Macmillan, 2003).

9   Memorandum of Conference with the President, July 10, 1959: https://history.state.gov/historicaldocuments/frus1958-60v08/d43. Memorandum of Conversation with Frol R. Kozlov, July 12, 1959: https://history.state.gov/his toricaldocuments/frus1958-60v10p1/d87.

10   Memorandum of Conference with the President, July 22, 1959: https://history.state.gov/historicaldocuments/frus1958-60v08/d467. Editorial note, Khrushchev visit: https://history.state.gov/historicaldocuments/frus1958-60v10p1/d85. Dwight D. Eisenhower, *Waging Peace, 1956–1961* (London: Heinemann, 1966), 407.

11   Jean Edward Smith, *Eisenhower: In War and Peace* (New York: Random House, 2013), 748–50.

12   Memorandum of Conversation at Camp David (Dillon and Khrushchev), September 27, 1959: https://history.state.gov/historicaldocuments/frus1958-60v10p1/d132

13   Michael R. Beschloss, *Kennedy v. Khrushchev: The Crisis Years,1960–1963* (London: Faber and Faber, 1991), 49–50. Harold Macmillan, *Pointing the Way, 1959–1961* (London: Macmillan, 1972), 279.

14   Memorandum of Conversation at Camp David (Dillon and Khrushchev), September 27, 1959. *New York Herald Tribune*, September 27, 1959.

15   Nikita Sergeevich Khrushchev and Sergeĭ Khrushchev, *Memoirs of Nikita Khrushchev. Volume 3: Statesman,1953–1964* (University Park: Pennsylvania State University Press, 2007). 160–4. Patricia Beard, *Douglas Dillon* (Cambridge, MA: Tidepool Press, 2018).

16   On the balance of payments deficit and gold losses, see the excellent study by

Francis J. Gavin, *Gold, Dollars, and Power: The Politics of International Monetary Relations, 1958–1971* (Chapel Hill; London: The University of North Carolina Press, 2004) and Gordon L. Weil and Ian R. Davidson, *The Gold War: The Story of the World's Monetary Crisis* (New York: Holt, Rinehart and Winston, 1970). Paper prepared in the Department of State, International Payments Position of the United States, July 24, 1959: https://history.state.gov/historicaldocuments/frus1958-60v04/d49.

17   Gavin, *Gold, Dollars, and Power*, 38. Minutes of Cabinet Meeting, August 7, 1959: https://history.state.gov/historicaldocuments/frus1958-60v04/d22. Record of Action on Items Presented at the Cabinet Meeting, August 19, 1959: https://history.state.gov/historicaldocuments/frus1958-60v04/d23. Press conference in Augusta, Georgia, October 22, 1959, Editorial Note: https://history.state.gov/historicaldocuments/frus1958-60v04/d184.

18   James Reston, "Cabinet's Strong Man – Anderson Prevailing on Foreign Policy," timesmachine.nytimes.com, October 28, 1959, https://nyti.ms/3au74jV. Memorandum of Conversation between Herter and Anderson, October 22, 1959: https://history.state.gov/historicaldocuments/frus1958-60v04/d24.

19   Douglas Dillon, interview by Robert Schulzinger, The Foreign Affairs Oral History Collection of the Association for Diplomatic Studies and Training, Library of Congress, April 28, 1987. E.W. Kenworthy, "'Buy-American' Policy on Loans Comes under Fulbright's Fire," timesmachine.nytimes.com, October 29, 1959, https://nyti.ms/2NDTAJo. Proposed United States Initiative to Mobilize Free World Resources for Development and to Strengthen Trade Relations, Memorandum from Secretary of State Herter to President Eisenhower, November 24, 1959: https://history.state.gov/historicaldocuments/frus1958-60v04/d26. Eisenhower sent his comments directly to Dillon as author of the paper. "Rap from Rich Uncle," *Time*, November 9, 1959.

20   Proposed United States Initiative to Mobilize Free World Resources for Development and to Strengthen Trade Relations.

21   Ibid.

22   Edwin L. Dale, "Europe Awaits a Visit by Dillon and His First-Hand Trade Study," timesmachine.nytimes.com, November 30, 1959, https://nyti.ms/2NiAngA.

23   Memorandum of Conversation, Brussels, December 10, 1959: https://history.state.gov/historicaldocuments/frus1958-60v07p1/d83. Arthur Olsen, "Dillon Stresses European Unity – Warns Common Market Six Not to Abandon Goal of Stronger Political Ties," timesmachine.nytimes.com, December 11, 1959, https://nyti.ms/37saAcE.

24   Summary of Dillon's visit to Europe, Editorial Note: https://history.state.gov/

historicaldocuments/frus1958-60v04/d27. Dillon to Herter, December 13, 1959: https://history.state.gov/historicaldocuments/frus1958-60v07p1/d88. Henry Giniger, "U.S. Seeks Talks by 2 Trade Blocs – Dillon, in Europe, Reported to Urge Bridging of Gap to Avoid Political Effects," timesmachine.nytimes.com, December 15, 1959, https://nyti.ms/2ZDAAgJ.Memorandum of Discussion at the 429th Meeting of the National Security Council, December 16, 1959: https://history.state.gov/historicaldocuments/frus1958-60v07p1/d91. Special Communiqué on the Economic Situation, Editorial Note: https://history.state. gov/historicaldocuments/frus1958-60v07p1/d92. Memorandum of Conversation, Meeting of Heads of Government, Paris, December 19, 1959: https:// history.state.gov/historicaldocuments/frus1958-60v07p1/d93. Douglas Dillon, interview by Schulzinger. Dillon had been fighting off the Treasury on the OEEC from the moment he arrived at the State Department. See Dillon to Dulles, June 17, 1957: Dillon Personal Papers, CDDPP-011-008, JFK Library.

25 Memorandum of Conversation with UK Chancellor of the Exchequer, Paris, January 11, 1960: https://history.state.gov/historicaldocuments/frus1958-60v07p1/d96. Dillon to Eisenhower, January 14, 1960: https://history.state.gov/ historicaldocuments/frus1958-60v07p1/d98. The Special Economic Committee, Editorial Note: https://history.state.gov/historicaldocuments/frus1958-60v07p1/d95.

26 Editorial, "The 'Dillon Era,'" timesmachine.nytimes.com, March 30, 1960, https://nyti.ms/3ukLK8x. C.L. Sulzberger, "The Meaning of the Dillon Plan," timesmachine.nytimes.com, January 20, 1960, https://nyti.ms/3aMQHPv.

CHAPTER SEVEN

1 "Address by Under Secretary Dillon at AFL-CIO Conference on World Affairs," timesmachine.nytimes.com, April 21, 1960, https://nyti.ms/2NUsPRe. AFL-CIO Conference on World Affairs, For World Peace and Freedom: Proceedings, Internet Archive (AFL-CIO Conference on World Affairs [1960: New York], 1960), https://archive.org/details/AFLCIO/page/n67/mode/2up.

2 "Address by Under Secretary Dillon at AFL-CIO Conference on World Affairs." AFL-CIO Conference on World Affairs, For World Peace and Freedom: Proceedings. A.H. Raskin, "Dillon Says West Rejects 'Slavery' for West Berlin,'" timesmachine.nytimes.com, April 21, 1960, https://nyti.ms/2OokZFr. "Dillon: Khrushchev 'Skating on Very Thin Ice,'" New York Daily News, April 21, 1960: Clippings File, Dillon Fund Archive.

3 Summary of Kremlin politics and Khrushchev quoted in Michael R. Beschloss,

Mayday: Eisenhower, Khrushchev, and the U-2 Affair (New York: Perennial Library, 1987), 240–1. Preparations for the summit, Editorial Note: https://history.state.gov/historicaldocuments/frus1958-60v09/d130.

4 "Eisenhower and His Time" conference, Institute of US and Canadian Studies, Moscow, October 1990. (I am grateful to Professor Mikhail Narinsky of the Moscow State Institute of International Relations, Russia, for providing me with a transcript of this conference.) The section that follows draws on my earlier work on the U-2 crisis and the Paris summit in *Macmillan, Eisenhower and the Cold War* (Dublin: Four Courts Press, 2005), 127–63, as well as Beschloss's account in *Mayday*.

5 Douglas Dillon, U-2 Incident, interview by John Lutter, June 28, 1972, Dillon Fund Archive. Presidential Memorandum for the Record (Goodpaster), April 25, 1960: Office of the Staff Secretary, Subject Series, Alphabetical Subseries, Box 15, Intelligence Matters (14, NAID 186630, Eisenhower Presidential Library. Beschloss, *Mayday*, 43–4. Francis Gary Powers and Curt Gentry, *Operation Overflight: A Memoir of the U-2 Incident* (Lincoln, NA: Potomac Books, Washington, DC, 2008), 56–63.

6 Douglas Dillon, interview by Robert Schulzinger, The Foreign Affairs Oral History Collection of the Association for Diplomatic Studies and Training, Library of Congress, April 28, 1987. Dwight D. Eisenhower, *Waging Peace, 1956–1961* (London: Heinemann, 1966), 543.

7 NASA press release on missing plane, May 5, 1960: Christian Herter Papers, Box 20, U-2 (1), NAID 12009392, Eisenhower Library. Douglas Dillon, interview by Schulzinger. Beschloss, *Mayday*, 51–2. Transcript of Press and Radio News Briefing, State Department, May 5, 1960: Herter Papers 20, U-2 (1), Eisenhower Library.

8 Douglas Dillon, interview by Schulzinger. Douglas Dillon, U-2 Incident, interview by Lutter. "US Heard Russians Chasing U-2," *Washington Post*, May 9, 1960.

9 Douglas Dillon, U-2 Incident, interview by Lutter.

10 Khrushchev quoted in Jean Edward Smith, *Eisenhower: In War and Peace* (New York: Random House, 2013), 752. Douglas Dillon, U-2 Incident, interview by Lutter. Herter and White quoted in Beschloss, *Mayday*, 246–50.

11 Diary, 9 May 1960: Whitman File, Whitman Diary Series 11, ACW Diary, May 1960, Eisenhower Library. On Eisenhower generally during these few days, I follow my own work in *Macmillan, Eisenhower and the Cold War*, 130–2.

12 Record of Actions by the National Security Council at its 44th Meeting, 9 May 1960: National Archives (Washington, DC), National Security Actions 1952–60; Beschloss, *Mayday*, 255. Diary, 9 May 1960: Whitman File.

13 Phyllis Collins, interview by Richard Aldous, April 18, 2022.

14 Statement by the President, May 11, 1960: Whitman File, International Series 11, Paris summit Meeting, May 1960 (1), Eisenhower Library.

15 Smith, *Eisenhower*, 753. Douglas Dillon, interview by Luter.

16 Memorandum for Ann Whitman, May 11, 1960: DDE Papers as President, DDE Diary Series, Box 50, Staff Notes, May 1960 (2), NAID 12010067, Eisenhower Library. Record of meeting between the four leaders, 16 May 1960, Paris, May 1960: PREM 11/2992, UK National Archives (TNA). Meeting of Chiefs of State and Heads of Government, Paris, May 16, 1960: https://history.state.gov/his toricaldocuments/frus1958-60v09/d168. William Taubman, *Khrushchev: The Man and His Era* (New York: W.W. Norton, 2002), 461. Beschloss, *Mayday*, 285. Macmillan, *Pointing the Way*, 204–5, Aldous, *Macmillan, Eisenhower and the Cold War*, 153–4.

17 Douglas Dillon, interview by Luter. Douglas Dillon, interview by Schulzinger. "Dillon Gets Award as a Top Jerseyan," timesmachine.nytimes.com, June 4, 1960, https://nyti.ms/3uGvOgW.

18 Memorandum of Conversation, Bipartisan Leaders Breakfast, May 26, 1960: DDE Papers as President, DDE Diary Series, Box 50, Staff Notes, May 1960 (1), NAID 12010079, Eisenhower Library. Special to the *New York Times*, "Dulles Testimony on U-2 Is Awaited," timesmachine.nytimes.com, May 28, 1960, https://nyti.ms/2PdH2ZZ. Murrey Marder, "Testimony on Spy Planes Reopens Shrouded Chapter of Cold War," *Washington Post*, December 13, 1982. Douglas Dillon, interview by Luter.

19 Memorandum of Conversation between Dillon and Tito, July 19, 1960: https://history.state.gov/historicaldocuments/frus1958-60v10p2/d165. Special to the *New York Times*, "GATT Acts to End Market Flooding," timesmachine. nytimes.com, June 1, 1960, https://nyti.ms/3bTS0M7. Kotaro Suzumura, "Japan's Industrial Policy and Accession to the GATT: A Teacher by Positive or Negative Examples?" *Hitotsubashi Journal of Economics* 38, no. 2: 101–23, https://core.ac.uk/download/pdf/6803319.pdf. Francine McKenzie, *GATT and Global Order in the Postwar Era* (Cambridge; New York: Cambridge University Press, 2020), 127–9.

20 Kohler to Herter, July 8, 1960: https://history.state.gov/historicaldocuments/ frus1958-60v09/d327. Dillon to Embassy in Austria, July 5, 1960: https://history. state.gov/historicaldocuments/frus1958-60v09/d326. M.S. Handler, "Dillon Counsels Austria on Trade," timesmachine.nytimes.com, July 16, 1960, https://nyti.ms/3qaS7YK. Embassy in Austria to Department of State, July 19, 1960: https://history.state.gov/historicaldocuments/frus1958-60v09/d328.

21 "An Outspoken Diplomat," *New York Times*, September 5, 1960.

22 Memorandum of a Conference with the President, February 8, 1960: https://history.state.gov/historicaldocuments/frus1958-60v05/d75. Stephen E. Ambrose, *Eisenhower, Volume 2: The President* (New York: Simon & Schuster, 1984), 558. Editorial Note, US regional economic policies with relation to Latin America: https://history.state.gov/historicaldocuments/frus1958-60v05/d4. Eisenhower to Kubitschek, July 8, 1960: https://history.state.gov/historical documents/frus1958-60v05/d29.

23 Dillon to Eisenhower, August 1, 1960, summarized in "Editorial Note, US regional economic policies with relation to Latin America."

24 E.W. Kenworthy, "In Washington: State Department Tries to Shape a New Policy of 'Collective' Action," timesmachine.nytimes.com, August 28, 1960, https://nyti.ms/2OhzG7m. Thomas C. Mann, interview by Thomas Zoumaras, Dillon Fund Archive, March 9, 1990.

25 Juan de Onis, "Dillon in Bogotá for Talks on Aid," timesmachine.nytimes.com, September 4, 1960, https://nyti.ms/3ejmr19. Special to *New York Times*, "Dillon Visits Church in Quito," timesmachine.nytimes.com, September 3, 1960, https://nyti.ms/3857QT2.

26 Juan de Onis, "U.S. Aid Plan Stirs Doubt on Eve of Bogotá Parley – Reaction Mixed as 500 Million Program Is Outlined," timesmachine.nytimes.com, September 5, 1960, https://nyti.ms/3cdQ7Kh. Juan de Onis, "Dillon's Popularity at Bogotá Adds to Backing for U.S. Plan," timesmachine.nytimes.com, September 9, 1960, https://nyti.ms/3v2G7Mq. "Text of Dillon Address on Inter-American Aid at Bogotá Talks," timesmachine.nytimes.com, September 7, 1960, https://nyti.ms/3t98E1f. Juan de Onis, "Bogotá Meeting Praises Aid Plan – Cuba Is Critical but Other Latins Hail U.S. Program as a Turning Point," timesmachine.nytimes.com, September 13, 1960, https://nyti.ms/3eoRzfx.

27 de Onis, "Bogotá Meeting Praises Aid Plan."

28 Kimber Charles Pearce, *Rostow, Kennedy, and the Rhetoric of Foreign Aid* (East Lansing: Michigan State University Press, 2001), 87. Burton Ira Kaufman, *Trade and Aid: Eisenhower's Foreign Economic Policy, 1953–1961* (Baltimore, MD: Johns Hopkins University Press, 1982), 208–11. Richard A. Melanson and David Allan Mayers, eds., *Reevaluating Eisenhower: American Foreign Policy in the 1950s* (Urbana: University of Illinois Press, 1989), 180–1.

29 C.L. Sulzberger, "The Next Secretary of State?," timesmachine.nytimes.com, October 31, 1960, https://nyti.ms/3rsg0wh. James Reston, "Beyond the Candidates – a National Government?" timesmachine.nytimes.com, October 30, 1960, https://nyti.ms/3bvEbEw.

30 Douglas Dillon, interview by Dixon Donnelly, JFKOH-CDD-01, John F. Kennedy Oral History Interviews, JFK Library, July 30, 1964. "Peter Flanigan Nixon's Mr-Fixit Adviser Dies," *Washington Post*, August 1, 2003. "Dillons Give $9,550 to G.O.P. Campaign," timesmachine.nytimes.com, October 6, 1960, https://nyti.ms/3bzoXya. John A. Farrell, *Richard Nixon: The Life* (New York: Doubleday, 2017), 84. Conrad Black, *The Invincible Quest: The Life of Richard Milhous Nixon* (Toronto: McClelland & Stewart, 2007), 412. Memorandum of Discussion at the 464th Meeting of the National Security Council, October 20, 1960: https://history.state.gov/historicaldocuments/frus1958-60v06/d596. Memorandum of a Conference with the President, October 17, 1960: https://history.state.gov/historicaldocuments/frus1958-60v06/d593.

31 White quoted in Farrell, *Richard Nixon*, 296. Black, *The Invincible Quest*, 422. Theodore C. Sorensen, *Kennedy* (London: Pan Books, 1965), 303.

CHAPTER EIGHT

1 Arthur M. Schlesinger, *Journals, 1952–2000* (London: Atlantic, 2008), 94–6. Gregg Herken, *The Georgetown Set: Friends and Rivals in Cold War Washington* (New York: Vintage Books, 2015), 254.

2 Katharine Graham, *Personal History* (New York: A.A. Knopf, 1997), 271. Herken, *The Georgetown Set*, 254.

3 Douglas Dillon, John F. Kennedy Oral History Interviews, interview by Dixon Donnelley, JFKOH-CDD-01, JFK Library, July 30, 1964. Graham, *Personal History*, 271.

4 Robert A. Lovett, John F. Kennedy Oral History Interviews, interview by Dorothy Fosdick, JFKOH-ROAL-01, JFK Library, July 20, 1964. Graham, *Personal History*, 271. Schlesinger, *Journals*, 95–6. Arthur M. Schlesinger, *The Letters of Arthur Schlesinger, Jr.*, ed. Stephen Schlesinger and Andrew Schlesinger (New York: Random House, 2013), 234. Robert F. Kennedy, *Robert Kennedy, in His Own Words: The Unpublished Recollections of the Kennedy Years*, ed. Edwin O. Guthman and Jeffrey Shulman (New York: Bantam Books, 1989), 40.

5 Joan (Dillon) Duchess of Mouchy to Richard Aldous, Email and unpublished memoir, July 5, 2018. Douglas Dillon, interview by Donnelley.

6 Douglas Dillon, interview by Donnelley.

7 Arthur Krock, "Embarrassing Prospect for High G.O.P. Personages," timesmachine.nytimes.com, December 13, 1960, https://nyti.ms/3cwI3Vg. "Nixon Battles JFK Effort to Lure GOPer Dillon to Treasury," *New York Daily News*, December 12, 1960.

8   OEEC Ministerial Meeting held December 13–14 in Paris, editorial note: https://history.state.gov/historicaldocuments/frus1958-60v07p1/d130. Douglas Dillon, interview by Donnelley.

9   "The Super Blooper," *New York Herald Tribune*, November 28, 1960.

10 Douglas Dillon, interview by Donnelley.

11 Ibid. Eisenhower to Dillon, December 15, 1960, quoted in Patricia Beard, *Douglas Dillon* (Cambridge, MA: Tidepool Press, 2018). Kennedy, *Robert Kennedy, in His Own Words*, 40. "Hagerty Silent on Dillon Job," timesmachine. nytimes.com, December 20, 1960, https://nyti.ms/3bRhvP2.

12 Douglas Dillon, interview by Donnelley.

13 Benjamin C. Bradlee, *Conversations with Kennedy* (New York: Norton, 1975), 38. Arthur M. Schlesinger, *Robert Kennedy and His Times*, (Boston: Mifflin, 1978), 242–3. Aurélie Basha i Novosejt, "C. Douglas Dillon, President Kennedy's Economic Envoy," *The International History Review* 40, no. 2 (April 24, 2017): 234–5, https://doi.org/10.1080/07075332.2017.1313297.

14 Wolfe quoted in Fritz Hahn, "JFK's D.C.," *Washington Post*, May 18, 2017.

15 "Messrs. Dillon, R. Kennedy," *Chattanooga Daily Times*, December 17, 1960. "Dillon Named despite Opposition in Both Parties, But Wall Street Is Reassured," *Washington Post*, December 17, 1960. Editorial, "From the Treasury Down," timesmachine.nytimes.com, December 17, 1960, https://nyti.ms/2OE ov6g. "The Dillon Era," *New York Herald Tribune*, December 17, 1960.

16 Douglas Dillon, interview by Donnelley. Kennedy, *Robert Kennedy, in His Own Words*, 40. "Hagerty Silent on Dillon Job." W.H. Lawrence, "Kennedy Denies Deal with Dillon," timesmachine.nytimes.com, December 24, 1960, https://nyti.ms/3cFWBSd. David Lawrence, "Eisenhower Never Requested Dillon to Decline Treasury Secretary Post," *US News & World Report*, December 27, 1960. Richard E. Mooney, "President Hails Dillon's Record," timesmachine.nytimes.com, January 5, 1961, https://nyti.ms/3qVxFLP.

17 Deane Heller and David Heller, *The Kennedy Cabinet: America's Men of Destiny* (Derby, CT: Monarch, 1961), 757. Douglas Dillon, interview by Donnelley.

18 James Reston, "Harmony on Capitol Hill," timesmachine.nytimes.com, January 14, 1961, https://nyti.ms/3lsgTmw. Heller and Heller, *The Kennedy Cabinet*, 73.

19 John D. Morris, "Senate Confirms Cabinet Swiftly," timesmachine.nytimes.com, January 22, 1961, https://nyti.ms/3bWZtLG. "Treasury's New Chiefs Get Names on $1 Bills," timesmachine.nytimes.com, January 24, 1961, https://nyti.ms/3rX fO8l. John Kenneth Galbraith, *Ambassador's Journal: A Personal Account of the Kennedy Years* (Boston: Houghton Mifflin, 1969), 37.

CHAPTER NINE

1   On Dillon's office: Deane Heller and David Heller, *The Kennedy Cabinet: America's Men of Destiny* (Derby, CT: Monarch, 1961), 65–75.

2   Theodore C. Sorensen, *Kennedy* (London: Pan Books, 1965), 451. Arthur M. Schlesinger, *A Thousand Days: John F. Kennedy in the White House* (Boston: Houghton Mifflin, 1965), 654.

3   Douglas Dillon, interview by Dixon Donnelley, John F. Kennedy Oral History Interviews, JFKOH-CDD-02, JFK Library, November 10, 1964.

4   Douglas Dillon, Oral History transcript, LBJ Library Oral Histories, LBJ Presidential Library, interview by Paige Mulhollan, June 29, 1969, https://www.discoverlbj.org/item/oh-dillonc-19690629-1-74-12. Aurélie Basha i Novosejt, "C. Douglas Dillon, President Kennedy's Economic Envoy," *The International History Review* 40, no. 2 (April 24, 2017): 236, https://doi.org/10.1080/07075332.2017.1313297.

5   Douglas Dillon, interview by Donnelley. Erwin C. Hargrove and Samuel A. Morley, eds., *The President and the Council of Economic Advisers: Interviews with CEA Chairmen* (Boulder, CO: Westview Press, 1984), 189. Robert Dallek, *Camelot's Court: Inside the Kennedy White House* (New York: HarperCollins, 2013), 118.

6   Robert Sobel and Bernard S. Katz, eds., *Biographical Directory of the Council of Economic Advisers* (Westport, CT: Greenwood, 1988), 100–1.

7   Robert F. Kennedy, *Robert Kennedy, in His Own Words: The Unpublished Recollections of the Kennedy Years*, ed. Edwin O. Guthman and Jeffrey Shulman (New York: Bantam Books, 1989). JFK quoted in Richard Reeves, *President Kennedy: Profile of Power* (New York: Touchstone, 1994), 55. Sobel and Bernard, eds., *Biographical Directory of the Council of Economic Advisers*, 100–4.

8   Dillon to Kennedy, January 17, 1961: CDDPP-033-006, Dillon Personal Papers, JFK Library. Heller and Heller, *The Kennedy Cabinet*, 148–9. Shriver quoted in Dallek, *Camelot's Court*, 119. Douglas Dillon, interview by Donnelley. Hargrove and Morley, eds., *The President and the Council of Economic Advisers*, 190. David E. Bell, John F. Kennedy Oral History Interviews, interview by Robert C. Turner, JFKOH-DEB-01, JFK Library, July 11, 1964.

9   Raymond J. Saulnier, *Constructive Years: The US Economy under Eisenhower* (Lanham, MD: University Press of America, 1991), 222–37.

10 John F. Kennedy, *"Let the Word Go Forth": The Speeches, Statements, and Writings of John F. Kennedy 1947–1963*, ed. Theodore C. Sorensen (New York: Delacorte Press, 1988). "President John F. Kennedy's First State of the Union

Address, January 30, 1961," National Archives, accessed March 25, 2021, https://www.archives.gov/legislative/features/sotu/jfk.html. Special to *New York Times*, "Text of President's Message to Congress on U.S. Balance of Payments and on Gold," timesmachine.nytimes.com, February 7, 1961, https://nyti.ms/2N WqipT. Dillon to Kennedy, March 8, 1961: CDDPP-033-006, Dillon Personal Papers, JKF Library.

11 Douglas Dillon and Robert V. Roosa, John F. Kennedy Oral History Interviews, interview by Dixon Donnelley, JFKOH-CDRR-01, JFK Library, January 25, 1965.

12 Summary of Bretton Woods: Alan Greenspan and Adrian Wooldridge, *Capitalism in America: A History* (New York: Penguin Books, 2019), 306–7. "Gold Reserves in Metric Tonnes by Country 1845–1998," *World Gold Council Report*, 1998. Sorensen, *Kennedy*, 449. Ian Fleming, *Goldfinger* (London: Jonathan Cape, 1959). On the balance of payments crisis generally throughout this chapter: Francis J. Gavin, "The Gold Battles within the Cold War: American Monetary Policy and the Defense of Europe, 1960–1963," *Diplomatic History* 26, no. 1 (January 2002): 61–94, https://doi.org/10.1111/1467-7709.00300; Francis J. Gavin, *Gold, Dollars, and Power: The Politics of International Monetary Relations, 1958–1971* (Chapel Hill: The University of North Carolina Press, 2004); and Gordon L. Weil and Ian R. Davidson, *The Gold War: The Story of the World's Monetary Crisis* (New York: Holt, Rinehart and Winston, 1970).

13 Douglas Dillon, John F. Kennedy Oral History Interviews, interview by Seymour Harris, JFKOH-CDD-08, JFK Library, August 18, 1964.

14 Ibid.

15 Weil and Davidson, *The Gold War*, 54–6; 127–8. Douglas Dillon, interview by Harris.

16 Gavin, "The Gold Battles within the Cold War," 61–94, Sullivan to Dillon, August 23, 1961: RG56, A1–198D–Box 4C–ES, Memos to the Secretary 1961, Part 1, NACP. Dillon to Kennedy, September 14, 1961: Letters for the president 1961, RG56, A1-198-D-Box 1C-ES, NACP. Aurélie Basha I Novosejt, *"I Made Mistakes": Robert McNamara's Vietnam War Policy, 1960–1964* (Cambridge: Cambridge University Press, 2019), 97.

17 Dillon and Roosa, interview by Donnelley. Dillon to Kennedy, August 31, 1961: https://history.state.gov/historicaldocuments/frus1961-63v09/d48.

18 Richard E. Mooney, "Big World Fund Proposed by U.S," timesmachine.ny times.com, September 10, 1961, https://nyti.ms/3cBoBI7. Dillon and Roosa, interview by Donnelley. Dillon to Kennedy (from Embassy in Vienna), September 18, 1961: https://history.state.gov/historicaldocuments/frus1961-63v09/d51.

19   Dillon to Kennedy, July 5, 1961: Letters for the president 1961, RG56, A1-198-D-Box 1C-ES, Letters for the president, 1961, NACP. Summary of Heller's view: Gavin, *Gold, Dollars & Power*, 70–1.

20   Dillon to Kennedy, July 5, 1962: CDDPP-034-001, JFK Library. Dillon and Roosa, interview by Donnelley. Gavin, *Gold, Dollars & Power*, 68–9. Weil and Davidson, *The Gold War*, 58. Robert Triffin, *Gold and the Dollar Crisis: The Future of Convertibility* (New Haven, CT: Yale University Press, 1960).

CHAPTER TEN

1   Juan de Onis, "Dillon and Guevara in Uruguay for Americas Parley," times machine.nytimes.com, August 5, 1961, https://nyti.ms/3mcOoei. Editorial, "Cuba at Punta del Este," timesmachine.nytimes.com, August 17, 1961, https://nyti.ms/3uj75OR.

2   Dillon to JFK, August 9, 1961: https://history.state.gov/historicaldocuments/frus1961-63v12/d22.

3   Kennedy quoted in David Reynolds, *America, Empire of Liberty: A New History of the United States* (London: Allen Lane, 2009), 441–2 and Richard Reeves, *President Kennedy: Profile of Power* (New York: Touchstone, 1994), 103. Acheson and Schlesinger quoted in Arthur M. Schlesinger Jr., *Journals, 1952–2000* (London: Atlantic, 2008), 119–20. Schlesinger to JFK, April 5, 1961: Schlesinger Papers, AMSPP-WH69-002, JFK Library. Casualty figures: George C. Herring, *From Colony to Superpower* (New York: Oxford University Press, 2017), 706.

4   Dillon to Eisenhower, December 2, 1960: https://history.state.gov/historical documents/frus1958-60v06/d615. Special Group (5412 Committee), December 8, 1960: https://history.state.gov/historicaldocuments/frus1958-60v06/d62.

5   Douglas Dillon, John F. Kennedy Oral History Interviews, interview by Elspeth Rostow, JFKOH-CDD-04, JFK Library, August 4, 1964. Lawrence Freedman, *Kennedy's Wars: Berlin, Cuba, Laos, and Vietnam* (Oxford; New York: Oxford University Press, 2002), 153. Eisenhower quoted in Reeves, *President Kennedy*, 102–3. Aleksandr Fursenko and Timothy Naftali, *"One Hell of a Gamble": Khrushchev, Castro, and Kennedy, 1958–1964* (New York: Norton, 1998), 85. Schlesinger to JFK, February 11, 1961: Schlesinger Papers, AMSPP-WH69-002, JFK Library.

6   Edwin Williamson, *The Penguin History of Latin America* (London; New York: Penguin, 2009), 353–5. Dean Rusk, *As I Saw It: A Secretary of State's Memoirs* (London: I.B. Tauris, 1991), 247–348.

7   Williamson, *The Penguin History of Latin America*, 353–5. Arthur M.

Schlesinger Jr., *A Thousand Days: John F. Kennedy in the White House* (Boston: Houghton Mifflin, 1965), 759.

8   Richard N. Goodwin, *Remembering America: A Voice from the Sixties* (Boston: Little, Brown, 1988), 190. A. Lincoln Gordon, interview by Charles Stuart Kennedy, The Association for Diplomatic Studies and Training Foreign Affairs Oral History Project, September 3, 1987, https://adst.org/wp-content/uploads/2013/12/Gordon-Lincoln.1987.toc_1.pdf.

9   Bureau of Inter-American Affairs staff member quoted in Schlesinger, *A Thousand Days*, 760.

10 Ibid. Special to *New York Times*, "Stevenson's Return Spurs Overhaul of Latin Policies," timesmachine.nytimes.com, June 21, 1961, https://nyti.ms/3dHsWZF. Chairman of the Task Force on Latin America (Berle) to JFK, July 7, 1961: https://history.state.gov/historicaldocuments/frus1961-63v12/d16. Bowles to Rusk, July 25, 1961: https://history.state.gov/historicaldocuments/frus1961-63v12/d17. Douglas Dillon, interview by Rostow. John Leddy, interview by Willis C. Armstrong, The Association for Diplomatic Studies and Training Foreign Affairs Oral History Project (January 31, 1990), http://lcweb2.loc.gov/service/mss/mfdip/2004/2004led01/2004led01.pdf.

11 The account of events in Dillon's hotel suite: Goodwin, *Remembering America*, 192–4. Dillon to JFK, August 6, 1961: https://history.state.gov/historicaldocuments/frus1961-63v12/d20. Leddy, interview by Armstrong.

12 Dillon to Kennedy, August 6, 1961; Embassy in Montevideo to Department of State, August 6, 1961: https://history.state.gov/historicaldocuments/frus1961-63v12/d20. Goodwin, *Remembering America*, 192–4. "The Economy: Man with the Purse," *Time*, August 18, 1961. Herring, *From Colony to Superpower*, 716–17, 704. Herring links New Frontier foreign policy to Wilsonian idealism and the conviction that "destiny had singled out their nation and themselves to defend democracy."

13 Dillon to JFK, August 12, 1961: https://history.state.gov/historicaldocuments/frus1961-63v12/d28. A. Lincoln Gordon, interview by Paige Mulhollan, The Association for Diplomatic Studies and Training Foreign Affairs Oral History Project, July 10, 1969, https://www.adst.org/OH%20TOCs/Gordon,%20A.%20Lincoln.LBJ.pdf.

14 Dillon to Rusk, August 11, 1961: https://history.state.gov/historicaldocuments/frus1961-63v12/d26.

15 Douglas Dillon, interview by Rostow. Dillon to JFK, August 9, 1961: https://history.state.gov/historicaldocuments/frus1961-63v12/d22. Full text of the Charter of Punta del Este: https://avalon.law.yale.edu/20th_century/intam16.asp. Che Guevara, *Our America and Theirs: Kennedy and the Alliance for*

Progress: The Debate at Punta Del Este, ed. Maria del Carmen Ariet Garcia and Javier Salado (New York: Ocean Press, 2006). Schlesinger. *A Thousand Days*, 762. Goodwin, *Remembering America*, 196. Andrew Hoberek, ed., *The Cambridge Companion to John F. Kennedy* (New York: Cambridge University Press, 2015), 128–9. Dillon to Rusk, August 11, 1961: https://history.state.gov/historical documents/frus1961-63v12/d26. Dillon to JFK, August 25, 1961: Dillon Personal Papers, CDDPP-033-008, JFK Library.

16 Return of the Delegation to the Inter-American Economic and Social Conference at Punta del Este, 19 August 1961: KN-18579, JFKWHP-1961-08-19-A, JFK Library. Remarks on Secretary Dillon's return from Punta del Este conference, 19 August 1961: JFKPOF-035-037, JFK Library. Goodwin, *Remembering America*, 196.

17 "The Economy: Man with the Purse." Robert Alden, "Advertising: Magazine Circulation Climbs," *New York Times*, March 23, 1961.

CHAPTER ELEVEN

1 Douglas Dillon and Robert V. Roosa, John F. Kennedy Oral History Interviews, interview by Dixon Donnelley, JFKOH-CDRR-01, JFK Library, January 25, 1965.

2 Jacqueline Kennedy Onassis and Arthur Schlesinger Jr., *Jacqueline Kennedy: Historic Conversations on Life with John F. Kennedy*, ed. Michael R. Beschloss (New York: Hyperion, 2011), 116–17. Bobby Kennedy quoted in Patricia Beard, *Douglas Dillon* (Cambridge, MA: Tidepool Press, 2018), 143. "Red Room Now a Bright Fuchsia in Redecoration of White House," timesmachine.nytimes.com, January 17, 1962, https://nyti.ms/3e6biPh.

3 Arthur M. Schlesinger Jr., *A Thousand Days: John F. Kennedy in the White House* (Boston: Houghton Mifflin, 1965), 624. White House staff quoted in Richard Reeves, *President Kennedy: Profile of Power* (New York: Touchstone, 1994), 334.

4 Aurélie Basha I Novosejt, *"I Made Mistakes": Robert McNamara's Vietnam War Policy, 1960–1964* (Cambridge: Cambridge University Press, 2019), 55. W. Elliot Brownlee, *Federal Taxation in America: A Short History* (Cambridge: Cambridge University Press, 2016), 166–7.

5 Herbert Stein, *Presidential Economics: The Making of Economic Policy from Roosevelt to Clinton* (Washington, DC: American Enterprise Institute for Public Policy Research, 1994), 94–101.

6 "Text of Report to the President-Elect on Prospects for Nation's Economy in 1961," timesmachine.nytimes.com, January 6, 1961, https://nyti.ms/3sniBXR.

Samuelson quoted in Lawrence A. Kudlow and Brian Domitrovic, *JFK and the Reagan Revolution: A Secret History of American Prosperity* (New York: Portfolio, 2016), 57. Stein, *Presidential Economics*, 94–101.

7   Arthur M. Schlesinger Jr., *Journals, 1952–2000* (London: Atlantic, 2008), 102. Summary of report and Surrey quoted in Kudlow and Domitrovic, *JFK and the Reagan Revolution*, 55–6.

8   Douglas Dillon, John F. Kennedy Oral History Interviews, interview by Dixon Donnelley, JFKOH-CDD-01, JFK Library, July 30, 1964. Stein, *Presidential Economics*, 95–7. Douglas Dillon, John F. Kennedy Oral History Interviews, interview by Harvey Brazer, JFKOH-CDD-06, JFK Library, September 21, 1964.

9   Erwin C. Hargrove and Samuel A. Morley, eds., *The President and the Council of Economic Advisers: Interviews with CEA Chairmen* (Boulder, CO: Westview Press, 1984), 196. Stein, *Presidential Economics*, 102–3. Kudlow and Domitrovic, *JFK and the Reagan Revolution*, 69–70. Robert Dallek, *An Unfinished Life: John F. Kennedy, 1917–1963* (Boston: Little, Brown, 2003), 332–5.

10 Theodore C. Sorensen, *Kennedy* (London: Pan Books, 1965), 443–4.

11 Douglas Dillon, interview by Harvey Brazer. Kudlow and Domitrovic, *JFK and the Reagan Revolution*, 79. President of the United States and Council of Economic Advisers, *Economic Report of the President, 1962*, https://fraser.st louisfed.org/title/economic-report-president-45/1962-8133.

12 Herbert Stein, *The Fiscal Revolution in America* (Washington: AEI Press, 1990), 384. Hargrove and Morley, eds., *The President and the Council of Economic Advisers*, 200.

13 Roy Hoopes, *The Steel Crisis* (New York: J. Day Co, 1963), 221. Dallek, *An Unfinished Life*, 483–7. Douglas Dillon, John F. Kennedy Oral History Interviews, interview by Seymour Harris, JFKOH-CDD-08, JFK Library, August 18, 1964.

14 Seymour Harris to Dillon, June 7, 1962: C. Douglas Dillon Personal Papers, CDDPP-033-013, JFK Library. Douglas Dillon, interview by Harris.

15 Council of Economic Advisers (Walter Heller), John F. Kennedy Oral History Interviews, interview by Joseph Pechman, JFKOH-CEA-01, JFK Library, August 1, 1964. Harris to Dillon, June 7, 1962. A good account of the dispute between the Treasury and the CEA in the summer of 1962 is given in Seiichiro Mozumi, "The Kennedy-Johnson Tax Cut of 1964, the Defeat of Keynes, and Comprehensive Tax Reform in the United States," *Journal of Policy History* 30, no. 1 (December 19, 2017): 25–61, https://doi.org/10.1017/s0898030617000379.

16 Dillon to JFK, June 6, 1962: C. Douglas Dillon Personal Papers, CDDPP-033-013, JFK Library.

17 "Transcript of the President's News Conference on Domestic and Foreign

Matters," timesmachine.nytimes.com, June 8, 1962, https://nyti.ms/3gzxDYB. Editorial, "Action on Taxes," timesmachine.nytimes.com, June 8, 1962, https://nyti.ms/3asTKMr.

18 Council of Economic Advisers (Walter Heller), interview by Pechman. Paul Samuelson, "Time Has Come to Cut Taxes," *Financial Times*, July 11, 1962. Dillon to JFK, July 12, 1962; July 27, 1962: C. Douglas Dillon Personal Papers, CDDPP-034-001, JFK Library. H. Ladd Plumley to JFK, July 13, 1962: C. Douglas Dillon Personal Papers, CDDPP-034-001, JFK Library. Schlesinger to JFK, July 17, 1962: "Tax Reform," Dillon Fund Archive. John Kenneth Galbraith, *Ambassador's Journal: A Personal Account of the Kennedy Years* (Boston: Houghton Mifflin, 1969), 393.

19 Dillon to JFK, July 12, 1962; July 16, 1962; July 27, 1962: C. Douglas Dillon Personal Papers, CDDPP-034-001, JFK Library.

20 Memorandum for the President, Monthly review by Treasury, CEA, and Budget Bureau, July 27, 1962: C. Douglas Dillon Personal Papers, CDDPP-034-002, JFK Library. Douglas Dillon, interview by Brazer. Council of Economic Advisers (Walter Heller), interview by Pechman.

21 Wilbur Mills, John F. Kennedy Oral History Interviews, interview by Joseph E. O'Connor, JFKOH-WDM-01, JFK Library, April 14, 1967. Meeting with Wilbur Mills on the Tax Cut Proposal, August 6, 1962: White House Tapes, Miller Center, UVA, https://millercenter.org/the-presidency/secret-white-house-tapes/meeting-wilbur-mills-tax-cut-proposal. Reeves, *President Kennedy*, 333–5. Julian E. Zelizer, *Taxing America: Wilbur D. Mills, Congress, and the State, 1945–1975* (Cambridge; New York: Cambridge University Press, 1998), 194–6.

22 Paul Samuelson to JFK, August 10, 1962: "Tax Reform," Dillon Fund Archive. "The Range of Tax Choices before Us" quoted in Reeves, *President Kennedy*, 334–5. Ira Stoll, *JFK, Conservative* (Boston: Houghton Mifflin Harcourt, 2014), 130–2. Radio and television address to the nation on the economy, 13 August 1962: Papers of John F. Kennedy, Presidential Papers, President's Office Files, JFKPOF-039-030, JFK Library.

23 Mills, interview by O'Connor. Meeting with Wilbur Mills on the Tax Cut Proposal, August 6, 1962 (14'). Council of Economic Advisers (Walter Heller), interview by Pechman.

CHAPTER TWELVE

1 Tom Wicker, "Eisenhower Calls President Weak on Foreign Policy," times machine.nytimes.com, October 16, 1962, https://nyti.ms/3evwY7L.

2   Douglas Dillon, John F. Kennedy Oral History Interviews, interview by Elspeth
    Rostow, JFKOH-CDD-04, JFK Library, August 4, 1964.

3   Joan (Dillon), Duchess of Mouchy, to Richard Aldous, Email and unpublished
    memoir, July 5, 2018. Dillon's family often referred to him as CDD—shorthand
    for C. Douglas Dillon.

4   "The JFK White House Tape Recordings," www.jfklibrary.org, accessed April
    28, 2021, https://www.jfklibrary.org/learn/about-jfk/jfk-in-history/white-
    house-tape-recordings. Robert Bouck, John F. Kennedy Oral History Inter-
    views, interview by Dan Fenn Jr., JFKOH-RIB-01, JFK Library, June 25, 1976.

5   Ernest R. May and Philip D. Zelikow, eds., *The Kennedy Tapes* (Cambridge,
    MA: Belknap Press, 1997), 42.

6   Kingston Reif, "13 Days – and What Was Learned," *Bulletin of the Atomic
    Scientists*, June 22, 2012, https://thebulletin.org/2012/06/13-days-and-what-was-
    learned/.

7   Meeting in the Cabinet Room, 11:50 am, October 16, 1962: May and Zelikow,
    The Kennedy Tapes, 45–76.

8   Serhii Plokhy, *Nuclear Folly: A History of the Cuban Missile Crisis* (New York:
    W.W. Norton, 2021), 141. Bruce J. Allyn, James G. Blight, and David A. Welch,
    "Essence of Revision: Moscow, Havana, and the Cuban Missile Crisis,"
    International Security 14, no. 3 (1989), 155, https://doi.org/10.2307/2538934.
    Meeting in the Cabinet Room, 6:30 p.m., October 16, 1962; Dillon to JFK,
    October 17, 1962, quoted in May and Zelikow, *The Kennedy Tapes*, 93, 120–1.
    Martin J. Sherwin, *Gambling with Armageddon: Nuclear Roulette from Hiro-
    shima to the Cuban Missile Crisis*, 1945–1962 (New York: Alfred A. Knopf, 2020),
    245–6, 264.

9   Barnaby J. Feder, "Robert H. Knight, 87, Influential Lawyer Who Served Several
    Presidents, Is Dead," *New York Times*, October 2, 2006, sec. Business. Douglas
    Dillon, interview by Rostow.

10 Inter-American Economic and Social Council of the Organization of Ameri-
    can States, October 22–27, 1962, Editorial note: https://history.state.gov/
    historicaldocuments/frus1961-63v12/d48.

11 Minutes of NSC meeting, October 20, 1962: https://history.state.gov/historical
    documents/frus1961-63v11/d34; May and Zelikow, *The Kennedy Tapes*, 193–203.
    Plokhy, *Nuclear Folly*, 154. Robert McNamara, John F. Kennedy Oral History
    Interviews, interview by Arthur Schlesinger Jr., JFKOH-RSM-01, JFK Library,
    April 4, 1964.

12 Minutes of NSC meeting, October 20, 1962; May and Zelikow, *The Kennedy
    Tapes*, 193–203.

13 Theodore C. Sorensen, *Kennedy* (London: Pan Books, 1965), 767. Minutes of

NSC meeting, October 20, 1962; May and Zelikow, *The Kennedy Tapes*, 193–203. Timothy J. Naftali, Philip Zelikow, and Ernest R. May, eds., *John F. Kennedy: The Great Crises. Vol. 2: September–October 21, 1962* (New York; London: Norton, 2001), 608.

14 Douglas Dillon, interview by Rostow.

15 James M. Lindsay, "The OAS Endorses a Quarantine of Cuba," Council on Foreign Relations, October 23, 2012, https://www.cfr.org/blog/twe-remembers-oas-endorses-quarantine-cuba-cuban-missile-crisis-day-eight. Edwin M. Martin, John F. Kennedy Oral History Interviews, interview by Leigh Miller, JFKOH-EMM-02, JFK Library, May 19, 1964. "Dillon Cautions on 'Miracles,'" timesmachine.nytimes.com, October 21, 1962, https://nyti.ms/3nDbI4g. Douglas Dillon, interview by Rostow. Thomas C. Mann, John F. Kennedy Oral History Interviews, interview by Larry Hackman, JFKOH-TCM-01, JFK Library, March 13, 1968. National radio and television address, October 22, 1962: JFKWHA-142-001, JFK Library.

16 Dillon's speech summarized and quoted in Paul P. Kennedy, "Dillon Reassures Latin Aid Parley," timesmachine.nytimes.com, October 24, 1962, https://nyti.ms/3nzDXAJ. Douglas Dillon interview by Rostow Mann, interview by Hackman. Summary Report on the Alliance for Progress, undated: https://history.state.gov/historicaldocuments/frus1961-63v12/d49.

17 Douglas Dillon, interview by Rostow.

18 National Security Action Memorandum 196, October 22, 1962: RG56-A1-198D-Box 1C-ES, Files of Secretary Dillon, Kennedy 1962, NACP. Plokhy, *Nuclear Folly*, 193. RFK quoted in Arthur M. Schlesinger Jr., *Robert Kennedy and His Times* (Boston: Mifflin, 1978), 534, 537. Sherwin, *Gambling with Armageddon*, 213.

19 Meeting of ExCom, Wednesday October 24, 10 a.m.: May and Zelikow, *The Kennedy Tapes*, 347–66. Reif, "13 Days – and What Was Learned."

20 Douglas Dillon, interview by Rostow.

21 Dillon to JFK: RG56-A1-198D-Box 1C-ES, Files of Secretary Dillon, Memos to President 1962 (2), NACP. Edward T. O'Toole, "Second Consecutive Drop Put the Level at $15,978,000,000," timesmachine.nytimes.com, November 2, 1962, https://nyti.ms/2RqPV3x.

22 Dillon to JFK, November 1, 1962; November 14, 1962: RG56-A1-198D-Box 1C-ES, Files of Secretary Dillon, Memos to President 1962 (2), NACP.

23 Summary Record of the Fifth Meeting of the Executive Committee of the National Security Council, October 25, 1962, 5 p.m.: https://history.state.gov/historicaldocuments/frus1961-63v11/d73.

24 Summary Record of the Sixth Meeting of the Executive Committee of the

National Security Council, October 26, 1962: https://history.state.gov/historical
documents/frus1961-63v11/d79. McCone quoted in Michael R. Beschloss,
Kennedy v. Khrushchev: The Crisis Years, 1960–1963 (London: Faber and Faber,
1991), 508–9. Phone call with Macmillan, October 26, 1962: May and Zelikow,
The Kennedy Tapes, 480.

25 Listen to Dillon's intervention here (13'): https://millercenter.org/the-presi
dency/secret-white-house-tapes/executive-committee-meeting-national-
security-council-8. Ball quoted in Paul Nitze's ExCom notes: https://archive.
org/details/PaulNitzeNotesOfExCom1962/page/n23/mode/2up.

26 Paul Nitze, interview by Thomas Zoumaras, November 13, 1990, Dillon Fund
Archive. Walter Rostow, interview by Thomas Zoumaras, June 2, 1993, Dillon
Fund Archive. Michael Mandelbaum, *The Nuclear Question: The United States
and Nuclear Weapons, 1946–1976* (Cambridge: Cambridge University Press,
1985), 46–7. Raymond Garthoff, The Association for Diplomatic Studies and
Training Foreign Affairs Oral History Project, interview by Horace Torbert,
June 22, 1989, https://adst.org/OH%20TOCs/Garthoff,%20Raymond%
20L.toc.pdf.

27 McGeorge Bundy and James G. Blight, "October 27, 1962: Transcripts of
the Meetings of the ExCom," *International Security* 12, no. 3 (1987): 30–92,
https://doi.org/10.2307/2538801. Dillon group discussion paper, "Scenario for
Airstrike against Offensive Missile Bases and Bombers in Cuba," undated
[October 25–26, 1962]: https://nsarchive2.gwu.edu//nsa/cuba_mis_cri/1962
1025dillon.pdf.

28 Meeting of ExCom, Saturday, October 27, 1962, 11 a.m.: May and Zelikow, *The
Kennedy Tapes*, 492–518. Record of the Fourth Meeting of the Berlin-NATO
Subcommittee of the Executive Committee of the National Security Council,
October 27, 1962, 11 a.m.: https://history.state.gov/historicaldocuments/frus
1961-63v11/d92. Kennedy quoted in Reeves, *President Kennedy*, 415–16. Lincoln
quoted in Beschloss, *Kennedy v. Khrushchev*, 530.

29 Meeting of ExCom, Saturday, October 27, 1962, 4 p.m.: May and Zelikow,
The Kennedy Tapes, 519–604. Summary Record of the Eighth Meeting of the
Executive Committee of the National Security Council, October 27, 1962,
4 p.m.: https://history.state.gov/historicaldocuments/frus1961-63v11/d94.
Graham T. Allison and Philip Zelikow, *Essence of Decision: Explaining the
Cuban Missile Crisis* (New York: Longman, 2010), 119–20.

30 Bundy quoted in Plokhy, *Nuclear Folly*, 250. Dean Rusk and Jupiter missiles,
Editorial note, https://history.state.gov/historicaldocuments/frus1961-63v11/d99.

31 Meeting of ExCom, Saturday, October 27, 1962, 9 p.m.: May and Zelikow, *The
Kennedy Tapes*, 605–28.

32 Kennedy to Powers quoted in Beschloss, *Kennedy v. Khrushchev*, 540. Summary Record of the Tenth Meeting of the Executive Committee of the National Security Council, October 28, 1962, 11:10 a.m.: https://history.state.gov/his toricaldocuments/frus1961-63v11/d103. Pierre Salinger, *With Kennedy* (New York: Doubleday, 1966), 273. Sorensen, *Kennedy*, 793.

33 Douglas Dillon, interview by Rostow.

34 Nitze, interview by Zoumaras.

35 Douglas Dillon, interview by Thomas Zoumaras, January 19, 1990, Dillon Fund Archive.

36 Rostow, interview by Zoumaras. Robert F. Kennedy, *Robert Kennedy, in His Own Words: The Unpublished Recollections of the Kennedy Years*, ed. Edwin O. Guthman and Jeffrey Shulman (New York: Bantam Books, 1989), 269. Sorensen, *Kennedy*, 793.

CHAPTER THIRTEEN

1 Dillon to JFK, November 6, 1962: RG 56-A1-198D-Box 1C-ES, "Memos to the President 1962," NACP. The pioneering work of Francis J. Gavin is particularly important for this chapter: see *Gold, Dollars, and Power: The Politics of International Monetary Relations, 1958–1971* (Chapel Hill: The University of North Carolina Press, 2004) and "The Gold Battles within the Cold War: American Monetary Policy and the Defense of Europe, 1960–1963," *Diplomatic History* 26, no. 1 (January 2002): 61–94, https://doi.org/10.1111/1467-7709.00300.

2 Douglas Dillon, interview by Seymour Harris, John F. Kennedy Oral History Interviews, JFKOH-CDD-08, JFK Library, August 18, 1964. Dillon to Kennedy, July 5, 1962: C. Douglas Dillon Personal Papers, CDDPP-034-001, JFK Library. On the Kennedy Round, see Francine McKenzie, *GATT and Global Order in the Postwar Era* (Cambridge; New York: Cambridge University Press, 2020), 129–37.

3 Gordon L. Weil and Ian R. Davidson, *The Gold War: The Story of the World's Monetary Crisis* (New York: Holt, Rinehart and Winston, 1970), 58. Ball is quoted in Gavin, "The Gold Battles within the Cold War," 79.

4 James A. Bill, *George Ball: Behind the Scenes in U.S. Foreign Policy* (New Haven, CT: Yale University Press, 1998), 1, 20. However, Dillon's daughter Phyllis notes, "He did not shop. My mother arranged for the tailor to come and take his measurements. She selected the style and the material from the swatches." Email to author, February 25, 2022.

5 Robert Dallek, *Camelot's Court: Inside the Kennedy White House* (New York: HarperCollins, 2013), 103. Bill, *George Ball*, 104–8.

6 Memorandum of Conversation (Ball and Giscard d'Estaing), July 20, 1962: https://history.state.gov/historicaldocuments/frus1961-63v13/d258. Gavin, "The Gold Battles within the Cold War," 79. George W. Ball, John F. Kennedy Oral History Interviews, interview by Larry Hackman, JFKOH-GWB-04, JFK Library, March 28, 1968. Fowler to Dillon, August 7, 1962: C. Douglas Dillon Personal Papers, Memoranda to the President, 1961–1965, CDDPP-034-003, JFK Library.

7 Fowler to Dillon, August 7, 1962. Dillon to JFK, August 7, 1962: C. Douglas Dillon Personal Papers, Memoranda to the President, 1961–1965, CDDPP-034-003, JFK Library. Douglas Dillon, interview by Harris.

8 Heller to JFK, August 9, 1962: https://history.state.gov/historicaldocuments/frus1961-63v09/d57.

9 JFK to Dillon and Ball, August 24, 1962: https://history.state.gov/historicaldocuments/frus1961-63v09/d58. Dillon and Ball to JFK, September 12, 1962; Memorandum for Secretary of the Treasury and the Under Secretary of State, September 10, 1962: https://history.state.gov/historicaldocuments/frus1961-63v09/d59.

10 Dillon to JFK, January 16, 1963: https://history.state.gov/historicaldocuments/frus1961-63v09/d66. Dillon to JFK, January 8, 1963: RG 56-A1-198D (2)-Box 12C-ES, "Memos to the President 1963," NACP.

11 JFK quoted in Gavin, *Gold, Dollars, and Power*, 89.

12 De Gaulle quoted and summarized in Julian Jackson, *Charles de Gaulle: A Life* (Cambridge, MA: Belknap, 2018), 59.

13 Summary Record of NSC Executive Committee Meeting No. 38 (Part II), January 25, 1963: https://history.state.gov/historicaldocuments/frus1961-63v13/d169.

14 David Coleman, ed., *The Presidential Recordings: John F. Kennedy. Volume VI: The Winds of Change, December 1, 1962–February 7, 1963* (New York: W.W. Norton, 2016).

15 Coleman, ed., *Presidential Recordings, JFK, Volume VI*, 373–96.

16 Douglas Dillon, interview by Harris. Gavin, "The Gold Battles within the Cold War," 74. Robert Dallek, *Camelot's Court: Inside the Kennedy White House* (New York: HarperCollins, 2013), 103.

17 Dean Acheson, John F. Kennedy Oral History Interviews, interview by Lucius Battle, JFKOH-DGA-01, JFK Library, April 27, 1964. Richard Reeves, *President Kennedy*, 77.

18 Dillon to JFK, February 11, 1963: RG 56-A1-198D (2)-Box 12C-ES, "Memos to the President 1963," NACP.

19 Meeting between the President and Dean Acheson on Balance of Payments,

February 26, 1963: https://history.state.gov/historicaldocuments/frus1961-63v09/d20. Acheson, interview by Battle.

20 Acheson, interview by Battle.

21 Ball, interview by Hackman. Acheson, interview by Battle.

22 Meeting with the President, Balance of Payments, April 18, 1963: https://history.state.gov/historicaldocuments/frus1961-63v09/d24.

23 Deborah Shapley, *Promise and Power: The Life and Times of Robert McNamara* (Boston: Little, Brown, 1993), 225–6. Francis J. Gavin, "The Myth of Flexible Response: United States Strategy in Europe during the 1960s," *The International History Review* 23, no. 4 (2001): 847–75, http://www.jstor.org/stable/40108839. Meeting with the President, Balance of Payments, April 18, 1963.

24 Meeting with the President, Balance of Payments, April 18, 1963. Dillon to JFK, May 31, 1963: RG 56-A1-198D-Box 12C-ES, "Kennedy 1963," NACP. Memorandum from President Kennedy to the Cabinet Committee on Balance of Payments, April 20, 1963: https://history.state.gov/historicaldocuments/frus1961-63v09/d25.

25 McNamara to JFK, July 16, 1963: https://history.state.gov/historicaldocuments/frus1961-63v09/d28. Eileen Shanahan, "Chronic Gold Outflow: Its Causes and Effects," timesmachine.nytimes.com, July 21, 1963, https://nyti.ms/3cenUnB.

26 Douglas Dillon, interview by Harris. McNamara to JFK, July 16, 1963. Dillon to JFK, May 31, 1963. "Dollar Trouble," timesmachine.nytimes.com, July 21, 1963, https://nyti.ms/3yFYY1L. Shanahan, "Chronic Gold Outflow." "The Text of Kennedy's Message Proposing a Plan to Cut Balance of Payments," timesmachine.nytimes.com, July 19, 1963, https://nyti.ms/3yzQ71D.

27 Quoted in Gavin, "The Myth of Flexible Response," 860–2, http://www.jstor.org/stable/40108839. President's European Tour, June 1963, https://history.state.gov/historicaldocuments/frus1961-63v09/pg_186.

28 Galbraith to JFK, The Balance of Payments, August 28, 1963: https://history.state.gov/historicaldocuments/frus1961-63v09/d32.

29 Aurélie Basha I Novosejt, *"I Made Mistakes": Robert McNamara's Vietnam War Policy, 1960–1964* (Cambridge: Cambridge University Press, 2019), 95.

30 John Kenneth Galbraith, *Ambassador's Journal: A Personal Account of the Kennedy Years* (Boston: Houghton Mifflin, 1969), 587. Memorandum from the President, May 31, 1963: RG 56-A1-198D-Box 12C-ES, "Kennedy 1963," NACP. Ball, interview by Hackman. Gavin, *Gold, Dollars, & Power*, 110. National Security Action Memorandum No. 270, October 29, 1963: https://history.state.gov/historicaldocuments/frus1961-63v09/d38. Thurston Clarke, *JFK's Last Hundred Days: An Intimate Portrait of a Great President* (London: Allen Lane, 2013), 311. Otto Feinstein, "Disarmament: Economic Effects," *Current History*

47, no. 276 (1964): 81–7, https://www.jstor.org/stable/45311156. "Death Came as Kennedy Sought to Shape a New Foreign Policy Geared to Changes in the World Outlook," *New York Times*, November 23, 1963. Robert S. McNamara, "Spectrum of Defense," *Survival* 6, no. 1 (January 1964): 2–8, https://doi.org/10. 1080/00396336408440441.

CHAPTER FOURTEEN

1   Dillon to JFK, May 31, 1963: RG 56-A1-198D-Box 12C-ES, "Kennedy 1963," NACP.
2   Herbert Stein, *Presidential Economics: The Making of Economic Policy from Roosevelt to Clinton* (Washington, DC: American Enterprise Institute for Public Policy Research, 1994), 428.
3   Theodore C. Sorensen, *Kennedy* (London: Pan Books, 1965), 471–2.
4   Henry Fowler, Memorandum on Conference with Chairman Mills, November 15, 1962: "Tax Reform," November 1962, Dillon Fund Archives. Julian E. Zelizer, *Taxing America: Wilbur D. Mills, Congress, and the State, 1945–1975* (Cambridge; New York: Cambridge University Press, 1998), 196–7.
5   David Coleman, ed., *The Presidential Recordings: John F. Kennedy. Volume VI: The Winds of Change, December 1,1962–February 7,1963* (New York: W.W. Norton, 2016), 129–34.
6   Address to the Economic Club of New York, 14 December 1962: https://www. jfklibrary.org/asset-viewer/archives/JFKWHA/1962/JFKWHA-148/JFKWHA-148. Coleman, ed., *Presidential Recordings: John F. Kennedy, Volume VI*, 129.
7   Seiichiro Mozumi, "The Kennedy-Johnson Tax Cut of 1964, the Defeat of Keynes, and Comprehensive Tax Reform in the United States," *Journal of Policy History* 30, no. 1 (December 19, 2017): 25–61, https://doi.org/10.1017/s0898030617000379. Erwin C. Hargrove and Samuel A. Morley, eds., *The President and the Council of Economic Advisers: Interviews with CEA Chairmen* (Boulder, CO: Westview Press, 1984), 202–3.
8   Hargrove and Morley, eds., *The President and the Council of Economic Advisers*, 204. Zelizer, *Taxing America*, 200.
9   Council of Economic Advisers (Walter Heller), John F. Kennedy Oral History Interviews, interview by Joseph Pechman, JFKOH-CEA-01, JFK Library, August 1, 1964.
10 Douglas Dillon, John F. Kennedy Oral History Interviews, interview by Dixon Donnelley, JFKOH-CDD-02, JFK Library, November 10, 1964. Walter Rostow, interview by Thomas Zoumaras, June 2, 1993, Dillon Fund Archives.

11 Special Message on Tax Reduction and Reform, January 24, 1962: "Tax Reform," Dillon Fund Archives. State of the Union message, reading copy, 14 January 1963: JFKPOF-042-021, JFK Library.

12 John D. Morris, "Democrats Split; Separate Bills Backed," timesmachine.ny times.com, January 25, 1963, https://nyti.ms/34Pcana.

13 Dillon's Testimony Given before House Ways and Means Committee, February 6, 1963: *Congressional Digest* 42, no. 4: 108–10, Dillon Fund Archives. Stein, *The Fiscal Revolution in America*, 440. Mozumi, "The Kennedy–Johnson Tax Cut of 1964," 47. John D. Morris, "Dillon Stresses Need for Reform with Tax Slash," timesmachine.nytimes.com, February 7, 1963, https://nyti.ms/2SZG5qo.

14 President Reverses Position," *Wall Street Journal*, February 28, 1963; "Kennedy Pulled Tax Boner," *Philadelphia Inquirer*, February 28, 1963: Clippings file, Dillon Fund Archive. Council of Economic Advisers (Walter Heller), interview by Pechman. Stein, *The Fiscal Revolution in America*, 438–9. Evelyn Lincoln to Dillon, March 25, 1963: "Tax Reform," Dillon Fund Archives.

15 *Philadelphia Inquirer*, February 6, 1963: Scrapbook, Dillon Fund Archives.

16 Dillon to Kennedy, April 1, 1963: "Tax Reform," Dillon Fund Archives. "Treasury Accepts Plan to 'Cut' Debt," timesmachine.nytimes.com, May 1, 1963, https://nyti.ms/3xctSxj. Remarks by Dillon, Chamber of Commerce, April 30, 1963: RG 56-A1-198D (2)-Box 12C-ES, "Memos to the President 1963," NACP.

17 Remarks by Dillon, Chamber of Commerce, April 30, 1963.

18 Treasury Department memo, "Analysis of Recent Editorial Comment on the President's Tax Proposals," May 29, 1963; Dillon to JFK, June 3, 1963: "Tax Reform," Dillon Fund Archives.

19 Andrew Cohen, *Two Days in June: John F. Kennedy and the 48 Hours that Changed History* (Toronto: Random House, 2004), 105–10. Lawrence A. Kudlow and Brian Domitrovic, *JFK and the Reagan Revolution: A Secret History of American Prosperity* (New York: Portfolio, 2016), 128–9.

20 Jordyn Holman and Marisa Gertz, "Black Americans Who Broke Barriers on Wall Street – and Beyond," www.bloomberg.com, February 17, 2020, https://www.bloomberg.com/news/photo-essays/2020-02-17/black-americans-who-broke-barriers-on-wall-street-and-beyond. James Willard Hurst, *The Negro in the Navy: First Draft Narrative* (Washington, DC: Historical Section, Bureau of Naval Personnel, US Navy, 1947), 83–5.

21 Douglas Dillon, interview by Donnelley. Dillon to Kennedy, April 28, 1961: CDDPP-033-006, Dillon Personal Papers, JFK Library. Dillon to Heads of Bureaus, July 17, 1961: CDDPP-033-007, Dillon Personal Papers, JFK Library. Nick Bryant, *The Bystander: John F. Kennedy and the Struggle for Black Equality* (New York: Basic Books, 2006), 211–14.

22 Dillon to Kennedy, February 8, 1961: CDDPP-033-006, Dillon Personal Papers, JFK Library. Douglas Dillon, interview by Donnelley. Douglas Dillon, interview by Thomas Zoumaras, Dillon Fund Archive, January 19, 1990. Morris J. MacGregor Jr., *Integration of the Armed Forces, 1940–1965* (Washington, DC: Center of Military History, U.S. Army, 1981), https://web.archive.org/web/20100721102246/http://www.history.army.mil/books/integration/iaf-fm.htm.

23 Douglas Dillon, John F. Kennedy Oral History Interviews, interview by Harvey Brazer, JFKOH-CDD-07, JFK Library, September 22, 1964. "11 Billion Tax Cut Voted by House Group," *New York Herald-Tribune*, September 11, 1963: Clippings files, Dillon Fund Archives. Dillon to JFK, September 16, 1963: "Tax Reform," Dillon Fund Archives.

24 John D. Morris, "Tax Cut Is Voted by House, 271–155," timesmachine.nytimes.com, September 26, 1963, https://nyti.ms/2TiTl9i. Edwin L. Dale Jr., "Dillon Stressing Speed on Tax Bill," timesmachine.nytimes.com, September 16, 1963, https://nyti.ms/3waXECq. Henry H. Fowler to JFK, September 30, 1963: "Tax Reform," Dillon Fund Archives.

25 The meeting between Dillon and Byrd is recounted in *Newsweek*, October 7, 1963. Fowler to JFK, September 30, 1963: "Tax Reform."

26 Henry H. Fowler to JFK, September 23, 1963: "Tax Reform," Dillon Fund Archives.

27 Robert A. Caro, *The Years of Lyndon Johnson: The Passage of Power* (New York: Alfred A. Knopf, 2012), 470–2.

28 Henry H. Fowler to JFK, September 22, 1963; Fowler to JFK, September 30, 1963: "Tax Reform." Douglas Dillon, interview by Brazer.

29 Sweeney, James R. "Whispers in the Golden Silence: Harry F. Byrd, Sr., John F. Kennedy, and Virginia Democrats in the 1960 Presidential Election." *The Virginia Magazine of History and Biography* 99, no. 1 (1991): 3–44. https://www.jstor.org/stable/4249197.

30 "The Congress: Slow Going," *Time*, October 25, 1963. Kermit Gordon to JFK, October 1963: Papers of John F. Kennedy, Presidential Papers, President's Office Files, Departments and Agencies, Bureau of the Budget, 1963, October-November, JFK Library. Bureau of the Budget: 1965 Proposed Planning Figures, August 8, 1963: Papers of John F. Kennedy, Presidential Papers, President's Office Files, Departments and Agencies, Bureau of the Budget, JFK Library. Fowler to JFK, September 30, 1963: "Tax Reform." Dillon to JFK, October 17, 1963; Statement of Secretary of the Treasury before the Senate Finance Committee, October 15, 1963: RG 56-A1-198D (2)-Box 12C-ES, "Memos to the President 1963," NACP.

31 Fowler to JFK, September 30, 1963: "Tax Reform." Walter Heller and Kermit

Gordon, John F. Kennedy Oral History Interviews, interview by Larry Hackman and Joseph Pechman, JFKOH-KGWH-02, JFK Library, September 14, 1972. John D. Morris, "Heller, in Senate Hearing, Urges Speed on Tax Cut," timesmachine.nytimes.com, November 13, 1963, https://nyti.ms/3q3QQEg. Dillon to JFK, October 24, 1963: RG 56-A1-198D (2)-Box 12C-ES, "Memos to the President 1963," NACP.

32   Remarks at AFL-CIO convention, New York, November 15, 1963: Papers of John F. Kennedy, Presidential Papers. President's Office Files, Speech Files, JFKPOF-048-008, JFK Library. Fowler to JFK, September 30, 1963: "Tax Reform."

33   John D. Morris, "Senators Kill Hope for Adopting Tax-Cut Legislation This Year," timesmachine.nytimes.com, November 16, 1963, https://nyti.ms/3wz6cDl. Arthur Krock, "In the Nation; Tax Legislation with the Next Budget in Hand Grounds of Mutual Suspicion," timesmachine.nytimes.com, November 22, 1963, https://nyti.ms/3vzJomY.

34   Fowler to JFK, October 28, 1963: RG 56-A1-198D (2)-Box 12C-ES, "Memos to the President 1963," NACP. Douglas Dillon, interview by Brazer.

35   Clarke, *JFK's Last Hundred Days*, 326. William Manchester, *The Death of a President: November 20–November 25, 1963* (New York: Harper & Row, 1967).

CHAPTER FIFTEEN

1   Joan (Dillon), Duchess of Mouchy, interview by Richard Aldous, July 10, 2018. William Manchester, *The Death of a President: November 20–November 25, 1963* (New York: Harper & Row, 1967), 460.

2   Douglas Dillon, Robert F. Kennedy Oral History Interviews, interview by Larry Hackman, RFKOH-CDD-01, JFK Library, August 18, 1970.

3   Max Holland, Robert David Johnson, and David Shreve, eds., *The Presidential Recordings, Lyndon B. Johnson: The Kennedy Assassination and the Transfer of Power, November 1963–January 1964*, vol. 1 (New York: Norton, 2005), 156–7.

4   Douglas Dillon, interview by Hackman. Dillon to JFK, January 31, 1961: C. Douglas Dillon Personal Papers, Memoranda to the President, "January–June 1961," Folder 1, CDDPP-033-007, JFK Library. Manchester, *The Death of a President*, 362–3. "World Banker Moved Fast Nov. 22 to Nip Raid on Dollar," *Boston Herald*, December 5, 1963: Clippings files, Dillon Fund Archives. Dillon to LBJ, December 3, 1963: EX FG 110, Box 148, "11/22/63 - 12/25/63," WHCF, LBJ Library.

5   On the Secret Service and the assassination: Carol Leonnig, *Zero Fail: The Rise and Fall of the Secret Service* (New York: Random House, 2021), 50–70. James J.

Rowley, Truman Library Oral History Interview, interview by Niel M. Johnson, September 20, 1988, https://www.trumanlibrary.gov/library/oral-histories/rowleyj. James J. Rowley, LBJ Library Oral Histories, LBJ Presidential Library, interview by Paige Mullhollan, January 22, 1969, https://www.discoverlbj.org/item/oh-rowleyj-19690122-1-74-243. Manchester, *The Death of a President*, 460. LBJ phone call with Hoover, November 29, 1963: Michael R. Beschloss, *Taking Charge: The Johnson White House Tapes, 1963–1964* (New York: Simon & Schuster, 1997). Dillon to Chief Justice Earl Warren, December 18, 1963, "Report of the Secret Service on the Assassination of President Kennedy": The Assassination Archives and Research Center, https://aarclibrary.org/publib/jfk/wc/wcdocs/pdf/wcd3v1.pdf. "Hero's Medal Given Secret Service Man for Dallas Bravery," timesmachine.nytimes.com, December 4, 1963, https://nyti.ms/3dpoHQ8. The following day Johnson presented a medal to Rufus Youngblood, the agent who had thrown himself on top of the then vice president during the assassination in Dallas.

6   Memorandum on Project Star, March 4, 1964: EX FG 110, Box 148, "2/20/64 - 4/24/64," WHCF, LBJ Library. Agent figures, Silvio Conte and Dillon quoted in Leonnig, *Zero Fail*, 51, 60–1, 68–9. Rowley, interview by Mulhollan. Testimony of C. Douglas Dillon, Warren Commission, September 2, 1964: http://mcadams.posc.mu.edu/russ/testimony/dillon.htm. Dillon to LBJ, June 12, 1964: FG 110, Box 148, "6/10/64 – 9/14/64," WHCF, LBJ Library. Telephone conversation # 5696, sound recording, LBJ and McGeorge Bundy, 9/27/1964, 2:55 p.m., Recordings and Transcripts of Telephone Conversations and Meetings, LBJ Presidential Library, https://www.discoverlbj.org/item/tel-05696.

7   Holland et al., eds., *The Presidential Recordings, Lyndon B. Johnson*, vol. 1, 106.

8   Henry H. Fowler to JFK, September 22, 1963; Henry H. Fowler to JFK, September 30, 1963: "Tax Reform," Dillon Fund Archives. Fowler to JFK, October 28, 1963: RG 56-A1-198D (2)-Box 12C-ES, "Memos to the President 1963," NACP.

9   Robert A. Caro, *The Years of Lyndon Johnson: The Passage of Power* (New York: Alfred A. Knopf, 2012), 393; 421–4. Julian E. Zelizer, *The Fierce Urgency of Now: Lyndon Johnson, Congress, and the Battle for the Great Society* (New York: Penguin Press, 2015), 77.

10 Erwin C. Hargrove and Samuel A. Morley, eds., *The President and the Council of Economic Advisers: Interviews with CEA Chairmen* (Boulder, CO: Westview Press, 1984), 210. Caro, *The Years of Lyndon Johnson*, 423. Robert Dallek, *Flawed Giant: Lyndon Johnson and His Times, 1961–1973* (New York: Oxford University Press, 1999), 72.

11 Dillon to LBJ; Fowler to Dillon, both undated [filed December 6, 1963]: EX LE

FI 11, Box 51, "LE FI 11 11/22/63-12/20/63," WHCF, LBJ Library. Manchester, *The Death of a President*, 544. Hargrove and Morley, eds., *The President and the Council of Economic Advisers*, 210–11.

12 Dillon to LBJ; Fowler to Dillon, both undated [filed December 6, 1963].

13 Holland et al., eds., *The Presidential Recordings, Lyndon B. Johnson*, vol. 1, 164–71.

14 Jack Valenti quoted in Dallek, *Flawed Giant*, 73. McNeil and Byrd quoted in Caro, *The Years of Lyndon Johnson*, 470, 476–7. Ronald L. Heinemann, *Harry Byrd of Virginia* (Charlottesville: University Press of Virginia, 1996), 400–1. Holland et al., eds., *The Presidential Recordings, Lyndon B. Johnson*, vol. 2, 82–3.

15 Holland et al., eds., *The Presidential Recordings, Lyndon B. Johnson*, vol. 2, 367–73.

16 Dillon to LBJ, December 13, 1963: LE FI 11, Box 51, "11/22/63-12/20/63," WHCF, LBJ Library. Arthur M. Schlesinger Jr., *Robert Kennedy and His Times* (Boston: Mifflin, 1978), 101. Zelizer, *The Fierce Urgency of Now*, 79. Letter to Tom Johnson, February 5, 1973, quoted in Patricia Beard, *Douglas Dillon* (Cambridge, MA: Tidepool Press, 2018), 186.

17 Dillon to LBJ, December 21, 1963: RG 56-A1-198D-Box 12C-ES, "Memos to the President 1963," NACP.

18 Holland et al., eds., *The Presidential Recordings, Lyndon B. Johnson*, vol. 3, 292–3. Caro, *The Years of Lyndon Johnson*, 552–3. Zelizer, *The Fierce Urgency of Now*, 79–81.

19 Holland et al., eds., *The Presidential Recordings, Lyndon B. Johnson*, vol. 3, 298–301, 745–7.

20 Ibid. John D. Morris, "Tax Bill Is Voted by Senate Panel," timesmachine.ny times.com, January 24, 1964, https://nyti.ms/2Ub4fPj.

21 Lawrence A. Kudlow and Brian Domitrovic, *JFK and the Reagan Revolution: A Secret History of American Prosperity* (New York: Portfolio, 2016), 149. Douglas Dillon, Oral History transcript, LBJ Library Oral Histories, LBJ Presidential Library, interview by Paige Mulhollan, June 29, 1969, https://www.discoverlbj. org/item/oh-dillonc-19690629-1-74-12.

CHAPTER SIXTEEN

1 Max Holland, Robert David Johnson, and David Shreve, eds., *The Presidential Recordings, Lyndon B. Johnson: The Kennedy Assassination and the Transfer of Power, November 1963–January 1964*, Vol. 3 (New York: Norton, 2005), 232–45. Douglas Dillon, Oral History transcript, LBJ Library Oral Histories, LBJ

Presidential Library, interview by Paige Mulhollan, June 29, 1969, https://www. discoverlbj.org/item/oh-dillonc-19690629-1-74-12. Robert F. Kennedy, *Robert Kennedy, in His Own Words: The Unpublished Recollections of the Kennedy Years*, ed. Edwin O. Guthman and Jeffrey Shulman (New York: Bantam Books, 1989), 420.

2   Michael R. Beschloss, *Taking Charge: The Johnson White House Tapes, 1963–1964* (New York: Simon & Schuster, 1997), 374–5, 392.

3   Herbert Stein, *Presidential Economics: The Making of Economic Policy from Roosevelt to Clinton* (Washington, DC: American Enterprise Institute for Public Policy Research, 1994), 113. Edwin L. Dale, "Economic Shifts Hailed by Dillon; Policy Changes Called 'Most Significant in Decades,'" timesmachine.ny times.com, June 7, 1964, https://nyti.ms/3BbWE3O.

4   Analysis and speech quoted in Dale, "Economic Shifts Hailed by Dillon." Milton Friedman, Letters, *Time*, February 4, 1966.

5   Statistics quoted in Julian E. Zelizer, *Taxing America: Wilbur D. Mills, Congress, and the State, 1945–1975* (Cambridge; New York: Cambridge University Press, 1998) 210–11, Charles Hicks, "Average and Marginal Tax Rates, 1980 Individual Income Tax Returns" (1980), https://www.irs.gov/pub/irs-soi/80inintrav matr.pdf, and Julian E. Zelizer, *The Fierce Urgency of Now: Lyndon Johnson, Congress, and the Battle for the Great Society* (New York: Penguin Press, 2015), 81. Mills quoted in Zelizer, *Taxing America*, 210. See also Judith Stein, *Pivotal Decade: How the United States Traded Factories for Finance in the Seventies* (New Haven, CT: Yale, 2010), Daniel T. Rodgers, *Age of Fracture* (Cambridge, MA: Belknap Press, 2012), and Zachary D. Carter, *The Price of Peace, Money, Democracy, and the Life of John Maynard Keynes* (New York: Random House, 2020).

6   LBJ to Dillon, July 7, 1964: FG 110, 11/22/63, Box 148, "6/10/64 - 9/14/64," LBJ Library. Telephone conversation # 4185, sound recording, LBJ and Dillon, 7/8/1964, 3:46 p.m.: Recordings and Transcripts of Telephone Conversations and Meetings, LBJ Presidential Library, https://www.discoverlbj.org/item/tel-04185 [author's transcription].

7   Michael R. Beschloss, *Reaching for Glory: Lyndon Johnson's Secret White House Tapes, 1964–1965* (New York: Simon & Schuster, 2001), 103. Robert Dallek, *Flawed Giant: Lyndon Johnson and His Times, 1961–1973* (New York: Oxford University Press, 1999), 183–4.

8   Johnson, Reston, and Burns quoted in James T. Patterson, *The Eve of Destruction: How 1965 Transformed America* (New York: Basic Books, 2012), xi–xii.

9   Arthur Schlesinger Jr., *Journals, 1952–2000*, ed. Andrew Schlesinger and Stephen C. Schlesinger (New York: Penguin, 2008), 232, 235.

10　Luke A. Nichter, *The Last Brahmin: Henry Cabot Lodge Jr. and the Making of the Cold War* (New Haven, CT: Yale University Press, 2020), 284. Oral history transcript, C. Douglas Dillon, interview 1 (I), June 29, 1969, by Paige E. Mulhollan, LBJ Library Oral Histories, LBJ Presidential Library, https://www.discoverlbj.org/item/oh-dillonc-19690629-1-74-12.

11　Dillon to LBJ, November 2, 1964: FG 110, Box 149, "9/15/64 – 12/14/64," WHCF, LBJ Library. Telephone conversation # 6133, sound recording, LBJ and Dillon, 11/3/1964, 7:38 p.m.: Recordings and Transcripts of Telephone Conversations and Meetings, LBJ Library, https://www.discoverlbj.org/item/tel-06133 [author's transcription].

12　Telephone call with Abe Fortas, November 4, 1964: Beschloss, *Reaching for Glory*, 122.

13　Ibid. Telephone conversation # 6309, sound recording, LBJ and Dillon, 11/9/1964, 12:56 p.m., Recordings and Transcripts of Telephone Conversations and Meetings, LBJ Presidential Library, https://www.discoverlbj.org/item/tel-06309 [author's transcription].

14　Telephone call with Abe Fortas, November 4, 1964: Beschloss, *Reaching for Glory*, 122.

15　Telephone conversation # 6321, sound recording, LBJ and Sidney Weinberg, 11/11/1964, 1:32 p.m., Recordings and Transcripts of Telephone Conversations and Meetings, LBJ Presidential Library, https://www.discoverlbj.org/item/tel-06321. Telephone call with Abe Fortas, November 4, 1964: Beschloss, *Reaching for Glory*, 122. Dillon to LBJ, January 13, 1964: FG 110, Box 149, "12/15/64 – 3/19/65," WHCF, LBJ Library. Douglas Dillon, interview by Mulhollan.

16　Reuters, "Excerpts from Remarks by President de Gaulle," timesmachine.nytimes.com, February 5, 1965, https://nyti.ms/3BzQfzD. Julian Jackson, *Charles de Gaulle: A Life* (Cambridge, MA: Belknap, 2018), 651–3. De Gaulle press conference, editorial note: https://history.state.gov/historicaldocuments/frus1964-68v08/d36. Dillon to LBJ, March 17, 1964: https://history.state.gov/historicaldocuments/frus1964-68v08/d53.

17　Jackson, *De Gaulle*, 653.

18　"Treasury Assails de Gaulle Bid; Plan Is Called 'Drastic,'" timesmachine.nytimes.com, February 5, 1965, https://nyti.ms/3i19RVz. "Dillon Puzzled by France's Bid; Says Gold Plan Contradicts View Endorsed Earlier," timesmachine.nytimes.com, February 6, 1965, https://nyti.ms/3ztBJHF. "Overseas Stock Markets Fail to React to de Gaulle Statement," timesmachine.nytimes.com, February 6, 1965, https://nyti.ms/3rxTUcp. Edwin L. Dale Jr., "Johnson Urges Restraint in U.S. Investing Abroad to Cut Payments Deficit,"

timesmachine.nytimes.com, February 11, 1965, https://nyti.ms/3zIyE71. Francis
J. Gavin, *Gold, Dollars, and Power: The Politics of International Monetary
Relations, 1958–1971* (Chapel Hill: The University of North Carolina Press,
2004), 125.

19 Dillon to Johnson, March 27, 1965: https://history.state.gov/historicaldocu
ments/frus1964-68v08/d56. Gavin, *Gold, Dollars, and Power*, 117–18; 128–9.

20 Carl Kaysen, Chairman of the Task Force on Foreign Economic Policy to LBJ
[enclosing report], November 25, 1964: https://history.state.gov/historical
documents/frus1964-68v08/d18.

21 Gavin, *Gold, Dollars, and Power*, 117. Dillon to LBJ, October 30, 1964: https://
history.state.gov/historicaldocuments/frus1964-68v08/d17.

22 Gordon L. Weil and Ian R. Davidson, *The Gold War: The Story of the World's
Monetary Crisis* (New York: Holt, Rinehart and Winston, 1970), 90–2. Briefing
Paper, "International Economic Situation," December 4, 1964: https://history.
state.gov/historicaldocuments/frus1964-68v08/d19.

23 Gavin, *Gold, Dollars, and Power*, 117–18, 126–7. "Nixon and the End of the
Bretton Woods System, 1971–1973," Department of State Milestones: https://
history.state.gov/milestones/1969-1976/nixon-shock. Michael Mandelbaum,
"Fifty Years Ago: A Landmark Day in Economic History," Review of *Three Days
at Camp David: How a Secret Meeting in 1971 Transformed the Global Economy*
by Jeffrey E. Garten, *American Purpose*, August 13, 2021, https://www.american
purpose.com/articles/fifty-years-ago-a-landmark-day-in-economic-history/.

24 On Cook, see especially Dale L. Flesher and Gary J. Previts, "Donald C. Cook:
CPA, SEC Chairman, Corporate Legend, and Presidential Advisor," *Research in
Accounting Regulation* 30, no. 2 (October 2018): 131–7, https://doi.org/10.1016/
j.racreg.2018.09.008. Gene Smith, "Cook Declines Bid to Succeed Dillon;
Johnson's Treasury Choice to Remain with Utility," timesmachine.ny
times.com, March 11, 1965, https://nyti.ms/3i5MCtl. Gene Smith, "Personality:
Man Who Can – and Did – Say No," timesmachine.nytimes.com, March 14,
1965, https://nyti.ms/2THMLKm. Telephone conversation # 7070, sound
recording, LBJ and Everett Dirksen, 3/16/1965 [misdated], Recordings and
Transcripts of Telephone Conversations and Meetings, LBJ Presidential
Library, accessed July 27, 2021, https://www.discoverlbj.org/item/tel-07070
[audio] and Beschloss, *Reaching for Glory*, 228–30.

25 Oral history transcript, C. Douglas Dillon, interview 1 (by Mulhollan).

26 "Johnson Selects Dillon Successor; Donald Cook, Utility's Chief, Is Choice for
Treasury," timesmachine.nytimes.com, February 12, 1965, https://nyti.ms/3iX7ySu.
Notes of Telephone Conversation, LBJ and Robert Carswell, February 5, 1965:

https://history.state.gov/historicaldocuments/frus1964-68v08/d37. Telephone conversation # 7057, sound recording, LBJ and ROBERT ANDERSON, 3/11/1965, 9:16 a.m.: Recordings and Transcripts of Telephone Conversations and Meetings, LBJ Presidential Library, accessed May 23, 2019, https://www.discover lbj.org/item/tel-07057.

27 Charles Mohr, "Fowler Is Named Dillon Successor," timesmachine.nytimes. com, March 19, 1965, https://nyti.ms/3f5JBr4. Oral history transcript, C. Douglas Dillon, interview 1 (by Mulhollan).

28 Dorothy McCardle, "Dillons Illuminate Evening," *Washington Post*, March 26, 1965. Dorothy McCardle, "Dillon's Dozen Are Due to End," *Washington Post*, February 2, 1965. Dorothy McCardle, "Dillon's Bigger Than $," *Washington Post*, March 25, 1965. Henry Fowler to Bill Moyers, February 23, 1965: WHCF, Name File, Box 187 (Dillon, Douglas), LBJ Library.

29 Maxine Cheshire, "Dinner-Dance – as in Douglas Dillon," *Washington Post*, April 2, 1965. Max Hastings, *Vietnam: An Epic Tragedy 1945–1975* (New York: Harper Perennial, 2019), 214–15.

30 LBJ to Dillon, March 30, 1965: WHCF, Name File, Box 187 (Dillon, Douglas), LBJ Library.

31 Richard Rutter, "Boom Is Entering Its 50th Month; Longest Surge in Peacetime Catches the Seers with Their Forecasts," timesmachine.nytimes.com, March 28, 1965, https://nyti.ms/2WrD3Nc. Editorial quoted in McCardle, "Dillon's Bigger Than $." Paul Samuelson, "A Word to the Wise: On Pitfalls for Secretaries of Treasury and Appreciation for Dillon's Work," *Washington Post*, April 25, 1965.

32 Eileen Shanahan, "Dillon Discusses U.S. Problems as He Leaves Job at Treasury," timesmachine.nytimes.com, April 1, 1965, https://nyti.ms/3zCv3qI. Special to *New York Times*, "Henry H. Fowler Is Sworn in to Head Treasury," timesmachine.nytimes.com, April 2, 1965, https://nyti.ms/3idMfNL. Editorial, "Truly Notable," *Washington Post*, April 2, 1965. 1965, https://nyti.ms/3l7gF5S. The unemployment rate in 1966 was 3.9 percent: Arthur F. Neef and Rosa A. Holland, "Comparative Unemployment Rates, 1964–66," *Monthly Labor Review* 90, no. 4 (1967): 18–20, http://www.jstor.org/stable/41836807.

33 Shanahan, "Dillon Discusses U.S. Problems as He Leaves Job at Treasury." Special to *New York Times*, "Truly Notable." Eileen Shanahan, "Tax Cut for Poor Urged by Dillon," timesmachine.nytimes.com, March 27,

34 Dillon to LBJ, April 30, 1965: WHCF, Name File, Box 187 (Dillon, Douglas), LBJ Library. "Henry H. Fowler Is Sworn in to Head Treasury."

EPILOGUE

1   LBJ to Dillon, March 30, 1965: WHCF, Name File, Box 187 (Dillon, Douglas), LBJ Library.

2   Figures and Pham Van Dong quoted in Max Hastings, *Vietnam: An Epic Tragedy, 1954–1975* (London: William Collins, 2018), 282. Robert Dallek, *Flawed Giant: Lyndon Johnson and His Times, 1961–1973* (New York: Oxford University Press, 1999), 369, 380–1.

3   Telephone conversation # 10590, sound recording, LBJ and Douglas Dillon, 8/8/1966, 12:38 p.m., Recordings and Transcripts of Telephone Conversations and Meetings, LBJ Presidential Library, accessed October 25, 2021, https://www. discoverlbj.org/item/tel-10590. Telephone conversation # 10591, sound recording, LBJ and Douglas Dillon, 8/8/1966, 12:38 p.m.: Recordings and Transcripts of Telephone Conversations and Meetings, LBJ Presidential Library, accessed October 25, 2021, https://www.discoverlbj.org/item/tel-10591. Luke A. Nichter, *The Last Brahmin: Henry Cabot Lodge Jr. and the Making of the Cold War* (New Haven, CT: Yale University Press, 2020), 311.

4   Telephone conversation # 10597, sound recording, LBJ and Douglas Dillon, 8/9/1966, 10:05 a.m., Recordings and Transcripts of Telephone Conversations and Meetings, LBJ Presidential Library, accessed October 25, 2021, https://www. discoverlbj.org/item/tel-10597. Editorial note, Vietnam, January–August 1968, https://history.state.gov/historicaldocuments/frus1964-68v06/d155. Phyllis (Dillon) Collins, interview by author, November 3, 2021.

5   Michael Woodsworth, *Battle for Bed-Stuy: The Long War on Poverty in New York City* (Cambridge, MA: Harvard University Press, 2016), 236, 240, 303.

6   Alan Brinkley, *Liberalism and Its Discontents* (Cambridge, MA: Harvard University Press, 2000), 259. Patricia Beard, *Douglas Dillon* (Cambridge, MA: Tidepool Press, 2018), 132. Arnold A. Offner, *Hubert Humphrey: The Conscience of the Country* (New Haven, CT: Yale University Press, 2018), 301–2. Phyllis (Dillon) Collins, interview by author.

7   This summary of the Rockefeller Commission is drawn from the following: Kenneth Kitts, *Presidential Commissions & National Security: The Politics of Damage Control* (Boulder, CO: Lynne Rienner, 2006), 47, 52–61. Tom Wicker, "Destroy the Monster," timesmachine.nytimes.com, September 12, 1975, https://nyti.ms/3pX1xdK. Daniel Schorr, "The Rockefeller Commission Has Been Forced to Add It to the Agenda; Assassination Is a Subject That Just Won't Go Away," timesmachine.nytimes.com, May 4, 1975, https://nyti.ms/ 3bz7c1n. United States President's Commission on CIA Activities within the United States, Rockefeller Commission Report (CIA Activities), Internet

Archive, 1975, https://archive.org/details/Rockefeller-commission-report-to-the-president-by-the-commission-on-cia-activiti.

8   Robert C. Perez and Edward F. Willett, *Clarence Dillon: A Wall Street Enigma* (Lanham, MD.: Madison Books, 1995), 137–8. Nicholas F. Brady, *A Way of Going* (Privately published, 2008), 93–4.

9   "The Douglas Dillon Legacy: Chinese Painting for the Metropolitan Museum," Exhibition, Metropolitan Museum of Art, March 12–August 8, 2004: https://www.metmuseum.org/exhibitions/listings/2004/chinese-painting. Beard, *Douglas Dillon*, 222.

10   Nichter, *The Last Brahmin*, 348–9. Paul Nitze, interview by Thomas Zoumaras, November 13, 1990.

11   Rick Perlstein, *Nixonland: The Rise of a President and the Fracturing of America* (New York: Scribner, 2009), 747.

12   Telephone conversation # 6133, sound recording, LBJ and Dillon, 11/3/1964, 7:38 p.m.: Recordings and Transcripts of Telephone Conversations and Meetings, LBJ Library, https://www.discoverlbj.org/item/tel-06133 [author's transcription]. Michael A. Cohen, *American Maelstrom: The 1968 Election and the Politics of Division* (Oxford; New York: Oxford University Press, 2018), 8–9. George F. Will, *The Conservative Sensibility* (New York: Hachette Books, 2020), 328. Sam Roberts, "Serving as Ford's No. 2, Rockefeller Never Took His Eye off the Top Job," *New York Times*, December 31, 2006.

13   Robert D. Dean, *Imperial Brotherhood: Gender and the Making of Cold War Foreign Policy* (Amherst & Boston: University of Massachusetts Press, 2001), 15–16. Perlstein, *Nixonland*, 747. Bell quoted in Kevin Boyle, *The Shattering: America in the 1960s* (New York: W.W. Norton, 2021), xii.

14   Boyle, *The Shattering*, xiii. Michael Knox Beran, *WASPS: The Splendors and Miseries of an American Aristocracy* (New York: Pegasus Books, 2021), 383. See also Richard Aldous, "'Richard Hofstadter' Review: An Egghead and Proud of It," *Wall Street Journal*, August 8, 2020.

15   Richard Rorty, *Achieving Our Country: Leftist Thought in Twentieth-Century America* (Cambridge, MA: Harvard University Press, 2003).

16   W.L. Burn, *The Age of Equipoise* (London: George Allen & Unwin, 1964), 15–19, 42. Press release with text of the Farewell Address, January 17, 1961: Eisenhower Library, https://www.eisenhowerlibrary.gov/sites/default/files/research/online-documents/farewell-address/1961-01-17-press-release.pdf.

17   Jakob Grazzini and Domenico Massaro, "Great Volatility, Great Moderation and Great Moderation Again," *Review of Economic Dynamics* 44 (April 2021), https://doi.org/10.1016/j.red.2021.04.003. Janan Ganesh, "How the Temperature of US Politics Came Down," *Financial Times*, February 14, 2023, https://www.ft.

com/content/3577cdd2-159e-4981-8ca3-49de7f0c228a. Peter Baker and Susan Glasser, *The Man Who Ran Washington: The Life and Times of James A. Baker III* (New York: Anchor Books, 2021), 266–8. Buck Chapoton, interview by author, December 14, 2021.

18 Address by Under Secretary Dillon, AFL-CIO Conference on World Affairs, For World Peace and Freedom: Proceedings, Internet Archive, AFL-CIO Conference on World Affairs (New York: 1960), https://archive.org/details/AFLCIO/page/n67/mode/2up.

Index